Praise for *Becoming Yourself*

"In Becoming Yourself, *Robert expertly reveals how the Enneagram offers an exquisite blend of ancient wisdom and modern psychology to help you become your True Self. I recommend his book wholeheartedly to you."*
— **Richard Rohr**, author of *Immortal Diamond: The Search for Our True Self*

*"*Becoming Yourself *is a work of spiritual brilliance. Robert Holden leads people into the wondrous world of the Enneagram with mystical precision, describing human nature and archetypal patterns within the framework of the cosmic power of numbers. This book is truly a spectacular accomplishment."*
— **Caroline Myss**, author of *Anatomy of the Spirit* and *Conversations with the Divine*

"For years, I battled with the habits and behaviors that kept me from realizing my full potential. Then I found the Enneagram. Thanks to Robert Holden, I became a grateful student of the nine Types and learned to see myself and others as both human and divine. In Becoming Yourself, *Robert's passion for the Enneagram is evident on every page. Written with his signature warmth, humor, and good sense, this book has added a new, important resource to the field—one I'll use for years to come. If you struggle to understand why you do what you do, let the Enneagram help. Take the test, learn about your Type, and let the transformation begin!"*
— **Cheryl Richardson**, author of *The Art of Extreme Self-Care*

"In Becoming Yourself, *Robert brings the Enneagram to life. Through music, art, poetry, and pop culture, you learn about the 'Types' and their gifts in a way that's very relatable. This book is like spending time with a close friend who knows your story, your history, and is rooting for you to be your most authentic self—because becoming yourself is the greatest gift you can give the world."*
— **Kyle Gray**, author of *Angels Are with You Now*

"Studying the Enneagram has been one of the greatest tools for understanding myself and my fellow humans. Whether you're a newbie to the Enneagram or an experienced practitioner, please give yourself the gift of learning about the Enneagram with Robert. It will change your life and your relationships for the better—forever."
— **Sonia Choquette**, author of *The Answer Is Simple . . . Love Yourself, Live Your Spirit!*

"Profound, illuminating, and full of heart. In this book, Robert Holden brings the timeless wisdom of the Enneagram to life, guiding us home to a deeper understanding of who we truly are and how we can love more fully, ourselves and each other."
— **Rebecca Campbell**, author of *Your Soul Had a Dream, Your Life Is It*

"This book is a masterclass in integrating your personality with your soul—helping you to be fully human and fully divine. If you are ready to stop fighting the world and start living with authentic purpose, let Robert be your guide."

— **Gabrielle Bernstein**, #1 *New York Times* best-selling author

"Unequivocally the best book on the Enneagram! Robert has a way to make complex concepts digestible and practical. I saw myself so clearly in this book. Highly recommended!"

— **Colette Baron-Reid**, author of *The Map: Finding Meaning and Magic in the Story of Your Life*

"An astonishing achievement. Robert's new book makes the rich complexity of the Enneagram accessible to all, guiding us toward a greater understanding of ourselves and others. It is a deeply wise companion for life's journey—profound in its insight and beautifully clear in its expression."

— **Liz Trubridge**, producer of *Downton Abbey* series and films

"*Becoming Yourself* celebrates the Enneagram as a model for self-awareness that helps us better understand ourselves and each other. It honors the 'original goodness' of the soul and how the Enneagram helps us meet our basic fear, heal old wounds, open our hearts, find our essential qualities and talents, while offering a path of lifelong learning and growth. Another substantive gift from Robert Holden to the healing of humans and the world! A classic in its genre."

— **Matthew Fox**, author of *Original Blessing* and *Creation Spirituality: Liberating Gifts for the Peoples of the Earth*

"Robert Holden has written a book that feels like a homecoming for the soul. *Becoming Yourself* is a radiant reminder that the Enneagram is not about fixing what's broken, it's about remembering the wholeness that has always been within us. With his signature warmth, humor, and deep spiritual insight, Robert offers a loving guide for anyone seeking to live as their truest self. . . . It invites us to see ourselves and one another through the eyes of grace."

— **Dr. Deborah Egerton**, author of *Know Justice, Know Peace: A Transformative Journey to Awareness, Healing, and Wholeness* and *The Enneagram Made Easy*

"While most books on the Enneagram seem to shrink us down to a number and a type, Robert Holden's beautiful exploration of this ancient model opens us up to the richness of our being and the possibilities for our life. If you're ready to become more of who you really are, this book will become your companion and your guide!"

— **Michael Neill**, author of *The Inside-Out Revolution* and *The Space Within*

BECOMING
YOURSELF

ALSO BY ROBERT HOLDEN

Authentic Success

Be Happy

Finding Love Everywhere

Happiness NOW!

Higher Purpose

Holy Shift!

Life Loves You (with Louise Hay)

Loveability

Shift Happens!

All of the above are available at your local bookstore, or may be ordered by visiting:

Hay House UK: www.hayhouse.co.uk
Hay House USA: www.hayhouse.com®
Hay House Australia: www.hayhouse.com.au
Hay House India: www.hayhouse.co.in

***

BECOMING YOURSELF

A JOURNEY OF SELF-DISCOVERY USING THE WISDOM OF THE ENNEAGRAM

ROBERT HOLDEN

HAY HOUSE

Carlsbad, California • New York City
London • Sydney • New Delhi

Published in the United Kingdom by:
Hay House UK Ltd, 1st Floor, Crawford Corner,
91–93 Baker Street, London W1U 6QQ
Tel: +44 (0)20 3927 7290; www.hayhouse.co.uk

Text © Robert Holden, 2026

Cover design: Jemima Giffard-Taylor
Interior design: Julie Davison
Interior illustrations: Jemima Giffard-Taylor
Indexer: J S Editorial, LLC

The moral rights of the author have been asserted.

All rights reserved. No part of this book may be reproduced by any mechanical, photographic or electronic process, or in the form of a phonographic recording; nor may it be stored in a retrieval system, transmitted or otherwise be copied for public or private use, other than for 'fair use' as brief quotations embodied in articles and reviews, without prior written permission of the publisher.

The information given in this book should not be treated as a substitute for professional medical advice; always consult a medical practitioner. Any use of information in this book is at the reader's discretion and risk. Neither the author nor the publisher can be held responsible for any loss, claim or damage arising out of the use, or misuse, of the suggestions made, the failure to take medical advice or for any material on third-party websites.

A catalogue record for this book is available from the British Library.

Excerpts from the poetry of Hafiz from the Penguin publication *The Gift: Poems by Hafiz*, by Daniel Ladinsky, copyright 1999, used by permission.

Tradepaper ISBN: 978-1-83782-482-3
E-book ISBN: 978-1-4019-9713-7
Audiobook ISBN: 978-1-4019-7767-2

10 9 8 7 6 5 4 3 2 1

This product uses responsibly sourced papers, including recycled materials and materials from other controlled sources. For more information, see www.hayhouse.co.uk

The authorized representative in the EU for product safety and compliance is
Penguin Random House Ireland, Morrison Chambers, 32 Nassau Street,
Dublin D02 YH68, Ireland. https://eu-contact.penguin.ie

Printed and bound by CPI Group (UK) Ltd, Croydon CR0 4YY

*Dedicated to
Laura Samuel, Diane Haworth,
and Sohini Sinha*

Contents

Foreword by Russ Hudson xi
Introduction xix

Type One: The Reformer 1
Type Two: The Helper 35
Type Three: The Achiever 71
Type Four: The Individualist 107
Type Five: The Investigator 141
Type Six: The Loyalist 177
Type Seven: The Enthusiast 211
Type Eight: The Challenger 245
Type Nine: The Peacemaker 279

Glossary of Terms 317
Frequently Asked Questions 321
Bibliography 323
Index 324
Acknowledgments 334
About the Author 337

Foreword

At first glance, it is not always obvious how the Enneagram, which is usually introduced as a simple typology of personality, could be of great benefit on our journey of spiritual awakening and psychological healing. How does knowing a description of my personality help me? Is it real? Is it practical? Many of these questions naturally arise for people discovering this approach to human development, and the plethora of novice teachers of the Enneagram, who may or may not be well versed in its context and background, can sometimes add to the confusion. But make no mistake. The Enneagram, in its core, is a support system for our inner journey, and a way to discover what is most beautiful and sacred in our lives, in our work, and in our relationships.

As you may know, the Enneagram describes nine ways of being in the world, nine ways of coping with our emotions and navigating life's challenges. But it is also connected with a symbol that is here to remind us that we are not looking at a filing system for human beings, but rather exploring ways to become more self-aware and connected through understanding the dynamic complexities of the human condition. The symbol of the Enneagram is important, and provides much of the context for what we learn about our personality patterns.

The symbol, and teachings associated with it, were introduced at the beginning of the 20th century by the Greek-Armenian spiritual teacher George Gurdjieff. Gurdjieff did teach about human types, but he did not explicitly teach nine personality types connected with the Enneagram. Rather, he taught about the Enneagram as a mandala of universal processes—ways we can better understand the laws that operate in our consciousness and in the world. One of these principles he called *The Law of Seven*, and explained that it was a way of understanding how complete processes work—the ways that things develop or deteriorate, and the idea that nothing in the manifested universe is static. Everything is changing and becoming, BUT according to laws. In a sense, science is also an endeavor to discover and describe these laws.

Particular to Gurdjieff's Law of Seven is the idea of *shocks*. In this teaching, nothing in reality manifests in a straight line or in a smooth continuum. There are points in a process in which other forces must enter the process in order for it to continue. We might see the ways that our body functions, with respiration, blood flow, and many other processes to grasp that processes are not independent and depend upon the interaction with other processes. Without those interactive shocks, a process will tend to stall or to even reverse itself. Gurdjieff went further in teaching that any discrete process has two shocks in it—one that appears after the process has been going for a while, and another that occurs near the culmination and conclusion of the process. This can all seem rather heady, but it has a great deal of practical impact and application. In other words, if we want to attain a certain goal, we need to know how to navigate shocks and sometimes *to create them* for ourselves.

In applying the Law of Seven to the process of spiritual development, what Gurdjieff called *inner work*, he denoted two major shock points that arise in the spiritual/psychological process of integration. The first of these he called *self-remembering*—this is remembering to come back to our direct experience in the living moment, *to be present*. To emerge from the ongoing inner chatter of our personality and to become awake and aware to felt sense of the moment is a shock—it is not a continuation of what was already happening in us. This can sound deceptively easy, and one of the great barriers to presence is believing we are already fully here. But inner work provides exercise and experiences to show us that we are not nearly as present as we might imagine, and shocks to help us come back to ourselves. It takes years of dedicated practice to cultivate the capacity to live from greater presence, and most of the inner teachings of spiritual growth from around the world know and understand this. We do spiritual practices such as meditation or centering prayer or sacred dance for the sake of cultivating this capacity, and also to be *better able to remember to be here*. We learn that part of what makes this difficult is that the trance of our personality causes us to forget our deeper nature and that other ways of being in the world are possible. The lack of self-remembering leads us to forget our spiritual, essential nature, and to believe that what we are is the ego self—the personality.

It was the spiritual teacher Oscar Ichazo, who was well acquainted with the Enneagram and its purpose, who took it further and related it to traditional understandings of the roots of egoic suffering—what he called the passions. He took this knowledge and correctly assigned the classical ideas of the passions, arising from the earliest forms of monastic Christianity in Egypt, to the Enneagram symbol. This was a tremendous realization and nearly all of the contemporary Enneagram teachings spring from this initial and amazing understanding. (He created a number of other Enneagram patterns, or as he called them, Enneagons, to further elucidate the emerging teaching he was working with.)

In this context, the value of the Enneagram becomes clearer. The personality patterns that we study are not a final statement of who we are, but *a study of what we have taken ourselves to be*. When we are not self-remembering, when we are not present, our personality type functions as a kind of autopilot and determines most of what we do in our lives. Much of the art of working with the Enneagram is to create more moments of self-remembering in which we can see our personality operating, much like a computer program. But when we really see these psychological patterns from presence, we see them with kindness, mercy, and a lack of rejecting or judging ourselves. Our essential nature helps us see what has captured us, and helps us bear being with the painful truth of this with greater kindness and courage.

This leads us to the second shock, which is the deeper heart rising to meet what we encounter through our presence practice. We begin to feel the suffering that has been created through our history, and through our separation from our source, whatever we choose to call that. Then our presence functions as an inner "yes"—as a call to Grace to hold and heal what has been driving us. Gurdjieff called this the arising of *organic conscience*—where we feel in our heart our longing to be real and true, and to no longer forget ourselves in the trances and illusions of our ego patterns. We might also say that this is the birth of authentic compassion, and ultimately, of real love. Not attachment, or clinging, or infatuation, or jealousy, or sentimentality, but the kind of love that Jesus and Buddha taught us about. This is the love we have been seeking our entire lives.

So, from this point of view, we can see how the knowledge of our personality patterns can function not as a reinforcement of our historic self-concepts, but as an ongoing reminder that we are falling asleep to ourselves and to our true nature. We gain more moments of awakening and are brought back to our deeper heart again and again. Crucially, this helps us to have more moments of awakening in life—when we are working and functioning and relating with others—not just when we are meditating or hanging out with our spiritual friends! Then our inner nature begins to consistently encounter the life we are living, and begins a process of integrating these two seemingly separate worlds. This is the great call of our time, and the way in which we begin to take our place in serving the process of awakening in this world.

As we continue we will notice a few very interesting things. One is that hidden in our personality patterns are great spiritual gifts—akin to the idea of gifts of the spirit as described in the Christian Bible. We discover that these gifts have been used to help maintain our personality, as a basic way of coping with the vicissitudes of our childhoods. As we see this with understanding and kindness, these gifts become freed up to do what they are actually for and become part of our love offering to our world. As you will see in this wonderful book, the liberation of your particular spiritual gifts will help you better understand yourself and your purpose in this world.

You will also begin to understand and experience that being present is an act of love. It is saying *yes* to reality, to Grace, and to being with whoever or whatever is here. What sense is there in speaking of love if we are not really here? What could love really mean if we are lost in the trances and dreams of our ego patterns? We learn that as we are more present, we enter a greater and deeper sense of what love actually is, and it guides and motivates us in our choices in life and in our inner work. We come to a direct and experiential knowing that presence, awareness, and love are really of one fabric, and that this fabric is what we are most fundamentally. This is the experience of the great "I AM."

It is here that this beautiful book from Robert Holden comes in and shines. Robert has been a devoted student of the Enneagram for many years, and has learned the intricate details of the system very well. Crucially, he has applied these teachings to himself and learned them from the inside out. Thus, he has learned to convey the specific teachings of the Enneagram through the matrix of his own spiritual journey, which has been most powerfully the exploration of the nature of love.

In these pages, you will find a very comprehensive compendium of Enneagram wisdom, including most of the finer points of the teaching—the wings, the subtypes, the inner lines, the healthier aspects of each point as well as its fears and trouble spots. But you will learn these particularities in the context of an inner journey to the very core of yourself, which is to say, a discovery of your soul nature, rooted in love. Robert presents each of the teachings with clarity and honesty but also with a wealth of kindness and compassion. This is a remarkably generous book.

When my dear co-traveler and co-author Don Richard Riso and I set about to write *The Wisdom of the Enneagram*, some 30 years ago, we had three aims that supported us in delivering that book. First, that is be as true as we could make it and that it reflected truths that we really knew from experience. Second, while there were a great many things we could say about each of the types, *we wanted to focus on what would be the most helpful*. What would actually help readers see through their illusions and come to more direct awareness of their true nature? What would help them heal and find greater awareness in the relationships? Third, we wanted to communicate these ideas in ways that could be more easily understood and received by readers. We wanted them to know that what we were speaking about was already there in them, albeit hidden beneath the veils of personality. We wanted them to recognize themselves in what we were writing. As a result, that book was well received and has remained so decades later.

I was totally delighted and moved to see how thoroughly Robert Holden has carried on with those aims. You will find in this book truths he has learned through his own inner journey and culled from years of helping many other people to find their way into this work and to find more of their life purposes. As you read Robert's words, you will feel how deeply he is speaking from experience and with the relaxed authority that this can bring. You will note too how this book is offered as a help, and holds to the elements of the system that will help us awaken our nature and possibly to our true place in this world. We cannot miss the friendly, intimate, and inviting tone with which the book reaches out to us. And Robert goes to great lengths to make what can be daunting information into clear and receivable wisdom. He has a great gift for speaking into the heart and intelligence of the reader and inviting them into this great journey. Further, Robert lives this teaching in his everyday life. He is a devoted father and husband and has integrated these wisdom teachings into the beautiful ways he attends to his family.

So, while there are a great many books on the Enneagram these days, and many that are introductory in nature, you will find *Becoming Yourself* a great companion in your Enneagram studies, and a very sturdy source of authentic teachings that are understandable and applicable to the life you are living. It can function as an excellent introduction, but also as a resource you will return to again and again as you explore the inner territories that this book reveals.

I am thrilled to know that this book has arrived, and that the deeper wisdom of what the Enneagram is really about is going to be known by many more people. Gurdjieff stated that the teachings connected with the Enneagram had arrived in the world just in time to help us make a major crossing in our civilization—one of those big "shocks" that we mentioned earlier. We human beings are in a time of great technological and sociological advancement, but have also arrived at a crossroads—perhaps a time of crisis. In a real way, our inner life, our soul's maturity level, has to catch up with the marvels that our intellects have unleashed so that these nearly miraculous innovations do not end up serving the undigested pain and fury born from our psychological suffering. The Enneagram is here to invite you and me to discover a deeper truth of who and what we are—literally becoming ourselves—and to find new ways of encountering and connecting with each other to create the kind of world that we sense is possible. We know that the old ways are no longer sustainable and that something new is required. In this context, *Becoming Yourself* is a significant step in finding what in us is capable to meet this challenge, for ourselves, for our loved ones, and for those who will follow after us.

I wish you a beautiful journey. With this book, you are in good hands.

— Russ Hudson
New York City
November 11, 2025

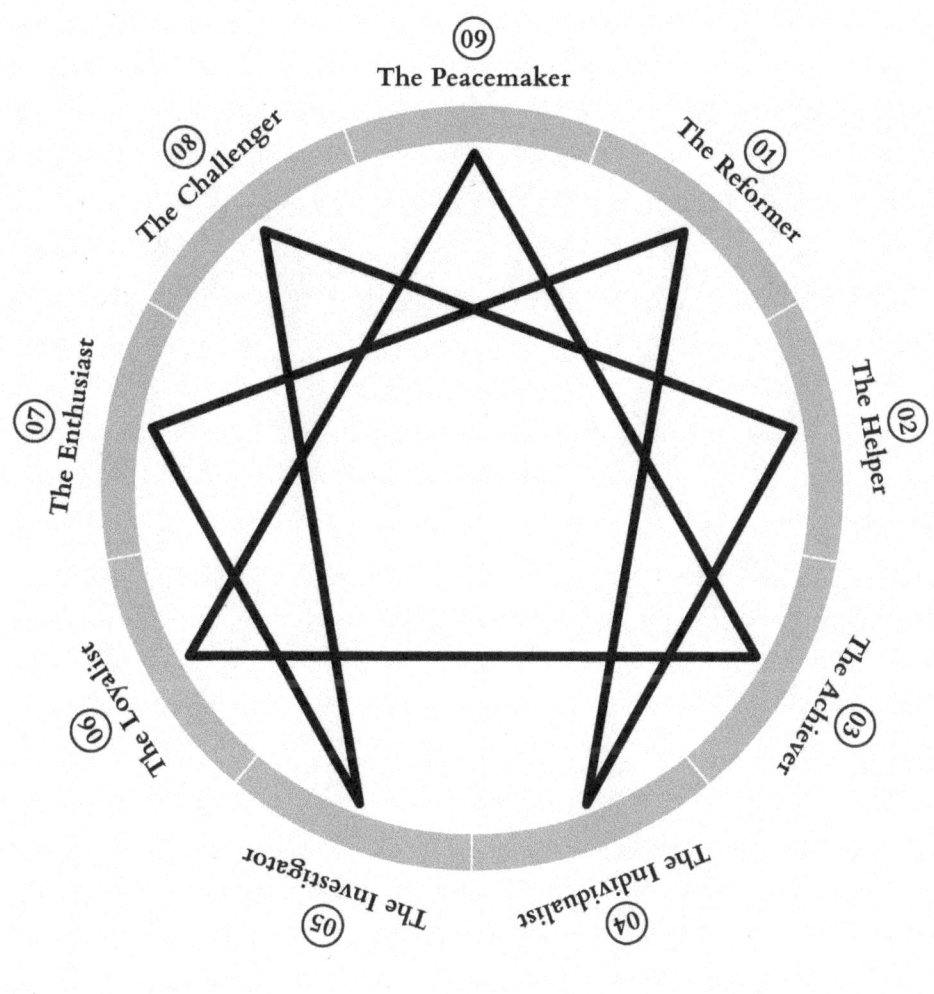

Introduction

Welcome to the Enneagram, and to a journey of Self-discovery that will help you become the full expression of yourself.

The Enneagram has an ancient history, and it is fast becoming the most popular self-awareness tool in the world today.

Millions of people use it daily to understand themselves better, realize their strengths, increase mental wellness, attract loving relationships, live their purpose, and grow spiritually.

In *Becoming Yourself*, I've packed in 20 years' experience of teaching the Enneagram to people from all walks of life, including psychologists, educators, authors, leaders, entrepreneurs, mums and dads, and anyone interested in personal growth.

My aim is to help you use the Enneagram to know yourself and become yourself. As you will see, the Enneagram offers a powerful mix of ancient wisdom and modern psychology to help you realize your potential and be your True Self.

The Enneagram doesn't try to fix you or change you; it helps you to grow. It recognizes that your True Self is already whole, complete, and perfectly made. You have within you everything you need to flourish and become yourself. Therefore, *if you think something is missing in your life, it is probably more of the real you.*

WHAT IS THE ENNEAGRAM?

When I first saw the name *Enneagram*, I wasn't sure how to say it. It sounded a bit Greek to me (pardon the pun!). For the record, you pronounce it "any-a-gram."

The Enneagram is a nine-pointed symbol. The word *Enneagram* comes from two Greek words: *ennea,* meaning "nine," and *gram,* meaning "drawing" or "figure." The symbol contains a circle with a triangle, a set of six inner lines called a hexad, and the nine points. It is based on universal laws, sacred mathematics, and spiritual principles that combine to help you cultivate a healthy ego and know your soul.

Think of the Enneagram as a mandala, like the ones you find in sacred art and spiritual traditions. I know that the Enneagram doesn't look like much at first. *It's just a bunch of lines, isn't it?* However, I promise you that every detail of the Enneagram offers precious insights, lessons, and gifts that give you a deeper understanding of yourself and others.

The Enneagram offers a map of growth. And it takes you on a journey that helps you in every major life domain—a term used by psychologists—to enjoy better mental health, more loving relationships, greater abundance and prosperity, authentic happiness, and inner peace.

The Traditional Enneagram

The Traditional Enneagram is at least 2,500 years old. The precise origin of the Enneagram is unknown, but its teachings can be traced back to Plato and Pythagoras; to Plotinus, who wrote a book called *The Enneads*; to the Desert Fathers and Mothers of Egypt; and to ancient wisdom schools in Spain, Turkey, and Persia. In short, the Enneagram has a paperless trail. It is deeply spiritual, but it doesn't belong to any religion, and it has existed for a very long time.

What we know for sure is that the Enneagram was introduced to Europe and America in the early 20th century by George Ivanovich Gurdjieff, a Greek Armenian philosopher and spiritual teacher. In 1915, Gurdjieff met P. D. Ouspensky, a philosopher in Moscow. Ouspensky, who was a kind of Indiana Jones character, was traveling through Europe, India, and Egypt in search of ancient knowledge.

Ouspensky studied with Gurdjieff for 10 years, and he later wrote an account of this in his classic work *In Search of the Miraculous*, published in 1949. When Gurdjieff first told Ouspensky about the Enneagram, he said,

> Everything can be included and read in the Enneagram. A man may be quite alone in the desert, and he can trace the Enneagram in the sand and in it read the eternal laws of the universe. And every time he can learn something new, something he did not know before.

The Traditional Enneagram focuses its attention on the nine Points of the symbol. Think of the nine Points as nine meditation seats. Each Point offers an education of the soul, teachings on the universal laws of life, and a pathway of spiritual growth. For example, Point One teaches the original goodness of the soul and holy perfection of creation; Point Two plugs you in to unconditional love and the holy will of creation; and Point Three focuses on higher purpose and playing your part in the Great Work of creation.

Gurdjieff used the Enneagram as a tool to help people wake up to themselves, to be more soul-centered, and to be less constrained by their ego. "One of the most important things to be understood about man is that man is asleep. Even while he thinks he is awake, he is not," wrote Gurdjieff. Gurdjieff taught that the soul is your essence, and the ego is merely an image or mask. When we are too ego-bound, we become mechanical and automatic. "We function like robots," he said. Learning from all nine Points on the Enneagram helps you to recover your soul and become your True Self.

When I teach courses and trainings on the Enneagram, I use the nine Points on the Enneagram as nine lenses through which to focus on key subjects such as relationships, health, prosperity, spiritual growth, and purpose. In this book, we will visit all nine Points. For now, what you need to know about them is:

- The nine Points are connected by the circle in the Enneagram symbol.
- You have a relationship to all nine Points.
- All nine Points live in you.
- The nine Points have no ranking of importance.
- One Point is not better than another.
- Each Point has a vital lesson and a gift for you.
- The nine Points are home to the nine personality types of the Enneagram.

The Modern Enneagram

The Modern Enneagram focuses on nine personality types that are referred to as Ennea-Types. In the 1960s, Oscar Ichazo, a Bolivian psychologist, was the first person to map the nine Types onto the Enneagram. His outstanding work was developed by other modern Enneagram teachers, including Claudio Naranjo, Helen Palmer, Don Riso, Russ Hudson, and others whom you will learn more about in this book.

The goal of the Modern Enneagram is the same as that of the Traditional Enneagram: *know thyself.* Just as Gurdjieff taught, the Modern Enneagram recognizes that we have both a psyche (or soul) and a persona (or ego). Oscar Ichazo wrote, "We have to distinguish between a man as he is in essence, and as he is in ego or personality. In essence, every person is perfect, fearless, and in a loving unity with the entire cosmos; there is no conflict within the person between head, heart, and stomach or between the person and others."

The Modern Enneagram offers a synthesis of spiritual wisdom and modern psychology. This blend of ancient and modern is what makes the Enneagram so powerful and practical. Each of the nine Types on the Enneagram has a name, and the name gives you a clue as to the life outlook and common social role of each one. Here are the nine Types, with a brief description of each:

The Reformer - *The Highly Principled, Idealistic Type*
Purpose-led, conscientious, ethical, dutiful, and perfectionistic.

The Helper - *The Heart-Centered, Interpersonal Type*
Warm-hearted, loving, generous, caring, and self-sacrificing.

The Achiever - *The Achievement-Oriented, Doing Type*
Dynamic, driven, hard-working, adaptable, and image conscious.

The Individualist - *The Highly Individual, Feeling Type*
Introspective, creative, artistic, expressive, and melancholic.

The Investigator - *The Highly Perceptive, Cerebral Type*
Observant, independent-minded, analytical, innovative, and remote.

The Loyalist - *The Highly Intuitive, Anxious Type*
Watchful, loyal, faithful, security oriented, and skeptical.

The Enthusiast - *The Highly Enthusiastic, Adventurous Type*
Positive, upbeat, fun-loving, optimistic, and restless.

The Challenger - *The Strong-Willed, Assertive Type*
Self-reliant, forceful, direct, big-hearted, and in charge.

The Peacemaker - *The Peaceful, Easygoing Type*
Positive, affirming, even-tempered, self-effacing, and stubborn.

KNOWING YOUR TYPE

How do you know what your Type is? The Enneagram has become so popular, the chances are someone you know will offer to tell you what your Type is. Has that happened to you yet?

Introduction

People like to guess each other's Type, and their guesses can be hit or miss. For example, *you like purple; you must be a Four. You work hard; you must be a Three. You get anxious; you must be a Six.* Back in 2009, when I gave a keynote speech on The JOY of the Enneagram at the International Enneagram Association's annual conference, I had Enneagram teachers tell me I must be a Seven because I spoke about joy. I'm not a Seven, though.

It's easy to mistype each other (and ourselves) because the nine Types are not that different from each other. Physically, we all have a nose and a head. Emotionally, we all want to be happy and be loved. Mentally, we all have fears and worries. Hence, the unwritten code in the Enneagram world is *don't tell anyone their Type; help them to work it out for themselves.*

There are three ways to find out what Type you are. First, take a test. I created the Enneagram Quiz, which is published by Hay House. We beta tested the quiz with over 10,000 people before we launched it. My Enneagram Quiz has a unique design. It takes less than five minutes, is easy to follow, and has a high accuracy rating. You get a free 1,500-word report written by me, and there is an option to purchase a longer 3,000-word profile that includes additional teaching videos and exercises. Turn to the back pages of this book to find out how to access the quiz.

> *Finding your Type is not the end of the journey; it is the start of the journey.*

Second, read a book on the Enneagram. The one you have in your hands is pretty good. As you read it, you'll see that I refer to other Enneagram books I've studied, and I've also compiled a bibliography of my favorites for you in the back of the book.

Third, take an online program. I've created an audio series that gives you practical ways to work with your Type in relationships and work, for instance. Better still, come to a live event or a training program. Learning about the Enneagram with other people helps you go deeper, and it can transform your life.

ANATOMY OF THE TYPE

This book features an in-depth profile of the nine Ennea-Types. Each chapter is laid out in the same way. I begin with an overview of the Type and share with you some examples of family and friends who are that Type. For example, my dad was an Eight, my mum was a Four, Louise Hay was a Six, and Caroline Myss is a One. I also share famous examples of each Type from philosophy, the arts, TV, and film to help you get to know their essential qualities.

After the overview, I take you through **the basic anatomy** of each Type. I start with the essential qualities, which is the term commonly used to describe the healthy traits, core strengths, and innate gifts of each Type. When a person is in touch with their True Self, they display these essential qualities naturally. For example, a Two is generous and humble; a Five is bright and insightful; an Eight is strong and kind; and a Nine is engaged and present.

Next, I go into the **ego operating system** of each Type. This is where we work on inner blocks to happiness and love. I start with the basic fear for the Type. For example, the basic fear for Threes is having no self-worth or intrinsic value; for Fours it is the fear of being without significance; for Sixes it is self-doubt and not feeling safe; and for Sevens it is the fear of missing out. The basic fear for each Type arises from a feeling of separateness, which is the basic wound that we all must deal with.

After the basic fear, I look at **the childhood story** of each Type. I focus especially on the social role each Type plays in their family constellation. For example, a One will commonly play the role of the "Good Child" who never has to sit on the naughty step; for Twos it is the role of "Little Helper" and "Cheerful Giver"; and for an Eight it is the "Strong Child" who never admits to feeling hurt or being tired. I'll also tell you about **the ego-drivers** of each Type, such as the "Be Perfect" driver in Ones; the "Try Harder" driver in Threes; and the "Hurry Up" driver in Sevens.

Next, I focus on the **passion** of the Type, which is the emotional wound in the heart. For example, the passion for Fours is envy and negative comparing; for Fives it is avarice and hoarding; for Sevens it is gluttony and forever wanting more; and for Eights it is lust and being too forceful. After that, I tell you about the **fixation**, which is a mental habit that upsets our psychology and mental well-being. For instance, for a One it is judging; for a Three it is deceit; for a Six it is overthinking; and for a Nine it is daydreaming.

Finally, I lay out the **path of growth** for each Type. This is where I introduce you to the virtue or superpower of your Type, and also **the wings**, the **three centers**, the **inner lines** of growth, and the **holy idea**. Now, if your head is spinning with all of this information, please don't worry. Take it a page at a time. Also, I have included a glossary at the back of this book to explain what passions, fixations, wings, virtues, and holy ideas mean. All will be revealed!

READING THIS BOOK

This is a book about you, and about your friends and family too. So my encouragement is that you read about all nine Types, not just the Type you think you are.

Remember, you have a relationship to all nine Points on the Enneagram. You are also connected to all nine Types. For example, if you are a Two, you have a 3-Wing and a 1-Wing, and so it's good to learn about Type Threes and Type Ones. Also, as a Two, you have lines of growth to Point Four and Point Eight, and so it is helpful to learn about Fours and Eights. As a Two, there is a lesson and gift that each of the nine Types is offering you. And this is true for whatever Type you are.

As you read about each Type, apply the learning to yourself and think about people in your life. What are your parents' Types? What Types are your partner and your kids? What Type is your colleague at work? What Type is the President of the United States? What Type is your favorite author? If you work in mental health or coaching, for instance, the Enneagram will help you practice greater empathy. In leadership, the Enneagram helps you to better understand your team. If you're an author or a film producer, you can use the Enneagram to bring to life the characters you create.

"The Enneagram is in perpetual motion," taught Gurdjieff. It is a dynamic system. Therefore, don't just read about the Enneagram. Scribble in the margins and make notes on every page. If that doesn't feel right, it might be you're a Type One and you prefer to keep your book neat and tidy. In that case, get yourself a journal and do the inquiries and exercises I have set out for you.

Whichever Type you are, commit to doing the inner work. The Enneagram isn't just for spiritual entertainment. Working with the Enneagram will give you the wisdom and courage to be a more complete expression of yourself and be a loving presence in the world.

Robert Holden
London, 2025

Type One
THE REFORMER

*Your goal is not to make a perfect self,
it is to see that you are perfectly made.*

The Ennea-Type One is commonly called The Reformer or Perfectionist. Other names for Ones include the Crusader, the Good Soul, Moralist, Advocate, and Idealist.

Type Ones are the *Highly Principled, Idealistic Type*. As a One, you believe in the sanctity of life and in the basic goodness of human nature. You uphold traditional values, and you are committed to making the world a better place. You have a strong moral compass. You are guided by a firm sense of right and wrong. You are conscientious and ethical, dutiful and self-disciplined, wise and

> *Just to be is a blessing;
> just to live is holy.*
>
> — Abraham Heschel

discerning, stoic under pressure, and you always try to better yourself. You are the Type most likely to color-coordinate your wardrobe. You are offended by typos and grammatical errors. You use the word *should* a lot. You can also be self-critical and a tad perfectionistic.

Ones aim to live a good life. They have a strong sense of mission. They aim to lead by example and to serve the common good. They hope to earn a good standing in their community and to be valued as a good representative of the human family. Ones wish to be seen as someone who is full of integrity, who lives their values, is true to their word, and is striving to do a good deed for the world. They pride themselves on being rational and objective, and they believe they are right about everything most of the time, if not always. They are full of good intentions, but good intentions are not always enough. Ones do well to heed the philosopher Aldous Huxley's warning: "Hell isn't merely paved with good intentions; it is walled and roofed with them. Yes, and furnished too."

> *You can start changing our world for the better daily, no matter how small the action.*
> — Nelson Mandela

When Ones meet the Enneagram, they cast their critical eye over it. They cross-examine the Enneagram to discern if it is good or not. *Is this another New Age fad? Who testifies for it? What are its flaws?* A religious One might want to know if the Enneagram is approved by their rabbi, their minister, or the pope. They don't want to get involved with a cult. Ones are usually pleased to learn that the Enneagram's roots can be traced back to the beginning of classical philosophy and to Plato. When Ones take an Enneagram test, they don't mess around. They will do it correctly or not at all. They want to know what the rules are. They don't want to make any mistakes. They want to get it right.

Working with the Enneagram can be a great blessing for Ones. It helps them to align with the highest good in themselves, to be less self-critical and judgmental, to forgive themselves for their mistakes, to remember to have fun, and to succeed in their mission to make the world a better place.

INTRODUCING TYPE ONE

Are you a Type One on the Enneagram? Maybe you have a family member, a friend, or a work colleague who is a One.

My grandfather, on my mother's side of the family, was a One. He resembled the hard-working and serious-minded Mr. Banks in *Mary Poppins*. He worked in a bank. He had a brown leather briefcase with his initials printed on it. He always wore a jacket and tie, even on Saturdays. He was rather stern, but also kind. He read *The Financial Times* newspaper. He didn't smoke. He enjoyed a glass of claret. He attended church on Sundays. "Hello, old boy," he'd say to me, even when I was only five years old. We both shared a love of cricket, and my happiest memories of Grandpa were when he laughed, which was approximately twice a year.

My younger brother, David, is also a One. Like Grandpa, he is set in his ways. As a young boy, he was very orderly and kept his room neat and tidy. He insisted on ironing his shirts and cleaning his shoes. He was obsessive compulsive, even by his own admission. When he was 10 years old, he got poor grades on his school report. "We are very disappointed in you," Mum and Dad told him, and David replied, "Not as disappointed as I am in myself." The next day, David went straight to the headmaster's office and organized an emergency meeting with his teachers to discuss what had gone wrong and how he could do better.

A challenge Ones often face is the impossibly high standards they set for themselves. Type Ones have a "Be Perfect" driver installed in their E.O.S—ego operating system—that is both a blessing and curse. In my book *Higher Purpose*, I tell the story of Claire, a Christian minister, who took my Spiritual Growth and the Enneagram program. Claire told me how she "put herself through hell" each week to deliver the perfect Sunday sermon. "It's just never good enough," she wept. When I asked her if her congregation were critical of her "not good enough" sermons, she laughed, and said, "No! They tell me that they love my sermons!"

> *Integrity is your destiny. It is the light that guides your way.*
> — Plato

"I'm going to give you some homework," I told Claire at the end of our first mentoring session. I know how much Ones enjoy being given an assignment and that they will always do a good job. I told Claire that I wanted her to think carefully about this question: *What is even better than giving the perfect sermon?* A week later, Claire came back with a revelation to tell. "I've been trying so hard to get everything right that I've been doing it all wrong!" she confessed. She then told me, "Your question helped me to realize that the purpose of a sermon is not to get it right or be clever, it's to feel God's love and to share that love with each other." When Ones stop trying to be perfect, their life often works out better for them.

Healthy Qualities of Ones

When Ones are healthy and well-balanced, they display essential qualities that we all love and appreciate. Here are a few things healthy Ones have told me about themselves.

- "Above all, I try to be a good person."
- "I have a strong sense of mission."
- "I want to leave the world a better place."
- "I am an advocate for positive change."
- "My mantra is: Just do right!"
- "Every day I try to do better."
- "I always try to live my values."
- "I want to be on the right side of justice."
- "I like to see the goodness in others."
- "I know that goodness wins the day."

Unhealthy Qualities of Ones

When Ones are out of balance, they struggle with self-criticism, fault-finding, and perfectionism. Here are a few things Ones have told me about themselves.

- "I suppose I can be a bit of a perfectionist."
- "I have a harsh inner critic."
- "My report card reads: 'Could do better.'"
- "I often take on too many responsibilities."
- "I crucify myself when I make mistakes."
- "I forget to relax, smile, and enjoy myself."
- "I know I could let my hair down more."
- "I wish I wasn't so hard on myself."
- "Sometimes, I lose sight of my own goodness."
- "I'm learning to be less self-critical."

RECOGNIZING TYPE ONES

In philosophy, Plato exemplifies the outlook of the One. In *The School of Athens*, a fresco painted by Raphael, in the Apostolic Palace in Vatican City, Plato stands at the center of a congregation of philosophers, mathematicians, and scientists. He is engaged in conversation with Aristotle, his first disciple. He holds his book *Timaeus* in his left hand and is pointing up to the heavens with his right hand. In *Timaeus*, Plato describes the creation of a well-ordered universe based on universal laws that are perfect, eternal, and changeless. In *The Republic*, Plato described God as "The Good" and God's universal laws as the "Form of the Good." Living with integrity, and being in alignment with these universal laws, is how we experience wholeness, truth, and beauty.

In the Bible, the apostle Paul was most likely a One. His many writings emphasize the nature of goodness. In his letter to the Galatians, he included goodness among the nine fruits of the Spirit: he wrote, "But the fruit of the Spirit is love, joy, peace, forbearance, kindness, goodness, faithfulness, gentleness, and self-control. Against such things there is no law." In his letter to the Romans, he urged his readers to be good and do good. He wrote, "Do not conform yourselves to this age, but be transformed by the renewal of your mind, that you may discern what is the will of God, what is good and pleasing and perfect."

> *Let us not become weary in doing good.*
> — Apostle Paul, Galatians 6:9

The Stoic philosophers, beginning with Marcus Aurelius, Seneca the Younger, and Epictetus, are particularly appealing to Type Ones. Stoicism offers teachings and maxims on how to be virtuous, resilient, happy, and wise. The Four Virtues of Stoicism are justice, self-control, wisdom, and courage. The aim of Stoicism is to live a good life. "Life is short, the fruit of this life is a good character and acts for the common good," wrote Marcus Aurelius in his *Meditations*. The emphasis of Stoicism is on turning philosophy into action and ethics into love. "Waste no more time arguing what a good man should be," wrote Marcus Aurelius. "Be one."

> *If it is not right, do not do it; if it is not true, do not say it.*
> — Marcus Aurelius

In leadership, the signature style of Ones is to lead by example. "Be the change you wish to see in the world," is a maxim attributed to Mahatma

Gandhi, the Indian lawyer and civil rights leader. It's not certain that Gandhi said these exact words. However, in his *Collected Works*, Gandhi did write,

> We but mirror the world. All the tendencies present in the outer world are to be found in the world of our body. If we could change ourselves, the tendencies in the world would also change. As a man changes his own nature, so does the attitude of the world change toward him. This is the divine mystery supreme. A wonderful thing it is and the source of our happiness. We need not wait to see what others do.

Nelson Mandela, the first President of South Africa, and Michelle Obama, attorney and former First Lady of America, also display strong One traits in leadership. Like Gandhi, Mandela believed in the goodness of humanity. In the fight for freedom and justice, he said, "A good head and a good heart are always a formidable combination." Michelle Obama works tirelessly to inspire a new generation of advocates and activists. In her memoirs *Becoming* and *The Light We Carry*, she encourages everyone to play their part in making the world a better place. How do we do this? Michelle said, "Be a good person every day" and "work continuously towards a better self."

> *Man's goodness is a flame that can be hidden but never extinguished.*
> — Nelson Mandela

Ones show up wherever they can do some good. Silvia Lagnado, former president of Dove and the Real Beauty Campaign, is a One. Silvia created an ethical purpose-driven brand, challenged beauty stereotypes, and led a campaign to raise the self-esteem of young girls around the world. I was Silvia's coach for three years, and I taught the Enneagram to her leadership team. Silvia always led by example. Her aim was to reform the beauty industry. "Everyone has the right to feel beautiful," she said. I also worked briefly with Dame Anita Roddick, the founder of The Body Shop, who had lots of One energy. Anita was a businesswoman, human rights activist, and environmental campaigner. In *Business as Unusual* she shared her vision of business as a force for good in the world. She wrote, "The business of business should not just be about money, it should be about responsibility. It should be about public good, not private greed."

> *Being good is good for business.*
> — Anita Roddick

Type One

In the arts, composer Johann Sebastian Bach was most likely a One. He has been described as a "theologian among composers" and as the "fifth evangelist." His much-loved compositions, such as the *Goldberg Variations*, are known for their intricate complexity and mathematical precision. In dance, think of Dame Margot Fonteyn, the prima ballerina assoluta of the Royal Ballet company, who was lauded for her long and exemplary career in classical ballet. Her iconic performances in *Swan Lake* and *Sleeping Beauty* were elegant, refined, and breathtaking.

In literature, the quintessentially English nanny Mary Poppins who is "practically perfect in every way" has bags of One energy. Played by Julie Andrews in the film, she is prim and proper, strict and kind, a disciplinarian, and she uses her magical powers to exert control over the physical world. P. L. Travers, who wrote *Mary Poppins*, was a keen student of George Gurdjieff, who introduced the Enneagram to the West. In the opening scene of the film *Saving Mr. Banks*, P. L. Travers, played by Emma Thompson, sits before her typewriter, and director John Lee Hancock gives us a close-up of a book on her desk, the *Teachings of Gurdjieff*.

> *I have found it is the small deeds of ordinary folk that keeps the darkness at bay. Simple acts of kindness and love.*
>
> — Gandalf, *The Lord of the Rings*, J. R. R. Tolkien

In J. R. R. Tolkien's *The Lord of the Rings*, Gandalf the Wizard is most likely a One. Tolkien imagined Gandalf as a Christ figure and described him as an "angel incarnate." Typical of a One, Gandalf is a true mentor who is quick to anger but also full of encouragement and praise. "It is important to fight and fight again, and keep fighting, for only then can evil be kept at bay though never quite eradicated," said Gandalf. A similar character to Gandalf is Professor Albus Dumbledore in the Harry Potter stories. "It is my belief . . . that the truth is generally preferable to lies," he said in his wise and whimsical way. Dumbledore represents the basic goodness in Harry Potter and in all of us.

In TV, Captain Jean-Luc Picard from *Star Trek: The Next Generation*, played by Sir Patrick Stewart, is probably a One. His favorite drink is "Tea. Earl Grey. Hot." He is highly principled and committed to making the universe a more accepting and kinder place to live. In the pilot episode of the first series, Captain Picard finds himself being cross-examined in a courtroom by a fiery entity called Q, who resembles the Old Testament God. Q has put humanity on trial as "a dangerous, savage child race" that is corrupt and evil and should be terminated. Picard concedes that humanity has made mistakes and committed crimes, but he insists that humanity is basically good, has a right to exist, and will come good in the end. "The trial never ends," says Q.

In the sitcom *Friends*, Monica Geller, played by Courteney Cox, is the Mother Hen of the group. She is bossy, compulsive, a neat freak, who loves to clean and is upset by the slightest mess in the apartment. Monica believes there is a right way to do things. "If I'm harsh on you, it's because you are doing it wrong," she tells her friends. In the sitcom *Modern Family*, Claire Dunphy, played by Julie Bowen, is the disciplinarian mother who was a wild child as a teenager. My favorite line from Claire is when she tells her husband, Phil, "Sweetheart, I would love to be wrong. I just don't live with the right people for that."

In *Downton Abbey* there is a strong Type One plot running through both the series and films. Violet Crawley, Dowager Countess of Grantham, played by Dame Maggie Smith, is very much a One, with her traditional views, her acerbic wit, her caustic insults, her tender heart, and, it must be said, her wild youth. Violet Crawley is wary of change. "First electricity, now telephones. Sometimes I feel as if I were living in an H. G. Wells novel," she says.

> Isobel: *How you hate to be wrong.*
> Violet Crawley: *I wouldn't know. I'm not familiar with the sensation.*
> — Downton Abbey

In Shakespeare's play *Twelfth Night*, Malvolio is steward to Olivia, a noblewoman in Illyria. He is a lampoon of a Type One. He is described as "a kind of Puritan" who is a party pooper, a spoiler of fun, and a killjoy. As a Puritan, Malvolio's main character flaw is his holier-than-thou attitude. He looks down on Sir Toby Belch and Sir Andrew Aguecheek for their hedonistic ways, and yet Malvolio fantasizes over Olivia, the lady he serves. Shakespeare often made fun of the Puritans for their pious and sanctimonious outlook. The Puritan ethic has good intentions, but it can easily descend to self-righteousness, smugness, and moral superiority.

ORIGINAL GOODNESS

And God saw all that God had made, and behold, it was very good.

— Book of Genesis 1:31

The circle in the Enneagram diagram represents the Original Goodness of the soul, which is whole, complete, and perfect. Original Goodness is in your spiritual DNA. It is the substance of the soul. Plato recognized the good in each of us, and he encouraged everyone to find out about it. Original Goodness is a universal idea. It is recognized in the Book of Genesis, the Psalms of Judaism, the poetry of Sufism, the Yoga Sutras of Patanjali, the Way of Taoism, and in the doctrine of basic goodness in Buddhism.

> *We all have the seeds of basic goodness within us. We only have to nourish them.*
>
> — Pema Chödron, Tibetan-Buddhist nun

Richard Rohr, the Franciscan priest, is a Type One and an excellent teacher of the Enneagram. In his book *The Enneagram: A Christian Perspective,* he tells us, "ONEs are originally joyfully enthralled with the goodness and perfection of the Really Real." He writes, "The primal knowing of ONES is that the world and we are deeply good." Ones know in their bones that we are all made of something good and that our mission is to align with our Original Goodness, which can be forgotten, denied, betrayed, or hidden, but never spoiled or erased.

My dear friend Deborah Egerton is a One, and she uses the Enneagram in her mission to end racism and bend the moral arc toward justice. Deborah has served as the president of the International Enneagram Association, and I've co-presented with Deborah on many programs, including The Enneagram of (G)Race series in which she skillfully coached us on how to heal the prejudices and biases of each Ennea-Type. Her work has earned her the affectionate moniker "Enneagram JEDI" (Justice, Equity, Diversity, Inclusion). In her book *Know Justice Know Peace*, Deborah tells us,

> As an enneagram One, I value goodness, integrity, and doing the right thing even if it involves conceding something of personal value. For me personally, honoring the dignity of every human being is the way that I choose to move through the world. I believe that who I am when on one is watching should be who I am when there is an audience. I don't want to be a version of myself. I want to be my true authentic self.

When Ones are aligned with their Original Goodness, they embody essential qualities and healthy traits that are plain for all to see. Here are a few of these qualities.

Original Blessing. Ones believe that life is a blessing, and that we are here to be a blessing to each other. Matthew Fox, author of *Original Blessing*, wrote, "We enter a broken and torn and sinful world—that is for sure. But we do not enter as blotches on existence, as sinful creatures, we burst into the world as 'original blessings.' And anyone who has joyfully brought children into the world knows this." The holy affirmation at Point One is *I am blessed as a Child of God.*

Life Is Good. Ones believe that *life is good,* and this motivates them to want to do a good deed for the world. Ones recognize that life is a mix of good times and bad, but they also have faith that goodness wins the day. My mentor Tom Carpenter had a favorite teaching from *A Course in Miracles*: "Child of God, you were created to create the good, the beautiful and the holy." Doing good deeds inspires others to do good deeds too.

Self-Acceptance. There's a lot of talk in the Enneagram how Ones are judgmental and perfectionistic, but this arises in Ones only when they forget their Original Goodness. Healthy Ones are known for their self-acceptance, compassion, and serene outlook on life. When Ones are aligned with their Original Goodness, they are able to love and accept themselves on good days and bad days, and when they overcook the Sunday roast, send a text message with a typo, or fail again at being the perfect parent.

Living Your Values. Ones are known for living their life according to a clear set of principles and values. They align themselves with universal values that promote the welfare of everyone. They adhere to universal laws like the Golden Rule. "As you live your values, your sense of identity, integrity, control, and inner-directedness will infuse you with both exhilaration and peace," wrote Stephen Covey, author of *Principle-Centered Leadership*, who was most likely a One.

Bettering Yourself. "Every day represents a new opportunity to become a better 'me,' a better partner, and a better contributor to the larger world," said Michelle Obama in *Becoming*. Ones are known for their commitment to inner work, personal development, and spiritual growth. They are dedicated to continuous improvement and to improving themselves. By bettering yourself, you help to make the world a better place.

On a Crusade. Ones are on a crusade. They fight the good fight. They can be fiery, highly driven, and fueled by a strong sense of duty. Ones often feel they've been given a specific task or divine assignment that they must fulfill. They are inspired by a higher purpose and a soul calling. "My personal creed is to do something each day that improves the world," says Caroline Myss in *Sacred Contracts*.

Social Activism. Ones are drawn to the kind of work that helps to reform laws, institutions, relations, and expectations in society. Ones are known for their social activism and for their work as environmentalists, justice makers, Earth keepers, diplomats, educators, teachers, and leaders. "Activism is my rent for living on the planet," says, Alice Walker, novelist, poet, and social activist.

LOSS OF GOODNESS

Forgetting about our original blessing, and the basic goodness of our soul, is the only "sin" or "mistake" we need to atone for.

– Matthew Fox, *Original Blessing*

Everyone has Original Goodness in their bones. Every newborn child is "clothed in goodness," to quote Julian of Norwich, the 14th-century mystic. If you've ever held a newborn child in your arms, you know this is true. Children are "made in heaven," so to speak. A baby looks and feels perfect, even if they have a limb missing. Nobody judges a newborn baby. An infant doesn't have a bad attitude. Little children don't criticize themselves. They don't say things like, "My legs are too chubby" or "My smile isn't perfect" or "This diaper doesn't look good on me."

Your Original Goodness is always with you, no matter how many mistakes you make or how much trauma or chaos you experience. That said, your awareness of your Original Goodness can be forgotten or obscured, and that's when you experience a sense of separation from your original nature. Psychologists observe that the separation phase happens between one and three years old, which is when a child begins to think of themselves as an "I," a "me," and "myself." The nine Types on the Enneagram experience the separation phase differently. For example, a Three feels a loss of intrinsic value and self-worth; a Six is overwhelmed by self-doubt and anxiety, and a Nine senses a lack of inner peace. And a One experiences a loss of goodness.

Type Ones experience the separation as a "fall from grace," like in the Bible story of Adam and Eve. The metaphysical meaning of "fall from grace" is a descent from a state of divine blessing and holy perfection. For Ones, this loss of good standing is a visceral feeling. They feel it in their bones. "As a One, I feel like heaven is 'up there' and I am 'down here,'" said Jo, a One, who took my Purpose and the Enneagram program. This split between heaven and earth, and psyche and persona, is how the story of Original Sin begins. *Did I do something wrong? Have I been bad? How can I make this right?* Ones will not rest until they are redeemed and recover their original goodness.

> *The first and primary meaning of salvation is this: to preserve things in the good.*
> — Thomas Aquinas

Basic Fear: Not Good Enough

When Ones forget their Original Goodness, a basic fear emerges that affects their self-image, emotional well-being, mental health, and close relationships. The basic fear for Ones is *the fear of not being good enough.*

Everyone can relate to the fear of not being good enough. We've all had moments when we've told ourselves, "I'm not a good enough parent" or "My best is not good enough" or "I'm not good enough to succeed," for instance. In my book *Happiness NOW!* I described the belief of "not being good enough" as the ego's greatest addiction and a major block to self-acceptance and happiness. For Ones, it can lead to harmful behaviors like unrelenting self-criticism, over-judging, self-directed anger, perfectionism, and an addiction to self-improvement.

> *There is more in you of good than you know, child of the kindly West.*
> — Torin to Bilbo, *The Hobbit*, J. R. R. Tolkien

The fear of "I am not good enough" is based on a judgment. Where does this judgment come from? Does it come from an angry God, a disappointed God, or a God that has put you on trial? Is God a bearded man in the sky who judges you? As children, most of us were taught stories about the fall from grace, the Original Sin, and the last judgment. *Is God really judging you?* "I'm not sure if God is judging me or not, but what I do know is that no one has judged me more than I've judged myself," said Graham, a One, who took my Spiritual Growth and the Enneagram program.

As we will see, this basic fear of not being good enough has a significant effect on a One's emotional wellness and their way of being. Here are a few things that Ones have told me about living with this basic fear:

- "I have a persistent 'Be Perfect' driver."
- "I set myself very high standards."
- "My report card reads: 'Could do better.'"
- "My superego makes me feel I am on trial."
- "My inner critic finds fault in everything I do."
- "I pick holes in my appearance."
- "I get easily frustrated with myself."
- "I can be very strict with myself and others."
- "I struggle to feel good about myself."
- "I wish I didn't judge myself so much."

Childhood Story: The Good Child

When young Ones fear they are not good enough, they will typically try to reclaim the feeling of "I am good" by modeling good behavior and presenting themselves to others as a good child. Here's what Richard Rohr, a One, said about his childhood in his book *Discovering the Enneagram*:

> From early childhood we ONEs have generally tried to be model children. Even in our first years we internalized those explicit or implicit voices that demand, "Be good! Behave yourself! Try hard. Don't be childish! Do it better!" Back then we decided to earn the love of the people around us by meeting their expectations and being "good." We tried to find, develop and stick to standards for judging what was good and bad, right and wrong. This demanding voice in us never falls silent.

In their family, young Ones typically take on the role of the Good Child to gain approval and earn love. They present themselves as "a good little adult" who is very sensible, always good, and never has to sit on the naughty step. Being a "good little boy" or a "clever little girl" is not always easy. For starters, adults have different ideas about what good is. For instance, your mum is strict and plays "Bad Cop," but your dad is easygoing and he plays "Good Cop." Your grandparents are more liberal than your parents, and they let you "get away with murder," which drives your parents crazy. Your teachers don't sing from the same hymn sheet, and your schoolmates often behave like children, which they are. Also, people contradict themselves, which is very disappointing and unfair.

Hermione Granger in the Harry Potter stories is a good example of a One. Hermione starts out as a rather bossy, perfectionistic, annoying, Goody Two-shoes. She always gets good grades and not surprisingly is made a prefect, a role that she takes very seriously. She's always correcting her best friends Harry Potter and Ron Weasley. "It's Leviosa, Not Leviosar!" she tells Ron when they are learning the Wingardium Leviosa levitation spell. Fortunately, Hermione changes for the good as she grows up. She becomes less rigid, she challenges her ideas of right and wrong, and she learns how to be a truly good friend to Harry and Ron.

> *The challenge itself is to exceed certain high standards you've set for yourself.*
> — Dimple Kapadia

When Ones play the role of the Good Child, they are trying to make themselves into a good person instead of simply being good naturally. The superego command *"I must be good"* sucks the joy out of them. Being good becomes a duty, an obligation, and a cross to bear. It makes a young One want to rebel and turn bad. Just like the "Bad Tuesday" chapter in *Mary Poppins*, in which young Michael wakes up one day with an urge to be naughty. Mary Poppins tells him he's got out of the wrong side of bed. Michael doesn't care, though. That day, he performs several misdeeds, including tying the tail of Miss Lark's dog to a fence and scribbling on his father's blotter. At bedtime, Michael reflects on his naughty ways.

"Isn't it a funny thing, Mary Poppins," he said drowsily. "I've been so very naughty and I feel so very good."

The "Be Perfect" Driver: Ones are known for having a persistent "Be Perfect" driver in their ego operating system. The ego-ideal for Ones is to be "better than good" and "even more perfect." Your "Be Perfect" driver has the "good intention" of realizing your highest potential and making you a better person. The upside of the "Be Perfect" driver is that it helps you to be focused and disciplined, pay attention to detail, hold yourself accountable, and deliver high-quality work. It helps you to aim high, to drive continuous improvement, and to excel at what you do.

The "Be Perfect" driver also has a downside with plenty of "not-so-good" side-effects. Ones who put pressure on themselves to be perfect often feel incapacitated, oppressed, and unable to enjoy their lives. *How many happy perfectionists do you know?* Setting impossibly high standards reinforces the One's basic fear of "I am not good enough." Their perfectionism is a form of self-attack. They find fault in everything they do. They are afraid of making mistakes. Nothing they do is ever good enough. "I wanted to be perfect so that I could stop judging myself, but the harder I tried to be perfect, the more I judged myself," said William, a One, a lawyer who took my Love and the Enneagram program.

Gill Edwards, a clinical psychologist, was a One. In her book *Wild Love,* she gave a very personal account of what it was like growing up with a "Be Perfect" driver and living with the fear of not being good enough. She wrote:

> Looking back, I had always tried to be good. As a child, I was helpful and self-contained. I cared for my younger brother. I was academically bright. Like many too-good children, I rarely expressed anger, hurt, sadness or other negative emotions. Somehow, I got the message that I must always be good, perfect and happy, and I did my best to succeed at that impossible task. At the age of 19, I became anorexic—aiming to be perfectly slim, perfectly in control, perfectly self-denying, perfectly free from any "messy" needs or emotions.

Let's look at some examples of how the "Be Perfect" driver operates for Ones in the three biological instincts: (1) Self-Preservation Instinct, which is mostly about lifestyle, material matters, and self-care; (2) Social Instinct, which is about relating to family, society, and the world; and (3) Sexual Instinct (also called One-to-One Instinct), which is about attraction, relating style, and romance.

Self-Preservation Instinct (SP) *Healthy:* Your lifestyle is well organized and orderly. You keep your home tidy, or at least how *you* like it. You control your calendar and manage your time wisely. You are responsible with money. You never miss a Pilates class or gym visit. You keep yourself in good shape. *Not-so-healthy:* You try to impose order on your physical surroundings. You have a lot of rules. For example, there's a right way and wrong way to store food in the refrigerator, the car keys should always be put in their proper place, and attendance for Sunday lunch is mandatory. SP Ones are most likely to set a rota for household chores. Family and friends wish you weren't so uptight, rigid, and controlling. They love it when you let your hair down and play. *Unhealthy*: You suffer from neurotic perfectionism. You are a control freak. You crucify yourself for making mistakes. You pick holes in your appearance. You abstain and binge. You deny yourself pleasure. You never rest.

Social Instinct (SO) *Healthy:* Your aim is to be a good daughter, good friend, a good partner, a good parent, a good and faithful servant, and a good citizen. You join organizations that follow tradition, have a code of conduct, and aim to do something good in the world. You are most likely involved in neighborhood projects, social reform, the school PTA, your local church, and charity work. *Not-so-healthy:* the role of being a "good person" can be a burden and a strain on you. You take on too many responsibilities and duties. For instance, you are a school governor, a trustee of your local theater, and a course marshal at your golf club. *Unhealthy:* You set high standards for yourself and others. No one meets your expectations. You wag your accusing finger at them. You have a hard stare of disapproval. Someone is always in your bad books. Your loved ones feel not good enough around you. You act superior. You are prone to outbursts of moral outrage. You can be cruel and inhumane.

Sexual Instinct (SX) *Healthy:* SX Ones are typically more overtly passionate and intense than an SP One or SO One. They are attracted to people who share similar values. They look for a marriage made in heaven. They are inspired by people who are virtuous and represent something good. They seek to pledge their allegiance and to betroth themselves to a person or a cause that is good and pure. *Not-so-healthy:* You are looking for Mr. Right or Miss Perfect, but no one meets your standards. You conduct a date with a potential mate more like a job interview or a court proceeding. You rule out opportunities because of your perfectionism and high standards. You are too idealistic to make a positive difference in the world. *Unhealthy:* You are Utopian and idealistic. You fall in love with ideas and ideologies. You put others on a pedestal. You idealize them, only to be disappointed later. You can be very critical and controlling of loved ones. You are authoritarian. You have a wild side. There is no pleasing you. People fear your wrath. You condemn and punish those who don't live up to your ideals.

Passion: Anger

All nine Types on the Enneagram experience a *passion*, or cause of suffering in the heart, that emerges from a sense of separation and from the basic fear. The passion for Ones is anger. It is closely associated with the sin of wrath, which is one of the so-called cardinal sins. Wrath is uncontrolled anger.

> *Anger is the deadly sin I've had most difficulty with.*
> — John Cleese, interview for *The Guardian*

Everybody gets angry. All nine Types in the Enneagram have their hot buttons. For instance, Eights have a fire in their belly and a short fuse; Nines can be passive-aggressive and stubborn; Sevens will "throw their toys out of the pram" when upset; and Threes get angry when they don't feel valued and esteemed by others. For Ones, anger is more than just an emotion; it is a chief feature of their personality structure. For Ones, anger is a wound and a constant thorn in their side.

Claudio Naranjo, in his classic work *Ennea-Type Structures*, gives an insightful account of how anger is experienced in the heart of Ones. He describes anger as the "generalized emotional background and original root" of the character structure of Ones. He writes, "The passion of anger permeates the whole of ennea-type 1 character and is the dynamic root of drives or attitudes such as . . . criticality, demandingness, dominance and assertiveness, perfectionism, over-control, self-criticism and discipline." Anger is not just an occasional thing for Ones; it is ever present, and Ones must learn how to transform their relationship to anger if they are to reclaim their Original Goodness.

"Be angry, and do not sin," wrote the apostle Paul in his letter to the Ephesians 4:26. Look carefully at Paul's words and you will see that Paul is not saying, "Don't be angry," and he's also not saying, "Anger is a sin." Ones often get into trouble with anger because they try so hard not to be angry. Ones typically judge anger as a "negative emotion," but anger is negative only when it is managed badly, so to speak. Being angry doesn't mean you have an anger problem, but suppressing anger, denying anger, or festering in anger is a problem. The sin of anger is being controlled by it. That's why Paul says to the Ephesians, "Do not let the sun go down on your wrath, nor give place to the devil."

Being angry is not a sin. Richard Rohr, who is a One, encourages Ones, and all nine Types, to see anger as a call to action. Anger mobilizes your energy. Anger brings out the activist in you when you see injustice, discrimination, malpractice, and wrongdoing. In the *The Enneagram and Grace*, which is a recording of a program co-presented by Richard Rohr and Russ Hudson, Rohr reminds us that Jesus got angry. "Anger can be deserved, and even virtuous, particularly when it motivates us to begin seeking necessary change," says Rohr. The inner work for Ones is to use anger as an invitation for healing and as a path of growth. Anger is an energy that can be transformed into compassion and love.

Let's look more closely at five common ways that the passion of anger plays itself out in Ones.

Anger Directed at Myself. Ones experience a lot of self-directed anger. "We ONES are angry at ourselves," wrote Richard Rohr in *Discovering the Enneagram*. Anger is activated in Ones when they don't feel good about themselves. They get angry for failing to live up to their ego-ideal of a saint who never gets angry, a bodhisattva who is always compassionate, a parent who raises a model child, or a leader who never makes a mistake. *Who is such a person? Have they ever existed? Might your ego-ideal be a mistake?*

Anger Expressed as Grief. Richard Rohr observed, "After a lifetime of counselling and retreat work—not to mention my own spiritual direction—I have become convinced that most anger comes, first of all, from a place of deep sadness." Grief, or sadness, for Ones relates to the perceived loss of Original Goodness and the fall from grace. It is a heartbreak that arises from the most wretched feeling of having messed up and having done something that can never be forgiven or atoned for.

Anger and Perfectionism. Ones feel disappointed and ashamed of themselves for not being more perfect. They are forever putting themselves on trial and punishing themselves for being human, for making mistakes, for getting things wrong, and for blotching their copybook. Their perfectionism never looks at what they do well or get right; it focuses only on their mistakes and what's wrong with them. *This so-called perfectionism is not kind or wise; it is a mistake that you must forgive yourself for and release.*

Anger and Resentment. Deborah Egerton, who is a One, and author of *Enneagram Made Easy*, writes about "the underlying current of resentment" that lives in the heart of Ones. For One's resentment can be a form of complaining, e.g., *Why is the world in such a mess? Where have all the good leaders gone? Why is it always me who washes the dishes? Why doesn't God do more?* Ones often feel like they are the only ones trying to make the world a better place.

Anger and Frustration. For Ones, anger arises from a feeling of disappointment and frustration. *All of my good works are not enough.* Anger is a reaction to a feeling of failure and futility. *My vocal range is only three octaves.* Anger stems from feelings of hopelessness and powerlessness. *We are destroying the planet. A good planet is hard to find.* Anger comes from a terrible fear of being forsaken and abandoned by God. Anger is an expression of anguish and deep despair.

Fixation: Judging

In the Enneagram, the *fixation* refers to a mental habit that causes an imbalance in your mental health and well-being. The fixation for Ones is judging.

Ones have a love-hate relationship with judging. They pride themselves on being good judges. They believe they're a better judge than others, including most other Ones. They use their judging faculty to help them be a good person and do good things in the world. Being a good judge helps Ones in the following ways:

> *Do not judge and you will not be judged; because the judgments you give are the judgments you will get.*
>
> — Matthew 7:1

Being ethical: telling the difference between good and bad.
Law and order: discerning between right and wrong.
Being organized: and not too chaotic, messy, and unruly.
Living with integrity: staying in alignment with personal values.
Self-discipline: enforcing good habits and breaking bad habits.
Justice: knowing what is right, fair, and just in every situation.
Being wise: being a good judge of character.

Judging becomes a problem for Ones when it is habitual and compulsive. Then it's as if their judging faculty has an energy of its own; it's a habit that is beyond their conscious control. Trevor, a One, who is a lawyer, told me, "When my Inner Judge is in control of my thinking, I judge the weather, I judge the news, I judge the economy, I judge my children. And, most of all, I judge myself for being so judgmental."

"All my thoughts turn into judgments," said Claire, a One, whom I mentored when she had writer's block. Her last novel had been critically acclaimed, and now she was putting herself under pressure to make sure her next book was even better. "I'm so self-critical that I can't finish a single sentence without deleting it and starting over," she told me. Claire was very frustrated with herself. "Nothing I write feels right!" she said. I told Claire that trying to "get it right" was blocking her creativity. "You might be right," she said with a twinkle in her eye. Claire's new book is soon to be published. I've just read it. It's amazing how much creativity is released in Ones when they judge and criticize themselves less.

Everyone judges. Take a close look at your psychology, and you will see that most of your thoughts and speech are judgments. *What bad weather we are having. Have a good day. You look pretty in that dress. What a good girl you are.* All nine Types on the Enneagram have their own flavor of judging. For Ones, their judging can be especially excessive and destructive, and that is why it is named as their fixation. Mindfulness breaks the habit of judging, especially for Ones. And mindfulness starts with self-awareness. Here are a few common ways that Ones experience the fixation of judging.

> **Being on Trial.** Ones are known for having a fussy super-ego—or internal judge—that assesses every thought and action as either good or bad and right or wrong. "Anybody who isn't a ONE can hardly imagine how exhausting it is to go through this endless inner trial," says Richard Rohr. The superego judges and shames Ones when they make a mistake or fail to live up to their ego-ideal of being a good person. *The good news for Ones is that the more you reclaim your inherent goodness, the less your superego rules over you.*
>
> **The Deforming Mirror.** The more judgmental Ones are, the more it distorts their thinking and perception. Anaïs Nin, the French novelist and essayist, observed: "Every one of us carries a deforming mirror where he sees himself too small or too large, too fat or too thin. . . . One discovers that destiny can be diverted, that one does not have to remain in bondage to the first wax imprint made on childhood

sensibilities. Once the deforming mirror has been smashed, there is a possibility of wholeness. There is a possibility of joy."

Log in Your Eye. "Why do you see the speck in your neighbour's eye, but do not notice the log in your own eye?" said Jesus in a parable that addresses the psychological concept of projection. When Ones judge they are "not good enough," "bad," or "wrong," they project their self-judgment on their work that is "not good enough," achievements that are "not good enough," loved ones who are "not good enough," and so on. Judging is not seeing; it is projection. When you judge a person, including yourself, you don't see who they are; you see only your judgments about them.

Addiction to Perfection. Perfectionism is a thorn in the side of Ones. Judging encourages perfectionism; and perfectionism makes you judge too much. Marion Woodman, the Jungian analyst, who was most likely a One, called perfectionism "a form of enslavement." In her classic work *Addiction to Perfection*, she wrote "perfection is an addiction to unreality." Ones struggle to give up perfectionism because they believe it is a good thing and that it makes them a better person. But when Ones are asked if they'd like their children to be perfectionists, they always say no.

Could Do Better. "Good, better, best. Never let it rest. 'Til your good is better and your better is best," is a saying attributed to Saint Jerome, who translated the Bible into Latin in the 4th century. The problem with superego commands that demand perfection is that they don't define what it is. Therefore, you always end up feeling "not good enough," which is the basic fear that drives this relentless self-judging. You never rest, you are never satisfied, and your report card always reads "could do better."

PATH OF GOODNESS

Our work is to reclaim our Original Goodness,
the Goodness that we are all made of.

– Matthew Fox

The Enneagram offers a path of growth for all nine Types that helps you to remember your original nature and be your True Self. For Ones, the path of growth is reclaiming your Original Goodness, and so I call it the Path of Goodness.

The Prodigal Son as told in the Gospel of Luke is a redemption parable that reminds us of our Original Goodness. Here is how I tell this story when I teach about Point One on the Enneagram:

> A father has two sons. The father represents God. He is a very healthy Type One, and he is unconditional love. The elder son is also a One, and the younger son is a Seven. The younger son doesn't want to wait for his inheritance, so he asks for it now. The father agrees and divides his estate between his two sons. The elder son stays at home, but the younger takes off on an adventure. He leaves the kingdom of his father. This action symbolizes the separation phase and the fall from grace.
>
> The younger son squanders his inheritance. He doesn't just lose all his money; he also forgets about his father's love, which is his real inheritance. A famine strikes the land. The famine represents a lack of food and a lack of spiritual nourishment and grace. His lowest point comes when he envies the pigs he is feeding. He has forgotten his sacred self and the goodness of his soul.
>
> The repentant younger son decides to return home. Along the way, he rehearses his speech to his father. He says, "I will arise and go to my Father and will say unto him, Father, I have sinned against heaven, and before thee, and am no more worthy to be called thy son: make me one of thy hired servants." The son expects to be punished for his mistakes. "But while he was still a long way off, his father saw him and was filled with compassion for him; he ran to his son, threw his arms around him and kissed him." The father does not condemn his son. "Let's have a feast and celebrate," he says. The message here is *God is unconditional love, and God does not judge you.*
>
> Meanwhile, the elder son, who is a One, has been working in the field, performing his duties. When he hears of his younger brother's return and that a party is in full swing, he gets angry because he believes it is unjust and unfair. "Look! All these years I've been slaving for you and never disobeyed your orders." And his father says, "My son, you are always with me, and everything I

have is yours." The message here is, *you don't have to make yourself good and perfect to earn unconditional love.* You are loved as you are.

Virtue: Serenity

Every Enneagram type has a virtue, or a superpower, that arises naturally as you do your inner work to heal the basic fear, the passion in the heart, and the fixation in your thinking. The virtue for Ones is *serenity*.

Serenity is linked to the Greek word *euthymia*. In Greek, the prefix *eu* means "good or well" and *thymia* comes from the word *thymus,* meaning "mind." So, *euthymia* means "a good state of mind." Imagine being in a good state of mind. This is what serenity is. What exactly is a good state of mind? Here are some answers I've collected from Ones who attended my Enneagram programs: *A mind free of judgment. Seeing the good in others. Accepting myself as I am. Good decision-making. Deep sense of inner peace. No bias or prejudice. Knowing that all is well. Compassionate and forgiving. Open to new ideas.*

Tom Carpenter, my spiritual mentor, who I mentioned earlier, was a living example of serenity. Tom had clear blue eyes. There wasn't a log or plank in either eye. Tom could see right through me. It was as if he could read my most private thoughts, including my worst fears and judgments about myself. Despite this, I always felt totally accepted by Tom. "The less you judge someone, the more you see who they really are," he told me. Tom was the first person to say to me, "There is nothing wrong with you." Whenever I was with Tom, I experienced a deep feeling of self-acceptance. I felt good in his company. I would forget to judge myself. The serenity in Tom activated serenity in me, and I felt good inside myself.

Serenity, or a good state of mind, has many facets to it. Here are a few ways that Ones experience serenity in their everyday lives.

> **A Mind Without Judgment.** Serenity is a mind that is free of habitual judging and criticizing. Imagine how much better you'd feel if you judged yourself less. *And can you think of someone you love who'd appreciate it if you didn't criticize them so much?* Rumi, a Sufi poet, gave a beautiful description of serenity. He said, as translated by Coleman Barks, "Out beyond ideas of wrongdoing and rightdoing, there is a field. I'll meet you there. When the soul lies down in that grass, the world is too full to talk about. Ideas, language, even the phrase 'each other' doesn't make any sense."

A Heart Without Shame. Serenity is a feeling in your heart that arises naturally when you're not shaming yourself with thoughts like "I have sinned," "I am bad," "There's something wrong with me," "I am not good enough," and "God doesn't love me." We all experience shame, but for many people, shame is compounded by the doctrine of Original Sin, a term coined by Saint Augustine, four centuries after Jesus was alive. Originally, the word *sin* referred to a mistake, not to a basic character flaw. Tom Carpenter, my mentor, taught, "Just beyond your belief in sin, is the awareness that there is no one in creation who does not love you, and whom you do not love too."

Miracle of Self-Acceptance. Ones are known for their commitment to self-improvement. As a One, you want to make yourself a better *you*. What's wrong with that? Nothing, if you also know how to practice self-acceptance. *No amount of self-improvement can make up for any lack of self-acceptance.* The miracle of self-acceptance is that when you accept your Original Goodness, you naturally judge yourself less, you are more creative, you are less perfectionistic, and you can do more good in the world.

Shoulding on Yourself. Serenity is an absence of superego commands that include a lot of "must," "ought," and "should." For Ones, their superego tells them that happiness is permissible only if you dress well, speak correctly, make no mistakes, get everything right, think no evil, and are a model citizen. Ones also do a lot of "shoulding on yourself." For instance, "I shouldn't get angry," "I must set a good example," and "I ought to know better." Imagine what good things could happen in your life if you eliminated the word *should* from your vocabulary.

All Is Well. Serenity arises from faith and a deep conviction that although there is sin, darkness, and evil, they will not triumph over you. Light is not overcome by darkness. There is no fear in perfect love. Every injustice can be reconciled through good works. Never lose heart, for goodness always prevails. The morning sun rises on a brand-new day. "All shall be well, and all shall be well, and all manner of things shall be well," said Julian of Norwich, the mystic who reminded us that we are clothed in God's Goodness.

Balancing Your Centers

Ones are called a Body Type, along with Eights and Nines on the Enneagram. As a One, your primary center of intelligence is your body center. This comes as a bit of a surprise to Ones who are typically more active in their head center than in their body center or heart center. Most Ones trust their logic more than their feelings. They prefer to be rational rather than intuitive. "Going with our gut" feels a bit risky for Ones. *Can I really trust the wisdom of my body?* Ones fear that their gut instinct is too impulsive, and that relying on the instinctual drives of their body might lead them astray.

Peter, a One, is a consultant surgeon at a London hospital. "My father was a strict and puritanical minister who believed that the body—or the 'flesh,' as he called it—is sinful and has no virtue," Peter told me. Peter's mother was a dancer, and she saw the body as a temple for the holy spirit. Working with the Enneagram has helped Peter to trust the wisdom of the body center. "In the operating theater, I experience a heightened sense of awareness from being aligned in my three centers. Each decision I make passes through a triple filter of (1) *Does this feel right in my body?* (2) *Does my heart feel good about this?* and (3) *Does my head* think *this is a sound judgment?* If it doesn't feel right in my body, I look for a better solution."

For a One it's important to know that there is goodness in all three centers. One center is not better than another. The centers need each other to function optimally. The key is to be in alignment with all three centers. A wise body, a good heart, and a sound mind will help a One to live a good life.

> **Head Center.** Being grounded in your body and connected to your heart helps you to think better. This is true for all nine Ennea-Types. When Ones are too "up in the head," their thinking often becomes flooded with judging. It's important for Ones to recognize that judging and wisdom are not the same thing. Too much judging blocks wisdom. Daniel Ladinsky, the poet, offers this story about Hafiz: "Once a young woman said to me, Hafiz, what is the sign of someone who knows God? I became very quiet, and looked deep into her eyes, and replied, 'My dear, they have dropped the

knife.' Someone who knows God has dropped the cruel knife that most so often use upon their tender self and others." *How can you drop the knife today?*

Body Center. Ones who are purpose-driven and have a strong sense of mission often sacrifice their physical well-being for the greater cause. I've coached a lot of Ones in leadership positions who carry chronic physical ailments. They routinely override messages their body sends them, such as muscle tension, back pain, a stiff neck, and tense shoulders. Marion Woodman, the Jungian analyst, who might be a One, wrote, "Often we listen to a cat with more precision than we listen to our body." She said, "Body work is soul work." She taught her students to respect the instinctual wisdom of the body, listen with love to the body's messages, and treat the body as a good friend. *What is your body trying to tell you?*

> *When the body is finally listened to . . . it becomes eloquent. It's like changing a fiddle into a Stradivarius.*
> — Marion Woodman

Heart Center. Ones often come across as being cold and heartless. This is because they favor reason over emotion and logic over feelings. And yet when Ones are "in their heart," they are warm, compassionate, loving, and wise. Gill Edwards, in *Wild Love*, gives us a great insight into the "good heart" of a Type One. She wrote, "When we are connected with Source, we are naturally 'good,' warm and loving—but it comes from the heart, not from a sense of duty or loyalty or approval-seeking. It is authentic. It is real. It is who we really are, and not what others think we should be." Ask your heart, *What would you like me to know today?* Listen. Feel. Take notes. And act accordingly.

> *The good person out of the good treasure of his heart produces good.*
> — Luke 6:45

Spreading Your Wings

Ones are situated at Point One, which is positioned between Point Nine and Point Two on the Enneagram. This means Ones have a 9-Wing and a 2-Wing. Typically, one wing is more dominant than the other, but the goal is to balance your wings. Working with the 9-Wing can help Ones to tap into the energy and wisdom of Point Nine and working with the 2-Wing can help Ones access the same at Point Two. Learning to live in balance with the wings, and drawing on the strengths of both, is certainly a good way to go for Ones.

One with a 2-Wing

Ones with a dominant 2-Wing (1w2) are called the Advocate. They show up in the world with the main characteristics of a One, plus some traits of Twos. For example:

> **Warm-Hearted.** As a 1w2, you combine the healthy qualities of Ones with the positive qualities of heart-centered Twos such as warmth, friendliness, and affection. Ones who are over-earnest in their efforts to make the world a better place, can inadvertently come across as overly serious, rational, cold-hearted, and unfeeling. The 2-Wing helps Ones to create more heart-to-heart connections with others. They come across to others as less of a scary schoolteacher and as more of a wise and good friend.
>
> **Relationship-Centered.** 1w2s tend to be more interpersonal and social than 1w9s. As a 1w2, you are typically active in your neighborhood. You attend meetings, get involved in conversations, and like to make your presence felt. You create a personal connection with the people you serve. You make yourself a close ally, an advocate, and a supporter of other people's good causes too.

> *Never believe that a few caring people can't change the world. For indeed, that's all who ever have.*
>
> — Margaret Mead

Nurturing Relationships. As a 1w2, you are busy making the world a better place, but you also manage to make time to enjoy and nurture your close relationships. You might be working all hours on a project that has a global impact, but you also prioritize playing in the sandbox with your son, taking your partner out on a date, calling on your neighbor, mailing a birthday card to an auntie, or having a night out with friends.

Making Amends. "Ones don't argue, they just explain why they are right!" said Kim, a One, who took my Love and the Enneagram program. As a One, you can come across as hard-edged, rigid, judgmental, and opinionated. *It's difficult even for a One to love someone who thinks they're always right.* We all make mistakes in relationships, and the 2-Wing can help 1w2s to be humble, to apologize, and to make amends when necessary.

Humble Up! Caroline Myss, a One, teaches the need for humility on the spiritual path. "Humble Up!" is one of her favorite sayings. Humility is the virtue for Twos, and it is very helpful for 1w2s. In *Intimate Conversations with the Divine*, Myss wrote, "Humility is a protection against our worst instincts, among them our tendency to judge situations and people we know nothing about." Humility can help 1w2s be more kind-hearted, practice better self-care, and ask for help when they need it.

One with a 9-Wing

Ones with a dominant 9-Wing (1w9) are often called the Idealist. They show up in the world with all the main characteristics of a One, plus traits of Nines. For example:

Inner Peace. As a 1w9 you embody the healthy qualities of Ones with positive qualities of Nines such as a tranquil mind, a calm disposition, and inner peace. Ones who have inner peace are much more effective than Ones who haven't any. "My Inner Peace is good for my family and for the world," says Jane, a 1w9, who works as a diplomat for the United Nations. "It helps me to soften my edges, slow down more often, and recharge my batteries. It also makes me more resilient and better at my job."

Positive Outlook. Nines are known for their positive outlook, their nonjudgmental nature, their respect for diversity, and their peace-loving attitude. *Seeing the good in each other is one of the greatest joys for Nines.* When 1w9s embody the positivity of Nines, they are less judgmental, critical, and self-righteous. It also makes them better at reconciling differences, resolving conflict, and making a positive difference in the world.

> *With our love, we could save the world.*
> — George Harrison

Going with the Flow. One of the wisdom teachings of Point Nine is effortless action. Healthy Nines can go with the flow. They follow the path of least resistance. "The highest good is like water. Water gives life to the ten thousand things and does not strive. It flows in places people reject and so is like the Tao," said Lao Tzu in the Tao Te Ching. As a 1w9, your 9-Wing makes you less rigid and more accommodating. You accomplish your mission with greater effortlessness and ease.

Periodic Rest. As a One, your aim is to do as much good as you can, and sometimes you push yourself too hard. Claire is a 1w2. She told me, "When I learned about the Enneagram, I realized that my 2-Wing needed the help of my 9-Wing. My 2-Wing helps me to serve and help others, but I often drive myself to the edge of exhaustion. Consciously engaging my 9-Wing has helped me be more disciplined in scheduling periodic rest and giving myself more 'time to be.'"

Down-to-Earth. 1w9s tend to be more withdrawn and introverted than 1w2s. They hang out on Cloud Nine with only their Utopian dreams for company. They social distance themselves when they want to avoid conflict. They also try to hide and suppress their anger from others. Engaging more of the 2-Wing helps 1w9s come down to earth and enjoy more connection, intimacy, and healing. It can also help them to balance their high ideals with more service and love in action.

Moving to Seven and Four

Following the Inner Lines of the Enneagram symbol, Ones move toward Point Four (home for the Individualist) and Point Seven (home for the Enthusiast). These Inner Lines invite you to visit these Points to explore the gifts and wisdom they have for you.

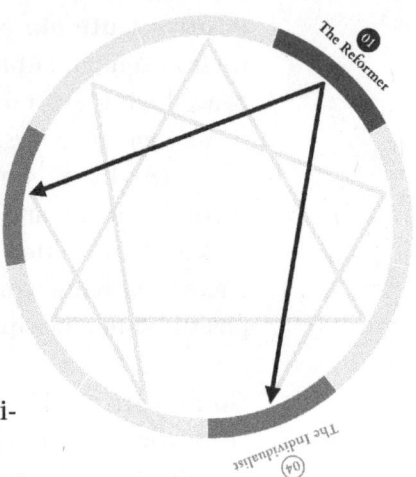

Moving to Four

When Ones are well-balanced and feel good about themselves, they embody some of the higher qualities that Fours are blessed with. For example:

Authentically You. When Ones embrace the energy of Point Four, it helps them to shift their focus from "be perfect" to "be authentic." Instead of trying to be a "better me," they focus more on being a "real me." "The more authentic I am, the better I feel about myself," said Kathy, a One, who took one of my Enneagram programs. Amazing things can happen when you remember what you are made of. And you don't have to be perfect to be amazing.

More Forgiving. The energy of Point Four helps Ones to be more self-forgiving. "Mistakes can be such friends," wrote Macrina Wiederkehr, a Four most likely, in *A Tree Full of Angels*. "They rough up my smooth edges, convincing me that I don't have to be perfect to be loved. What a freedom to be able to say, 'I was wrong'! What's wrong with being wrong? Now more than ever I can truly say, 'I like it like that.' It is such a burden to have to be right all the time."

Self-Acceptance. The virtue for Fours is equanimity, which promotes greater self-acceptance and compassion for self and others. When Ones and Fours are not busy judging or shaming themselves, they tap into the power of self-acceptance that helps them to admit their mistakes, forgive their blemishes, and remember their Original Goodness. With greater self-acceptance, you are less self-critical, you censor yourself less, you express yourself more freely, and creativity pours out of you.

When Ones are under stress, they may display some unhealthy qualities that are also common to Fours. Knowing about these unhealthy qualities can be a helpful warning sign for Ones. For example:

A Heavy Sigh. Ones and Fours are known for being melancholic and perfectionistic. They let out a heavy sigh of disappointment and frustration when dispirited and feeling low. Their heavy sigh is audible. Everyone around them hears it. Sad Ones and Fours long to withdraw from the maddening crowd. *Why aren't people better than they are? Nothing is as beautiful as it once was.* Their heavy sigh is a reaction to the perceived loss of goodness and beauty that Ones and Fours experience.

Downward Spiral. When Ones can't feel their inner goodness, and Fours have lost sight of their inner beauty, they spiral downward into depression and despair. Ones become very self-critical, and Fours compare themselves negatively with others. When Ones take on the unhealthy qualities of Four, they judge themselves mercilessly and they envy others for their goodness and beauty. *The more Ones judge themselves, the more they lose sight of their inherent goodness.*

Put to Shame. "Whatever is begun in anger ends in shame," is a quote attributed to Benjamin Franklin, who was most likely a Seven. Ones are known for their self-directed anger. Their anger arises from self-judgment "I am not good enough." The effect of their excessive self-judging is shame. When Ones are not compassionate with themselves, they can get caught in a destructive cycle of self-judging, self-shaming, and self-harming.

Moving to Seven
When Ones are well-balanced and healthy, they tap into some of the positive qualities that Sevens are blessed with. For example:

Joy Is Noble. "Joy is the noblest human act," said Thomas Aquinas, the 13th-century Italian philosopher and priest, who spoke often about the Original Goodness in everyone. Ones are so busy trying to make the world a better place that they often have no time to smile, to play, to laugh, and to enjoy themselves. "I habitually put joy on the backburner," Suzanne, a One, told me. When Ones integrate the wisdom at Point Seven, they recognize that their happiness helps to make the world a better place.

More Spontaneous. Sevens are known for their upbeat energy, positive outlook, and unrestrained enthusiasm. When Ones integrate the energy of Point Seven, they are less controlled and more spontaneous, less rigid and more flexible, less rule-bound and more open. *There are many "right" ways to do something.* They're more willing to break their routine, to say yes to new experiences, to entertain different points of view, and to act on the spur of the moment. They trust the Holy Plan for their life, and this gives them greater inner freedom and joy.

The Fun Child. Ones are known for being "good little adults" in their childhood. From an early age, they present themselves as someone who is good, responsible, and dutiful. They're often not as playful or free-spirited as other kids. "I was too busy being good to enjoy my childhood," said Tina, a One, who took my Love and the Enneagram program. The energy of Point Seven helps Ones to reclaim their inner fun child. It encourages them to lighten up, let their hair down, and come out to play. Point Seven energy gives you permission to follow your joy.

When Ones are under pressure and weighed down by life, they may display some of the unhealthy qualities of Sevens. For example:

Loss of Focus. "Your focus needs more focus," says Jackie Chan's character, Mr. Han, who is trying to introduce self-control and discipline of focus to his young wayward student, played by Jaden Smith, in the film *Karate Kid*. Both Ones and Sevens are known for taking on too many yeses and juggling too many priorities. This causes them to lack focus, to be scattered, to make mistakes, and to struggle to complete tasks.

No Time to Stop. "There is more to life than increasing its speed," is a quote attributed to Mahatma Gandhi. When Ones are out of balance, they tend to act like unhealthy Sevens: hurried, impatient, and restless. Ones who don't make time to stop are more ego-driven, and their impatience is flavored with hints of anger, annoyance, and irritability. They are not in their right mind. There is no time for rest and play. And the doctor's appointment or visit to the hair salon gets postponed again.

On the Wild Side. When the One's superego goes into overdrive, demanding that they "do better" and "be perfect," they crash and burn. Ones can be rebellious, rather like a Seven. They are impetuous and act like a drunk. They are rebellious and break the rules. They blow off steam. They disgrace themselves, like in the film *Chocolat*, when the town mayor, who is outspoken in his opposition to the sin of pleasure, ends up breaking into the chocolatier's shop and gorging himself on chocolate.

Holy Perfection

The nine Points on the Enneagram each offer a Holy Idea—a higher wisdom or universal teaching—that all nine Ennea-Types can contemplate and put into practice.

> *Deep within you is everything that is perfect, ready to radiate through you and out into the world.*
> — A Course in Miracles

The Holy Idea at Point One is called Holy Perfection. This is the idea that each of us is made in heaven, clothed in goodness, and fashioned out of perfect love. *God doesn't make junk.* Therefore, your goal is not to create a perfect self; it is to accept that you are perfectly made and already good. Knowing that Holy Perfection exists is a great relief to Ones. It helps them to relax and trust in their Original Goodness. "And now that you don't have to be perfect, you can be good," says Lee to Abra in the novel *East of Eden*, by John Steinbeck.

Holy Perfection recognizes that the universe is oddly perfect. There is an order that underpins the chaos of everyday life. It is difficult at times to trust that "All is in Order." *Why do bad things happen to good people?* That said, there is such a thing as grace. "Grace is not fairy dust," writes Caroline Myss in *Intimate Conversations with the Divine*. Grace is the "good glue" that holds the universe together. Grace does not have to be earned or deserved. It is freely given and always available to you. This is why grace is grace! You don't need to have had a perfect past or to earn a gold star. You only need ask, and grace will appear. "It is by grace that you become a whole person and discover what is holy in you and in all beings," says Caroline.

Holy Perfection helps you to embrace your so-called imperfections. *It gives you the courage to be imperfect.* Holy Perfection helps you to forgive yourself for your blemishes. It helps you to see that even your worst mistakes can be used for your highest good and for the greater good of all.

"The great and merciful surprise is that we come to God, not by doing it right, but by doing it wrong," writes Richard Rohr in *Falling Upward*.

> *Amazing grace,*
> *how sweet the sound*
> *That saved a wretch like me*
> *I once was lost, but now I'm found*
> *Was blind, but now I see.*
>
> — "Amazing Grace," hymn

Type Two
THE HELPER

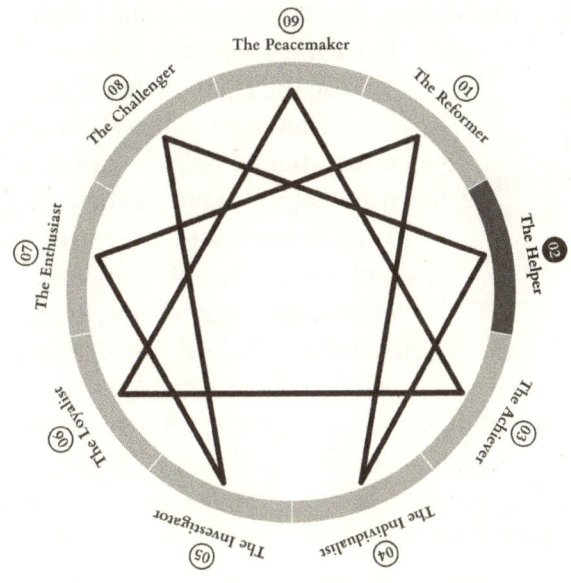

When two people relate to each other authentically and humanly, God is the electricity that surges between them.

— MARTIN BUBER

The Ennea-Type Two is commonly called the Helper or Giver. Other names for Twos include the Caretaker, Caring Soul, Servant, Altruist, and Martyr.

Type Twos are the *Heart-Centered, Interpersonal Type*. Twos feel a deep affiliation and connection with life. They recognize a basic relatedness in all of creation. Making connections is what makes

> *Life is a gift, not to possess, but to share.*
> — Henri Nouwen
> *You Are the Beloved*

life worthwhile for Twos. They have a genius for empathy. They are sensitively attuned to other people's needs. They are kind-hearted and friendly, warm and caring, and compassionate and loving. A Two's favorite greeting is *How are you?* They are the Type most likely to add a happy emoticon, smiles and hearts, to their text messages. They bring a gift for you when they visit. It feels good to be in the company of Twos. You feel seen by a Two. You feel loved by them, and you feel that they are here for you.

Twos are happiest when they are helping people, giving to others, and being of service. As we shall see, they have a strong "Be Helpful" driver installed in their ego operating system. Twos are the first to raise their hand when they hear a request for help. They are the Good Samaritan. They are genuinely skilled helpers, carers, and givers. Being truly helpful is one of their soul gifts. That said, Twos can overidentify with their role of helper and often overlook their own needs. They give more than they receive, resist asking for help, and struggle with self-care, all of which blocks the flow of love and connection with others.

> *Life becomes harder for us when we live for others, but it also becomes richer and happier.*
> — Albert Schweitzer

When Twos are taking an Enneagram test, they're already thinking about who to share the test with. *Mom would find this so helpful. Terry needs to know about this. The Enneagram could change Alex's life!* Twos are the Type most likely to gift an Enneagram book to a friend. I meet a lot of Twos on my Enneagram programs. They are especially drawn to my programs that focus on relationships, parenting, and coaching with the Enneagram. They want to use the Enneagram to understand their partner better, be a more skilled helper, and be a more loving person. Twos often need reminding that the Enneagram is also for self-awareness, for healing their own blocks to love, and for being more compassionate and caring toward themselves.

Working with the Enneagram can be a great gift for Twos, helping them to recognize their own needs, balance giving with receiving, serve without being in sacrifice, and be a magnet for greater abundance and love.

INTRODUCING TYPE TWO

Are you a Type Two on the Enneagram? Maybe you have a family member, a friend, or a work colleague who is a Two.

My aunt Joan, who was my father's younger sister, was a Two. My brother David and I loved our visits to Aunt Joan and Uncle Ken. Joan had a very big heart. She dispensed hugs freely, and she always burst into tears when she saw David and me. "Don't worry, boys, these are happy tears," she'd assure us. Aunt Joan gave us presents even when it wasn't our birthday. She had the biggest freezer ever, full of pizzas, french fries, chicken nuggets, and enormous tubs of ice cream. She always filled our pockets with candies and sweets before we went home. My dad, who was an Eight, would tell his sister to stop spoiling us. "I'm not spoiling them; I'm loving them," she'd say.

Aunt Joan drove Uncle Ken crazy because she didn't look after herself. "I'm too busy looking after you," she'd tell him, though Ken was perfectly content. "I don't need you to help me," he'd tell her. Joan neglected her own health and paid the price for it; she was overweight and suffered from diabetes. She fretted constantly about her son and daughter. "Stop fussing, Mum," said her son, Nick. "I'm okay, Mum," Sarah, her daughter, told her. "You need to look after you." It was sad to see Aunt Joan struggle with her physical mobility and health. It got to the point where she couldn't go out anymore. She became increasingly isolated. She didn't ask for help. If anyone asked her if she needed anything, she'd say, "I'm fine, thank you."

Maria, a Two, attended my program on *Love and the Enneagram*. "I knew I was a Two the moment I learned that the name for Twos is the Helper," she told me. Maria was in her 50s, a mother of two children and two foster children. She had two part-time jobs to cover for her husband, who was unemployed. Her elderly father lived at home with them, and she was his main carer. In her free time, she volunteered at a nearby dog rescue shelter. "I've had four heart attacks in the last five years," she told me. "Each time I was rushed into hospital, I was excited to be there. As the paramedics wheeled me onto the ward, I prayed to God, *How can I serve?* and *Show me who I can help.*"

> *Helper's Prayer*
> Dear God, please help me
> to ask for help more often.
> Thank you.
> Amen.

It was on her fourth visit to hospital that Maria experienced what she called "a miracle." As Maria lay on her hospital bed praying to God, *How can I help?* she heard a voice tell her, "My Beloved Child, it is you who needs the help." During her convalescence, she read a book on the Enneagram that a friend had given her five years earlier after her first heart attack.

Healthy Qualities of Twos

When Twos are healthy and well-balanced, they display essential qualities that we all love and appreciate. Here are a few things healthy Twos have told me about themselves:

- "I am very much a people person."
- "It is my joy to help and serve others."
- "I am called to be of service."
- "I want to make a contribution to life."
- "I believe a loving world starts with me."
- "Life is a gift, and I want to give back to life."
- "Being of service connects me to my purpose."
- "Making connections is why we are all here."
- "I can't take the last cookie on the plate!"
- "I'm getting better at prioritizing self-care."

Unhealthy Qualities of Twos

When Twos are out of balance, their generous and loving approach to life becomes more fearful, needy, and manipulative. Here are a few things Twos have told me about themselves:

- "I'm always looking for ways to be helpful."
- "I often say yes when I mean to say no."
- "I struggle to say no to requests for help."
- "I am prone to over-giving and burnout."
- "I'm afraid my needs will push friends away."
- "I feel guilty prioritizing my own well-being."
- "I have a fear that being happy is selfish."
- "I don't always follow my own helpful advice."
- "I wish I were better at asking for help."
- "I'm learning to be a better receiver."

RECOGNIZING TYPE TWOS

In the Bible, the parable of the Good Samaritan speaks to the heart of Twos. Jesus tells this story to illustrate his commandment to "Love your neighbor as yourself." On the road from Jerusalem to Jericho, a lowly Samaritan comes across a Jew who has been attacked by thieves and left for dead. A priest and a Levite have already passed by the Jew without stopping to help. Even though Samaritans were hated by Jews, the Samaritan does not hesitate to offer his help. He bandages the Jew's wounds, takes him to an innkeeper, pays for his board, and goes on his way without asking for anything in return. The Samaritan has performed an act of true kinship and unconditional love.

In Buddhism, the bodhisattva takes a vow to serve humanity and relieve the suffering of others. I imagine there is a bodhisattva for each of the nine Points on the Enneagram, and that the bodhisattva that sits at Point Two is the Maitreya Buddha, who is revered for being the "friend to all souls" and a "friend to the whole world." The name Maitreya is derived from the Sanskrit word *Maitri*, which means "friendliness." The Maitreya teaches that our dharma, our noble purpose, is "to support, hold, and bear" each other in friendship and love. There is a Tibetan prayer that begins, "I am Maitreya, the buddha of the sun; I shine with equal love upon all."

> *Differences are not intended to separate or to alienate. We are different precisely in order to realise our need of one another.*
>
> — Desmond Tutu

Archbishop Desmond Tutu, the much-loved South African anti-apartheid and human rights activist, was most likely a Two. "God's dream is that you and I and all of us will realize that we are family, and that we are made for togetherness, for goodness, and for compassion," he said. Archbishop Tutu taught the world about the Zulu African philosophy of Ubuntu, which means "humanity." The spirit of Ubuntu is expressed as, "I am because we are." Far more than a philosophy, it is a way of being. Archbishop Tutu said, "Ubuntu speaks particularly about the fact that you can't exist as a human being in isolation. It speaks about our interconnectedness. You can't be human all by yourself." Tutu went on,

> Ubuntu is the essence of being human. It speaks of the fact that my humanity is caught up and is inextricably bound up in yours. I am human because I belong. It speaks about wholeness; it speaks about compassion. A person with Ubuntu is welcoming, hospitable, warm and generous, willing to share. Such people are open and available to others, willing to be vulnerable, affirming of others, do

not feel threatened that others are able and good, for they have a proper self-assurance that comes from knowing that they belong in a greater whole.

In psychology, Erich Fromm, the humanistic philosopher and psychoanalyst, coined the term *biophilia*, which describes the human drive to connect with other people and with nature. Fromm outlined five essential human needs: a sense of identity, relatedness, rootedness or unity, a frame of orientation, and transcendence, all of which help a person to be less self-centered and more deeply connected with the world. In his classic work *The Art of Loving,* he wrote, "The deepest need of man, then, is the need to overcome his separateness and to leave the prison of his aloneness. The absolute failure to achieve this aim means insanity." Fromm went on,

> If it is true, as I have tried to show, that love is the only *sane and satisfactory answer to the problem of human existence,* then any society which excludes, relatively, the development of love, must in the long run perish of its own contradiction with the basic necessities of human nature.

In poetry, Hafiz, the 14th-century Sufi poet, is the perfect fit for Point Two. Hafiz is the most popular poet in Iran today and *The Divan of Hafiz,* his collected works, is in every Iranian home. The core themes of his poetry resonate deeply with how a Two typically sees things. For instance, Hafiz says God is Unconditional Love and that in God's eyes we are the beloved. He describes the soul as the Friend, and he encourages us "to kiss the Friend" often, which means to give yourself the gift of time alone with your soul. I especially like Daniel Ladinsky's renderings of Hafiz. In *The Gift*, he includes a poem: "Your Mother and My Mother." The last two stanzas read:

> *The heart is a thousand stringed instrument that can only be tuned with love.*
>
> — Hafiz

<blockquote>
Your soul and my soul
Once sat together in the Beloved's womb
Playing footsie.
Your heart and my heart
Are very, very old
Friends.
</blockquote>

In leadership, the signature style of Twos is to lead by being of service. When I teach about Point Two on my Leadership and the Enneagram program, I feature the work of Robert Greenleaf, who created the Servant Leadership model. In his essay "The Servant as Leader," first published in 1970, Greenleaf wrote, "The servant-leader is servant first. . . . It begins with a natural feeling that one wants to serve, to serve first," as opposed to wanting power, influence, fame, or wealth. In his second essay, "The Institution as Servant," Greenleaf encouraged organizations to embrace a service ethic, to profit-share more generously, and help build a society that is more just and more loving.

> *This is my thesis: caring for persons, the more able and the less able serving each other, is the rock upon which a good society is built.*
>
> — Robert Greenleaf

In the arts, Stevie Wonder's music resonates with all nine Points on the Enneagram, and especially at Point Two. Stevie Wonder is most likely a Two, and in his ballads, such as "Ribbon in the Sky," "Love's in Need of Love Today," and "As," Stevie serenades us with a love that is unconditional and forever. The storytelling and lyrics in "For Once in My Life," "You Are the Sunshine of My Life," and "Signed, Sealed, Delivered, I'm Yours" have strong Two themes such as looking for love, needing to be needed, the pain of rejection, and giving your heart to someone special. Stevie Wonder is also a humanitarian who uses his music to support AIDS awareness, anti-apartheid, anti-racism, ending global poverty, and other causes.

> *Use your heart to love somebody. And if your heart is big enough, use your heart to love everybody.*
>
> — Stevie Wonder

Dolly Parton is one of the best-selling country music artists of all time and is loved by her fans for being warm-hearted, empathetic, and real. A talented actress, she played Shirlee Kenyon, a Two, in the romantic comedy *Straight Talk*. Shirlee excels at giving life advice, even though her own life is a mess. While working as an assistant on a popular call-in radio show, she is mistaken for a clinical psychologist and goes live on air as Doctor Shirlee. Her show becomes very popular, but she has plenty of mishaps, and her helpful advice gets her into trouble. In real life, Dolly Parton is also a most generous philanthropist and tireless campaigner for causes close to her heart.

> *Get down off the cross honey, somebody needs the wood!*
>
> — Dolly Parton as "Dr." Shirlee Kenyon in *Straight Talk*

In film, Samwise Gamgee in *The Fellowship of the Ring* is the best friend of Frodo, who has volunteered to take the evil Ring back to Mount Doom, a volcano in Mordor. Frodo tells Sam, "I'm going to Mordor alone!" And Sam replies, "Of course you are! And I'm coming with you." The friendship between Frodo and Sam is one of the most inspiring and heart-warming plots in this epic tale. On the way to Mordor, Sam and Frodo learn to help each other, and when Frodo can't continue physically, Sam tells him, "I can't carry it [the Ring] for you, but I can carry you." Sam carries his friend Frodo on his shoulders as they make the ascent up Mount Doom. Tolkien said it was Sam's love for Frodo that protected Frodo from the evil of the Ring, and it was love that ultimately destroyed the Ring.

In Christopher Nolan's Batman trilogy, Michael Caine plays Alfred Pennyworth, a Two, who is the butler to Bruce Wayne, a.k.a. Batman, a One. Alfred remains devoted to the Wayne family, years after Bruce's parents were tragically killed. He is a father figure to Bruce and is willing to put their friendship on the line to save him. In the original *Star Trek* TV series, Dr. Leonard McCoy, "Bones," is a Two. He is passionate, emotional, and ready to save the galaxy at the drop of a hat. He trusts his heart and is wary of technology. And in the Harry Potter series, Rubeus Hagrid, the big, friendly wizard, played by Robbie Coltrane, is a Two. He is the groundskeeper at Hogwarts, a confidant and special aide to Dumbledore, and he is ready to put his life on the line to help Harry and his friends.

> *Compassion: that's the one thing no machine ever had. Maybe it's the one thing that keeps men ahead of them.*
>
> — Dr. Leonard McCoy

The film *Clueless* is a comedic adaptation of Jane Austen's novel *Emma*. Cher Horowitz, played by Alicia Silverstone, is a modern Emma and is very Two-like. At first, her focus is on helping others find love. She is well meaning but overestimates her matchmaking skills and meddles too much in others' affairs. Cher's arc of growth begins when she humbles up, asks for help, and sorts her own life out. And then there is Stephen King's fictional character, Annie Wilkes, played by Kathy Bates, in the film *Misery*. Annie is a chilling example of a very unhealthy Two who saves a person's life, nurses him back to health, but then becomes possessive, manipulative, and unable to let go.

> *I go out of my way for you! I do everything to try and make you happy. I feed you, I clean you, I dress you, and what thanks do I get?*
>
> — Annie Wilkes in *Misery*

In Shakespeare, Juliet Capulet, in *Romeo and Juliet*, is a Two. She is a young and innocent woman who is wise, decisive, and ready to follow her heart. She loves Romeo wholeheartedly and unconditionally. She tells him, "My bounty is as boundless as the sea. My love as deep; the more I give to thee, the more I have, for both are infinite." Also, there is King Lear, an unhealthy Two, who attempts to manipulate, seduce, and buy the love of his three daughters Goneril, Regan, and Cordelia. The proud King Lear wishes to be flattered by his daughters. His fatal flaw is his pride, which he must overcome to know real love. In the opening scene, he says,

> Tell me, my daughters
> (Since now we will divest us both of rule,
> Interest of territory, cares of state),
> Which of you shall we say doth love us most,
> That we our largest bounty may extend
> Where nature doth with merit challenge.

A CONNECTED UNIVERSE

The world is not formed of things but of encounters.

— Martin Buber

The Enneagram, with its ancient Greek origins, teaches that we live in a connected universe. The circle of the Enneagram symbolizes wholeness, unity, and connection. Every wisdom tradition perceives a fundamental unity that underpins the periodic table of elements and atoms. Modern science recognizes we live in an entangled universe in which everything is related to everything. Physicist Erwin Schrödinger, who coined the term *entanglement*, said that entanglement is "not *one* but rather *the* characteristic trait of quantum mechanics." At Point Two on the Enneagram, we are invited to meditate on the unity that links heaven and earth, sun and moon, spirit and matter, body and soul, "I" and "thou," and so on. Every appearance of duality is held in perfect unity.

Here at Point Two, we recognize the interconnectedness of all things on the level of pure being. We sense this basic unity in our body and in our heart. What is it that unites us? "Love is the cause of unity of all things," said Aristotle. Love is the fabric of creation. Love is the cause of creation. Love is the sacred hoop, a

> *To be human is to live in relation, to exist in constant dialogue with others and the world around us.*
>
> — Martin Buber

term used in Native American teachings. It is the medicine wheel. It is our reason for being. "Love is indivisible," wrote Erich Fromm in *The Art of Loving*. "Love is what inseparably connects us to each other."

"Love is the greatest medicine," said Tom, a Two, who is a cardiac surgeon. I met Tom at the Heart and Beyond conference in Prague, attended by 1,000 cardiologists. I gave a keynote speech on "The Wisdom of the Heart," and Tom spoke to me afterward. "My parents introduced me to the Enneagram," he told me. Tom's mother, a psychologist, also a Two, secretly packed an Enneagram book in his suitcase when he went to Africa to work for the humanitarian aid organization Médecins Sans Frontières (Doctors Without Borders). "The Enneagram has made me a better doctor because I see all nine Types in my clinic, and I can relate to them with greater empathy and love," said Tom. "Learning about Two has also encouraged me to practice better self-care."

Twos personify loving-kindness. My friend Cheryl Richardson is a Two. Cheryl served as the first president of the International Coach Federation. She was also team leader for the Lifestyle Makeover Series on *The Oprah Winfrey Show*. I first met Cheryl at a Hay House I CAN DO IT! event in Las Vegas in 2009. I was the new kid on the block. "Welcome to the Hay House family!" said Cheryl, sensing my shyness. Cheryl took me under her wing. "Ask for what you need," she told me. She made sure I was taken care of. Cheryl has been a great coach and mentor to me. I know I can call upon her friendship at any time. When we meet up, she always asks me, "How is your self-care, Robert?"

When Twos are soul-centered, and connected with their essence, they display essential qualities and healthy traits that are appreciated and loved by all. Here are a few of these qualities.

> *Treat people with kindness because behind every face is a story that could use a little more love.*
>
> — Cheryl Richardson

Life Is a Gift. Twos see that life is gift and that each new day is a gift to be cherished. Living life as a gift helps Twos to be receptive, abundant, and present. *"Yesterday is history, tomorrow is a mystery, today is a gift. That's why we call it the present,"* is a quote attributed to Eleanor Roosevelt, who had many Two traits. Gifts are everywhere, even in the most challenging situations and painful times.

In every relationship there is a gift. And the greatest gift of all is the love we share with each other.

Generosity of Spirit. Healthy Twos have a generosity of spirit that enables them to give without it costing them anything. They help without expecting anything in return. They volunteer their services freely. "The more you love, the more loving you become. That's just the way it works. It is a generosity of spirit," says Jean Houston, a Two, and author of *The Search for the Beloved*.

A Caring Soul. A Two's favorite way of saying *"Hello"* is *"How are you?"* Twos are caring and considerate. They call on you when you're unwell, they remember your birthday, and they celebrate you. "We are wired to be caring for the other and generous to one another," wrote Desmond Tutu in *The Book of Joy*. Being a caring person means you also take care of yourself. L. R. Knost, author of *Two Thousand Kisses a Day*, understood this and clarified it in Type Two terms: "Taking care of others doesn't mean me first; it means me too."

Soul Gift. Twos often work hard to cultivate a soul gift that they can share with others. Their soul gift might be a specific talent for singing, cooking, accountancy, networking, or a knack for languages, for example. They may be a gifted teacher, a skilled caregiver, or a brilliant personal assistant. Their soul gift might be a natural quality such as a gardener with a "green thumb." "The meaning of life is to find your gift. The purpose of life is to give it away," said Picasso.

Being of Service. Twos recognize that we are here to honor, love, and serve each other. They ask *How can I serve?* and are naturally drawn to community service, charity work, volunteering, doing good, and acts of kindness for others. "One thing I know; the only ones among you who will be really happy are those who will have sought and found how to serve," said Albert Schweitzer, the humanitarian, who might well have been a Two.

The Helper's High. Twos are often skilled helpers who are highly resourced and capable. They experience great joy and upliftment from being a helper. They know about the "helper's high," which is the feeling of well-being that comes from helping others. The term *helper's high* was coined by Allan Luks in *The Healing Power of Doing Good*. In a YouTube film Luks says, "Being a helper improves the lives of others, and it improves your life too." He says, "If you want to be a happier you, then helping others will do that for you."

Unconditional Love. Healthy Twos have a love-centered approach to life. They are altruistic and unselfish. They give of themselves freely and with no strings attached. "Love is love's reward," wrote John Dryden, the poet. Being loving is inherently rewarding for a Two. Their love is not a bargain; it is freely given. Hafiz, the Sufi poet, wrote, "The Sun never says to the Earth, 'You owe me.' Look what happens with a love like that. It lights the whole sky."

LOSS OF CONNECTION

When we seek for connection, we restore the world to wholeness. Our seemingly separate lives become meaningful as we discover how truly necessary we are to each other.

– Margaret J. Wheatley

Thomas Berry, a Catholic priest, who described himself as a "geologian," dedicated his life to helping humanity recognize our connectedness with the universe. "The universe, by definition, is a single gorgeous celebratory event," he observed. Berry had a strong Two energy, and his central message was "We are connected!" In a lecture he gave at the Schumacher College, in England, Berry told us, "The universe must be experienced as the Great Self. Each is fulfilled in the other: the Great Self is fulfilled in the individual self, the individual self is fulfilled in the Great Self." He also said, "The destiny of humans cannot be separated from the destiny of earth."

"Connection is a basic human need and vital for a person's well-being," said Thomas Berry. Psychologists who study early childhood development recognize that children need a daily dose of heart-to-heart connection to flourish and grow. Adults also need this. Our immune system functions better when we mix and mingle. A hug and a smile boost physical health and emotional wellness, even for introverts. Medical research recognizes that social isolation increases the risk of depression, anxiety, cardiovascular disease, and strokes. Whereas connecting with others boosts our heart-brain coherence, cognitive ability, and mental wellness. The bottom line is our connectedness makes us human, and it brings out the best in us.

> *The universe is a communion of subjects, not a collection of objects.*
> — Thomas Berry

Loss of connection is humanity's first wound. Erich Fromm, the psychologist whom I mentioned earlier, described disconnection as humanity's most basic problem, causing alienation, depression, and even insanity. Likewise, Thomas Berry described loss of connection as a "radical discontinuity" and as our "central pathology." In his classic book *The Great Work*, he said that humanity's greatest need is to realize the deeper connection we have with each other, with the Earth community, and with the larger story of the Universe. Berry taught that connection is our only hope for our survival. He said, "We will go into the future as a single sacred community, or we will all perish in the desert."

Basic Fear: Not Being Loved

When Twos experience a loss of connection, a basic fear arises in them that affects their self-worth, their mental well-being, and their relationship with others. The basic fear for Twos is feeling unloved and not wanted by others.

We can all relate to this fear. We've all had moments when we felt "I am not lovable" or "I am not loved." All nine Types have a basic fear, and although the basic fear is described differently for each Type, it is connected to the fear of not being loved or feeling unlovable. For instance, Threes don't feel lovable when they experience their basic fear of being unworthy, and it the same for Ones when they don't feel good enough, for Sixes when they have self-doubt, for Nines when they experience conflict and upset, and for Eights when the don't feel strong or capable.

When Twos feel disconnected and unloved, it brings up secondary fears of feeling helpless, not being cared for, not getting their needs met, and being rejected. Twos often work hard at building connection with others so as to avoid feeling unloved. Wendy is a Two. She is a single mother, in her mid-40s, and I met her on my Love and the Enneagram program in London. This is what Wendy said about living with her basic fear.

My favorite coffee mug says, "I ♥ connections." As a Two, my first waking thought is, *Who shall I connect with today?* Before I get out of bed, I usually hop on social media, check for birthdays on my calendar, and message at least five people. Not feeling connected brings up a lot of fear for me. For example, my daughter is studying at university now. She's an Enneagram Eight and is very independent. When I text her, and she doesn't get back to me right away, I get panicky. I want to phone her immediately, but she hates it when I'm needy. When I'm desperate, I send her psychic messages telling her, "Call me," "Call Mom," and "Phone home."

Here are a few things that Twos have commonly told me about what it's like to live with their basic fear:

- "I hate not feeling connected to others."
- "I make a lot of effort to stay in touch with friends."
- "I worry when I don't feel close to people I love."
- "I live with a constant fear of rejection."
- "I've never been good at asking for help."
- "I focus more on other people's needs."
- "I worry that my needs will push others away."
- "I feel indebted when people are nice to me."
- "I don't tell people I'm unhappy or not well."
- "I don't pray for myself, only for others."

Childhood Story: The Helpful Child

Infants are entirely dependent on others for help and care. Before they can speak, they must develop lots of "engagement cues" to communicate their needs. They cry, make cooing sounds, lick their lips, look directly at you, hold out their arms, and tell you what they want. It's their way of saying, "I'm a baby, and I have needs." There's no shame in this; it's natural. Donald Winnicott, the English pediatrician and psychoanalyst, used the term *holding environment* to describe a loving atmosphere created by parenting figures who are "good enough" at caring for a child's physical and emotional needs. For as long as the holding environment is good enough, all is well.

When the Two child feels a loss of connection, also referred to as a "loss of holding," the basic fear arises of not being loved. Sadly, this loss of holding is inevitable. Parents may be "good enough," but no parent is perfect. Also, the loss of holding can be exacerbated by traumatic events such as parents divorcing or the death of a grandparent, for example. It may also be disrupted by the arrival of a sibling. *Who will give me what I need? Who will help me? How much love is there for me?* Twos fear that their environment cannot cater for all their needs. *Maybe, I have too many needs,* thinks the Two child. *Maybe, I should not have any needs at all.*

Susan, a Two, is a psychoanalyst who works closely with children. I met her on my Coaching and the Enneagram program. Here's how she described the helpful child paradigm in her own life:

> As a young girl, I imagined that our family had a lovely cream cake to feed us all. It was an imaginary cream cake, and my job was to serve everyone a slice. In my mind, I served Mum and Dad first because they worked so hard and needed it the most. Next, I served my brother Finn, because he was the eldest, and then my two younger brothers, Declan and Connor. My plan was to serve myself last, but I didn't like taking the last slice, and so I'd save it just in case anyone wanted a second slice. I thought I was being generous and selfless. In fact, I was training myself not to need anything and therefore not be rejected or unloved.

The Two child believes that to stay connected to people, they must choose between their own needs or the other person's needs. To achieve this, they must try to forget about their own needs and hide their needs from others. They present an ideal self-image that wants for nothing and is a fountain of generosity. They live off the release of endorphins, the "feel-good hormone," and oxytocin, the "love-drug" from the "helper's high" and from caring and giving to others.

The "Be Helpful" Driver: Twos typically have a persistent "Be Helpful" driver installed in their ego operating system. In childhood, they commonly take on the role of "Mummy's little helper" or "Daddy's little angel" and are happy to take the initiative in being helpful, doing household chores, and performing family duties. Their "Be Helpful" driver can be positive in that it helps Twos to learn how to be genuinely helpful, care for others, and express their love. But the "Be Helpful" driver can also be a cover for seeking connection and earning love. It can lead to over-helping, getting stuck in the role of helper, and blocking reciprocity and the flow of love. In short, too much "being helpful" can cause you to put others first, second, and third; and to place yourself last.

"I don't find it easy to put myself first," said Tim, a musician and a Two, who came to me for coaching after he was offered his first big record deal. "At school, I started a rock band, and we mostly played covers to be popular. After school, I studied music, and I got paid writing songs for other artists. I've helped a lot of artists be successful, but not me." Tim and I met up several times. In one session Tim shared, "Writing my own songs brings up the fear of being rejected by others, but if I don't do it, I'm rejecting myself, which is worse." Eventually, Tim made a change that helped him to perform more of his own songs. He realized that it was his job to like his own songs, and this helped him not to worry so much about other people's opinions. He trusted that if he wrote songs that he loved and felt connected to, that would be enough.

The "Be Helpful" driver for Twos also operates in the three main biological instincts (1) Self-Preservation Instinct (SP), which is mostly about the body, material matters, and self-care; (2) Social Instinct (SO), which is mostly about relating to family, society, and the world; and (3) (SX) Sexual Instinct (also called One-to-One Instinct), which is mostly about attraction, relating style, and romance.

>**Self-Preservation Instinct (SP)** *Healthy:* Your lifestyle reflects your image of yourself as a helper, carer, and giver. You prioritize family and a close circle of friends. You create a living space that is warm and inviting. You are a generous host. You like to help in practical ways (i.e., with financial support, nutrition advice, cooking meals, household chores, and help with personal care). You also manage to fit in some "me time." You like to stay in shape, keep youthful, and treat yourself to nice things. Giving gifts is your love language. *Not-so-healthy:* When you over-give you get drained physically as well as emotionally. Your efforts at self-care are a compensation for being in unhealthy sacrifice. You indulge in "love substitutes" such as chocolate and wine, beauty treatments, and buying yourself expensive gifts. "I've earned it," you tell yourself. *Unhealthy:* You wear yourself out taking care of everything. You sacrifice your physical well-being for others. You don't ask for help when you

need to rest, are feeling unwell, or are struggling financially. You play the role of martyr.

Social Instinct (SO) *Healthy:* You have a wide social circle and a busy social calendar. You know everyone in your neighborhood. You are an active community member. You serve and are involved in circles of influence, e.g., on the school PTA, as a trustee for a charity, a work committee, or social secretary at the golf club. *Not-so-healthy:* You have a lot of names in your contacts book, but not many friends whom you can be vulnerable and honest with. You need to feel you belong. You work hard to stay in the inner circle. You make yourself indispensable to others. Your family and kids feel rejected by you because you're always out. *Unhealthy:* You don't pay attention to your emotional needs. You avoid solitude and connecting more deeply with yourself. You don't know how to be when it's only you. You are more sensitive than people realize. You don't tell anyone when you are feeling blue. You are constantly afraid of being rejected.

Sexual Instinct (SX) *Healthy:* You more assertive than the SP and SO subtypes and invest a lot of time and energy in special relationships such as a special teacher at school, a BFF (best friend forever) from school days, an exclusive partnership at work, friends who are rich or famous, and a soulmate or life partner whom you give all your love to. *Not-so-healthy:* Your "I-thou" balance leans more toward "thou" than "I." You work hard to win people over. You ingratiate others with your attentiveness, offers of help, words of praise, and "I'm here for you" approach. You work overtime to make your significant other feel special. You make yourself into a "gift." *Signed, sealed, delivered, I'm yours. Unhealthy*: You are deliberately seductive. You bribe others with your flattery. You know how to please others. You also get angry when you don't feel appreciated. *After all I've done for you!* You can be possessive, manipulative, and jealous. You demand compensation. You take revenge by showering someone else with your attention and love.

Passion: Pride

All nine Types on the Enneagram experience a *passion*, or cause of suffering in the heart, that emerges from a sense of separation and from the basic fear. The passion for Twos is pride, which is one of the so-called cardinal sins.

Pride has been described as "the original sin" and "everybody's sin." It has been called the "mother of sins," the "root of all sins" and the "most shameful of sins." "It was pride that changed angels into devils; it is humility that makes men as angels," wrote Saint Augustine. He was referring to the story of Lucifer, the most prideful of angels, who said "I" before God, and who asserted his own will over the Will of God. What was one, became two. A rip had appeared in the fabric of universe. Now there were two separate competing wills in Creation: "God's will" and "my will."

Pride is the sin we can see readily in others but not in ourselves. It can be a blind spot for all nine Types, and especially for Twos. Beatrice Chestnut, the renowned Enneagram teacher, and a Two, addresses pride in her opus *The Complete Enneagram*. She points out that the sin of pride "does not mean the healthy, good feeling we have about ourselves as when we 'take pride in' a job well done. Rather, it is the false pride of self-inflation." She goes on to say,

> Over time, Twos may recognize the pride underlying the sense of power they feel from their imagined capacity to meet everyone's needs and the sense of superiority that goes along with not having conscious needs themselves. Pride manifests itself in Type Twos as a feeling of power in independence—a fantasy that they do not need to depend on the very people they have manipulated into depending on them.

"Learning about the sin of pride was a dagger in my heart," said Karen, a Two, who attended my Love and the Enneagram program. The sin of pride brings up a lot of shame for Twos. When I teach Twos about the sin of pride, I explain to them that the word for *sin* in ancient Greek is *hamartia* and was first used by Aristotle in *Poetics*. Interestingly, hamartia is an archery term that means "to miss the mark." Hamartia was also used to refer to a basic mistake or error made by the protagonist in Greek tragedy. Seen through this lens, sin is not a punishable offense as is commonly thought; rather, it is a source of suffering that is caused by a misdirection or mistake.

For all nine Ennea-Types, the sin of pride is caused by trying to live up to an idealized self-image. For instance, when Ones try to make themselves into a good person who is always right and never makes a mistake; when Threes try to make themselves valuable by being a success in the eyes of others and by avoiding failure; when Eights try to make themselves totally independent, always strong, and never weak; and when Fours create a unique self-image that is more special than others. For Twos, the idealized self-image is having no needs and not ever needing help. Remember, Twos are afraid that having needs increases their chances of being rejected by others. They're also ashamed of having needs because they think it blocks their ability to love unconditionally and without needing anything in return.

The good news for Twos is that being honest about your pride helps to heal the fear and shame about it. Meeting pride with honesty and compassion also helps to create more intimate and loving relationships with others. So, let's take a compassionate look at how the sin of pride plays out in Twos. Here are five examples I highlight in my Enneagram programs.

Role of Helper. When Twos are prideful, they appoint themselves as "the helper" in every relationship. They may also take on similar roles such as healer, rescuer, and savior. Twos mistakenly believe that the role they play is what makes them lovable and valuable. However, these social roles, if held too tight, can block the flow of connection, intimacy, and love in relationships. A helpful practice for Twos is to take a day off—or at least an hour—from their role of helper or carer and to notice how this benefits them and others.

Denial of Needs. Pride has been described by Enneagram teacher Claudio Naranjo as "a passion for the self-aggrandizement of the self-image." The idealized self-image for Twos is a self that doesn't need anything from others. This denial of needs makes Twos a very "pride-centered character," in Naranjo's words. When Twos are honest about having needs—*I need love, I need friendship, I need help,* etc.—it makes them less prideful and less isolated. It also helps them to enjoy the gifts of intimacy such as connection, emotional support, trust, gratitude, and love.

"I don't need help." Twos are often too proud to ask for help. "I'm fine, thanks," is their standard reply to offers of help. Their pride is a defense against fear of rejection ("What if I ask and they say no?"); unworthiness ("I don't want to be a burden to others"); feeling vulnerable ("What if people think less of me?"); independence ("Asking for help is a weakness"); old wounds ("I don't want to get hurt again"); skepticism ("No one can help me"); competitiveness ("Accepting help is a failure"); arrogance ("I know what they're going to say"); and control ("I'd rather take my own advice").

"I know what help is." Prideful Twos insist they know best how to help others, better even than other Twos. They act as Chief Help Officer of the universe. They dispense advice for free, and a cost is incurred only if the advice is not taken. In truth, being helpful requires humility and openness. "I start every session with a prayer: 'Dear God, show me how to help this person today,'" said Karen, a Two, who is a psychotherapist. Karen told me, "I didn't used to pray for help, because I thought I didn't need to. But one time I had a client who I couldn't help. In mid-session, when she visited the restroom, I said a quick prayer: 'God, please help me.' Immediately, I knew how to proceed. We were both helped."

Earning Love. Pride comes from the mistaken belief that *you earn love as a reward rather than receive it as an act of grace*. "God's love is not earned; it is a gift," said Henri Nouwen, theologian and author of *You Are the Beloved*, who was most likely a Two. God's love cannot be earned, and a person's love can't be brought, because true love is given freely. Love is not a bargain; it has no price. As a Two, you must be willing to see that you can't make someone love you. In a loving relationship, you are loved for who you are.

Fixation: Flattery or Ingratiation

In the Enneagram, the *fixation* refers to a mental habit that causes an imbalance in your mental health and well-being. The fixation for Twos is commonly called *flattery* or *ingratiation*. My name for it is *othering*. Othering for a Two is when they habitually think about and prioritize the needs of others before their own needs. Othering is when the primary focus of attention is on "you, not me," or on "thou before I" as Martin Buber, the philosopher, put it.

Martin Buber recognized the vital need for human connection in his classic work *Ich und Du* (*I and Thou* in English). "All real living is meeting," wrote Buber.

He made a distinction between two modes of relating: *I-Thou* and *I-It*. The I-Thou mode is a way of being that allows two people to meet "through grace," as Buber put it, and as equals to one another, both inherently worthy, both fully present, both active and open, and both giving and receiving. The I-It mode is more like a transaction between two people who do not recognize their mutual importance to each other. They either ignore each other, treat each other like an object, or use each other to get something.

Healthy Twos exemplify the I-Thou mode beautifully in relationships. They enjoy what Buber calls "a continuous dialogue" in which they celebrate the "Thou" without losing connection with their "I." They receive from a "Thou" without trying to grasp or possess anything. This is possible for Twos when they are connected to their heart and feel lovable. But when Twos don't feel lovable, the fear of rejection arises, the passion of pride stirs, and the fixation of othering begins to distort their thinking and relating. This is also when the I-It way of relating takes over. Here are five ways in which unhealthy othering is exhibited by Twos, and by all of us for that matter.

> *To enter into true relation, one must give up the urge to possess, to control, and to manipulate.*
> — Martin Buber

People Pleasing. A people pleaser is someone who habitually puts others' needs before their own. People pleasing disrupts the mutuality and reciprocity of the "I-Thou" mode of relating. It idolizes the "Thou" and sacrifices the "I." It is not a sustainable friendship model, so to speak. "When you engage in people pleasing you are out of integrity with yourself, your goals, your dreams, and your life's mission," warns Eileen Anglin, actress and artist.

Other-Enhancement. Psychologists recognize different styles of ingratiation, one of which is called *Other-Enhancement*. The healthy version of Other-Enhancement is using positive strokes, like compliments and words of praise, to boost the self-esteem of another person. The unhealthy version is using Other-Enhancement to make others feel good about themselves so that they will feel good about you too. This tactic can be very seductive and manipulative. It is not unconditional love, and most people see through it eventually.

Acquisitive Ingratiation. Social psychologist Edward E. Jones is known as the Father of Ingratiation. He made a lifelong study of relationships and observed ways we attempt to connect with people through ingratiation. Jones noted a style of ingratiation he called *acquisitive ingratiation.* This is when a person focuses their attention on "a target individual" with a view to acquiring something from them. This person is using ingratiation to win favor and to get their needs met. It is a strategy of "giving to get."

Emotional Invoices. Claudio Naranjo, the Enneagram teacher, uses the terms *egocentric generosity* and *false abundance* to describe the "giving-to-get" strategy of unhealthy Twos. Giving to get is a trait of the I-It mode of relating. Here, the other person is not a Thou; they're an investment. Giving to get is an example of egoic generosity because the giver isn't giving something for free; they want a return on their investment. Their egoic generosity comes with emotional invoices attached. Every act of love has an IOU. Acts of kindness are a loan that must be paid back.

Asking Indirectly. Unhealthy Twos struggle to ask for anything directly from others because they fear it will lead to rejection and disconnection. Instead of making a straight request, Twos will ask indirectly by making suggestions, dropping hints, being coercive, nudging, and manipulating others into giving. The trouble with indirect asking is that receiving feels more like getting, and the kindness of others feels more like a win or a gain rather than a gift.

In summary, too much othering creates unhealthy one-sided relationships with lots of "Thou" and no "I." For Twos, this one-sidedness reinforces the fear of not being worthy of love and not being loved for who you are. Friends and family don't see the real you; they see only the role you play and what you allow them to see. You believe that the only way to stay in a relationship is to be in sacrifice. You give more than you receive, and this lack of reciprocity blocks genuine connection and relatedness. And the more you refuse offers of help, the lonelier and more impoverished you feel.

PATH OF CONNECTION

> *All spiritual paths are paths of connection,
> leading from separateness to union.*
>
> — Steve Taylor, *DisConnected*

Cheryl Richardson, author and coach, whom I mentioned earlier, is a Two. I introduced Cheryl to the Enneagram when we were on a speaking tour of Australia. Cheryl had recently published *The Art of Extreme Self-Care*, and her latest book was *You Can Create an Exceptional Life*, co-written with Louise Hay. If memory serves me right, we were in Melbourne Botanic Gardens when we sat down to talk about the Enneagram. We had spent the morning getting foot massages, which is one of Cheryl's favorite things to do. "If everyone got a regular foot massage, it would help save the world," says Cheryl.

Cheryl connected deeply with the wisdom of the Enneagram, and she soon incorporated it into her spiritual practice and daily life. After our speaking tour, she invited me on her *Coach on Call* radio show to talk about the Enneagram. Cheryl told her listeners, "The Enneagram is offering us a sacred gift. Our work is to be humble enough to recognize and accept this gift." Cheryl has since given many talks and workshops on the Enneagram, including Self-Care and the Enneagram and the Enneagram as a Path to Wholeness. Cheryl teaches, "When you study the Enneagram, ask yourself, *What gift is the Enneagram offering me?* and *How is the Enneagram inviting me to grow?*"

The Enneagram offers a path of growth for all nine Types that helps you to remember your original nature and be your True Self. The path of growth for Twos, which I call the Path of Connection, focuses on a deeper connection with yourself and a more abundant connection with others. The better we connect with ourselves and each other, the healthier we are. How does this connection happen? It all comes down to love. Leo Buscaglia, the professor and author who was known as "Dr. Love," was most likely a Two. He taught, "Love creates an 'us' without destroying a 'me.'"

> *Only love has the power to unite without taking away another's dignity, another's self.*
>
> — Leo Buscaglia, *Bus 9 to Paradise*

To have a real connection with others, you must have a real connection with yourself. "You can love others only as much as yourself," wrote Buscaglia. The Enneagram encourages Twos, and all nine Types, to connect with their

True Self. For a Two, this includes taking care of your body, listening to what your heart tells you, giving yourself "soul time," and making decisions that are authentic and loving. In *The Art of Extreme Self-Care*, Cheryl Richardson wrote: "If you want to live an authentic, meaningful life, you need to master the art of disappointing and upsetting others, hurting feelings, and living with the reality that some people just won't like you. It may not be easy, but it's essential if you want your life to reflect your deepest desires, values, and needs."

For Twos, it's important to realize that your connection with others exists already and that you don't have to sacrifice yourself to keep the connection alive. "Fall in love in such a way that it frees you from any connecting," said Rumi in the poem "Taste of Morning." At the deepest level, our basic relatedness with each other is continuous and cannot be broken. For Twos, it's important then not to force the connection or try to manipulate it or control it. "Love one another but make not a bond of love," wrote Khalil Gibran, the Lebanese poet and philosopher in *The Prophet*. He also wrote, "Let there be spaces in your togetherness, And let the winds of the heavens dance between you."

Virtue: Humility

Every Ennea-Type has a virtue, or a superpower, that arises naturally as you do your inner work to heal the basic fear, the passion in the heart, and the fixation in your thinking. The virtue for Twos is humility.

> *A person's pride will humble him, but a humble spirit will gain honor.*
> — Proverbs 29:23

Humility has been described as the beginning and end of all virtues. Aristotle considered humility to be a moral virtue and a cornerstone for living a good and ethical life. Dante Alighieri described humility as the first virtue in his classic work *The Divine Comedy*. Humility is the starting point on Dante's journey through nine levels of purgatory. Saint Thomas Aquinas named humility as the first of seven heavenly virtues. And Saint Augustine of Hippo described humility as the foundation of all other virtues. He said, "Humility must accompany all our actions, must be with us everywhere." In one of his letters to Dioscorus the Great, pope of Alexandria, he wrote,

> This way is first humility, second humility, third humility, and however often you should ask me I would say the same, not because there are not other precepts to be explained, but, if humility does not precede and accompany and follow every good work we do, and

if it is not set before us to look upon, and beside us to lean upon, and behind us to fence us in, pride will wrest from our hand any good deed we do while we are in the very act of taking pleasure in it.

Humility is an uber virtue that all nine Types can work with to be less ego-driven and more soul-directed. For example, humility helps Ones to accept that we all make mistakes, to be less judgmental, and to be open to God's benevolence and grace; humility helps Eights to accept that life is fragile, to recognize our strengths and weaknesses, and to surrender to a higher power; humility helps Fives to accept that life is a mystery, that you can't learn everything from a book, and to be more open to inspiration and learning from others; humility helps Sevens to accept that life has its ups and downs, to see boredom as a gift, and trust in a higher plan for your life. The point is, we all need to practice humility, not just Twos.

For Twos to practice humility, they need to discern between false humility and true humility. We all need to do this, but especially Twos because the passion for Twos is pride, which generates false humility. False humility is an effort to make yourself superior or "holier than thou" by giving more than you receive, refusing offers of help, trying to win praise for being a martyr, never accepting a compliment, always putting yourself last, and pretending you have no needs. *There is nothing wise or spiritual in denying your own needs.* Humility helps us to practice self-acceptance and have compassion for ourselves. Philosopher Simone Weil wrote in *Gravity and Grace* that "compassion directed towards oneself is true humility."

Humility is a godsend for Twos. It is a virtue born of love for self and others. It requires daily practice, and it can be cultivated only with help from others. Here are five ways that Twos can practice the virtue of humility in daily life.

The First Love. Henri Nouwen, the theologian, wrote, "The spiritual life starts where you dare to claim the first love. 'Love one another because I have loved you first' (see John 4:19)." Humility is the acceptance that you are loved by God as you are. You are loved even before you try to make yourself lovable. What is lovable about you is not your image or the role you play; it is the essence of you. Nouwen said in one of his talks, "When you accept that you are God's beloved child, you are able to give and receive love in abundance, and you can help to make God's unconditional love more visible in the world."

We All Have Needs. Humility helps Twos to feel less ashamed about their personal needs. Having needs, such as food and shelter, safety and security, friendship and love, is what makes us human. Our needs connect us to each other. Our needs also show us our path of growth in this lifetime, e.g., the need for friendship and community, acceptance and intimacy, healing and beauty, and belonging and love. Being honest about your needs helps you to be vulnerable and open and to feel loved by others. A good practice for Twos is to put your hand on your heart, and ask, *What do I need today, and who can help me with this?*

The Gift of Relationships. In every relationship, we are both the giver and the receiver. This reciprocity between giving and receiving is what helps us to connect deeply with one another. Relationship coach Chuck Spezzano, who is a Two, wrote, "If someone is in your life, it's because you have a gift for them, and they have a gift for you." A helpful exercise for Twos is to make a list of friends and loved ones and name specific gifts that each relationship has given you and/or is offering you at present. For example, *The greatest gift I have received from my mother is . . .*

God Is the Giver. One of the names for God early Christians commonly used was the Giver. "Every day is a gift from God. Learn to focus on the Giver, and enjoy the gift!" teaches Joyce Meyer, a minister and author. Meyer also said, "Humble people ask for help." Humility for Twos is accepting God's help in your everyday affairs. In Islam, humility is the acceptance that "La ilaha illallah," or "There is no God, but God." God is One, and God is the Giver that supplies our every need. It is our connection with God and with each other that helps us to flourish and grow.

Joy of Receiving. How good a receiver are you? Do you drink life in? Are you open-minded? Can you accept a compliment with a simple "Thank you"? Humility helps Twos to experience the joy of receiving. Hafiz, the Sufi poet, encourages us to become better receivers so that we are even more abundant and generous in our giving. In the poem "So Many Gifts," Hafiz tells us:

> There are so many gifts
> still unopened from your birthday,
> there are so many hand-crafted presents
> that have been sent to you by God.
> The Beloved does not mind repeating,
> "Everything I have is also yours."

Balancing Your Centers

Twos are called a Heart Type, along with Threes and Fours on the Enneagram. As a Two, your primary center of intelligence is your heart center. Twos typically identify more with their heart center than with their body center or head center. But when Twos rely too much on their heart center, and neglect the other two centers, it puts a strain on the heart. For the heart center to be healthy, it must be in right relationship with the whole system. The heart center cannot function well on its own; it needs a healthy mind-body-heart connection.

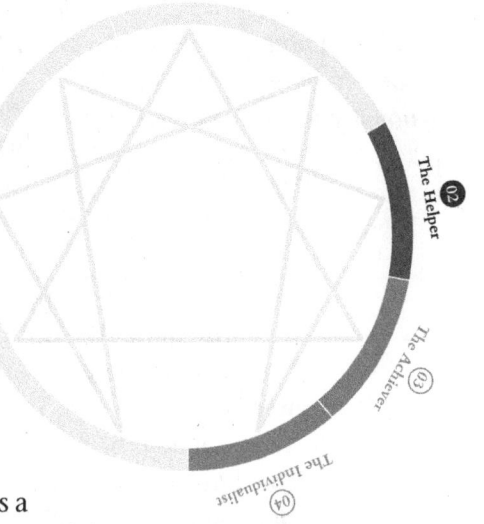

Heart coherence is a term used by doctors to describe the healthy connection between the heart, head, and body. Doctors at the HeartMath Institute in America were the first to use the term heart coherence. The HeartMath Institute mission statement is: To help awaken the heart of humanity. One of its main slogans is "Uncover what your heart is capable of." For the past 30 years, HeartMath has conducted scientific research on the benefits of heart coherence that includes increased physical vitality and immunity, emotional stability and enhanced creativity, and improved decision-making and clear thinking.

"As a Two, I like to think of my three centers as three friends who need each other to perform well," said George, a Two, a medical doctor who has trained at the HeartMath Institute. George has a morning spiritual practice that includes a check-in with the three centers. "First, I connect with my body, and I ask what my body needs to be healthy and well," George told me. "Next, I place my hand on my heart center, and I listen for any message or wisdom that my heart has for me," explained George. Lastly, George focuses on his head center. "Here, I ask for inspiration and guidance for the day ahead, and I always get an answer."

Heart Center. Twos are heart-centered people. They seek heart-to-heart connections with others. They have a giving heart. They are also the Type most prone to giving their heart away to others. Working with the Enneagram encourages Twos to make a deeper connection with the heart. The heart is the seat of the soul. "Listen to your heart. It knows all things, because it came from the Soul of the World and it will one day return there," wrote Paulo Coelho in *The Alchemist*. Deep within the heart is an inner voice that helps you to be true to yourself and to love yourself and others. "Intelligence and intuition are heightened when we learn to listen more deeply to our own heart," wrote Doc Childre in *The HeartMath Solution*.

> *When you say "yes" to others make sure you are not saying "no" to yourself.*
> — Paulo Coelho

Body Center. "Before I found the Enneagram, I was an unhealthy Two who didn't take proper care of my body," Tracy told me. Tracy is a senior nurse at a London hospital. "In my nurse training, we were taught to care for others, but not for ourselves," she said. Tracy invited me to teach a Well-Being and the Enneagram program for her staff. In her team of 20 people, 12 were Type Twos. Together we created a self-care program that included actions such as filling the refrigerator with foods that say, "I love you," taking breaks during the day, going to bed an hour earlier, giving yourself more "me time," getting a foot massage, and growing flowers and herbs in your garden. "Taking care of my body helps my body to take better care of me," Tracy told her team.

> *Gardening is an active participation in the deepest mysteries of the universe.*
> — Thomas Berry

Head Center. "I never thought of myself as a great thinker," said Claire, a Two. "But in my late twenties I worked as a PA for a boss who kept asking me, 'What do you think, Claire?' He saw a potential in me I didn't know I had. He valued my opinion, and eventually, he made me a partner in his company." My hunch is that Claire's boss might be a Two also. One of the soul gifts

> *Follow your heart, but take your brain with you.*
> — Alfred Adler

Twos have is seeing potential in others. Twos typically identify more as a "feeling type" than a "thinking type." But, when Twos experience coherence between all three centers, they make great thinkers. They combine the gut instinct of the body center with the intuition in their heart center and with logic and reasoning in the head center to be healthy, helpful, and wise.

Spreading Your Wings

Twos hang out at Point Two, which sits between Point One and Point Three on the Enneagram symbol. This means Twos have a 1-Wing and a 3-Wing. Typically, one wing is more dominant than the other, but the goal is to balance your wings. Working with the 1-Wing can help Twos to tap into the essential qualities and wisdom of Point One, and working with the 3-Wing can help Twos access the same at Point Three. Learning to live in balance with your wings, by drawing strengths and lessons from both, can be very helpful for Twos.

Two with a 1-Wing

Twos with a dominant 1-Wing (2w1) are called the Servant. They show up in the world with the main characteristics of Two, plus some traits of Ones. For example:

> **A Good Heart.** You combine the heart-centered qualities of Two with the healthy qualities of Ones who wish to live a good life, act with a moral compass, be on the right side of justice, and do a good deed for the world. "We are each made for goodness, love and compassion. Our lives are transformed as much as the world is when we live with these truths," said Desmond Tutu.
>
> **A Sense of Duty.** For a 2w1, the joy of helping and being of service is supported by a strong sense of duty and responsibility. It feels good to do good for others. However, you must take care that the

joy of giving doesn't turn into an obligation, a burden, or a drudgery. "Each one must give as he has decided in his heart, *not reluctantly or under compulsion,* for God loves a cheerful giver," teaches the Bible in 2 Corinthians 9:7, from the English Standard Version.

The Greatest Good. 2w1s want to serve a higher purpose and contribute to the greater good. They don't need recognition or applause for their efforts. Wendell Berry, the poet, said, "The real work of planet-saving will be small, humble, and humbling, and (insofar as it involves love) pleasing and rewarding. Its jobs will be too many to count, too many to report, too many to be publicly noticed or rewarded, too small to make anyone rich or famous."

The Inner Critic. The "Be Perfect" driver in Ones can cause 2w1s to be too idealistic and perfectionistic. When 2w1s are not connected to their heart, they criticize and judge themselves for not helping enough and not doing enough to save the world. They forget that small things done with great love make a big difference. "I alone cannot change the world, but I can cast a stone across the waters to create many ripples," said Mother Teresa.

Playing the Martyr. 2w1s often confuse "giving yourself wholeheartedly" with "giving yourself away." Giving yourself wholeheartedly to a good cause means you engage the wisdom of your heart so that you are an instrument, not a martyr. Giving yourself away leads to a lack of self-care, unhealthy sacrifice, and burnout. As the saying goes, *You can't pour from an empty cup; first you must fill yourself up.*

Two with a 3-Wing

Twos with a 3-Wing (2w3) are called the Enabler. They show up in the world with the main characteristics of Two, plus some traits of Threes. For example:

Authentically You. 2w3s combine healthy qualities of Two with the healthy qualities of Threes such as authenticity, genuineness, and being true to yourself. Your 3-Wing helps you to be more inner-directed, be less of a people pleaser, not lose yourself in the role of helper, and be more up front and honest in your communicating style, for instance. Being yourself is your greatest gift to yourself and to others.

Personal Best. Healthy Threes are motivated to bring out the best in themselves. A 2w3 wants to be the best partner, best dad, best mum, best friend, best colleague they can be to others. They work hard to cultivate their talents and skills so that they can share them with others. "Your talent is God's gift to you. What you do with it is your gift back to God," wrote Leo Buscaglia in *Living, Loving and Learning.*

Enabling Others. As a 2w3 you combine the gifts of the Helper and the Achiever. You have a genuine gift for helping others to achieve success. You are a great coach and enabler who helps others to be in their element, to believe in themselves, and to live their best life. Oprah Winfrey, who is most likely a Three, said, "My constant prayer for myself is to be used in service for the greater good."

Image Conscious. 2w3s tend to be more image-conscious than 2w1s, which can be healthy or unhealthy. On the healthy side, 2w3s care about how they come across to others, and this helps them to be sociable, empathic, and adaptive. On the unhealthy side, they may be too self-serving and suffer from too much vanity, pride, and narcissism.

Lonely Hearts Club. 2w3s are a combination of two Heart Types on the Enneagram. Heart Types get disconnected from their heart center when they habitually prioritize the needs of others before their own. When 2w3s focus too much attention on gaining a place in other people's hearts, they become a stranger to themselves, and end up feeling very lonely, heartbroken, and disconnected from their True Self.

Moving to Eight and Four

Following the Inner Lines of the Enneagram symbol, Twos move toward Point Eight (home for the Challenger) and Point Four (home for the Individualist). These Inner Lines invite you to visit these Points to explore the gifts and wisdom they have for you.

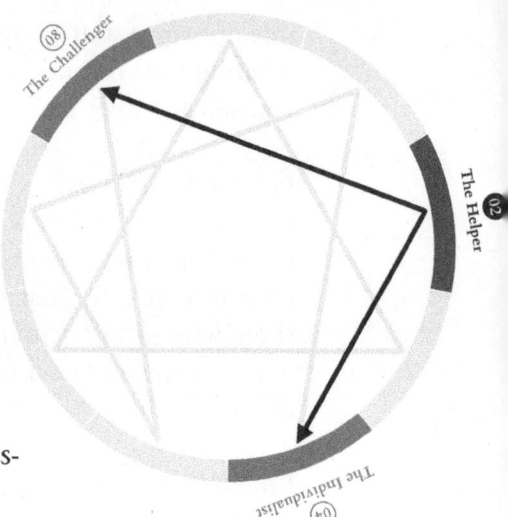

Moving to Eight

When Twos tune in to Point Eight, they access some of the higher qualities that Eights are blessed with. For example:

> **Self-Empowerment.** When Twos integrate the energy of Point Eight, they tap into an inner strength they've always longed for. The Eight energy helps Twos to connect with their inner power. Like an Eight, they operate from the core of their being. They discover an inner strength that gives them self-confidence and a feeling of empowerment. They feel connected to their True Self, and this connection also helps them to surrender to a higher power.
>
> **More Direct.** Eights are known for their direct communication style and candor. When Twos tune in to the energy of Point Eight, it helps them to be more direct in expressing their needs, sharing their feelings, and asking for help. They get straight to the point rather than being indirect or sugarcoating things. Twos discover that being up-front and honest helps to create deeper connections, closer friendships, and a stronger bond with others.
>
> **Healthy Boundaries.** When Twos embody the energy of Point Eight, it helps them to be more grounded and rooted in themselves. They find it easier to be assertive, to stand up for themselves, and to set clear and healthy boundaries. The Eight energy helps Twos be true to themselves. They stand their ground when they need to, they don't have a problem saying no, and they won't be manipulated or shamed into doing something if it doesn't feel right.

Type Two

When Twos are having a difficult time, they may take on some of the unhealthy qualities common in Eights. Knowing about these unhealthy qualities can be a helpful warning sign for Twos. For example.

Too Independent. Twos, like Eights, build emotional walls around their heart so as protect themselves from hurt and pain. They try to make themselves strong by being independent and not needing help from others. For an Eight, asking for help can feel like a weakness; and for a Two, accepting help feels like a failure. Too much independence disrupts the reciprocal flow of giving and receiving. It also increases feelings of disconnection and loneliness.

Feeling Rejected. Both Eights and Twos are prone to overidentifying with the social role they play in their family, at work, and with friends. For example, Twos see themselves as the Helper or Giver; and Eights are the Provider, the Rock, or the Strong One. But too much role-playing causes inequality and blocks genuine togetherness and intimacy. When Eights and Twos are too role bound, they believe they are loved only for the role they play, and fear being rejected or abandoned if they were more vulnerable.

Plotting Revenge. Twos can act quite Eight-ish when they feel underappreciated for what they give, how much they help, and for what a good martyr they are. They get angry when they feel taken advantage of. *How dare you! After all I've done for you! So, this is the thanks I get!* Like an unhealthy Eight, Twos will be vengeful and want to settle the score. They will present the ingrates with emotional invoices that must be paid or else.

Moving to Four
When Twos tune in to Point Four, they access some of the higher qualities that Fours are blessed with. For example:

Time for Self. When Twos embrace the energy of Point Four, it helps them to create a healthy balance between focusing on themselves and focusing on others. Point Four energy helps Twos to turn their attention inward, connect with their heart, and find the

Deeper Self. Here, in an atmosphere of solitude, they can ask themselves questions like, *How am I feeling today? What do I need? What does my soul want me to know?*

Expressing Needs. Beatrice Chestnut, a Two, writes in *The Complete Enneagram*, "By consciously drawing on the strengths of type Fours, Twos can expand their access to their authentic emotions, reclaim a healthy ability to self-reference (to balance out their disproportionate focus on others), and accept and express their needs with more confidence." It is very healing for a Two to realize that expressing their feelings and needs deepens their connection with others.

Emotional Honesty. The communication style of Fours is to be self-referencing and emotionally honest. When Twos integrate the energy of Point Four, it helps them to be more self-revealing and more truthful with others. Being more emotionally honest helps Twos be more compassionate with themselves and empathic. Emotional honesty boosts intuitive wisdom and spiritual clarity. It helps Twos to be more authentic, inspired, and creative.

When Twos are struggling, they may take on some of the unhealthy qualities of Fours. Knowing about these unhealthy qualities can be a helpful warning sign for Twos. For example:

Negative Comparisons. Fours and Twos are called image types on the Enneagram, along with Threes. Image types are overly identified with their self-image, and on their down days they will compare themselves negatively with others. Fours see themselves as flawed, wounded, and not special. Threes fear they are not successful enough. Twos think others are more gifted, talented, and lovable. And because Twos focus more on others than themselves, they are also prone to the passion of envy that Fours suffer with.

Self-Compassion. The invitation at Point Four is for all nine Types to practice equanimity and be more compassionate to self and others. Healthy Fours exemplify these beautiful soul qualities, but when Fours are unhealthy, their self-compassion turns into self-pity. Like unhealthy Fours, Twos can wallow in self-pity. Both Types identify with a sad story they tell. *No one loves me. No one can help me. No one is here for me.* They secretly hope to be helped and rescued one day, but fear it will never happen.

Making It Difficult. Both Fours and Twos are known as Heart Types on the Enneagram, along with Threes. When these Types are not connected to their heart, they typically accuse others of not valuing, appreciating, or loving them enough. However, these Types can also make it difficult for others to love them. For example, when Twos are not emotionally honest, won't express their needs, and don't ask for help. A good exercise for Twos is to ask yourself, *How can I make it easier for others to love me?*

Holy Will and Holy Freedom

The nine Points of the Enneagram each offer a Holy Idea—a universal teaching and higher wisdom—that all nine Types can contemplate and practice. Point Two has two Holy Ideas: Holy Will and Holy Freedom.

Holy Will teaches that the Universe is an expression of a single Unified Will. This One Will connects heaven and earth, spirit to matter, and soul to ego. The spiritual laws of God and the natural laws of Creation are coherent and fair. We are created in unity; God does not play favorites. We are made to serve a higher will, and there is an infinite supply of gifts and graces for each of us to enjoy. The law of reciprocity, in which giving and receiving are the same, makes it possible for the universe to supply your every need. It is the Holy Will of the Universe that there be no lack for anyone.

Holy Freedom describes the feeling of joy that arises when you accept that your individual will is not separate from the Holy Will of Creation. "My will" and "Thy will" are not two opposing forces. Jane, a Two, is a permaculture gardener whom I met at an Enneagram talk I gave at St. James's Church, Piccadilly. She told me, "Permaculture taught me how to work with nature, not against it. And likewise, the Enneagram showed me that 'my will' and 'Thy will' are an expression of 'One Will.'" Jane also told me, "I used to pray to God, *Thy Will be Done*, but now I like to say, *Our Will Be Done*, because it helps me to feel closer to God."

> *Behold, how good and how pleasant it is for brethren to dwell together in unity!*
> — Psalm 133

> *God's Will for me is perfect happiness.*
>
> — *A Course in Miracles*

Holy Freedom teaches that your nature and the nature of Creation are the same. It frees you from the thought of separateness, and from the fear that you must take care of your needs all by yourself. The Holy Will of Creation wants to look after you. Knowing this is a great freedom. It helps you to give and receive more freely and to experience unconditional love. As Hafiz the poet said, it helps you to "let God pour a universe of love into your heart." And also to "carry your heart through this world like a life-giving sun." To close, here is a Hafiz poem, translated by Daniel Ladinsky, called "A Cushion for Your Head."

>Just sit there right now
>Don't do a thing
>Just rest.
>
>For your separation from God,
>From love,
>Is the hardest work
>In this
>World.
>
>Let me bring you trays of food
>And something
>That you like to
>Drink.
>
>You can use my soft words
>As a cushion
>For your
>Head.

Type Three
THE ACHIEVER

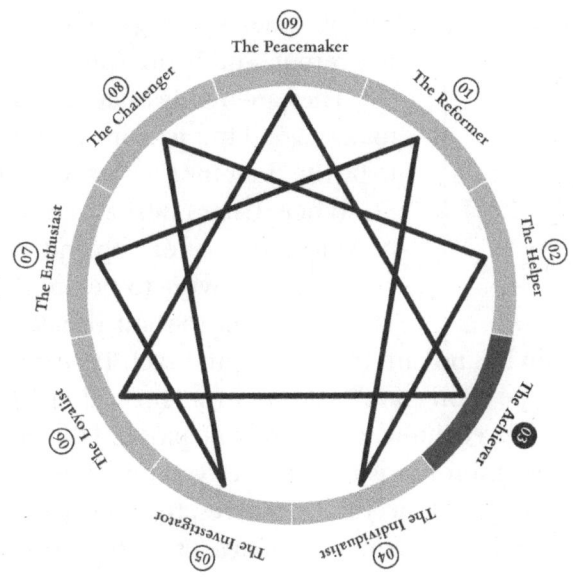

The greatest human quest is to know what one must do in order to become a human being.

— IMMANUEL KANT

The Ennea-Type Three is commonly called the Achiever. Other names for Threes are the Performer, Golden Soul, Doer, Motivator, and Status-Seeker.

Type Threes are the *Achievement-Oriented, Doing Type.* Threes have a strong work ethic, a positive "can do" attitude, and a winning mentality. They display an energetic pursuit of achievement and are highly motivated to succeed at something worthwhile and valuable. They have an urge for greatness and want to do something meaningful with their lives. Threes strive to be their best self. They work hard to bring out the best in themselves, and they also have a talent for bringing out the best in others. Threes are known as the star performers of the Enneagram. They hate to fail, and despite their many accomplishments, they often struggle with self-worth and rarely feel they are a true success.

Threes want to live a successful life. They are goal oriented and results driven. They are assertive and task focused. They are called to be fruitful and productive. As we will see, Threes like to be recognized for their achievements and admired for their successes. They like to look good and seek validation from others. Threes are the Type most likely to dream of seeing their name up in lights, being inducted into a Hall of Fame, winning a gold medal, walking the red carpet, and being featured in a Who's Who list. They are highly image conscious and love to make a good impression. They like to shine and to be the "best in show" at what they do.

> *Always do your best. What you plant now, you will harvest later.*
> — Og Mandino, *The Greatest Salesman in the World*

When Threes take an Enneagram test, they hope to come out on top and be one of the best Types. Threes wish to be seen in a good light. They want to be the best, or at least above average. But the Enneagram has no ranking system, and each Type is valued equally. "I kept thinking 'I hope I don't fail,'" said Susan, a Three, after taking her test. But the Enneagram is not a contest, and there is no pass or fail mark. The real prize for taking an Enneagram test is that it takes you on a journey to know yourself better and achieve real success. For Threes, this journey will require them to rethink success and disassemble the image of a "successful self" in order to expand their thinking and become more of their True Self.

INTRODUCING TYPE THREE

Are you a Type Three on the Enneagram? Maybe you have a family member, a friend, or a work colleague who is a Three.

I was introduced to the Enneagram by my dear friend Marika Borg, who is a Three, and a much-loved Enneagram teacher. Marika and I had been friends before she discovered the Enneagram. We first met when she was at the height of her fame and success. Marika was a household name in Finland, her home country. She had her own TV talk show, she was editor in chief and the public face of a health magazine *Voi Hyvin* (*Be Well*, in English), and she was the author of several best-selling books. When Marika found the Enneagram, she told me that she was stepping back from her public life to do some deep inner work on herself and to imagine what success might look like in the next chapter of her life.

A year later, I met up with Marika when I was in Helsinki. She took me to a café called Robert's Coffee in Helsinki city center. "I've brought you here for two very important reasons," Marika told me. "The first reason is that I know how much you love good coffee, and this coffee is very good, and it has your name on it. The second reason is that I want to introduce you to the Enneagram." Marika drew the nine-pointed Enneagram symbol on a napkin, and for the next three hours she told me about her own journey with the Enneagram. She told me, "The Enneagram is a map that shows you where your treasure is. It offers you a path of growth that helps you to find your inner gold and be your authentic self."

Marika gave me an Enneagram test to take. "I already know what Type you are," she told me with a twinkle in her eye. I took the test that night. I must confess I secretly hoped I'd get a high score and avoid a low ranking of some kind. Anyway, I discovered that I am a Type Three, the same as Marika. "Congratulations! Threes are definitely the best Type," said Marika, who was obviously joking. Marika told me that if I studied the Enneagram, and did the inner work, it would help me to flourish in every area of my life. She told me, "Working with the Enneagram will help you to stop chasing success, to listen to your heart, and to be more true to yourself."

Healthy Qualities of Threes

When Threes are healthy and well-balanced, they display essential qualities that we all love and appreciate. Here are a few things healthy Threes have told me about themselves:

- "I aim to do something great with my life."
- "I do work that feels meaningful to me."
- "I am always working toward a goal."
- "I don't have a job; I have a purpose."
- "Success is being true to myself."
- "Authenticity brings out the best in me."
- "I always strive to give my personal best."
- "I like to bring out the best in others."

- "I know we're here for a higher purpose."
- "My success is my gift to others."

Unhealthy Qualities of Threes

When Threes are out of balance, they become competitive, put on a show, and seek success through appearances. Here are a few things Threes have told me about themselves:

- "I strive for significance and success."
- "I work harder than anyone I know."
- "I am very competitive and love to win."
- "I feel a constant pressure to perform."
- "I want to be the best version of myself."
- "I'm afraid 'my best' isn't good enough."
- "I struggle to know my own self-worth."
- "I'm not sure what my real value is to others."
- "I experience fraud guilt and imposter syndrome."
- "I wish I could enjoy my successes more."

RECOGNIZING TYPE THREES

In Greek philosophy, Aristotle's work sits well at Point Three. In his classic work *Nicomachean Ethics*, he set out his thoughts on how best to live. He wrote about *arete*, a concept in ancient Greek thought that means "personal excellence and moral virtue." A person of *arete* is living up to their potential, achieving high levels of effectiveness, and fulfilling their purpose. *Arete* denotes inherent function and noble effort in which human and divine tendencies combine to achieve real results. Aristotle wrote, "Excellence is never an accident. It is always the result of high intention, sincere effort, and intelligent execution; it represents the wise choice of many alternatives—choice, not chance, determines your destiny."

Khalil Gibran, the Lebanese poet and philosopher, was most likely a Three. His classic work *The Prophet* has been translated into over 100 languages and is one of the best-selling books of all time. It features 26 soul meditations given by a prophet, Al Mustafa. Though *The Prophet* took many years to write, Gibran managed to remain patient with himself and never forced the words to come. In an interview after the publication of *The Prophet*, Gibran was asked how he wrote it. "Did I write it?" he replied. "It wrote me." In *The Prophet* there is an inspiring meditation on the nature of work, in which Al Mustafa declares, "And all knowledge is vain save when there is work / And all work is empty save when there is love; / And when you work with love you bind yourself to yourself, and to one another, and to God."

> *The secret to success is this: Do one thing at a time, and while doing it put your whole Soul into it to the exclusion of all else.*
> — Vivekananda

Swami Vivekananda first appeared on the world stage when he addressed the Parliament of Religions in Chicago in 1893. He spoke about Karma Yoga, which is the yoga of work and action. Journalists hailed him as a "golden presence," "the greatest figure," and the "most popular" speaker there. Typical of a healthy Three, Vivekananda had a gift for synthesizing and making practical the esoteric wisdom of the Bhagavad Gita and of his mentor Sri Ramakrishna. His name is from two Sanskrit words, *viveka* and *ânanda*, meaning "the bliss of discerning wisdom." In *The Secret of Work*, Vivekananda taught that the purpose of work is not to glorify the self-image; it is to realize your divine potential and make your work an expression of love. He wrote:

> No great work can be achieved by humbug.
> It is through love, a passion for truth, and tremendous energy,
> that all undertakings are accomplished.

In psychology, Donald Winnicott, the English psychoanalyst and pediatrician, presented a lot of Three traits in his work. Winnicott made a distinction between True Self and False Self. He described the True Self as the "authentic self," "original self," and "vulnerable self," and the False Self as a "learned self" and "narcissistic self" that worries about being superior or inferior, accepted or rejected. In *Playing and Reality*, Winnicott observed that the True Self is what you are born with, and it expresses itself as "the heart's action," "genuine aliveness," and "spontaneous authenticity." By contrast, the False Self is a "show of being real." It is a defensive façade, developed in infancy, when children believe they must work hard to win approval and be loved. Winnicott believed our life's work is to remember

> *Only the True Self can be creative and only the True Self can feel real.*
> — D. Winnicott

the True Self so that we can rediscover our innate self-worth and experience real love.

In leadership, Threes who are at the top of their game are success focused, heart centered, action oriented, and results driven. They model authentic leadership and seek to bring out the best in themselves and others. They are genuine in their efforts and strive constantly to move the needle from good to great. They typically make great teachers and coaches, communicators and motivators. Think of Deepak Chopra, author of *The Seven Spiritual Laws of Success*; Tony Robbins, "Success is taking massive, determined action!"; and Wayne Dyer, "Don't die with your music still in you," who inspire and energize us with their Three-like traits and qualities.

> *The true self, once discovered, is the source of creativity, intelligence and personal growth. No external solution has such power.*
> — Deepak Chopra

In sport, while all nine Types make great athletes, Threes in particular often make great champions and have their name etched on honors boards. Examples of sports stars with strong Three energy include golfer Tiger Woods, winner of 82 official PGA Tour events; Michael Jordan, named NBA's most valuable player (MVP) five times; Lewis Hamilton, the Formula One champion who holds the record for most wins and podium finishes; and Serena Williams, the tennis champion who is hailed as the GOAT and as a living legend. On the darker side of the Threes' desire for success, we find cyclist Lance Armstrong, winner of the Tour de France seven times, who was later stripped of his titles after a doping scandal. Armstrong denied all allegations at first before coming clean in a 2013 interview with Oprah Winfrey. "This story was so perfect for so long," he told Oprah. "It's this myth, this perfect story, and it wasn't true."

> *The success of every woman should be the inspiration to another.*
> — Serena Williams

In the arts, Threes typically work hard at their craft. They are great performers and entertainers. They are gifted artists. They have a great stage presence. And they bring something authentic and real to what they do. In popular music, think of David Bowie's song "Heroes," Lady Gaga's *The Fame Monster* album, and Sting's songs "Shape of My Heart" and "Fields of Gold." Also, Paul McCartney, whom Ringo Star described as "the workaholic of the band [the Beatles]"; and Taylor Swift, the multitalented singer-songwriter

> *I've always strived to be successful, not famous.*
> — Taylor Swift

and global superstar who has won more music awards than any other artist. And spare a thought for Elvis Presley, singer of "An American Trilogy (Glory, Glory Hallelujah)," and Whitney Houston, singer of "The Greatest Love of All," who both shone so bright but were tragically undone by their fame and success.

In poetry, the work of Kabir sits well at Point Three. Kabir (1440–1518) was an Indian mystic and saint who is revered equally by Hindus, Muslims, and Sikhs. Through his poetry he encourages you to listen to the wisdom of the soul—what he called the Inner Self—and to let divine love work *in you, through you,* and *as you.* "A drop of divine love can turn you to gold," said Kabir. I especially like Andrew Harvey's two collections of Kabir poems: *Turn Me to Gold* and *Engoldenment.* Kabir used the word *gold* to describe the substance of your Inner Self. Engoldenment is the journey you make to contact your Inner Self and live a soul-centered life.

> *If you want the truth,*
> *I'll tell you the truth:*
> *Listen to the secret sound,*
> *The real sound,*
> *which is inside you.*
> — Kabir

In literature and film, there are plenty of Three-like characters that feature in storylines and plots to do with fame and fortune, winning and losing, truth and deceit, and hero and anti-hero. Jay Gatsby, lead character in *The Great Gatsby*, by F. Scott Fitzgerald, is a quintessential Three who at the age of 17 invented an image of himself to succeed at life; as Fitzgerald writes, "To this conception he was faithful to the end." Think of Tom Cruise, who plays the sports agent in *Jerry Maguire.* "Show me the money!" is his famous success mantra. And Will Smith, who plays Chris Gardner, the homeless man who chases after success in *The Pursuit of Happyness.* Also, Meryl Streep, who plays the cold-hearted and ruthless editor in chief at the fictional *Runway* magazine in *The Devil Wears Prada.*

> *I've spent many birthdays on a movie set, all great days.*
> — Tom Cruise

In *Harry Potter and the Chamber of Secrets*, Gilderoy Lockhart, the new Defense Against the Dark Arts Professor, played by Kenneth Branagh, is a lampoon of an unhealthy Three. He is vainglorious, immoderate, and narcissistic. He hands out signed pictures of himself. He is the five-times winner of *Witch Weekly*'s Most-Charming-Smile Award. His curriculum vitae is full of boasts,

> *Fame's a fickle friend, Harry. . . . Celebrity is as celebrity does, remember that.*
> — Gilderoy Lockhart's advice to Harry Potter

fabrication, and lies. In an interview, J. K. Rowling described her character Lockhart as "hollow" and full of deceit.

In *The Lord of the Rings*, Boromir, the warrior of Gondor, displays a lot of Three traits. Tolkien described Boromir as "a strong and esteemed warrior, and a proud and valiant man." Boromir is a great leader and is also vain and image conscious. Boromir is tempted by the corruptive powers of the Ring, but he is honest enough to admit it, and his veracity and self-sacrifice helps the Fellowship of the Ring to succeed at their task. Another example of a Three is James T. Kirk, the gallant captain of the USS *Enterprise* in the *Star Trek* series. Captain Kirk, played by William Shatner, can be vain and arrogant, but his heart is in the right place, and his spirited leadership helps his crew to succeed, often against all odds. "I don't believe in a no-win scenario," said Kirk when faced with an impossible test in *Star Trek II: The Wrath of Khan*.

In Shakespeare, the tragedy *Macbeth* is a cautionary tale of ego-ambition for status, fame, and power. At the start of the play, three witches tell Macbeth, a noble man, that he is destined to be King of Scotland. Macbeth and Lady Macbeth, who both have strong Three traits, soon show impatience and a lack of faith in their destiny. They decide to wear a "false face" and a "false heart" and plot to kill the good King Duncan. After the murder, Macbeth is racked with shame and remorse, because he realizes he has given away his "eternal jewel" (his soul) to the "common enemy of man" (ego ambition). Macbeth tells us,

> . . . my soul is clog'd with blood—
> I cannot rise! I dare not ask for mercy—
> It is too late, he drags me down; I sink,
> I sink,—my soul is lost forever!—Oh!

THE GOLDEN SOUL

> *You went out in search of gold far and wide, but*
> *all along you were gold on the inside.*
>
> — Rumi

One of the names for Threes is the Golden Soul. In Greek philosophy, gold represents the substance of the soul. The goal of life is to excavate this inner gold, to realize your inherent value, and be your authentic self.

Jungian analyst Robert Johnson wrote an inspiring book, *Inner Gold*, that I often quote from when I teach about Point Three. His insightful work speaks to all nine Types on the Enneagram, and especially to Threes. In the first paragraph of *Inner Gold*, he writes:

> Inner gold is the highest value in the human psyche. It is our soul, the Self, that innermost part of our being. It is us at our best, our twenty-four-karat gift to ourselves. Everyone has inner gold. It isn't created, but it does have to be discovered. When I speak about gold this way, I am also speaking about God.

Healthy Threes have a golden quality about them. We all have this inner gold, as Johnson says, but Threes often excel at expressing it. Deep down, Threes know that they have been given everything they need to live a golden life. Taylor Swift, who has strong Three energy, sings about "golden feelings," "gold sky," "golden thread," and true love that "shines golden" in her songs such as "Best Day," "Dress," and "Gold Rush." To live a golden life is to realize your inner gold, which is the substance of your soul, and let it guide you in all you do. Your inner gold offers you a way of being that money cannot buy. It helps you to know the difference between real gold and fool's gold. Not all that glitters is gold.

Robert Johnson explains that our inner gold lives in our unconscious and that our inner work is to make it conscious. He observes that our first glimpse of inner gold typically comes from seeing the inner gold in others: "When we awaken to a new possibility in our lives, we often see it [the inner gold] in another person. A part of us that has been hidden is about to emerge, but it doesn't go in a straight line from our unconscious to becoming conscious." He continues, "You put your own gold onto somebody until you're able to hold it yourself." This is the great work, to see the inner gold in everyone and in ourselves. This is how we come to know our soul and to live a soul-centered life.

Mary Hulnick is a Three, and she is a wonderful example of a person who has found her inner gold. Mary and her husband, Ron Hulnick, are pioneers in the field of spiritual psychology. For 40 years, they served as co-founders and co-directors of the University of Santa Monica (USM) and graduated over 6,000 students from their soul-centered programs. Their book *Loyalty to Your Soul* is a modern classic in spiritual literature. Mary and Ron are keen

> *We are not human beings with Souls; we are Souls having a human experience.*
>
> — Mary & Ron Hulnick
> *Loyalty to Your Soul*

students of the Enneagram and invited me to teach a five-day retreat on the Soul-Centered Enneagram at USM. "The Enneagram helps you to discover your inner gold and live a soul-centered life," said Mary. "As a Three, I work with the Enneagram to help me honor my human journey, to know my heart, and to follow my soul's calling."

When Threes are soul-centered and connected with their heart, they display essential qualities and healthy traits that are plain for all to see. Here are a few of these healthy qualities.

True to Yourself. Healthy Threes present their True Self to others. They are the genuine article, always true to themselves, present no falsity to others, do not hide behind a mask, are typically modest and honest, and have no need to impress or "dress for success." "To shine your brightest light is to be who you truly are," wrote Roy T. Bennett, author *The Light in the Heart*.

Inherent Self-Worth. As a Healthy Three, you are in touch with the heart of who you are. You are self-assured and know your intrinsic worth as a child of God. You recognize the inner gold of your true nature. And, therefore, you don't need to sell an image of yourself to win love, to achieve happiness, or to buy success. "Your self-worth is determined by you. You don't have to depend on someone telling you who you are," said Beyoncé, the singer, who displays a lot of Three traits.

Doing Great Work. Threes feel most alive and on purpose when participating in a Great Work that is meaningful and significant. The term *Great Work*, as used in Hermeticism, is about spiritual endeavor and your *reason for being*. The Great Work isn't only about a job, a career, or a salary; it's about being an instrument for a greater purpose. Most of all, the Great Work is becoming your True Self. "Be who God intended you to be, and you will set the world on fire," said Saint Catherine of Siena.

Your Best Life. "Live your best life!" is a success mantra that Oprah Winfrey made popular. Threes are motivated to give life their best shot. As a Three, you are willing to do the inner work to bring out the best in yourself, and be the best parent, best friend, best partner, and best *you* that you can be. "Living your best life is your most important journey in life," said Oprah.

Authentic Success. For a Three, real success is knowing who you are and being true to yourself. Your ideas about success are your own, and not a copy or secondhand version of what your parents told you or you learned at school. Your success comes from being inner-directed, listening to your heart, and making authentic choices no matter how difficult or unpopular they might be.

Acts of Service. As a Three, you don't sit on the sidelines waiting for your name to be called. You are keen to play your part and do something great with your life. In your heart, you have an intrinsic desire for greatness. Martin Luther King Jr., whom we meet at Point Eight, said, "Not everybody can be famous, but everybody can be great, because greatness is determined by service." He also said, "Acts of service are never too small to count." Being of service makes a big difference to how Threes show up in the world and operate in life.

Love Made Visible. In my book *Authentic Success*, I wrote, "If your definition of success has little or no mention of love, get another definition." When Threes pour their heart into their work, they become an instrument for love. They embody love in action by helping others to learn, heal, grow, and succeed. They are a presence of love in the world. They exemplify Khalil Gibran's famous words: "Work is love made visible."

CLOUDS OF GLORY

Let your light shine before others, so that
they may see your good works and
give glory to your Father who is in heaven

– Matthew 5:16

William Wordsworth's poem "Ode: Intimations of Immortality from Recollections of Early Childhood" offers an excellent meditation for Point Three on the Enneagram. It is a poem about glory. In ancient Greek, "glory" describes the majesty of God, splendor of the universe, and divine nature of the soul. Humans are made in the image of God. The term *Glory of Man* refers to the inherent dignity and worth of every human being. Glory is the visible manifestation of God's presence in us. Our work is to express this glory, not for self-gain, but as an act of love. This is why Jesus said, "I seek not my own glory" and why he credited all his great works to the Glory of God.

In his poem, Wordsworth charts the journey of the soul from heaven to earth and the sense of separation we go through. He described the newborn as "heaven born," "Nature's Priest," a "Mighty Prophet," and a "Seer Blest." As an infant, we shine with an "innocent brightness," with "new-fledged hope," and we are "appareled in celestial light." "Heaven lies about us in our infancy!" said Wordsworth. Shortly, our experience of our own glorious self begins to fade. "Shades of the prison-house begin to close upon the growing boy," he wrote. The "prison house" refers to the ego-self which believes it is separate from the glory of creation. All of this is summed up in Wordsworth's famous verse:

> Our birth is but a sleep and a forgetting:
> The Soul that rises with us, our life's Star,
> Hath had elsewhere its setting,
> And cometh from afar:
> Not in entire forgetfulness,
> And not in utter nakedness
> But trailing clouds of glory do we come

Every child is born in glory. They are a reminder to us that we were also born in glory. This is why our hearts leap for joy when we hold a baby in our arms. We feel blessed to be in their presence. In each child, there is what Wordsworth calls "A Presence which is not to be put by." What is this Presence with a capital *P*? It is your own glorious, divine nature. It is the I AM of your soul. After you are born into a body, the awareness of the soul begins to fade. Your Holy Work is to remember the glory of your true nature, so that you might be born again, and become your True Self.

Basic Fear: Not Being Worthy

When we forget who we are, and are estranged from our soul, we experience what Wordsworth describes as "a thought of grief," and with this grief a basic fear arises in us.

The basic fear for Threes is the fear of being unworthy. Each Ennea-Type experiences low self-worth in their own way. For Threes, it is a loss of value, a sense of being insignificant and feeling worthless. It's common for a Three to feel empty inside. "My heart is like an empty jewelery box. It looks pretty on the outside, but there's nothing of value on the inside," said Tracy, a Three, who took my Love and the Enneagram program. The feeling of having no intrinsic value causes Threes to search outside of themselves for approval and love. They seek external validation by looking attractive, impressing the boss, proving themselves to others, and getting more "likes" from a social media audience, for instance.

As a Three, I've had a long struggle with self-worth. As a child, I believed something was missing in me. I felt like I had a hole in my heart. I coped with my unworthiness by being determined to succeed. I put a superhuman effort into everything I did. I tried to be the best version of myself. I wrote several best-selling books. I had my own radio show. I was a TV celebrity. But no amount of success was enough. Like a Type One, I didn't feel "perfect" or good enough. Like a Seven, I kept thinking *there must be more to life than this*. Like a Four, I felt unseen and a fake. Not to be defeated, I continued to work hard. Agents kept knocking on my door. "We'll make your image into a brand!" they told me. I felt as if I was selling my soul to the devil. And the fear of being unworthy didn't go away.

> *For what is a man profited, if he shall gain the whole world, and lose his own soul? or what shall a man give in exchange for his soul?*
>
> — Jesus, Matthew 16:26

A Three's ambition to succeed is driven by an urge for greatness and by a fear of being worthless and insignificant. In Wes Anderson's animated film *Fantastic Mr. Fox*, which is an adaptation of Roald Dahl's famous children's tale, the protagonist Mr. Fox might easily be a Three. George Clooney is well cast as the voice for Mr. Fox, who is known as "Foxy." He is suave, charming, and incorrigible. When things go from bad to worse, he confesses to his wife, Mrs. Fox, "I think I have this thing where everybody has to think I'm the greatest, the quote unquote 'Fantastic Mr. Fox.' And if they aren't completely knocked out and dazzled and slightly intimidated by me, I don't feel good about myself."

Mr. Fox is the hero who saves the day, but only after he comes through an existential crisis. "Who am I?" Mr. Fox asks himself. It was Mr. Fox's pride that got everyone into trouble in the first place. To succeed, Mr. Fox must be less fantastic and more authentic. My favorite scene is when Mrs. Fox, played by Meryl Streep, tells him, "In the end we all die, unless you change." Everyone must learn, not just Threes, that there is more to us than our self-image. Our inner work is to graduate from being an image of ourselves to being our True Self. This journey from being ego-driven to soul-centered is described in ancient Greek as a *metanoia*, which means "a change of heart." It is the death of the self-image and birth of the Real You.

Here are a few comments from Threes about what it's like to live with the basic fear of being unworthy and not feeling valuable.

- "I need to feel significant and successful."
- "I am highly conscious of my self-image."
- "I feel like I have to prove myself to others."
- "I want people to see the best version of me."
- "I often feel like life is an audition."
- "I work hard to earn and win love from others."
- "I don't want to be second best."
- "I am highly driven and need to be productive."
- "I wish I didn't have to work so hard at life."
- "I don't know who I am without my accomplishments."

Childhood Story: The Star Child

Psychologists recognize that every child needs some positive mirroring in the early years. Mirroring gives a child a sense of self. It establishes rapport and empathy. It is a positive affirmation. Mirroring sends a message of "I see you," "You are lovable," "You are good," "You matter to me," and "You are safe." Young Threes experience mirroring from a father figure's warm words of love and especially from the admiring gaze of a mother figure. "In individual emotional development the precursor of the mirror is the mother's face," wrote D. W. Winnicott, in the chapter of his book *Playing and Reality* titled "Mirror-Role of Mother and Family in Child Development." Mirroring helps a child to remember the inner gold that Robert Johnson speaks about. It also helps them to know they are not alone.

When a Three child has positive mirroring, they feel seen and loved for who they are. They are not loved because one day they might be a CEO or appear on *The Oprah Winfrey Show*. A baby doesn't need a curriculum vitae to impress us. But when the positive mirroring is lacking, or doesn't happen at all, then the Three child decides to do something about it, and this is when they make an extra special effort to be lovable. Typically, they take on a role, and a common role for Threes is what psychologists call the Star Child or Actor Child, that helps them put on a show to win attention, admiration, and applause.

The Star Child believes, "When I am outstanding, I am lovable." For a Star Child, love is an Oscar, and you must give your best performance to win one. I was a Star Child in my family. I was athletic and sporty, and I played a lot of football and cricket, which were my dad's favorite sports. As a teenager, I played guitar in a school rock band called I AM 7. We had about 20 fans. We gave each of them an I AM 7 badge. We played a few live gigs, and I remember that the applause made me feel golden. I also spent a lot of time practicing my autograph. I once got a detention for using up an entire notebook in Geography trying out new autograph styles.

> *Be gentle with yourself. You are a child of the universe and no less than the trees and the stars.*
>
> — Max Ehrmann

Threes also commonly play the role of Family Hero or Family Mascot. From a young age, they set out to impress everyone. They are the "poster child" who exemplifies the values of their society. They win achievement awards at school. They are highly commended for their efforts. They give their family a good name. Born into a musical family, they will be a virtuoso. In a family of doctors, they become a surgeon. In a family of teachers, they become a professor. In a farming community, they become the best farmer ever. In my case, I hoped that my work as a psychologist would help my mother to heal her depression and cure my father of his alcoholism. I put a lot of pressure on myself to succeed, and I hoped that my efforts would somehow save our family.

The "Try Harder" Driver: Threes typically have a dominant "Try Harder" driver installed in their ego operating system. Threes are known for being industrious and hard working. Most Threes relate to the mantra: *Success is 99 percent perspiration and 1 percent inspiration.* Their "Try Harder" driver does have its pluses. It can help them to excel at a sport or a hobby, be top of the class at school, drive continuous improvement at work, and distinguish themselves in their

> *I will be great or nothing.*
>
> — Amy March in *Little Women*, by Louisa May Alcott

career. That said, trying too hard can also be a block to success. For example, I find that when I try too hard to write an article or a book, it stops the creative flow. Have you noticed that what you work hardest at often causes you the most struggle and pain? There can a big difference between working harder and working smarter.

Chloe, a Three, a real estate agent who took my Leadership and the Enneagram program, speaks very honestly about how her "Try Harder" driver was a double-edged sword for her.

> When I was 10 years old, I had a lightbulb moment when I realized that if I worked hard enough, I could be a success at anything I wanted. From that time on, I decided to work harder than anyone else I knew. At school, I wasn't the smartest, but I got the best grades. At work, I broke every sales record in the company. "Hard work is my secret to success," I told everyone. In my marriage, I made myself into the model wife. And with my children, I was supermom.
>
> Hard work got me everything I wanted, but it came at a high price. I was afraid that if I stopped working so hard, the life I'd made would collapse. I was successful and on the edge of burnout when I was diagnosed with breast cancer. My diagnosis made me face my biggest fear that without hard work I'm nothing and I don't deserve anything. For the first time in my life, I had to meet this fear and stop compensating for it. My therapist gave me an Enneagram book. As I read it, I had another lightbulb moment, and I realized that my "Work Harder" driver was blocking happiness and success.
>
> The Enneagram was my invitation to enjoy a deeper and more authentic success that comes from slowing down, valuing each day, and being more present in my life.

Let's look at some examples of how the "Try Harder" driver operates for Threes in the three biological instincts: (1) Self-Preservation Instinct (SP), which is mostly about the body, material matters, and self-care; (2) Social Instinct (SO), which is mostly about relating to family, society, and the world; and (3) (SX) Sexual Instinct (also called One-to-One Instinct), which is mostly about attraction, relating style, and romance.

Self-Preservation Instinct (SP) *Healthy:* You have a strong work ethic and strive to achieve a lifestyle you've always dreamed of. You focus on material success, on financial abundance, and on being able to afford the best things in life. You work hard to make things happen. *Not-so-healthy:* You are typically career-driven. You have a never-ending To Do list. Your work-life balance isn't healthy. Your loved ones rarely get your best energy. You take work with you on holiday. You believe you can't afford to rest. You're afraid your net worth might fall if you took a day off. *Unhealthy:* You are a workaholic. You're the last to leave the office. You often miss telling your children bedtime stories. You neglect your health, forfeit old friendships, and haven't had a date night in ages. You promise you will be less busy next year, but that's what you said last year.

Social Instinct (SO) *Healthy:* You enjoy being in the public eye, being in the spotlight, and being recognized for your success by your peers. You aim to be a valuable member in your town, at church, or on the parent-teacher association at school. Social ranking means a lot to you. VIP status, the best tickets, and Gold memberships are very appealing. "Success is boarding an airplane and turning left towards Business Class," said Mike, a Three. *Not-so-healthy*: You believe your value is determined by social status. You strive to be the best among peers. For example, best baker of cakes at the county fair, best lifeguard on the beach, and best monk in the monastery. At the very least, you want to be above average. "I'm intimidated by the fear of being average," said Taylor Swift. *Unhealthy:* You are a status-seeker. Life is an achievement contest. You can be opportunistic and competitive, ruthless and self-serving, self-promoting and narcissistic. You pay a heavy price for "keeping up with the Joneses" and standing out from the crowd.

Sexual Instinct (SX) *Healthy:* You are more assertive than SP and SO Threes. You seek to work with the best, to learn from the best, and hang out with the best. You like to be admired and desired by others. You display your feathers like a peacock. You know how to work your sex appeal. *Not-so-healthy:* You know how to model an image or style that gets results. You are good at impression management. You stay in good shape. You know how to turn on the charm. You feel a pressure to perform. Life is an audition. You must always be "on." *Unhealthy:* You're afraid that you are loved only for your "best" self. You try always to present the best version of yourself to others. You need external validation to feel special. You look for narcissistic supplies to top up your social worth. You flirt. You are promiscuous. You are easily jealous. You sell yourself to the highest bidder.

Passion: Vanity

All nine Types on the Enneagram experience a *passion*, or cause of suffering in the heart, that emerges from a sense of separation and from the basic fear. The passion for Threes is vanity, or vainglory, which is another of the so-called cardinal sins in Christian theology.

We all can relate to vanity. "There are no grades of vanity, there are only grades of ability in concealing it," wrote Mark Twain. Vanity arises in Threes when they forget about the inner gold of their true nature. Vanity masks the terrible fear of "I am unworthy," "I have no value," and "I am without significance." Vanity is an effort to make a shiny self-image and look like a million dollars. Vanity is all about image; it has no soul. No one has ever become happier and more successful by being even more vain. Vanity is a mistake.

> *A knowledge of thyself will preserve thee from vanity.*
> — Miguel de Cervantes, *Don Quixote*

In Greek mythology, Narcissus was a handsome youth who fell in love with his own reflection. The story of Narcissus, also known as the "Myth of Vanity," is the origin of the term *narcissism*, which describes a self-obsessed personality disorder. The story is told in Ovid's epic poem of transformation called *Metamorphoses*. Narcissus makes his own image into an idol, and this leads to his demise. Narcissus fails at life because he is obsessed with his outer image, and has no awareness of his inner gold. He is so self-absorbed that he is unable to love others or be loved by them. He doesn't do anything valuable or worthwhile for others. Even at his death, as he crosses the Styx, the river between this life and the next, he is still staring at his reflection.

> *Gotta kiss myself, I'm so pretty.*
> — Mark Ronson, "Uptown Funk"

In *Ennea-Type Structures*, Claudio Naranjo presents an insightful portrait on the passion of vanity. In the chapter entitled "Success Through Appearance*s*," Naranjo writes:

> Vanity is a passionate concern for one's image, or a passion of living for the eyes of others. Living for appearances implies that the focus of concern is not in one's own experience, but in the anticipation or fantasy of the experience of another, and thus the insubstantiality of the vain pursuit. Nothing could be more appropriately called "vanity of vanities," of which the preacher in Ecclesiastes speaks, than living for an ephemeral and insubstantial image (rather than out of oneself).

Vanity is the ambition to succeed at life by creating an image that others value and love. The tragedy is that the more you live "for the eyes of others," the more you lose sight of who you really are. Vanity is hell because it distances you from yourself. The focus on *external validation* takes you further away from your *intrinsic value*. You pin your hopes for happiness and success on the positive estimation of others. You are ambitious, work hard, and remain hopeful you will eventually be valued by others, but this misguided effort increases the feeling of inner emptiness and no self-worth. In Latin, the word *vanitas* means "emptiness" and "nothingness."

> *Vanity is definitely my favorite sin.*
> — Al Pacino, the devil in *Devil's Advocate*

Let's take a closer look at how Threes may display their vanity and how it causes heartache and a deep sense of deficiency and loneliness.

> **Success Through Appearances.** You work hard to present yourself in a favorable light. You are putting on a show. You are playing to the crowd. "Never play to the gallery," warned David Bowie in an interview about success and fame. "It's terribly dangerous for an artist to try to fulfil other people's expectations," he said. "Always remember that the reason you started working is that there is something inside yourself that if you could manifest it, would help you understand more about yourself and how you co-exist with society."

Selling an Image. Vanity is making an image of yourself to buy success and win love. You make yourself into an "attractive package" to sell on the "personality market," both terms coined by Erich Fromm in *The Art of Loving*. But vanity always fails because true love cannot be bought, and real success doesn't come from selling an image of yourself. Trying hard to make a good impression blocks intimacy and love. *You win at life by being yourself.* A helpful exercise for Threes is to ask your heart: *What one way can I be even more authentic and true to myself today?*

Imitation of Success. Vanity is an attempt to model society's values and other people's ideas about success. You are not being authentic; you are imitating others. You adapt yourself to be what you think others want. You become so socially modified that you don't recognize yourself in the mirror. "At the height of my success, I had lost touch with my core, and I was held together by an image I had made," said Mary, a Three, a retired businesswoman. Real success is not an imitation; it is being your True Self.

Fear of Being Original. In *Daybreak,* Friedrich Nietzsche wrote about vanity, conformity, and passion. He observed, "Vanity is the fear of appearing original." Too much vanity deceives you into believing that your self-image is more real and valuable than your essence. Nietzsche observed: "*The Vain*—we are like shop windows in which we are continually arranging, concealing or illuminating the supposed qualities others ascribe to us—in order to deceive *ourselves*." A good practice for Threes is to notice how your relationships improve and work flourishes when you are more authentic and genuine.

Seeking Glory for Yourself. Another name for vanity is *vainglory*. Vanity, or vainglory, arises when you forget about "the trailing clouds of glory" that is your original nature. Vainglory is an egoic attempt to glorify yourself, and to turn an image into gold. Your real glory comes not from what you make of yourself, but who you are in truth. This is what Jesus pointed to when he said in John 8:54, "If I glorify myself, my glory means nothing. My Father, whom you claim as your God, is the one who glorifies me."

Fixation: Deceit

In the Enneagram, the *fixation* refers to a mental habit that causes an imbalance in your mental health and well-being. The fixation for Threes is commonly called *deceit*. There are two main forms this takes: self-deception and deceiving others. Threes are prone to self-deception when they believe their value comes from what others think of them. Wayne Dyer, often called "The Father of Motivation," said, "Self-worth cannot be verified by others." He also said, "Don't equate your self-worth with how well you do things in life. You aren't what you do. If you are what you do, then when you don't . . . you aren't." Threes deceive others when they rely on their self-image to get a date, pass an interview, make a sale, get a promotion, and win people over.

Arthur Miller's play *Death of a Salesman* is a tale of deceit and lies and an indictment against the false hope of American capitalism. The protagonist, Willy Loman, is most likely a Three. He is 63 years old, and after 35 years of hard toil, his company dispenses with him as if he were a used-up cog in the machine. Willy has been a traveling salesman chasing after the American Dream of success all his life. Linda, his wife, doesn't know he has lost his job. He tells her he remains vital to the company. Willy tells his sons, Biff and Happy, that selling is "the greatest career a man could want" and that "the only thing you've got in this world is what you can sell." Willy is defeated, but he will not admit it. He is heartbroken and exhausted, but he isn't being honest with himself or his family.

Willy has been slowly working himself to death. With his life insurance policy in his hands, he says, "Funny, y'know? After all the highways, and the trains, and the appointments, and the years, you end up worth more dead than alive." Before his suicide, Willy tries to convince Biff and Happy they can both succeed at the American Dream. He tells them they are two Greek Adonises, and that they must "make an appearance in the world." At his father's funeral, Happy promises to follow his father's dream. "I'm gonna show you and everybody else that Willy Loman did not die in vain," he says. However, Biff is more self-aware than Happy. He is listening to his True Self when he says,

> Why am I trying to become what I don't want to be? What am I doing in an office, making a contemptuous, begging fool of myself, when all I want is out there, waiting for me the minute I say I know who I am!

Working with the Enneagram helps Threes to be more honest with themselves, so that they can tell when they're being authentic or false. Here are five ways deceit may arise in the thinking and behavior of Threes.

Forgetting Who You Are. How would you describe your True Self? How do you experience your soul? What is your soul's calling? Many of us, no matter our Ennea-Type, find it difficult to answer these questions. In *A Course in Miracles* it is written, "Uncertainty about what you must be is a self-deception on a scale so vast, its magnitude can hardly be conceived. To be alive and not to know yourself is to believe that you are really dead." What helps you to remember who you are?

Putting on a Face. In T. S. Eliot's poem "The Love Song of J. Alfred Prufrock," the protagonist is lonely and loveless, aging and insecure. Before going out, he takes a moment "to prepare a face to meet the faces that you meet." Self-deception is believing you are separate from others, and that your face is everything you are. "The bravest thing I ever did was let my fiancé see me without my make-up on," Sandra, a Three, told me.

I Am My Business Card. In the film *American Psycho*, there is a boardroom scene in which the corporate big shots compete for who has the most stylish business card: the best font, embossed lettering, subtle off-white coloring, a watermark, and other distinguishing features. Self-deception is believing you are defined by fine clothing, luxury brands, and the accessories you wear. And also by thinking that your work, your resume, and your business card makes you better than another person.

Valuing What Has No Value. The chief deceit is not knowing your intrinsic value. It is being unaware of your own eternal loveliness, your secret beauty, and your inner gold. Deceit is also valuing things that money can buy more than what money cannot buy. "You know the value of every article of merchandise, but if you don't know the value of your own soul, it's all foolishness," says Rumi in *Jewels of Remembrance*. Today, notice the treasures in your life that cannot be bought or sold, and that you don't have to deserve, earn, or work for.

Thinking You Are the Doer. Threes are doers. Their "To Do" is their bible. They often feel at a loss when they've got nothing to do. "Working with the Enneagram has helped me to be less of a human doing and more of a human being," says Chris, a Three, who is CEO of an advertising agency. In our coaching sessions, we talked about inspired work, enlightened action, God as the Doer, being an instrument, and the I AM, which in ancient wisdom is called "the activity of God." "I used to think I was the doer, but being an instrument is much more inspiring and far less exhausting," Chris told me.

PATH WITH HEART

You can't live a lie, you have to follow your heart.

— Paul Weller

The Enneagram teaches that everyone is a work of God and that we all are here to participate in the Great Work of Creation. You have a divine assignment and a holy purpose to fulfill. In Christianity, Jesus referred to the Great Work as "the glory of God" and "my Father's business." In Hinduism, it is Karma Yoga, the practice of selfless love and right action. In Buddhism, it is called the Dharma. In Taoism, it is the Way. In Sufism, it is your Soul Calling. And in Greek philosophy, the word *apotheosis* describes the spiritual goal of life, which is to realize your God-given talents, be a model of excellence, and be a loving presence in the world.

> *God and nature create nothing that does not fulfill a purpose.*
>
> — Aristotle

Carlos Castaneda, an anthropologist, wrote a best-selling book, *The Teachings of Don Juan: A Yaqui Way of Knowledge*, first published in 1968. His work was featured on the cover of *Time* Magazine, March 5, 1973. I have an original copy of it in my office. The book tells the story of how Castaneda met Don Juan, a Yaqui shaman, and their conversations about the meaning and purpose of life. Don Juan told Castaneda, "Never take a path that has no heart in it. You can't lose if your heart is in your work, but you can't win if your heart is not in it." He went on:

Before you embark on any path ask the question: Does this path have a heart? If the answer is no, you will know it, and then you must choose another path. The trouble is nobody asks the question; and when a man finally realizes that he has taken a path without a heart, the path is ready to kill him. At that point very few men can stop to deliberate, and leave the path. A path without a heart is never enjoyable. You have to work hard even to take it. On the other hand, a path with heart is easy; it does not make you work at liking it.

The Enneagram offers a path of growth for all nine Types that helps you to remember your original nature and be your True Self. Healthy Threes follow a path with heart. *A path with heart is the path your heart wants you to take.* Your heart tells you "Go here" and "Do this!" Where it leads you might seem irrational, and go against society's norms, but it feels right and so you do it. Oprah Winfrey is a great example of a person with Three traits who follows her heart. She and I talked about the Enneagram when I was a guest on *The Oprah Winfrey Show*. Oprah told me, "My message to everyone is *live from the heart of yourself.*" She also said, "My greatest achievement is that in my darkest moments, and I've had plenty of them, I never shut my heart down." The great work for all nine Ennea-Types, and for Threes especially, is to keep your heart open so you are able to turn lead into gold, wounds into wisdom, and fear into love.

> *Honor your calling. Everybody has one. Trust your heart and success will come to you.*
> — Oprah Winfrey

Virtue: Truthfulness

Every Ennea-Type has a virtue, or a superpower, that arises naturally as you do your inner work to heal the basic fear, the passion in the heart, and the fixation in your thinking. The virtue for Threes is commonly called truthfulness or veracity.

When Threes do "the work on oneself," as Gurdjieff described it, they gradually come to see that being authentic is much more impressive than putting on a show. Working with the Enneagram helps Threes to become a real person, and not just a pleasing image. The path of growth for Threes is authenticity, and it starts with taking the mask off, addressing feelings of low self-worth, and digging deep to discover the inner gold of your True Self.

> *If you want to be successful, you must respect one rule—never lie to yourself.*
> — Paulo Coelho

Being authentic is a journey of self-discovery. It requires an inward-facing gaze. You must pay attention to yourself, survey your inner landscape, and know where your I AM lives in you. Being authentic takes practice. Listening to your heart and recognizing your true voice are skills you might need to relearn. Being authentic also takes courage. Everyone experiences failure and defeat, for instance. However, failure can be a valuable learning curve, and being defeated can teach us how to succeed in the future. In his poem "Defeat," Khalil Gibran wrote, "Defeat, my Defeat, my solitude and my aloofness; You are dearer to me than a thousand triumphs. And sweeter to my heart than all world-glory."

What's vital for Threes is to remember your True Self exists already. It does not have to be manufactured or invented. Your I AM abides in your heart, and it is far greater than any image you make of yourself. "You are already that which you want to be, and your refusal to believe it is the only reason you do not see it," wrote Neville Goddard, the philosopher and mystic.

Here are a few ways that Threes—and all the Ennea-Types—can work with the virtue of veracity or truthfulness to be more of their True Self.

Sound of the Genuine. To be authentic, you must recognize within you "the sound of the genuine," a phrase coined by Howard Thurman, an African American theologian and philosopher who was a mentor to Martin Luther King Jr. He said, "The sound of the genuine is flowing through you. Don't be deceived and thrown off by all the noises that are a part even of your dreams [and] your ambitions that you don't hear 'the sound of the genuine' in you. Because that is the only true guide that you will ever have and if you don't have that you don't have a thing." *When you stop and listen to the sound of the genuine in you, what does it say to you?*

Speaking Your Truth. Veracity is from the Latin *vērāx* ("speaking truth") and *vērus* ("true, real"). Authenticity is a practice that happens one conversation at a time. As a Three, before I give a talk, sometimes to thousands of people, I pray, "Dear God, what is the most truthful thing I can say?" When I write, I follow Ernest Hemingway's advice to "write one true sentence" at a time. *What does speaking your truth mean to you? Who could you be more honest with?*

The Soul Made Visible. "The authentic self is soul made visible," said Sarah Ban Breathnach, author of *Something More: Excavating*

Your Authentic Self. What does contact with your soul feel like for you? What five words would you use to describe the presence of the soul? When I work with Threes, the goal I set them is to *add more soul to everything you do.* For Threes, this normally requires slowing down, being less of a doing machine, being heart-centered, and being more present. *How can you be more soulful today?* Name a few ways you might add more soul to your life.

From Ambition to Meaning. I often feature clips from Wayne Dyer's documentary *The Shift* when I teach on Point Three on the Enneagram. The original title of the documentary was *Ambition to Meaning: Finding Your Life's Purpose*. In it, Wayne teaches about the inner shift from ambition to meaning, which is essentially being less ego-driven and more soul-centered. Wayne observed, "Most of us are so attached to our personalities that we are immune to recognizing the LIGHT that is our true essence. That which you have come to think you are you are not!"

> The secret to success and happiness is WHO you are, not WHAT you do.
> — Wayne Dyer

Selling Yourself Short. "They say I tell the truth. Then they ask me to do a puppet show of myself in the bazaar. I'm not something to sell. I have already been bought!" wrote Rumi, the Sufi poet. Sometimes you must choose between being popular or being authentic. Being true to yourself connects you to your inner gold, and this gives you the sufficient self-worth not to betray yourself or sell yourself short. *Notice how you are typically tempted to betray yourself. Who and what can help you stay true to yourself?*

The Authenticity Solution. When I coach and mentor people, my work is to help them be even more of who they really are. "The solution to every problem is to be more authentic," I tell them. I once coached a politician who was working on a peace treaty with a foreign minister of another country. Their talks hit a stalemate. I asked him, "How might you solve this problem by being more authentic?" He instantly replied, "I'd invite him [the Foreign Minister] to my house for dinner." The next time they met was not at Government House, but at his home. Over dinner, they got to know each other, and they found a solution to their stalemate.

Balancing Your Centers

Threes are called a Heart Type (along with Twos and Fours) on the Enneagram. As a Three, your primary center of intelligence is your heart center. A Healthy Three is a heart-centered person who operates in all three centers of intelligence: heart, head, and body. Many Threes struggle to know their heart. They are typically overactive in their head center and body center, and underactive in their heart. Maybe this is because they don't realize how useful the heart is. The heart is more than just a muscle or a pump; it is also a wisdom seat and a portal for inspiration and divine works. Spending time with your heart helps you to know yourself, to recognize the "I AM," and feel your intrinsic worth as a human being. "For where your treasure is, there your heart will be also," said Jesus (Matthew 6:21).

The Heart Center. The greatest success for a Three is to know their own heart. Often, a Three is so busy trying to win the hearts of others with their dazzling performances and impressive works that they are estranged from their own heart. The Three's basic fear of having no intrinsic worth is a dark shadow that hovers over the surface of the heart. But deep within the heart there are no shadows; there is only perfect love. Henri Nouwen, theologian and author of *You Are the Beloved*, said, "The key to success in all your endeavors is to remember that you are a beloved child of a loving Creator. And that with God, all things are possible." When you are centered in your heart, you find yourself doing great works and living an inspired life.

> *Each of us was made for some particular work, and the desire for that work has been placed in our hearts.*
> — Rumi

Head Center. When Threes chase after success, they're often too busy to stop and think about what real success is. In my book *Authentic Success,* I wrote, "In a world full of front-page news, fast-tracked careers, designer clothing, and tragic sports results, you have to remember what is real." My work with my company Success Intelligence helps all nine Types on the Enneagram to meditate on the question, "What is a successful life?" To answer this question, you must consult your head and your heart. A regular inquiry into "What is success today?" helps you to think clearly, to be inner-directed, and to choose work that feels valuable and meaningful.

> *It is not enough to be busy. So are the ants. The question is: What are we busy about?*
> — Henry David Thoreau

Body Center. Threes are the type most likely to skip the Savasana pose at the end of a yoga class. Savasana is the pose of rest, and it helps you enjoy the harvest of your practice. Getting to a yoga class is already a big deal for Threes, as it takes them away from their busyness. Unhealthy Threes use their body primarily as a doing machine to exert willpower and keep active. But healthy Threes have learned to respect their body and to listen with love to their body's messages. For example, exhaustion is a sign you need to reconnect with your heart and elevate your thinking. Working with the innate intelligence of the body helps Threes to balance doing and being, to schedule rest, and to enjoy the fruits of their labor.

> *Half an hour's meditation each day is essential - except when you are very busy. Then a full hour is needed.*
> — Saint Francis de Sales

Spreading Your Wings

Threes are situated at Point Three, which sits between Point Two and Point Four on the Enneagram symbol. This means Threes have a 2-Wing and a 4-Wing. Typically, one wing is more dominant than the other, but the goal is to balance your wings. Working with the 2-Wing can help Threes to tap into the inherent qualities and wisdom of Point Two, and working

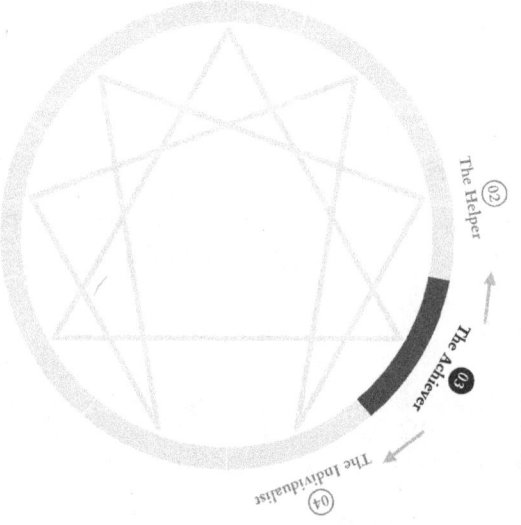

with the 4-Wing can help Threes to access the same at Point Four. Learning to live in balance with the wings, by drawing strengths and lessons from both, can be very helpful for Threes.

Three with a 2-Wing

Threes with a dominant 2-Wing (3w2) are called the Guide or Charmer. They show up in the world with the main characteristics of Three, plus some traits of Twos. For example:

How May I Serve? A 3w2 embraces the healthy qualities of Twos such as being helpful, caring, and service-minded. Being of service means a lot to a 3w2. Wayne Dyer asked, "What's the difference between our authentic self and the false self created by ego? Authentic self wonders: *How may I serve?* Ego's attitude on the other hand is: *Gimme, gimme, gimme—I need more, and I can never be satisfied.*"

Sociable and Outgoing. A 3w2 is typically more interpersonal and extroverted than a 3w4. They are more outward facing than a 3w4. They are warm, friendly, generous, and popular. They have a busy social schedule and a wide social circle. They are in their element when they have an audience. They love to teach, communicate, perform, and do their thing. They like to collaborate, do duets, and work in partnership with others for mutual success.

Coach and Mentor. A 3w2 is typically supportive and empathetic and enjoys helping others to succeed. They are skillful coaches and mentors who help others to realize their potential. They know how to motivate people to achieve their personal best. They are great cheerleaders and supporters who get a kick out of contributing to other people's success. Their mantra is "your success is my success too."

Relationships Come First. As a 3w2, you are ambitious, driven, and always working toward a goal, but you also make sure that your family and friends get some of your best energy and attention. Whenever you lapse, you are quick to apologize and make amends. "My success is my family," Celine Dion told *People* magazine in 2012. "My life is to be a mom. It is what I enjoy the most. It is my most amazing reward. I will take a chance with my music. I don't take risks with my family."

Doing What's Best for You. A 3w2 tends to focus their energy and attention more on others than self. They're described as chameleons who adapt themselves to other people's wishes. They make themselves into an image that matches other people's fantasies, but inside they feel empty and experience fraud guilt and imposter syndrome. "Live life for you, not for the audience in your head," teaches Cheryl Richardson, a life coach, who is a Two.

Three with a 4-Wing

Threes with a 4-Wing (3w4) are called the Professional or the Creative. They show up in the world with the signature qualities of Threes, plus some of the traits of Fours. For example:

Don't Imitate! 3w4s are motivated to be authentic and original. The American Trappist monk Thomas Merton, a Four on the Enneagram, wrote in *Love and Living*, "If I had a message to my contemporaries, it is surely this: Be anything you like, be madmen, drunks, and bastards of every shape and form, but at all costs avoid one thing: success. . . . If you are too obsessed with success, you will forget to live. If you have learned only how to be a success, your life has probably been wasted."

Be True to Your Art. A 3w4 typically wants to express themselves creatively and artistically. They have a unique sense of style and won't compromise themselves. They work hard to master their craft and be the best at what they do. They are creative and productive. "I'm going to make and release as many albums as is humanly possible," said Taylor Swift to her fans. They are the artist who creates from the inside out. *Don't write for an audience; write for yourself.* They love having an audience, but that's not the reason why they do what they do.

Time for Self-Reflection. A 3w4 is more introverted than the sociable 3w2. Being in solitude, having soul time, and writing a daily journal, for instance, help Threes connect more deeply to themselves and tap into the creative energy of Point Four. Petrarch, an Italian Renaissance poet, observed, "Solitude is not out to deceive anyone; it does not pretend or embellish; it has nothing to hide and invents nothing. It is completely naked and without adornment; it knows nothing of shows or the applause which poisons the mind."

Courage to Dig Deep. A 3w4 is willing to work with the energy of Point Four to be emotionally honest and resilient. They face their fears, are honest about how they feel, and are prepared to suffer for success. They dig deep during hard times. "The key to success is failure," says Michael Jordan, the NBA legend. "Heart is what separates the good from the great," says Jordan. Two more famous Jordan mantras are: "I've never been afraid to fail" and "Failure makes me work harder."

The Dark Side. 3w4s may experience the inner turmoil that Fours typically go through. Fours can become too self-obsessed when they are too withdrawn or introverted. They can be perfectionistic when they try too hard to be original or unique. Their thoughts turn dark when they procrastinate over their work and stop being creative. They can get caught up in emotional dramas and romantic tragedy when they won't surrender more deeply to their soul's calling.

Moving to Nine and Six

Following the Inner Lines of the Enneagram Symbol, Threes move toward Point Nine (home for the Peacemaker) and Point Six (home of the Loyalist). These Inner Lines invite you to visit these Points to explore the gifts and wisdom they have for you.

Moving to Nine

When Threes tune in to Point Nine, they access some of the higher qualities that Nines are blessed with. For example:

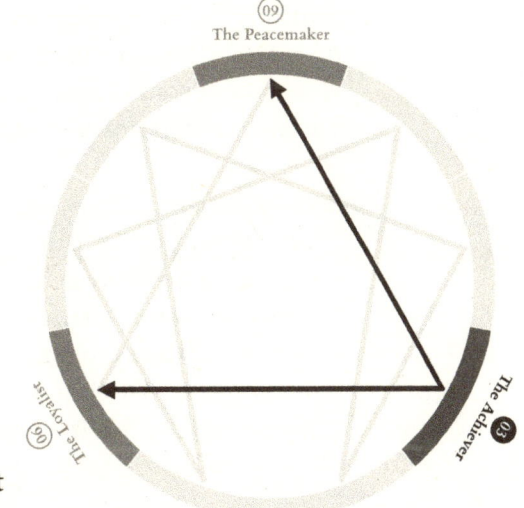

Being Yourself. The invitation at Point Nine is to center yourself in your being. First be, then do. Imagine how it would feel if all your doing came from your being and the essence of who you are. "The ground for action is to Be, and the quality of your Being determines the quality of your Doing," wrote Thích Nhất Hạnh, a Nine.

Tao of Success. Nines demonstrate an innate capacity to be in the flow and achieve effortless success. When Threes integrate the energy of Point Nine, their actions arise naturally from a place of inner calm and flow. Spontaneous action happens when you slow down and stop forcing it. "You can't hurry the Tao," said Wayne Dyer.

Holy Love. The Holy Idea at Point Nine is Holy Love. The invitation here is to be present and be guided by love. When Threes embody the energy of Point Nine, they love what they do and do more of what they love. "Let all that you do be done in love" (Corinthians 16:14).

When Threes are under stress, they may exhibit some unhealthy qualities also displayed by Nines. Knowing about these unhealthy qualities can help Threes to watch for self-defeating behaviors and attitudes. For example:

Zoning Out. When Threes are dispirited and feel like a failure, they experience the same temptation as a Nine, which is to disengage, close down, shut others out, and numb unpleasant feelings with busyness, entertainment, food, drugs, and other love substitutes.

Self-Forgetting. Nines and Threes are prone to self-forgetting. Nines often prioritize other people's wishes and forget about their own, and Threes may betray themselves when they focus only on the good opinion of others. Kabir, the poet, encouraged everyone to remember their inner gold. He called this self-remembering and remembrance. "Dwell in the house of remembering," said Kabir. "The essence of life is in remembering who you are before God."

Death Temptation. When Nines and Threes are dispirited, they get slothful, apathetic, and indecisive. Threes, like Nines, want to escape and disappear. *"Beam me up, Scotty!"* They want to exit their life and start over as someone else. They want to curl up and die. It's vital that Threes remember life is an endless cycle of death and rebirth. When it feels like your ego is dying, you need to ask yourself, *What is wanting to be born in me?*

Moving to Six

When Threes tune in to Point Six, they discover some of the higher qualities that Sixes are blessed with. For example:

Your Sixth Sense. When Threes integrate the energy of Point Six, it helps them to develop their sixth sense. Healthy Sixes and Threes practice inner listening. They listen to their Soul Voice. They follow their inner guidance. "The sound of the genuine is flowing through you," said Howard Thurman, the philosopher. Ask yourself, *what does my Soul Voice want me to know?*

A Team Player. Healthy Sixes are known for being loyal to a cause and for their loyalty in relationships. When Threes absorb the energy of Point Six, they embrace more of a win-win attitude, become more of a team player, and are less competitive and more cooperative.

Courage to Be. The virtue for Type Sixes is courage, and the greatest courage of all for Threes is to trust that your True Self is more valuable and lovable than any pleasing image you create. "Follow your own star! Follow your path, and let the people talk," said Dante Alighieri, whom we will meet again at Point Six.

Also at Point Six, Threes are made aware of the unhealthy qualities of Type Sixes. These act as a warning to Threes. For example:

Fear of Failure. Like Sixes, Threes can get incapacitated by the fear of failure. *What if I fail? What if I don't look good? What if I get egg on my face?* To be truly successful, Threes must develop the courage to face their fears. "Failure is a great teacher and, if you are open to it, every mistake has a lesson to offer," says Oprah Winfrey.

Self-Doubting. When Sixes don't listen to their inner wisdom—their sixth sense—they lack self-trust, are self-doubting, and are overwhelmed with anxiety and fear. William James, the Father of Western Psychology, observed, "There is but one cause of human failure. And that is man's lack of faith in his true Self." Ask yourself, *How can I be more centered in my True Self today?*

Life of Faith. Like Sixes, when Threes are stressed, it causes them to be indecisive, to avoid taking risks, and to play safe. The invitation at Point Six is to trust life and to affirm that life wants the best for you. "Follow your inner star. You have within you all the ingredients for success," taught Louise Hay, a Six.

Holy Law, Holy Harmony, and Holy Hope

The nine Points on the Enneagram each offer a Holy Idea—a higher wisdom and universal teaching—for all nine Ennea-Types to contemplate and practice. Point Three has three Holy Ideas. They are Holy Law, Holy Harmony, and Holy Hope.

Holy Law recognizes that the Great Work of Creation is happening everywhere, all at once, and according to universal laws. This Great Work is done through every person and all living beings including humans, worms, whales, bees, flowers, trees, stars, and galaxies. Holy Law teaches that you are here to play your part in the Great Work. No one is idle, there are no spare parts, and we all are equally valuable and necessary. Every person is *"capax universi,* capable of the universe," to quote Thomas Aquinas, who taught that everyone is capable of greatness if they will align their efforts with universal laws and work for a purpose greater than their own.

Holy Harmony teaches that every great work is a co-creation. There is no such thing as an independent doer. No one can perform a symphony on their own. "By myself I can do nothing," said Jesus, who credited his great works to the glory of God (John 5:30). Holy Harmony is the experience of aligning your individual efforts with the action for the Universe, and in doing so, becoming an instrument for universal inspiration and a higher purpose. The Italian composer Giacomo Puccini experienced Holy Harmony when he wrote his opera *Madama Butterfly*. He said, "The music of this opera was dictated to me

> *I myself do nothing.*
> *The Holy Spirit*
> *Himself accomplishes*
> *all through me.*
>
> — William Blake

by God. I was merely instrumental in getting it on paper and communicating it to the public."

In Khalil Gibran's classic work, *The Prophet*, a ploughman asks the prophet Al Mustafa to explain the higher purpose of work. The prophet said, "You work that you may keep pace with the earth and the soul of the earth. For to be idle is to become a stranger unto the seasons, and to step out of life's procession, that marches in majesty and proud submission towards the infinite." We find value and meaning in work because in doing our work—and following our soul's calling—we realize that we exist not only for ourselves, but for everyone.

> *When you work you are a flute through whose heart the whispering of the hours turns to music.*
> — Khalil Gibran

Holy Hope is a feeling of joy and optimism that arises in the heart when you align yourself with the one, unified purpose of creation. Beyond your ego, there is a universal field of inspiration and grace. When you make yourself an instrument for this universal inspiration, your chances of success and happiness increase exponentially. Holy Hope also recognizes that your worst failures and most heavy defeats can help you to succeed beyond your dreams, but only if you do the inner work and keep on growing. Your crowning achievement is to be your authentic self, and you are filled with Holy Hope when you connect with your I AM, live from your heart, and choose love over fear.

Type Four
THE INDIVIDUALIST

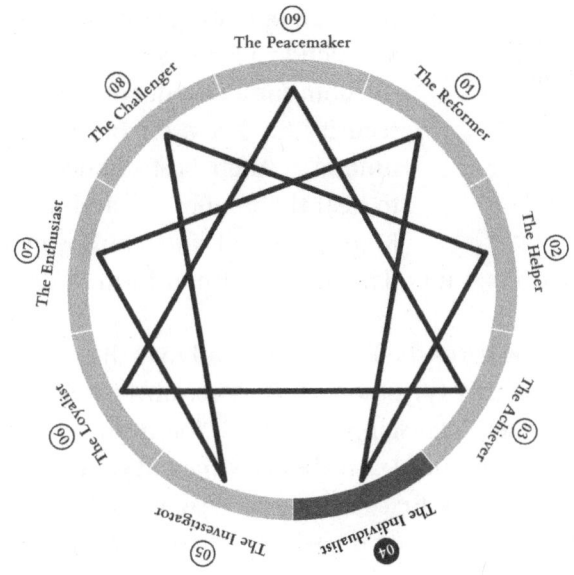

*And you? When will you begin that long
journey into yourself?*

– RUMI

The Ennea-Type Four is commonly called the Individualist. Other names for Fours include the Bohemian, Deep Soul, the Artist, Tragic Romantic, or Originality-Seeker.

Type Fours are the *Highly Individual, Feeling Type.* They are known as the deep-sea divers of the Enneagram. They explore the hidden depths of the soul, visit out-of-the-way places in the heart, and bring back pearls to share. They are naturally artistic and emotionally sensitive, self-expressive and withdrawn, self-revealing and shy, quirky and nonconformist, deeply romantic and melodramatic. Fours are lovers of beauty. They like films with sad endings. They probably keep a dream journal. Fours crave depth and intimacy. They value emotional honesty. They detest small talk. They believe in unicorns. They probably have a favorite font style that is distinctive and rare. They insist they have great taste. And Paris is always a good idea.

Fours seek originality and wish to be seen as one of a kind. They are one of the Ennea-Types that is most passionate to "find themselves" and express their True Self. As we shall see, Fours have a strong "Be Unique" driver installed in their ego operating system. Being unique means as much to a Four as does inner peace for a Nine, freedom for a Seven, connection for a Two, and security for a Six, for instance. Fours see being unique as their best chance to find their soul, to heal their suffering, and to know God. Søren Kierkegaard, a Danish philosopher who had a lot of Four and Five traits, said, "The most common form of despair is not being who you are."

> *While you had the chance to live, did you become your true self?*
> — Michael Meade

Fours are often wary of the Enneagram and may dismiss it at first glance as "just another personality type model." They certainly don't want to be pigeonholed or have another label slapped on their forehead. However, Fours warm to the Enneagram when they learn about its ancient roots and deeper purpose. Don Riso, a Four, was my first Enneagram teacher. He taught classes on the original purpose of the Enneagram, which is to discover your soul and become your True Self. He wrote several classic works on taking a deep inner journey with the Enneagram, including *Personality Types: Using the Enneagram for Self-Discovery,* in which he presents his model of nine levels of health and healing for each Ennea-Type.

Don Riso liked to say, "There is no such thing as a normal Type Four." Most Fours feel different from everyone, including other Fours. Fours want to be an original, not a copy. They want to be unique, and not to "fit the mold" or conform to expectations. *Being normal is not an aspiration for Fours.* Being unique helps a Four to be true to themselves, not get "lost in the crowd," and fully express who they are. That said, when Fours try too hard to be unique, it disconnects them from their essence, and they often end up making themselves into a copy or replica of something original.

> *The Enneagram doesn't put you in a box. It shows you the box you're already in and how to get out of it.*
> — Don Riso

"Working with the Enneagram helped me, as a Four, to stop trying to be unique and focus instead on being authentic," Don Riso told me in an interview shortly after we first met. "The more authentic I am, the more unique I feel and more connected I am to others. This change helped me to come home to myself and take my place in the world."

INTRODUCING TYPE FOUR

Are you a Type Four on the Enneagram? Maybe you have a family member, a friend, or a work colleague who is a Four.

My mother displayed many hallmark qualities of a Four. In her childhood, she felt very lonely, like the odd one out, and different from everyone else. She was born into an aristocratic British family, the youngest of four children, an unintended pregnancy, conceived on the eve of World War Two. Her siblings were much older than her, and she felt like the family misfit. She felt "not seen" by her parents. She was closer to Alice, the household cook, than to her mother. Her best friends growing up were Sally, an evacuee who came to stay during the war, and her beloved dog, Rupert, whom she said was the only one who really understood her.

Mum had a melancholic temperament and experienced recurring bouts of depression throughout her life. She was naturally beautiful and elegant, a debutante in London's high society in the 1960s, with a beehive hairdo, and frequently attended lavish balls and royal garden parties. She was courted by princes and proposed to by lords, but instead she fell for my dad, a working-class man. They had a whirlwind romance that caused quite a stir. Her story is similar to the first season of *Downton Abbey*, when Lady Sybil, the youngest of the family, marries the family chauffeur, Tom Branson. Mum was disinherited from the family fortune when she married Dad. When I asked her why she chose Dad, she said, "It was love, and somehow I knew he had come to take me away from the life I had been living."

> *I wandered lonely as a cloud, That floats on high o'er vales and hills.*
>
> — William Wordsworth

Like a lot of Fours, Mum was naturally artistic. She had beautiful handwriting. She was a gifted sketcher and painter. She knew the Latin name for flowers. She was always reading a novel. She could recite the romantic poets like Wordsworth, Shelley, and Keats. She adored Rimsky Korsakov's romantic symphony *Scheherazade*. She loved snooping around antique shops and had a great eye for a bargain. For years, she excavated an old Victorian bottle dump in the woods next to the house she was born in. Our garage was full of vintage perfume bottles, rare medicine bottles, and Codd-neck soda bottles—the ones with a marble in the neck—all perfectly preserved and worth a few pennies.

Healthy Qualities of Fours

When Fours are healthy and well-balanced, they display essential qualities that we all love and appreciate. Here are a few things healthy Fours have told me about themselves:

- "I want to be seen for who I am."
- "I value emotional depth and honesty."
- "I must be allowed to express myself."
- "I'm not very good at being normal."
- "I believe that life is a healing journey."
- "I often fantasize I am a character in a novel."
- "I worship at the altar of beauty."
- "I cry easily, and I love my tears for many reasons."
- "My wounds are my beauty marks."
- "I follow my soul's calling."

Unhealthy Qualities of Fours

When Fours are out of balance, they become more self-absorbed, full of self-pity, and melodramatic. Here are a few things Fours have told me about themselves:

- "I am obsessed with originality."
- "I often feel not seen or understood by others."
- "I can be self-obsessed and overly sensitive."
- "I can be contrary and quick to cut people off."
- "I can be too deep and forget to have fun."
- "I envy others for the life I imagine they have."
- "I make people walk on eggshells around me."
- "I find being sad easier than being happy."

- "I fantasize my real life will happen one day."
- "I am prone to bouts of melancholy."

RECOGNIZING TYPE FOURS

In philosophy, Fours are attracted to paths of mysticism that offer a heart-centered and direct approach to healing, wisdom, and love, such as Sufism, Gnosticism, Kabbalah, Advaita Vedanta, and Zen. Thomas Merton, an American Trappist monk, mystic, and social activist, showed a lot of Four and Five qualities in his teachings and best-selling memoir *The Seven Storey Mountain* (1948). Merton described the ego as the "false self" and "surface self," and the soul as the "True Self" and "Deep I." He taught that the real journey of life is interior, and that we come home to our True Self and to God by dropping deeper and deeper into the "secret beauty" of our heart.

> *For it is by the doors of his deep self that we enter into the spiritual knowledge of God.*
> — Thomas Merton

In psychology, Fours are drawn to Carl Jung's work on archetypes, mythology, dreams, and the search for the soul. Jung's Four Stages of Life maps how we become less ego-bound and more soul-centered as we grow and mature. Jung asked, "What is it, in the end, that induces a man to go his own way and to rise out of unconscious identity with the mass as out of a swathing mist?" He used the term *individuation* to describe the journey we take to recover our original wholeness. He taught that "The aim of individuation is nothing less than to divest the self of the false wrappings of the persona."

> *The world will ask you who you are, and if you don't know, the world will tell you.*
> — Carl Jung

Otto Rank, the early-20th-century Austrian psychoanalyst, is another psychologist whose work appeals to Fours. Like Jung, Rank recognized the mystery of God, the existence of the soul, and the need for creative self-expression. His works included *The Trauma of Birth* (1929), *Psychology and the Soul* (1930), and *Art and Artist* (1932). Rank recognized three phases of life that Fours can especially relate to. They are (1) the adaptive phase: suppressing one's individuality and conforming to society's norms; (2) the neurotic phase: fighting against society's norms, but getting lost in the drama of it all; and (3) the creative phase:

> *I'd say we [Apple Inc.] are the most creative of the technology companies and definitely the most artist-friendly.*
>
> — Steve Jobs

when a person finally succeeds at "winning his own individuality and in realizing his own creative potential."

In leadership, Fours are often charismatic and creative. Their work is an expression of who they are. They design their own workspace. They hate hot desks. They must be in the right mood to work, and their work must feel meaningful and have a deeper purpose, or else they will quit. The Apple Inc. brand is very Four-like. The brand strategy was meticulously crafted on beauty of design, an independent Mac operating system, and an intuitive user experience that appealed to artists, designers, and creatives. In my Leadership and the Enneagram program, I show at Point Four the film "Here's to the Crazy Ones" from the "Think Different" campaign by Apple Inc. It's 1.01 minutes long, and it celebrates 17 leaders in their field—featuring several Fours—who are described as "the crazy ones," "the misfits," and "the round pegs in the square holes" who changed the world.

The arts are a spiritual home for Fours who appreciate all art forms for their unique ability to touch souls, evoke emotions, heal wounds, transform pain into beauty, and, most of all, help us find love. Frédéric Chopin's Prelude, Op. 28, No. 4 could be a theme tune for Fours. It is the story of someone longing for home and that seeks reunion with a lost love. The E-minor key, known as "The Sad Key," the descending scale, and the moderate tempo help to convey grief, mourning, and restlessness. On the

> *Art enables us to find ourselves and lose ourselves at the same time.*
>
> — Thomas Merton

theme of longing and homecoming, I recommend listening to Judy Garland's performance of "Over the Rainbow," recorded at the Olympia Theater in Paris on October 28, 1960.

Fours bring something unique to the arts. They do what they do in their own special way. Think of Frida Kahlo, the Mexican painter known for her iconic self-portraits; Maria Callas, the opera singer, as Madama Butterfly; Van Gogh, the tortured artist who sold only one painting, *The Red Vineyard*, in his lifetime; Virginia Woolf, novelist and essayist, who wrote like an artist and pioneered stream of consciousness as a narrative device; and James Joyce, whose novels *Ulysses* and *Finnegans Wake*

> *No need to hurry. No need to sparkle. No need to be anybody but oneself.*
>
> — Virginia Woolf

are full of interior monologues that focus on the inner states of the characters. Joyce's works are recognized for their creative genius and for being notoriously difficult to understand. It is fitting perhaps that Joyce's alleged last words were "Does nobody understand?"

In poetry, go straight to Jelaluddin Rumi, the Sufi mystic and love poet with his 3,500 odes, 2,000 *rubayat*, which are four-line quatrains, and the epic *Mathnawi*, made up of six books of poetry that contains 25,000 verses. There is a Rumi poem for all nine Points on the Enneagram, but Rumi is most at home at Point Four. A central theme of Rumi's works is "holy longing." "All language is a longing for home," he wrote. He describes the soul as "a stranger trying to find a Home—somewhere that is not a where." The journey home is not to a place, but to the essence of who we are. "Do not feel lonely, the entire universe is inside you," said Rumi.

> *There is some kiss we want with our whole lives, the touch of spirit on the body.*
> — Rumi

In music, think of Joni Mitchell, "Woodstock"; Van Morrison, "Into the Mystic"; Bob Dylan, "Subterranean Homesick Blues"; Adele, "Rolling in the Deep"; Alanis Morissette, "Jagged Little Pill"; Eva Cassidy, "Songbird"; and Prince, "When Doves Cry." These singer-songwriters are artists, not popstars. Their music is packed with candid and self-revealing lyrics, with exquisite storytelling and imagery, and features recurring themes of nostalgia, heartache, melancholy, soul searching, and spiritual liberation. These artists work with artistic freedom and fiercely resist being labeled or categorized. Joni Mitchell said in a rare interview, "I have an aversion to being mislabeled. Here's a label I'd accept: I'm an 'individual.' I'm someone who can't follow and doesn't want to lead."

In film, the Scarlet Witch in the Avengers series is a being of unfathomable magic. She is dark, sensitive, introverted, mysterious, and very kind. In a scene with a character called Vision, she tells him, "You are my sadness and my hope. But mostly, you're my love." The film *Back to Black* is a biographical drama about the life and music of Amy Winehouse, who was most likely a Four. She was one of a kind, with her iconic look, beehive hair, expressive voice, and self-revealing lyrics in songs like

> *Every bad situation is a blues song waiting to happen.*
> — Amy Winehouse

"Rehab," "Wake Up Alone," "Love Is a Losing Game," and "You Know I'm No Good." Also in film, *Lady Bird,* the funny and poignant coming-of-age drama written and directed by Greta Gerwig. The lead character Christine "Lady Bird"

McPherson is a high school student who longs to express herself, feels misunderstood by her mom, and dreams of finding more culture in a place far away.

In Shakespeare's *As You Like It,* Jacques is one of Duke Senior's noblemen. He is known as "The Melancholy Jacques." Actor Alan Rickman, who was perhaps a Four, played a great Jacques. "I can suck melancholy out of a song, as a weasel sucks eggs," said Jacques, who also gives one of Shakespeare's best-known speeches, "All the world's a stage." In *Romeo and Juliet,* Romeo is very Four-like. He is a mopey teenager and a tragic romantic. At the beginning of the play, he is infatuated with Rosaline, and he suffers from her unrequited love. He is moody and melancholic and "makes himself an artificial night." His father, Montague, observes his son's "black and portentous" humor, and how Romeo's "deep sighs" have the effect of "adding to clouds more clouds."

THE ORIGINAL FACE

> *What is your substance, whereof are you made,*
> *That millions of strange shadows on you tend?*
>
> — Shakespeare, "Sonnet 53"

The Enneagram wants you to cultivate a healthy relationship to your psyche and persona. Your psyche is the essence of you. It is your soul, your Unconditioned Self, your Deep I, and your Original Face. And your persona is your self-image, a mask, and a story about you. Fours long to experience their natural, unfabricated self. "I am looking for the face I had before the world was made," wrote W. B. Yeats in his poem "Before the World Was Made." The person speaking in the poem is a young woman who is sitting before a mirror. She is painting her face to make it look beautiful, to be attractive, and to gain power over others, but deep down she longs to experience the inner beauty of the soul.

Original Face is a phrase used in Zen Buddhism to help you contemplate your original nature. The term is thought to originate from the 13th-century text *The Gateless Gate* that features a collection of 48 koans. In koan 23, a monk called Emyo is deeply envious of Eno, a fellow monk who has realized enlightenment, been ordained as the Sixth Patriarch, and bestowed the bowl and robes that once belonged to the Buddha. Monk Emyo pursues Eno and is set on stealing the bowl and

> *Show me your Original Face, the face you had before your parents were born.*
>
> — Zen meditation

robes from him. When Eno sees Emyo coming, he offers the bowl and robes to him. "You may take them now," he tells Emyo, but they are strangely too heavy for him to lift, and he realizes they are not his to take.

"I come for the teaching, not for the robe. Please enlighten me!" requests Emyo, ashamed of his envy. Eno, the Sixth Patriarch, offers Emyo medicine for his shame in the form of a question: *"Without thinking good or evil, in this very moment, what is your Original Face?"* Emyo takes the question deep into his heart and instantly realizes his true nature, which is the Buddha nature in each of us. Emyo is overjoyed and asks the patriarch to be his teacher, but the patriarch responds, "Once you have realized your own true self, the depths of Zen belong to you." Emyo keeps his gaze on his Original Face, and he experiences directly the eternal wisdom and boundless love at the core of his being.

Thomas Merton, a Christian mystic, used the term *Original Face* in his teachings. In *A Year with Thomas Merton*, Merton's entry for January 1 focuses on new beginnings and his wish to deepen his spiritual practice. He wrote, "It is certainly true that what is needed is to get back to the 'original face' and drop off all the piled-up garments of thought that do not fit me and are not 'mine'—but to take only what is nameless." Merton encouraged us to find our original, unconditioned Self. He often said, "Pray for your own discovery." He wrote:

> We are at liberty to be real, or to be unreal. We may be true or false, the truth is ours. We may wear now one mask and now another, and never, if we so desire, appear with our own true face. But we cannot make these choices with impunity. Causes have effects, and if we lie to ourselves and to others, then we cannot expect to find truth and reality whenever we happen to want them. If we have chosen the way of falsity, we must not be surprised that truth eludes us when we come to need it!

When Fours identify with their Original Self, their Deep I, they display essential qualities and healthy traits that we all appreciate and love. Here are a few of these healthy qualities.

> **The Original You.** To be original means everything to a Four. Your Original Self is the Self you truly are and that is without concepts, labels, and images. Being in touch with your Original Self helps you to feel at home with yourself wherever you are. It helps you to express yourself authentically and to find your true place in the world. *Always be yourself, because an original is worth more than a copy.*

Your Unique Style. Healthy Fours bring their own unique style and creative touch to everything they do. They embrace their uniqueness not to be different, but to be themselves. They also get a kick out of helping others to express their uniqueness and creativity. "Always remember you are absolutely unique. Just like everyone else," said Margaret Mead, a cultural anthropologist.

Not a Normal Life. "I tried to be normal once; it was the worst ten minutes of my life!" said Dotty, a Four, who took my Creativity and the Enneagram program. Dotty told me, "I used to think I was flawed, and that something was deeply wrong with me, because I had no interest in wanting to be normal. Working with the Enneagram finally gave me the permission to stop trying to be normal, and start being me!"

Creative Self-Expression. Creativity is a spiritual practice for Fours. It helps them to be present, to express themselves, and to connect in a deep and loving way with others. Fours create not only when standing at an easel, playing the piano, or writing a poem, but also in everyday tasks like making a handmade birthday card, growing a strawberry patch, painting butterflies on wellington boots, and making a decoration for the dinner table. Being creative is how Fours express their love for us.

A Lover of Beauty. Fours have a reverence for beauty. Noticing beauty is enlivening and consoling for Fours. Beauty is a way of seeing, not only with physical eyes, but with the *nous*, an ancient Greek word that means "the eye of the heart or soul." To find something beautiful is to see the essence of what you are looking at. To be beautiful means to be yourself. Appreciating beauty is how we experience intimacy with each other and with the universe.

> *Beauty is not in the face; beauty is a light in the heart.*
>
> — Khalil Gibran

Emotional Intelligence. Feelings are a Four's primary language. Fours are typically the most emotionally articulate people you will meet. They recognize the vital need to be in relationship with all their emotions, including sadness and joy, shame and innocence, anger and hope, fear and love. *A person cannot be a whole and complete expression of themselves if they suppress their feelings.* Feelings are the language of the soul. Every emotion has a message. "The wound is the place where the light enters you," said Rumi.

A Deep Soul. Don Riso, the Enneagram teacher, described Fours as "the deep-sea divers of the psyche." By going deep into themselves, they meet their fears and the source of their suffering, and they bring back pearls of love and wisdom. "Going deep" helps Fours to be gifted healers, wise teachers, inspiring artists, and, most of all, compassionate friends who are truly there for you in the best and worst of times.

THE ORIGINAL WOUND

> *Vitally, the human race is dying.*
> *It is like a great uprooted tree, with its roots in the air.*
> *We must plant ourselves again in the universe.*
>
> – D. H. Lawrence, *Lady Chatterley's Lover*

In mythology, the Garden is a symbol that represents our original home. The Garden is where we are from and where we return to. It is an experience of heaven. Entrance into the Garden is through a gateless gate, and everyone is welcome in the Garden because it is everybody's original home. Here we experience our Oneness with God. The Garden is our holy origin. Rumi, the poet, describes our planet Earth as a garden, and "God is the gardener," "Spring is Christ," "The Trees are Mary," and "Wind is the Holy Spirit."

In the Garden, we experience our Original Self. In Van Morrison's song "In the Garden," he tells us that there is no need for a guru, a method, or a teacher. Everything we long for is already here in the Garden waiting for us to return. Van Gogh found a way to paint heaven on a canvas in his garden portraits such as *The Garden at Arles* and *The Poet's Garden*. My favorite is his *Garden of the Asylum*, where his inner turmoil is transformed into a symphony of colors and his terrible loneliness is absorbed and taken in by beauty. "If you truly love nature, you will find beauty everywhere," said Van Gogh.

Every human being experiences a sense of separation, and for a Four the separation is being uprooted and exiled from the Garden. The Garden of Eden myth in the Bible marks the beginning of the story of separation, sin, and shame. Joni Mitchell's song "Woodstock" describes the terrible ache and longing for home. It's all in her beautiful lyrics: "stardust," "golden," and the need to "get ourselves back to the garden." Dua Lipa also explores the theme of leaving the Garden of Eden in her song "Garden." When we are not in the Garden, and connected with our Original Self, we feel a long way from home. "I was born very far from where I'm supposed to be, and so I'm on my way home," said Bob Dylan in the movie *No Direction Home*.

Otto Rank described our sense of separation as our original wound. All our traumas, heartache, and suffering stems from the original wound of separation. "At birth, the individual experiences the first shock of separation, which throughout his life he strives to overcome," he wrote. Rank observed that life is a succession of separations, and that our deepest longing is to experience a *unio mystica*, a mystical union (or reunion) between soul and nature. He maintained that our best chance to achieve this union is through art and love.

Basic Fear: No Special Identity

"I am obsessed with originality," said Annika, a lawyer from St. Petersburg, Russia, who attended my Soul of the Enneagram program in London. Annika liked to collect original works of art, antique jewelry, and vintage clothing. One of her prized possessions was a first edition of *Paradise Lost*, by John Milton. When I asked Annika about her obsession, she spoke with great self-awareness and was very self-revealing, which is typical for a Four. She told me, "Deep down, I'm afraid that there is nothing original about me. And yet I long to find something original inside myself—something God has given me—that I can give expression to. I must keep trying to find it or I will die."

> *I'm not a body with a soul, I'm a soul that has a visible part called the body.*
> — Paulo Coelho, *Eleven Minutes*

When Fours struggle to locate their Original Self, they are troubled by a deep sense of loss, and a basic fear arises in them of having no special identity or personal significance. "Who am I without my soul? I cannot exist without my soul, no more than my body can live without air," said Annika. When Fours are estranged from their soul, and lose sight of their Original Face, they feel a loss of identity. This loss of identity causes Fours to fear that something is missing in them, and that they are flawed and not beautiful in their own way.

The Four's basic fear of having no special identity may express itself as FOBO—the Fear of Being Ordinary. What is so frightening about being ordinary? For Fours, it may heighten the sense of having no personal significance and being without any distinguishing features. It is the fear of being lost in the crowd, of being unrecognizable, and having no spiritual DNA or fingerprint to prove that you exist. FOBO conjures up nightmare scenarios for Fours like living a normal life in suburbia, working at a hot desk for a large corporation, and being just another extra on a film set.

> *Somebody save my life. I'd rather be anything but ordinary, please.*
> — Avril Lavigne, "Anything but Ordinary"

And yet healthy Fours will tell you that there is no such thing as ordinary. Nothing is ordinary because everything comes from a single Holy Origin that is truly sacred. When I teach about Point Four on the Enneagram, I often quote Macrina Wiederkehr, a Benedictine nun with plenty of Four energy. In *A Tree Full of Angels*, she wrote, "Holiness comes wrapped in the ordinary. There are burning bushes all around you. Every tree is full of angels. Hidden beauty is waiting in every crumb."

Here are some insights that Fours have shared with me about living with their basic fear of having no special identity:

- "I've always felt a little homeless."
- "I don't feel like I fit in anywhere."
- "I often feel like I am dancing on my own."
- "I'm trying to find the person I really am."
- "I can be painfully self-conscious."
- "I crave intimacy, but I'm also shy."
- "I need to be seen for who I am."
- "I feel easily rejected and hurt by others."
- "My fear is I am the exception to the rule."
- "I'm a sad person, and I don't know why."

Childhood Story: The Misfit

Many Fours will tell you that they don't feel at home in the world. From an early age, they experience "a loss of origin," "a feeling of nostalgia," and "a deep longing for home." They identify with E.T. and his desire to "Phone home!" They also identify with Dorothy from *The Wizard of Oz*, who is not in Kansas anymore. *Where am I from? Is this my original home? Does anyone see me for who I am?* Young Fours often feel out of place in the world and feel very different from other family members. Don Riso offers an insightful portrait of a young Four in *Wisdom of the Enneagram*, co-written with Russ Hudson. He tells us,

> Fours feel that they are not like their parents. Many Fours report fantasizing that they were mistakenly switched at the hospital, or that they are orphans or some kind of changeling. They often express this as feeling that they have not been "seen" by their parents, that they did not connect sufficiently with their parents or their parents with them. In psychological terms, Fours feel that they have not had adequate mirroring of actual qualities and talents that they can make part of their developing identity. In family systems theory, Fours tend to identify with the Lost Child role.
>
> The result is that Fours believe that something must be profoundly wrong with them, launching them on a lifelong "search for self." They feel "If I am not like my parents and I cannot see myself in them, then who am I?" This also predisposes Fours to focus on what they lack—on what is missing in themselves, their lives, and their relationships. They feel abandoned and misunderstood by their parents and later by other significant people.

In childhood, Fours typically place themselves on the outer rim of the family constellation. As the Individualist, they identify with the role of "family misfit," "odd one out," and "the outsider." This self-assigned role may be reinforced and exacerbated by having a different temperament to others: *"I'm the only one who cries in my family,"* or by having different interests: *"I love to watch Indie movies, but my family only likes action movies,"* or by having different points of view in spirituality and politics; or by having a different taste in fashion, food, music, and art.

The "Be Unique" Driver: Most Fours will tell you they have a persistent "Be Unique" driver installed in their ego operating system. Fours get a kick out of being unique. They enjoy the feeling of being "an original" and are intent on being authentic and true to themselves. When Fours are in tune with their Original Self, they feel beautiful and are naturally authentic and unique. You don't have to try to be unique when you are being authentic. But when Fours lose sight of their originality, it can drive them to fabricate an idealized self-image that is special, different, exempt, and "more unique" than others.

> *Beauty begins the moment you decide to be yourself.*
> — Coco Chanel

Wanting to be unique can help a Four to find their Original Self, but it can also cause Fours to lose themselves in what Enneagram teacher Claudio Naranjo, a Four, calls "an excessive concern with the image of the self." The highly image conscious Four tries so hard to be unique that it blocks intimacy and depth with others, and as the need to be different intensifies, it plunges them into a realm of isolation, alienation, and abandonment. Here, in the depths of despair, Fours take on another role, the Special Case or Lost Cause, in which they play out the fear of being "the exception to the rule," e.g., the only one who will not find love, the only one who does not have a soul, and the only one who will not make their way back home to God.

Let's look at some examples of how the "Be Unique" driver operates for Fours in the three biological instincts: (1) Self-Preservation Instinct (SP), which is mostly about lifestyle, material matters, and self-care; (2) Social Instinct (SO), which is mostly about relating to family, society, and the world; and (3) (SX) Sexual Instinct (also called One-to-One Instinct), which is mostly about attraction, relating style, and romance.

Self-Preservation Instinct (SP) *Healthy:* You are typically more materialistic and earthy than other Fours. You design your lifestyle to be an expression of your unique self. You create spaces that mirror who you are and support your creativity, e.g., a rustic kitchen, an artist's garret, a creative workspace, a meditation room, a sewing room, a pottery shed, or a garden greenhouse. You appreciate ambiance and aesthetics and have your own signature style. *Not-so-healthy:* You are the most introverted of Fours. You enjoy solitude. You make time for your soul. You prioritize "me time." You can be so self-absorbed—with personal interests, creative pursuits, and self-healing work—that you "paint yourself into a corner" and are too solitary. *Unhealthy:* Self-indulgence. Lavish spending. Very particular taste. Drinking only the finest red Burgundy. A craving for luxury, even when you can't afford it. Identifying with brands that make you feel beautiful. You insist: *I am what I wear.* You suffer from terrible self-neglect, procrastination, and a refusal to address physical issues to do with work, money, and self-care.

Social Instinct (SO) *Healthy:* You are less insular and more socially active than SP and SX Fours. You have a close circle of friends. You feel appreciated and valued for your uniqueness. You are ultra-honest and relatable. You are compassionate and empathetic. People confide in you. It's okay to be a hot mess. You can stand with people in both their suffering and their joy. *Not-so-healthy:* On your down days, you compare yourself negatively with others. You score yourself below average in every imaginary poll. You feel like an outsider and a misfit. You fantasize that being a dolphin or a cat would be easier than being human. *Unhealthy:* You turn your feelings of being a misfit into an identity and a story. "I feel like an outsider" morphs into "I am an outsider." You withdraw from your social circle. You distance yourself from the crowd. You feel rejected by others, but maybe that's because you are rejecting them.

Sexual Instinct (SX) *Healthy:* You are known for being the most emotionally intense of all the Ennea-Types. You identify with your feelings. *I am my feelings!* At work, you pour your libido and sexual energy into your creative projects. You are deeply romantic. You are looking for *The One* that is your true love. Spiritually, you have a holy longing and wish for a mystical union with the divine. *Not-so-healthy*: You use your sexual energy to make yourself into an object of desire. You try to make yourself attractive. You cultivate an air of mystique. Your charisma is alluring, but it also blocks intimacy and depth. Do people love you for who you are, or only for the intriguing image you present? *Unhealthy:* You are known for being moody and melodramatic. People walk on eggshells around you. Your histrionics are notorious. You are a tragic romantic. You confuse infatuation with love. You are so infatuated with yourself, there is no room for anyone else in your life.

Passion: Envy

All nine Types on the Enneagram experience a *passion*, or cause of suffering in the heart, that emerges from a sense of separation and from the basic fear.

The passion for Fours is envy, which is another of the so-called cardinal sins. We can all relate to envy. Envy has a secret life in everyone. Envy has been described as "the lowest of sins" and "the most shameful sin" and the sin we try hardest to hide from others.

I once took a class with Claudio Naranjo, a Four, on the passions of the Enneagram. Naranjo described envy as the "most passionate of the passions" and as "the saddest of all sins." He said, "Envy arises from the fear that there is nothing original about you, and that you are only a poor imitation of someone that is truly beautiful." He explained how envy is "a satellite of vanity," which is the passion for Threes, and that when we are gripped by envy, we try desperately to make ourselves original, beautiful, successful, unique, perfect, and the list goes on. But envy cannot create; it only frustrates us. "Envy disappears when you meet your Original Face," Naranjo said. "Nothing is more beautiful than experiencing the essence of who you are."

In his classic work *Ennea-Type Structures*, Naranjo offers a most insightful portrait of what it is like for a Four to suffer envy. Here, in this passage, Naranjo reveals some of the underlying causes of envy in Fours.

> Possessed of a deep longing, dominated by nostalgia, intimately forlorn and sometimes visibly liquid-eyed and languorous, they are usually pessimistic, often bitter and sometimes cynical. Associated traits are lamenting, complaining, despondent and self-pitying. Of particular prominence in the painful landscape of the ennea-type IV psychology is what has to do with the feeling of loss, usually the echo of real experiences of loss and deprivation, sometimes present as a fear of future loss and particularly manifest as a proneness to suffering intensely from the separations and frustrations of life. Particularly striking is the propensity of ennea-type IV to the mourning response, not only in relation to persons but also pets. It is in this cluster, I think, that we are closest to the core of the character ennea-type, and particularly in the maneuver that it entails of focusing upon and expressing suffering to obtain love.

Let's take a closer look at some of the common threads of envy that Fours experience in their heart and in their relationships.

Loss of Originality. In Latin, the word *envy* is bound to the word *Invidia*, which is associated with "the evil eye," and is translated variously as "non-sight," "poor sight," and "looking against." In Ovid's *Metamorphoses*, Invidia, the goddess of envy, is portrayed as having "sickly pale" features, "a poisonous breast of a greenish hue," and it is said that "she squinted horribly." The point is that envy arises in you when you lose sight of your Original Face, your secret beauty, and your eternal loveliness. Macrina Wiederkehr, a Benedictine nun, has the perfect prayer for this loss of sight: *"O God, help me to believe the truth about myself no matter how beautiful it is!"*

A Missing Piece. Naranjo observed that envy comes from a "chronic sense of inner scarcity and badness" and from "a craving towards that which is felt lacking." Fours often describe themselves as feeling unfinished and incomplete. They strongly identify with this painful feeling of "something missing" and make it into a sad story about themselves. "I describe myself as a jigsaw puzzle with a missing piece," Brandon, a Four, told me. When I asked him, "Who would you be without this story?" he was silent for five minutes. Tears rolled gently down his cheeks. Eventually he said, softly, "Without this story, I would be whole."

Unfavorable Comparisons. Fours envy no one when in tune with their originality. In fact, Fours get a thrill out of seeing originality in others and will actively encourage others to express their talents and gifts. This is one of the soul gifts of Fours. But when Fours lose sight of their originality, they compare themselves unfavorably with others. They long to be more rational and objective (like Ones), warm and sunny (like Twos), disciplined and productive (like Threes), clear and luminous (like Fives), steady and courageous (like Sixes), upbeat and happy (like Sevens), strong and confident (like Eights), and more easygoing and calm (like Nines). Envy disappears when Fours are not comparing themselves to others.

My Outcast State. "I all alone beweep my outcast state," said the speaker in Shakespeare's Sonnet 29, which is known as the sonnet of envy. When Fours are estranged from their own soul, they feel out of place with themselves and the world. "All of life is foreign country," wrote Jack Kerouac, a Beat poet and author of the memoir *Lonesome Traveler*. A Four's saving grace is accepting that we all feel like outcasts from time to time, and that the more present we are to each other's suffering, the less alone we feel. "Practice kindness all day to everybody and you will realize you're already in heaven now," wrote Kerouac.

My Sad Story. Claudio Naranjo observed how Fours "seek happiness through pain," and that this causes Fours to feel envious of others who seem to have a much easier life. Fours recognize the need to accept their suffering, and to meet it with honesty and compassion, but when gripped by envy they can overidentify with suffering too. True happiness for Fours comes from recognizing the original cause of their suffering, but also from giving up their attachment to suffering.

Fixation: Melancholia

In the Enneagram, the *fixation* refers to a mental habit that causes an imbalance in your mental health and well-being. The fixation for Fours is melancholia, or melancholy. Hippocrates, the Greek physician and philosopher, named melancholy as one of the four basic temperaments, along with choleric, sanguine, and phlegmatic. Melancholia is associated with being dispirited, downhearted, and feeling blue. "Grief and fear, when lingering, provoke melancholia," observed Hippocrates. It is a mood that reflects a state of loss, heavy mourning, and deep longing.

Melancholia, or melancholy, sounds rather dreary and undesirable, and yet most Fours would not wish to live without it. My wife, Hollie, is a Four, and when she teaches about Point Four on the Enneagram, she happily speaks in praise of melancholy. "Melancholy does not have to be scary or depressing," she said. "I have learned to live with melancholy as a friend and a guide. Melancholy slows you down. It asks you to pay attention to your life, and to be a 'noticer of things.' It wants you to be emotionally honest, and not to stray from what is most real and meaningful to you. Having a healthy, all-embracing relationship with melancholy keeps you grounded, present, and authentic."

There are many shades of melancholy. For instance, there is a sweet melancholy for appreciating beauty and love, as found in John Keats's poems "Ode to Melancholy" and "Ode on a Grecian Urn." There is an artistic melancholy that inspires creativity in artists. "Melancholy is one of my muses," Van Morrison once told me. There is a romantic melancholy that Fours often experience in unrequited love or a past relationship. And there is a light melancholy for finding humor and hope in the most depressing situations. Actor Bill Murray portrays comedic melancholy expertly in his films such as, *Rushmore*, *Broken Flowers,* and *Groundhog Day*. He said, "Melancholy is kind of sweet sometimes, I think. It's not a negative thing. It's not a mean thing. It's just something that happens in life, like autumn."

> *I recommend you take time to make friends with melancholy. She will help you notice which areas of your heart need to be loved, reclaimed, and breathed back to life.*
> — Hollie Holden

Fours find melancholy seductive and pleasurable. Ask Fours to name their favorite Christmas carol, and the chances are that "In the Bleak Midwinter" will top the charts. And *Les Misérables* will most definitely be on their list of favorite musicals. Fours are also the Type most likely to compile a Melancholy play mix, featuring songs such as "Cry Me a River" by Julie London, "Strange Fruit" by Nina Simone, "Love Is a Losing Game" by Amy Winehouse, "Tears in Heaven" by Eric Clapton, and songs from the *Mellon Collie and the Infinite Sadness* album by Smashing Pumpkins, and anything by Coldplay. For classical music, Samuel Barber's *Adagio for Strings* and Henryk Gorecki's Symphony No. 3 bring tears to a Four's eyes.

Melancholy becomes a serious challenge for Fours when they are overidentified and fixated on it. This is when the passing clouds of melancholy gather up and turn into a dark storm that blots out the sun and may last for days on end.

The Sad Child. "In all our family pictures, I am the sad child who is staring down at the ground or facing the wrong way," said Connie, a Four, whom I met on a Parenting and the Enneagram program I taught with Hollie. Connie told us, "Melancholy is my birth mark. It's a scar on my heart, and I don't know how to be myself without it," Connie told us. Connie and I did some inner child work together. And as Connie connected more deeply with her inner child, her inner child became less sad. "My inner child's sadness was an invitation for me to connect more deeply with myself and love myself more," Connie told me.

Clouds of Nostalgia. Melancholia has heavy hints of nostalgia and grief. The word *nostalgia* denotes a yearning to return. It is made of two Greek words: *nostos*, which means "return" or "homecoming," and *algos*, which means "suffering" or "pain." Nostalgia is linked to the original wound of separation and is overlaid with feelings of paradise lost. Nostalgia also arises from the fear of not finding happiness where you are. Fours who are fixated on nostalgia live too much in the past. Their nostalgia robs them of the present. They don't allow themselves to be happy in real time, only in hindsight.

> *I prefer the mystic clouds of nostalgia to the real thing, to be honest.*
> — Robert Wyatt

A Chronic Sigh. William Shakespeare's Sonnet 30, called the Sonnet of Melancholy, begins with a heavy sigh of despair. The first four lines are: "When to the sessions of sweet silent thought / I summon up remembrance of things past, / I sigh the lack of many a thing I sought, / And with old woes new wail my dear time's waste." Enneagram teacher Russ Hudson, a Five, refers to the "the chronic sigh of melancholy" that Fours use to express their disappointment with the past and hopelessness about the future. Fours who are fixated on melancholy live life as a lament. They are so used to feeling blue, they don't know what to do when happiness comes to them suddenly and from out of the blue.

SOMO—Sadness of Missing Out. The British rock band The Who wrote a song, "Melancholia," that tells the story of a person whose "heart is born to melancholia." This person believes, "The sun is shining, but not for me." When Fours are fixated on melancholy, they wallow in the feeling of SOMO—Sadness of Missing Out. It's important for Fours to realize that SOMO is often self-imposed. For example, Fours make themselves sad by withdrawing from "normal people" and by waiting in their ivory tower for their prince to arrive. "There is no greater cause of melancholy than idleness," wrote Robert Burton, author of *The Anatomy of Melancholy*, first published in 1621.

Melancholic Depression. Melancholia can be a major contributing factor to major depressive disorders (MDD). Melancholic depression is a recognized MDD with symptoms of dark thoughts, loss of appetite, hopelessness, poor sleep, chronic fatigue, and thoughts of suicide. Otto Rank, the renowned psychologist whom I mentioned earlier, experienced life-long depression after he was sexually abused as a child by an uncle. He attempted suicide as teenager. His saving grace was helping others to heal their suffering and also his love of beauty, creativity, and art. In his personal journal, Rank wrote that he had to make a conscious choice every day to choose life, to choose the present moment, and to choose love. "I must either commit suicide or give birth every day," he wrote.

THE JOURNEY HOME

> *But if you travel far enough, one day you will recognize yourself coming down the road to meet yourself. And you will say—yes.*
>
> – Marion Woodman, *Coming Home to Myself*

The Enneagram offers a path of growth for all nine Types that helps you to remember your original nature and be your True Self. For Fours, the path of growth is a journey home.

Most Fours I know are soul-searchers. They are seeking a greater depth and intimacy with their soul. They want to *actualize the blueprint* of their Original Self and be a full expression of themselves. Carl Jung described this as the process of individuation. To do this we must go on what he called "a night-sea journey" deep into the underworld of the unconscious, beyond the ego-self, to where the soul lives.

When I teach about Point Four, I draw inspiration from Jung's *Liber Novus*, also known as *The Red Book*. This awe-inspiring work contains writings from Jung's notebooks and journals between 1914 and 1930, and it was not published or made accessible for public study until 2009, which was 48 years after Jung's death. In *The Red Book*, Jung describes his own night-sea journey, where he encountered what he called "the spirit of the depths," and engaged in a dialogue with the soul.

"I lived into the depths, and the depths began to speak," wrote Carl Jung in *The Red Book*. Jung's ego-self resisted the spirit of the depths at first: "I could not and did not want to listen to the depths. But on the seventh night, the spirit of the depths spoke to me: 'Look into your depths, pray to your depths, waken the dead.'" Jung ultimately surrendered to this spirit of the depths. He wrote, "Therefore the spirit of the depths forced me to speak to my soul, to call upon her as a living and self-existing being."

At first, Jung struggled to feel the presence of his soul. For nights on end, he addressed his soul directly and beckoned his soul to make an appearance. He wrote:

> My Soul, where are you? Do you hear me? I speak, I call you—are you there? I have returned. I am here again. I have shaken the dust of all the lands from my feet, and I have come to you, I am with you. After long years of long wandering, I have come to you again . . .

For Jung to commune more deeply with his soul, he realized it was necessary to let go of all his learned ideas and old concepts of what the soul is. "I had to accept that what I had previously called my soul was not at all my soul, but a dead system that I had contrived," he wrote. Jung had to take off every label he had put on himself and on the soul. Later, Jung wrote about how he found his soul. "You [the soul] announced yourself to me in advance in dreams," he wrote. " And you, my soul, I found again, first in images within men and then you yourself. I found you where I least expected you. You climbed out of a dark shaft. In the end, Jung recognized that what he called "self" was only an image, and that it is the soul that is our True Self.

Virtue: Equanimity

Each Enneagram type has a virtue, or a superpower, that blossoms and blooms in you as you do the inner work to heal the basic fear, the passion in the heart, and the fixation in your thinking. The virtue for Fours is *equanimity*.

Equanimity is a quality that arises from your depths and from spending time with your soul. Your ego can't manufacture equanimity by itself. It is a gift given to you by the soul. In Buddhism, equanimity is one of the Four Divine Abodes, along with kindness, compassion, and empathetic joy. Equanimity describes a boundless love and acceptance of ourselves. It is the feeling of a spacious heart—a heart as wide as the world—that wants you to embrace your human longing and your divine nature. Equanimity reunites you with your original innocence. It liberates you from self-judgment and attack. Equanimity is a soul without shame. It reveals to you your secret beauty.

Equanimity offers you a deep welcome. It is a radical self-acceptance that loves all of you, including the pieces of you that are broken and bent out of shape. Equanimity is represented by the Black Madonna, for instance, who embodies unconditional love. She meets you in the darkest places inside yourself. She sits with you during your dark night of the soul. She makes sure you do not go through hell alone. She helps you to meet fear with love, to bless your wounds, to turn grief into wisdom, and to offer compassion and loving-kindness to yourself and to the world.

> **Welcoming Your Pain.** Equanimity does not shout, "Leave me alone!" or "Go away!" to troubled guests such as pain, sorrow, grief, and despair. "These pains you feel are messengers. Listen to them," said Rumi. When teaching about equanimity, I often share Rumi's poem "The Guest House," translated by Coleman Barks, which encourages us to transform our experience of pain by welcoming it with love. In it, Rumi said, "The dark thought, the shame, the malice, meet them at the door laughing and invite them in." And also, "Be grateful for whoever comes, because each has been sent as a guide from beyond."
>
> **Facing Your Dragons.** Equanimity helps you to see everything through the eyes of love. In *Letters to a Young Poet*, Rilke advised, "What is happening in your innermost self is worthy of your entire love; somehow you must find a way to work at it." This includes facing your dragons and your darkest fears. Rilke observed, "Perhaps all the dragons in our lives are princesses who are only waiting to see us act, just once, with beauty and courage. Perhaps everything that frightens us is, in its deepest essence, something helpless that wants our love."
>
> **Honoring Your Wounds.** Equanimity is an aspect of love that does not judge you or shame you for your wounds. When you stop judging and shaming yourself, your wounds turn into beauty marks. Wounds

> *I am blooming from the wound where I once bled.*
>
> — Rune Lazuli, poet

and heartbreaks invite you to let more love in and be more loving. "Out of the shell of the broken heart emerges the new-born soul," wrote Hazrat Inayat Khan, the Sufi mystic.

Meeting Your Shadow. Equanimity gives you the emotional courage to enter the out-of-the-way places in your heart and meet your shadow. The shadow is often an unloved wound or fear, but it can also be a disowned talent or gift. The shadow is that aspect of yourself that you have refused to accept and love. Equanimity teaches you that healing your shadow is the greatest gift you can give to yourself and to your partner, your family, your friends, and the world.

Miracle of Forgiveness. Equanimity is a deep love that helps you to forgive your past and step into the present. Forgiveness helps you to remember that you are not defined by what happened to you in your past. No single failure is an entire biography. A heartbreak is only a story, and not the whole story. Pain may leave a scar, but it is not your identity. Forgiveness is a new beginning. "Forgiveness teaches you that nothing that happened yesterday can limit the miracles that are available today," said Marianne Williamson, author of *A Return to Love*.

Equanimity recognizes that we are different and the same in that we all suffer, we all feel lonely, we all can be foolish, and we all want to feel loved and be happy. This compassionate outlook is expressed beautifully in a Buddhist prayer called the Equanimity Prayer.

> May all beings have happiness
> and the causes of happiness.
> May all beings be free from suffering
> and the causes of suffering.
> May all beings never be separated from the
> supreme joy that is beyond all sorrow.
> May all beings abide in equanimity free
> from attachment and aversion.

Balancing Your Centers

The Enneagram encourages you to balance your three centers of intelligence—body, heart, and head—to be healthy, happy, and wise. Fours are called a Heart Type, along with Twos and Threes, because their primary center of intelligence is the heart center. It can be tempting for Fours to live mostly in the heart center and make only occasional visits to the head center and body center. However, healthy Fours know that that the three centers belong together. "As a Four, my work is about making a home for myself in all three centers," says Hollie Holden. The centers are like three jewels set in a beautiful, handcrafted ring, and the ring is complete only if each of the three jewels are loved, polished, and cared for.

> *I always find a love note, waiting, for me, in my heart. She is so sweet to me my soul.*
>
> — "So Sweet," a poem, Robert Holden

The Heart Center. It is in the heart center that Fours cultivate their soul gift of equanimity, and also compassion, empathy, and love. Fours relate to their heart in different ways. For some, the heart is a healing temple, a place you enter to do deep emotional healing work, to anoint your wounds with love, and to recover your exiled parts. For others, the heart is an artist's garret, a place to nurture your divine spark and creative self-expression. And for others, it is a secret garden, a place for solitude, for deep inner listening, and for a dialogue with your soul and with God.

The Body Center. Fours often neglect the body center, which can have a damaging effect on their emotional well-being and mental health. The Enneagram encourages Fours to listen with love to their body's messages, to take long walks in nature, to pay

> *God spoke today in flowers, and I, who was waiting on words, almost missed the conversation.*
>
> — Ingrid Goff-Maidoff

attention to the shape of clouds, to work on their garden patch, to dance their prayers, and make the body sweat every now and then in order to activate their life force, throw off their inertia, and turn creative ideas into actions. Marion Woodman, the Jungian analyst who described body work as soul work, wrote, "Give your body an hour a day. If it's not worth an hour a day, there's nothing your body can tell you and not much anyone else can do."

The Head Center. Most Fours will describe themselves as "feelers" and not "thinkers." Fours tend to process their life primarily through their feelings, not their thoughts. And yet many Fours are naturally deep thinkers who are intuitive and wise. They also like to engage in deep and meaningful conversations that require open-mindedness and outside-of-the-box thinking. This is especially true of Fours who have a dominant Five wing. The Enneagram encourages Fours to be more confident in their natural capacity to think deeply and clearly. A helpful journaling exercise for Fours is to meditate on these three questions: (1) *What is the most beautiful thought I can think today?* (2) *What is the most healing thought I can think?*" and (3) *What is the most kind and loving thought I can think?*

Spreading Your Wings

Type Fours home base is Point Four, which sits between Point Three and Point Five on the Enneagram symbol. This means Fours have a 3-Wing and a 5-Wing. Typically, one wing is more dominant than the other, but the goal is to balance your wings. Working with the 3-Wing helps Fours to tap into the essential qualities and wisdom of Point Three, and working with the 5-Wing helps Fours to access the same at Point Five. Learning to live in balance with your wings, by drawing strengths and lessons from both, can be very helpful for Fours.

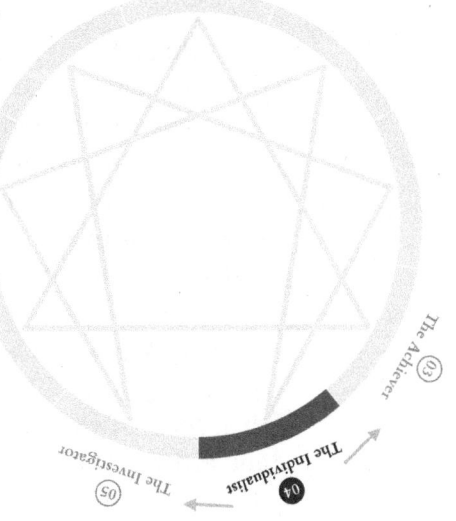

Four with a 3-Wing

Fours with a dominant 3-Wing (4w3) are called the Aristocrat. They show up in the world with the main characteristics of Four, plus some traits of Threes. For example:

Authentically Me. A 4w3 combines the healthy qualities of Fours and Threes, such as being authentic, genuine, and true to yourself. Both Fours and Threes are called Heart Types on the Enneagram, along with Twos. For a 4w3, their spiritual focus is to listen to the wisdom of the heart and to follow what Carlos Castaneda, in *The Teachings of Don Juan*, called "a path with heart." "Your heart knows the way, run in that direction," said Rumi.

Can-Do Attitude. The energy at Point Three connects you to your I AM, which is the mystical term for your Original Self. A 4w3 is typically self-assertive, inner-directed, and action oriented. They are more likely to have a To-Do list than 4w5s, and they work hard to turn ideas into actions and make their dreams come true. When 4w3s are centered in their I AM or Original Self, they feel the activity of God flowing through them. God works directly through the I AM in all beings.

Outgoing Energy. A 4w3 is typically more upbeat, energetic, and outgoing than a 4w5. They tend to live at a faster pace and are generally more active and whizzier than a 4w5. Most Fours like their own space, are private by nature, and tend to need a little nudge to "put themselves out there" in the world, but a 4w3 tends to find it easier than a 4w5 to step out on the stage, turn on their heart light, and make their unique mark on the world.

Creative Work. "Creativity is a drug I cannot live without," said filmmaker Cecil B. DeMille. Fours must have a creative outlet in their life. A 4w3 is driven to do work that is creative, expressive, and artistic. They look for the thing they are uniquely placed to do in the world. When they find it, they are in their element, and feel they have full permission to be themselves. It might be a job, a special talent, an artistic pursuit, or being a parent, for instance.

Special Attention. Both Fours and Threes (along with Twos) are called Image Types in the Enneagram. A 4w3 is typically more image conscious than a 4w5. They tend to create with an audience in mind. "One should either be a work of art, or wear a work of art," said Oscar Wilde. They want to be admired. They fear being insignificant. They can be attention-seeking, overly competitive, prone to bouts of envy, fearful of rejection, and may be deceptive and underhanded in how they go about winning love and success.

Four with a 5-Wing

Fours with a dominant 5-Wing (4w5) are called the Bohemian. They show up in the world with the main characteristics of Four, plus some traits of Fives. For example:

Creative Thinking. A 4w5 embraces the mental attributes of healthy Fives such as curiosity, perceptiveness, ingenuity, and inventiveness. A 4w5 engages both their heart and head in their creative pursuits. Hence, 4w5s are known for being creative thinkers who, with their "seeing mind," will regularly experience eurekas, epiphanies, and flashes of genius and inspiration in their work.

Think Different! "If you lend your consciousness to someone else, you're a robot," said, Prince, the singer-songwriter. Prince displayed a creative mix of Four and Five traits. "Art is about laying a new foundation, not just about laying something on top of what's already there," he said. Like many 4w5s, he was nonconformist, free-spirited, pioneering, and impossible to pigeonhole. "I like to open people's eyes," said Prince.

Going Within. Fours and Fives (along with Nines) are known as the Withdrawn Types on the Enneagram. A 4w5 is typically more introverted and insular than a 4w3. They value solitude, personal space, and quiet time for recharging themselves and being creative. "Solitude is creativity's best friend, and solitude is refreshment for our souls," said Naomi Judd, the country music singer and actress. A 4w5 also tends to be more of a reclusive artist, less interested in performing for an audience the way a 4w3 does.

Highly Sensitive Person. Both Fours and Fives will commonly describe themselves as being highly sensitive. And a 4w5 will claim they are the most sensitive of all Ennea-Types! "As a 4w5 I often feel like I am too sensitive to be in the world," said Tim, a graphic designer. "I feel like I have no skin or armoring, and my sensitivity to criticism and rejection and other people's opinions stops me from expressing my creativity, sharing my ideas, and being who I am."

Independent and Aloof. Fours and Fives are known for being independent and idiosyncratic. When you combine Four and Five energies, which is the case for a 4w5, you get a double dose of independence that may cause problems. For example, it can reinforce the story of being the outsider, a misfit, and the odd one out. It can also heighten schizoid feelings of isolation, alienation, and abandonment. And it can prevent 4w5s sharing their creativity and ideas more widely with the world.

Moving to One and Two

Following the Inner Lines of the Enneagram symbol, Fours move toward Point One (home for the Reformer) and Point Two (home for the Helper). These Inner Lines invite you to visit these Points to explore the gifts and wisdom they have for you.

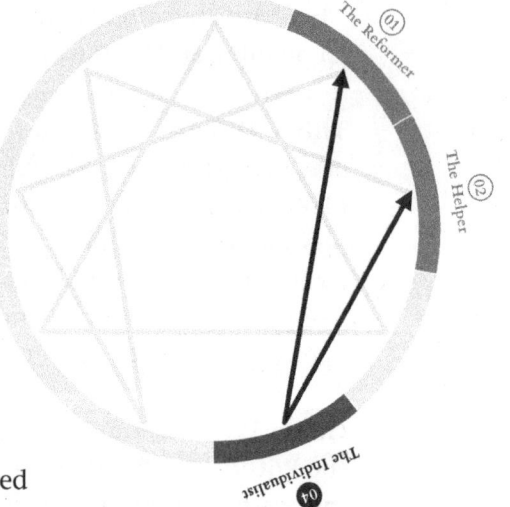

Moving to One

When Fours are well-balanced and feel good about themselves, they access some of the higher qualities that Ones are blessed with. For example:

I Am Blessed. At Point One, you are encouraged to meditate on your Original Goodness. The holy affirmation at Point One is: *I am a beloved child of God.* Aligning with our Original Goodness helps you to feel *I am blessed*. "Child of God, you were created to create the good, the beautiful and the holy. Do not forget this," teaches *A Course in Miracles*.

Self-Acceptance. The virtue at Point One is Serenity, which is a mind without judgment. "Coming home to ourselves is not a game of perfect," says Hollie Holden. "Greeting our fears with love, forgiving our mistakes, blessing our wounds, accepting God's love, is the way home to ourselves."

The Greater Good. The energy of Point One helps Fours to be less self-absorbed and more concerned with channeling their creativity for the greater good of all. Fours who embrace the energy of Point One inside themselves find it helps them to stand upright, live their values, embody compassion and justice, and play their part in making the world a beautiful place to live in.

When Fours are under stress, they may display unhealthy qualities common to Ones. Knowing about these unhealthy qualities can be a helpful warning sign for Fours. For example:

Judging Yourself. The more you judge yourself, the louder your basic fear yells in your head that you are imperfect, fatally flawed, not significant, and not beautiful in your own way. *Aiming for authenticity rather than perfection is more wholesome and healthier for both Fours and Ones.*

On a High Horse. When you struggle to love and accept yourself, you project your self-hate onto others. You get on your high horse and see yourself as superior to others. You act like a prima donna and dismiss others as ordinary. You are self-righteous and snobby. You reject others because you fantasize that they are rejecting you.

Poor Self Image. "When a Four cannot feel their Original Goodness, they develop a poor self-image and will attack themselves for feeling not good enough, flawed, ugly, unintelligent, repulsive, and rotten to the core," observed Claudio Naranjo. In desperation, Fours try to craft a more perfect self-image because they cannot see that the soul is already whole and perfect.

Moving to Two

When Fours are well-balanced and feel good about themselves, they access some of the higher qualities that Twos are blessed with. For example:

Warm-Hearted. At Point Two, Fours balance their melancholy "moon energy" with "sun energy" that is bright and shiny. Like Twos, Fours become more warm-hearted, generous, affectionate, and expressive of their love.

Soul Friend. Something that healthy Fours and Twos have in common is they both know how to be a soul friend to others. When Fours absorb the gifts of Point Two, they show up even more as a true friend, and we feel genuinely seen, cared for, and loved in their presence.

Being of Service. *The more I serve, the less depressed I feel!*—sign outside a coffee shop. Being of service is a saving grace for Fours. When Fours embrace the service ethos of Twos, it helps them to be less self-absorbed and less alienated. Fours prosper when they use their creativity to serve and love the world.

When Fours are under stress, they may suffer from some of the unhealthy qualities of Twos. Knowing about these unhealthy qualities can be a helpful warning sign for Fours. For example:

You Need Therapy! Like Twos, Fours can get stuck in the family role they played as a child. For Twos, it may be "the helper," and for Fours, "the healer." When Fours are too role-bound, they can be judgmental and bossy, demanding that every family member should get more healing, more therapy, more counseling, etc.

Crying for Help. Both Twos and Fours are known for crying easily and often being tearful. Twos are typically ashamed of their tears and try to hide them. Fours are not ashamed of tears, but when unhealthy, they will use their tears to get attention, manipulate others, and get their own way.

Type Four

Rescue Me! Like Twos, Fours are afraid of being rejected and abandoned. Both Types also secretly fantasize that one day someone will save them. Fours typically have a deep longing to be rescued. When Fours fantasize too much, they withdraw into themselves and miss out on real-life invitations for real connection, friendship, and romance.

Holy Origin

> *Click your heels together three times and say*
> *"There's no place like home," and you'll be there.*
>
> – Glinda, the Good Witch, *The Wizard of Oz*

The nine Points on the Enneagram each offer a Holy Idea, a higher wisdom, for all nine Ennea-Types to contemplate and put into practice. The Holy Idea at Point Four is Holy Origin, which is essentially an invitation to come home to your True Self.

Holy Origin is an awareness that there is one God, to which we all belong. We all come from the same Source, even though our outer appearances differ. Our being, which is the essence of who we are, connects us to a Holy Origin that we share with every other living being, including trees, angels, planets, whales, and flowers. Virginia Woolf, in *Moments of Being*, observed, "that behind the cotton wool [of daily life] is hidden a pattern; that we—I mean all human beings—are connected with this; that the whole world is a work of art; and that we are parts of the work of art."

We share the same Holy Origin, and we are made of the same cosmic substance. No two thumbprints or snowflakes are the same, but they are made by the same artist that uses the same basic materials. When we accept our Oneness, we can rejoice in our uniqueness without fear of being separated, cast out, or exiled from the Oneness. We can be the same and unique without fear of contradiction. "We are already one. But we imagine that we are not. And what we have to recover is our original unity. What we have to be is what we are," wrote Thomas Merton in *The Hidden Ground of Love*.

> *Why do you weep?*
> *The Source is within you,*
> *and this whole world*
> *is springing up from it.*
>
> — Rumi

> *The Kingdom of Heaven is inside of you, and it is outside of you.*
>
> — Jesus, Gospel of Thomas

Holy Origin teaches we are always connected to Divine Source, no matter where we are or how we feel about ourselves. You don't need to get to the end of the rainbow to come home to yourself or to find God. When you live in the present moment—this beautiful, ordinary moment—you find a "welcome home" sign hanging in front of you. *The Kingdom of Heaven is everywhere you are.* "You are at home in God, dreaming of exile but perfectly capable of awakening to reality," teaches *A Course in Miracles*. And your Original Self, which is already whole, beautiful, and complete, is waiting inside you to welcome you home.

Type Five
THE INVESTIGATOR

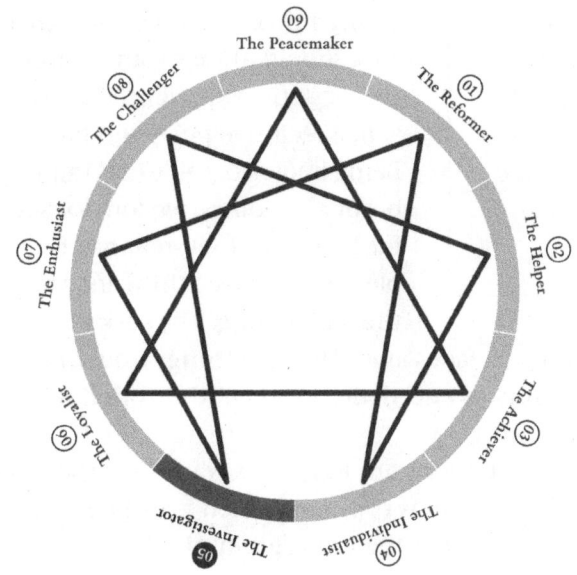

*Four thousand volumes of metaphysics will
not teach us what the soul is.*

—VOLTAIRE

The Ennea-Type Five is commonly called Investigator or Observer. Other names for Fives include Thinker, Luminous Soul, Gnostic, Specialist, and Knowledge-Seeker.

Fives are the *Highly Perceptive, Cerebral Type*. They are known for being naturally curious and inquisitive, observant and insightful, intellectual and imaginative, geeky and nerdy, aloof and sensitive, objective and skeptical. Fives pay close attention to their environment and will look deep inside a flower if it interests them to do so. They are the Type most likely to count the number of drupelets in a raspberry. They look up the etymology of words. They know how a microchip works. Fives are among the first in line to examine images of newborn stars and fossil galaxies from the James Webb Space Telescope. They've probably watched their favorite film over a hundred times, including the Director's Cut. And they've got a theory about how the world will end.

Fives are knowledge-seekers. At their best, Fives are very open-minded and attentive. Learning to see life as it really is, is what most fascinates Fives. They are blessed with the gift of sight. They have a seeing mind. They are life's great noticers. "The soul should always stand ajar, ready to welcome the ecstatic experience," wrote Emily Dickinson, a reclusive poet who had a lot of Five traits. Being knowledgeable is as important to Fives as is beauty for Fours, freedom for Sevens, inner peace for Nines, and self-reliance for Eights, for example. Fives are deep thinkers. They have a big appetite for learning. They ask a lot of questions. They don't accept things on face value. They see things from different angles. They acquire vast amounts of knowledge. And yet they often feel they don't know enough about anything.

> *Nobody sees a flower really; it is so small. We haven't time, and to see takes time, like to have a friend takes time.*
>
> — Georgia O'Keeffe

Before taking an Enneagram test, Fives want to gather more information about what the Enneagram is or is not. When a Five tells you they have done "a little bit of research" into the Enneagram, the chances are they've amassed 10 times more information than any of the other Ennea-Types. Fives will subject the Enneagram to their heavy scrutiny. They will be curious and cautious about what they're getting themselves into. They will acquire a small library of Enneagram books and spend hours on the Google Scholar search engine investigating the origins of the Enneagram, researching its precepts, and examining its efficacy to make certain the Enneagram is not a hocus-pocus new fad or a load of old nonsense.

> *When I get a little money, I buy books; if any is left, I buy food and clothes.*
>
> — Desiderius Erasmus

Many of the most insightful Enneagram authors and teachers are Fives, or they have a Five wing. Russ Hudson, a Five, has co-authored several excellent books with Don Riso (a 4w5), including *The Wisdom of the Enneagram*. Russ is a fountain of knowledge, and I always learn something fascinating and new on his Enneagram programs. Russ and I have also taught many Enneagram programs together. One time, when we were teaching a five-day program on Living with the Enneagram in London, Russ delivered a two-hour lecture, without notes, on the ancient history and esoteric knowledge of the Enneagram. It was a transmission of the highest order, and I have watched the recording many times. At one point, Russ told us,

> The Enneagram is not a flat circle; it is a sphere. When you step inside the Enneagram, you find yourself standing inside the Mind of the Universe. Working with the Enneagram will clean your lens of perception and open your mind to the wonders of the universe. It will give you greater knowledge of your being and help you to access the infinite intelligence of creation.

INTRODUCING TYPE FIVE

Are you a Type Five on the Enneagram? Maybe you have a family member, a friend, or a work colleague who is a Five.

My great uncle, Derek Hill, had a lot of Five energy. As a child, I found him to be the most interesting and unusual member of our family. He was artistic and erudite. He was sensitive and kind. He was childlike and a wise old soul. In my adulthood, we became very good friends, and he often stayed with me in my home in Oxford. Uncle Derek encouraged me to follow my love of learning, to expand my horizons, and to be a writer.

Derek Hill was a portrait and landscape painter. "I am a seer by nature, and I paint what I see," he told me. He painted portraits of many interesting people, including Noël Coward, the actor; Isaiah Berlin, the philosopher; Arthur Rubinstein, the composer; and Bernard Berenson, the art historian who specialized in the Renaissance. Derek had a knack for painting the essence—the spark of soul—of his subjects. His paintings of Irish and Tuscan landscapes capture the unique light in both places and are now collector's items. His favorite place to paint was on Tory Island, the most remote inhabited island of Ireland, about 10 miles out in the Atlantic Sea. "Here, on Tory Island, the light changes by the minute," he told me with a look of glee in his eye as we stepped off the boat and onto the harbor.

Uncle Derek had many interests. "I am an avid learner and intend to keep on learning until the end of my days here on Earth," he told me. On the Enneagram symbol, there is an inner line from Point Five to Point Seven, which, as we will see later in this chapter, stimulates curiosity, enthusiasm, and awe. Derek had a lot of Five and Seven energy. He studied theater design in Munich. He was an enthusiastic art collector. He wrote books about Islamic architecture and wallpaper. He was a gifted photographer. He was director of fine arts at the British School at Rome for five years in the 1950s. He was also an expert in botany and dendrology. Derek was full of learning, and I found his love of learning to be infectious and inspiring.

Uncle Derek was a generous and kind person. Fives like to share their love of learning, and he was a teacher and mentor to many people, including HRH the Prince of Wales (now HM King Charles III), with whom he traveled annually to Mount Athos, on the northeast peninsula of Greece, to study painting and philosophy. He set up the "Tory School" of artists on Tory Island that included James Dixon and Anton Meenan. He gave his home, Glebe House, situated in rural Donegal, and his collection of art at Glebe Gallery, to the Irish nation in 1982, 18 years before he died. His house is a collector's paradise. I stayed there several times as a child. I particularly love the William Morris wallpaper and fabrics.

Uncle Derek was very Five-like in that he was considered a genius, and yet he was incapable of (or simply not interested in) doing everyday tasks such as ironing a shirt, boiling an egg, writing a check, or booking a train ticket. His housekeeper, Gracie, did it all for him. Also, Derek was a loner. He never married and confessed that intimate relationships were too taxing and overbearing for him. He had a wide circle of interesting friends, including actress Greta Garbo and poet Seamus Heaney, but most of all he liked to be alone. In his biography, *Derek Hill: An Appreciation*, by Grey Gowrie, he told Gowrie, "I like people. I need to be stimulated by people. But I cannot have a day without the need to spend several hours entirely alone. Every day, and it goes through all my life too."

Healthy Qualities of Fives

When Fives are healthy and well-balanced, they display essential qualities that we all love and appreciate. Here are a few things healthy Fives have told me about themselves:

- "As a child, I asked a lot of questions about life."
- "My parents called me 'The Little Professor.'"
- "I like to count the number of spots on a ladybug."
- "I've always been interested in how things work."
- "I like to learn something new every day."

- "Solitude helps me to know myself better."
- "I enjoy dark humor, surrealism, and the absurd."
- "I relish deep and meaningful conversations."
- "I love to share and trade knowledge with others."
- "I think there's more to life than meets the eye."

Unhealthy Qualities of Fives

When Fives are out of balance, they become closed-minded, socially isolated, and locked inside their head. Here are a few things Fives have told me about themselves:

- "I had my first existential crisis at five years old."
- "I tend to overthink and overanalyze situations."
- "I withdraw from others when I get anxious."
- "My mind often takes me down the rabbit hole."
- "I often wonder if this is the day I will die."
- "My friends tell me to cut down on screen time."
- "People tell me I need to get out more."
- "Small talk isn't my cup of tea."
- "I find it hard to break out of my privacy."
- "It can get dark and lonely inside my mind."

RECOGNIZING TYPE FIVES

In philosophy, the so-called Enlightenment Period from 1685–1815—also known as the Age of Reason—still influences much of Western thought today. Many of Europe's Enlightenment thinkers had strong Five energy. Think of René Descartes's rationalist philosophy and his maxim "I think, therefore I am," the philosophical skepticism of David Hume, and Immanuel Kant's *Critique of Pure Reason*. The emphasis was on empiricism, "the evidence of the senses," and on strong reasoning. It was a time full of scientific discovery, new advances in human understanding, and the separation of church and state.

> *What is your aim in philosophy?*
> *To show the fly the way*
> *out of the fly-bottle.*
>
> — Ludwig Wittgenstein

Western philosophy is full of classic literature that most of us find impenetrable and difficult to understand. Interestingly, a challenge that many Fives have is learning how to translate their ideas into everyday life. Philosophers like Søren Kierkegaard, Arthur Schopenhauer, Ludwig Wittgenstein, and more recently Martin Heidegger, have delivered brilliant works that are simply too heady for most of us. We persist with this literature, however, because its purpose is to make us think about life, to wonder at existence, and to grapple with what Heidegger called the fundamental question of metaphysics, which is:

Why is there anything at all?
Or why is there something rather than nothing?

In Eastern philosophy, Siddhartha Gautama, who became known as the Buddha, had a lot of Five and Six energy. The Buddha has been described as a saint, a philosopher, and as the first cognitive psychologist, but he described himself as "someone who is awake." The name *Buddha* describes an "enlightened mind" that belongs to a person who has awakened from the sleep of ignorance and achieved liberation from suffering. The Buddha Mind is everyone's Original Mind, a mind that is bright and clear. Zen Buddhism, a school of Buddhism that originated in China, teaches that anyone can access their Inner Buddha and attain enlightenment. The term *Zen Mind* describes a state of pure awareness, unclouded by fear and judgment, that helps us to live in the present and see things as they really are.

> *When we first seek the truth, we think we are far from it. When we discover that the truth is already in us, we are all at once our original self.*
>
> — Dōgen (1200-1253), Buddhist philosopher and poet

On that note, I want to spotlight two more schools of thought that many Fives have a special interest in metaphysics and mysticism. Both schools encourage us to go beyond our physical senses, to empty the mind of all thinking, and to tap into the intelligence of the universe. Greek thinkers like Plato, Aristotle, and Pythagoras recognized two types of thinking: *dianoia* and *noesis*. Dianoia is discursive reasoning and points to intellectual knowledge that is collected from observation through the physical senses, while noesis is more immediate and is gained from flashes of illumination and direct knowing. Like noesis, the words *gnosis* and *Gnosticism* cite a spiritual knowledge that arises spontaneously when you contact the divine spark in your being.

Pythagoras was both a mathematician and a seer. His teachings sit well at Point Five. He saw that we live in an intelligent universe. "Astonishing! Everything is intelligent!" he declared. He observed creation as a wondrous display of geometry and mathematics. "All is number!" he said. After Pythagoras, there is a continuous line of mystics whose influence has stretched across the centuries to the present day. These seers have opened our eyes to a new way of seeing reality, and they include the German philosopher and mystic Meister Eckhart (1260-1328); Johann Wolfgang von Goethe (1749-1832), a German scientist and mystic hailed for his theory of observation; and Rudolf Steiner (1861-1925), a student of Goethe, who has inspired Waldorf education, biodynamic agriculture, and anthroposophical medicine.

> *The eye with which I see God is the same eye with which God sees me.*
> — Meister Eckhart

In psychology, Sigmund Freud, the neurologist, had a lot of Five energy. His pioneering work on personality theory, psychoanalysis, and ego defense mechanisms, for example, is taught in schools, universities, and institutes worldwide. He inspired many Neo-Freudians such as, Alfred Adler, Otto Rank, Anna Freud (his daughter), Erik Erikson, Karen Horney, and Carl Jung—all of whom I reference and quote in my Enneagram trainings. Carl Jung, whom I focused on at Point Four, is also a firm favorite among Fives. His work is considered by many to be more spiritual and complete than Freud's. His map of the psyche, and his psychology of the soul, is incorporated in the work of many practitioners of depth psychology.

> *Your vision will become clear only when you can look into your own heart. Who looks outside, dreams; who looks inside, awakes.*
> — Carl Jung

Fives are thought leaders. In science, they operate at the cutting edge of physics, chemistry, and biology. Think of quantum physicists such as Albert Einstein (who is a poster child for Fives), Erwin Schrödinger, Werner Heisenberg, J. Robert Oppenheimer, and Sir James Jeans, who revealed a universe that is more "mind-like" than "matter-like." Also, Stephen Hawking, who wrote *The Theory of Everything*, and said, "My goal is simple. It is a complete understanding of the universe, why it is as it is and why it exists at all." In technology, think of Bill Gates, Mark Zuckerberg, Elon Musk, and Sergey Brin, one of the

> *Not only is the universe stranger than we think; it is stranger than we can think.*
>
> — Werner Heisenberg

brains behind Google, who famously said, "We want Google to be the third half of your brain." Also, Dorothy Vaughan, mathematician and first African American NASA manager, known as a "human computer," whose story is featured in the book and movie *Hidden Figures*.

In the arts, Fives challenge us to look at life through their quirky and eye-opening lens of perception. Again, their aim is to provoke thinking. Think of David Lynch, the enigmatic filmmaker and creator of *Dune* and *Twin Peaks*. "New mysteries. New day. Fresh doughnuts," said Lynch. Think of the auteur, Werner Herzog, who has written, directed, and produced over 60 spellbinding films, such as *Fitzcarraldo*, and self-narrated documentaries such as *Antarctica: Encounters at the End of the World*. And Christopher Nolan, who explores reality and illusion in his films *The Batman Trilogy, Memento, Inception, Interstellar,* and humanity's dogged, self-destructive tendencies in his biopic *Oppenheimer*.

Elsewhere in the arts, Fives are drawn to the dark humor of the Theatre of the Absurd and to playwrights like Samuel Beckett, who wrote *Waiting for Godot*, Harold Pinter, who wrote *The Caretaker*, and Eugene Ionesco, who wrote *Exit the King*. In music, think of Peter Gabriel from Genesis and his song "Here comes the Flood," Roger Waters from Pink Floyd, who co-wrote "Shine On You Crazy Diamond," and the Canadian classical pianist Glenn Gould. In poetry, read the brilliant nature mystic Mary Oliver, "When Death Comes." In surrealism, think of the Monty Python animator Terry Gilliam and his film *Brazil*, and artist Salvador Dalí, with his melting clocks and works like *Metamorphosis of Narcissus* and *The Sacrament of the Last Supper*. "I'm not strange. I'm just not normal," Dalí insisted.

> *Every man should pull a boat over a mountain once in his life.*
>
> — Werner Herzog

Finally, in Shakespeare, think of Prospero, the Duke of Milan, from *The Tempest*, who is very Five-like. Prospero buried his head in books, which "I prize above my dukedom," he said. Alas for Prospero, he was so distracted with seeking knowledge from books that he failed to notice his brother Antonio's plot to overthrow him. Exiled on a small island, Prospero plots his revenge with his "rough magic" and sorcery learned from books. But with the aid of the spirit Ariel, he experiences

> *When it's over, I want to say all my life I was a bride married to amazement.*
>
> — Mary Oliver, "When Death Comes"

a conversion in his heart, a change at the core of his being. Prospero resolves to put away his books, to swap sorcery for forgiveness, and to rejoin society as a changed person. He tells us:

> I'll break my staff,
> Bury it certain fathoms in the earth,
> And deeper than did ever plummet sound
> I'll drown my book.

A UNIVERSAL MIND

> *The total number of minds in the universe is one.*
> *In fact, consciousness is a singularity phasing*
> *within all beings.*
>
> — Erwin Schrödinger

Type Fives are on a quest for knowledge and wisdom. The Enneagram teaches that every person is born whole and complete, and that we each have access to the infinite intelligence of creation. We are a microcosm of the universe. Knowledge of your True Self helps you to better understand the world you live in. You don't need a PhD to be wise; you simply need to have an open mind, a loving heart, and a willingness to see. "There is an inmost center in us all where truth abides in fulness," wrote Robert Browning in his five-part epic poem *Paracelsus*. Above all, Fives want to stay in contact with this "inmost center" of truth, to know how to think and how to live.

> *Knowledge is the food of the soul.*
>
> — Plato

A lot of my closest friends, teachers, and mentors have an Ennea-Type Five personality. They are very interesting to be around, not least because they take a deep interest in life. My first spiritual mentor was Avanti Kumar, a Five, whom I met when I was 18 years old. We both studied psychology, philosophy, and linguistics at Birmingham City University in England. Avanti was six years older than me. He was a playwright, a literary editor, a theosophist, a yogi, a cricket lover, and he meditated for up to six hours a day. His home was his cave, and he slept in a bedroom lined with bookshelves, a collection of classical music vinyl LPs, a desk to write at, and a small one-door wardrobe for a handful of clothes.

Avanti kindly loaned me books from his personal library on the strict condition that I'd return them by a specific date. His first recommendation was the Bhagavad Gita, and then the Upanishads, the Dhammapada, and the Tao Te Ching. Other books included Albert Einstein's *The World as I See It*, Franz Kafka's *The Metamorphosis*, and Aldous Huxley's *The Doors of Perception*. More than that, Avanti taught me how to meditate. He gave me my first spiritual practice, which was to gaze at a candle flame. "This will help you to concentrate your mind, to focus your attention, and learn to see," Avanti told me.

Avanti was the first person to talk to me about the soul. He gave me a spare copy of Carl Jung's *Modern Man in Search of a Soul*—this one to keep. "This book will introduce you to your Atman," he told me. The word *Atman* means "soul" or "mind" in Sanskrit, and is sometimes translated as "Self-light," or "Light of the Self." "When looking at the candle flame, see if you can connect to a light within you, the Self-light, that is the essence of who you are," instructed Avanti. The Christian mystic Thomas Merton described the soul as a "point of light." Meister Eckhart spoke of "a spark of the soul." For Fives, this inner light is not just a metaphor. The universe is a play of light, and we are made of light.

> *There is a light within you, it is the lamp of the being of God.*
>
> — John of the Cross

Fives are known for having a luminous mind, a spacious heart, and a clear lens of perception. Here are some of the healthy qualities of mature, well-rounded Fives.

A Bright Mind. "Meditation is light sitting in light," said Sister Elaine McGuiness, a Catholic nun and Zen master, who taught me Zen meditation in my 30s, when living in Oxford. Sister Elaine had a lot of Five energy. She had a bright mind, a razor-sharp intellect, and the kindest eyes. She explained that meditation is not about acquiring knowledge; it is about making yourself available to wisdom. "We learn to meditate so that we can experience the Buddha and the Christ in all of us," she told me.

Basic Openness. Fives can be the most open-minded or the most closed-minded people you meet. Healthy Fives display what psychologists call a "basic openness" that makes them intellectually curious, attentive to feelings, sensitive to beauty, highly imaginative, and inventive. They approach life with a "beginner's mind," a term used in Japanese Zen. "When I think about a problem, I imagine that the answer is already here. I open my mind, and what I need to know appears," says Helen, a Five, who is a kindergarten teacher.

Natural Observer. Learning to see life as it really is, is what most fascinates Fives. "Life is a tremendous gift, but most of us are missing it because we are watching a mental movie of our lives in our head instead of seeing reality," says Russ Hudson, my friend and Enneagram mentor. Fives have a "seeing mind" that enables them to gather eurekas and epiphanies, to make new discoveries, to gain greater understanding, and to cultivate a deep appreciation for life.

Knowledge-Seeker. Fives have a love of knowledge and are life-long learners. They have a talent for learning. They love to understand how things work. They use their time and energy to do research, to conduct experiments, to test hypotheses, to play with magnets, to dissect an insect, to build a telescope, and to gather information. They experience what Richard Feynman, who won a Nobel Prize in Physics, called "the pleasure of finding things out."

Independent Thinker. Fives like to make up their own minds about things. They trust in the power of their own mind to work things out. They are mistrustful of secondhand knowledge. Erwin Schrödinger, who pioneered quantum mechanics, put it this way: "The task is, not so much to see what no one has yet seen, but to think what nobody has yet thought, about that which everybody sees."

Great Conversationalists. Danah Zohar, an MIT physicist and philosopher, was my neighbor when I lived in Oxford. She has a Five-like mind and has authored many books, including her groundbreaking work *Spiritual Intelligence*. We enjoyed many great conversations long after midnight as we drank a red Bordeaux and ate cheese. Her cat, called Schrödinger, was curled on my lap as we talked about metaphysics, the Mind of God, and how humans must learn to think properly before we destroy ourselves.

Mindful Compassion. Fives understand that much of our suffering comes from ignorance and not knowing who we are. My mentor, Avanti, took me under his wing and taught me how to think. He was compassionate and patient with me as I took my baby steps into metaphysics and higher learning. His great joy was to open my eyes to life. One of our early adventures was a visit to a William Blake exhibition. "Look at this!" said Avanti as he hovered excitedly over an original manuscript of Blake's famous poem "Auguries of Innocence." The one that begins,

> To see a World in a Grain of Sand
> And a Heaven in a Wild Flower,
> Hold Infinity in the palm of your hand
> And Eternity in an hour.

A SEPARATE MIND

You are an aperture through which the universe is looking at and exploring itself.

– Alan Watts, philosopher

The Enneagram, rooted in ancient Greek thought, recognizes a basic Oneness behind every shape and form in the Universe. The circle of the Enneagram symbolizes the One Mind of Creation. Every being, including a fish, a star, a stone, and a human, is an expression of One Infinite Intelligence. Pythagoras observed: "We come from God. As the tree from the root and the stream from the spring; that's why we should always be in contact with Him, as the trunk from the root. Because the stream dries up when it is separated from the spring and the tree dies when is uprooted."

> *Quantum physics thus reveals a basic oneness of the universe.*
>
> — Fritjof Capra, *The Tao of Physics*

Albert Einstein, a theoretical physicist, was in accord with this ancient thinking. In his work on quantum theory, he saw the universe as a "unified whole" that operates with a "lawful harmony." He recognized what he called an "intelligence manifested in nature" and "a marvelous structure behind reality." Like Pythagoras, he also recognized that humanity suffers because of our sense of separateness from the basic oneness of the universe. This separateness may be convincing to our physical senses, but it is "an optical delusion," as Einstein put it. Einstein wrote in one of his letters:

> A human being is a part of the whole, called by us "Universe," a part limited in time and space. He experiences himself, his thoughts and feelings as something separate from the rest—a kind of optical delusion of his consciousness. The striving to free oneself from this delusion is the one issue of true religion. Not to nourish it but to try to overcome it is the way to reach the attainable measure of peace of mind.

The inner work of every Ennea-Type, including Fives, is to straighten out this "optical delusion" and free us from this ignorance and suffering. As Einstein said, "Our task must be to free ourselves by widening our circle of compassion to embrace all living creatures and the whole of nature and its beauty."

Basic Fear: Not Knowing Enough

When Fives experience the sense of separation, a basic fear arises in the mind of the ego. The basic fear for Fives is the fear of not knowing enough, which brings on feelings of insufficiency, being incapable, and general incompetence.

Russ Hudson, a Five, and Don Riso, a Four, were the first Enneagram teachers to map the basic fears to each of the nine Ennea-Types. In their book *Wisdom of the Enneagram,* they explain how the fear of not knowing enough can cause Fives to feel anxious, insecure, and to distance themselves socially from others. They write,

> Behind Fives' relentless pursuit of knowledge are deep insecurities about their ability to function successfully in the world. *Fives feel that they do not have an ability to do things as well as others.* But rather than engage directly with activities that might bolster their confidence, Fives "take a step back" into their minds, where they feel more capable. Their belief is that from the safety of their minds, they will eventually figure out how to do things—and one day rejoin the world.

The fear of "not knowing enough" can cause extreme anxiety and overwhelm for Fives on any topic. It may be about cosmic matters such as why we are alive, how to know God, reversing global warming, and the sixth mass extinction. It may also be about everyday matters like how to start a conversation, making new friends, falling in love, opening a bank account, or how to boil an egg. Fives must befriend their fear of not knowing enough if they are to come out of their shell and join in with life. They need to remember we are all participating in a great big mystery and that none of us have all the answers. If we keep an open mind, we will learn and grow, and, hopefully, have some fun along the way.

> *Lack of knowledge is the source of all pains and sorrows.*
> — B. K. S. Iyengar, *Light on Yoga*

Here's some things Fives have said to me in relation to living with their basic fear of not knowing enough:

- "I get anxious when I haven't enough information."
- "I never feel I am ready enough to begin things."
- "I think that life is a puzzle with missing pieces."
- "I am often overcome with a cloud of unknowing."
- "I tend to overanalyze situations."
- "I wish there were a manual for how to live."
- "I get migraines from too much thinking."
- "I wish I could switch off my mind more often."
- "I don't ever feel like I have enough information."
- "I wish someone would tell me why we are alive."

Childhood Story: The Loner

Fives enter the world full of wonder and awe. "It's truly astonishing to be alive if you think about it. Even after sixty years of being on this planet, I still wake up each morning feeling like a newborn baby," said Russ Hudson.

Young Fives are curious and inquisitive. *Why am I here? What is life for? What happens when we die? Why does God not stop the war?* Young Fives have a lot of questions about life and death. A Five's constant questioning is a quest for knowledge and safety. But no one has a complete instruction manual for living. In fact, Fives soon realize

> *The beginning of awe is wonder, and the beginning of wisdom is awe.*
> — Abraham Heschel, *Between God and Man*

that most adults and teachers don't know much at all. And so the young Five's astonishment at life is soon overshadowed by a cloud of unknowing, a sense of aloneness, a feeling of anxiety, and a desperate need to learn and acquire more information.

Young Fives are *philomaths*, lovers of learning and study. They are Little Einsteins, who have a bright mind, natural inquisitiveness, and great powers of concentration. Their bedroom is a library. Their computer is always on. They can gaze at a night sky for hours on end. They are typically quiet, private, introverted, self-sufficient, and happy to be left alone to pursue their interests. This lack of contact with the outside world enables Fives to know their own mind, but it may also cause feelings of isolation and alienation. Russ Hudson and Don Riso expounded on the withdrawn nature of Fives in *Wisdom of the Enneagram*. They wrote:

> *What a distressing contrast there is between the radiant intelligence of a child and the feeble mentality of the average adult.*
>
> — Sigmund Freud, *The Future of an Illusion*

> Young Fives typically spend long periods on their own; they are quiet children who shy away from playing with others, instead occupying their minds and imaginations with books, practicing a musical instrument or playing with a computer, collecting insects or plants, or playing with board games or chemistry sets. It is common to find young Fives who are exceptionally advanced in some areas (such as spelling or mathematics) but who are unwilling to even try other basic activities (such as riding a bike or going fishing). Others in the family, especially anxious parents who want their Five child to be more "normal," will typically try to pressure them into joining in social activities. These efforts usually meet with intense resistance.

Young Fives are known for their active imagination. Christopher Robin, of the Winnie-the-Pooh books by A. A. Milne, has a lot of Five energy. We meet Christopher Robin in his pre-school years, before he is sent away to boarding school and becomes more bookish. He has his own imaginary world, Hundred Acre Wood, and a host of imaginary friends. He is sensitive, kind, mature, and often the voice of reason. Interestingly, his friends map nicely onto the Enneagram. For example, Tigger, an exuberant and bouncy Seven; Eeyore, a melancholy Four; Pooh Bear, a laid-back and addicted-to-honey Nine; Owl, a know-it-all Five; Rabbit, a meticulous One, with his carefully tended garden; Piglet, an anxious and courageous Six; and Kanga, a caring and nurturing Two.

At school, Fives often struggle to find their place. They don't make friends easily, the curriculum isn't interesting, and the teachers are boring. "It is a miracle that curiosity survives formal education," said Einstein. School protest songs, such as Pink Floyd's "Another Brick in the Wall," and Supertramp's "The Logical Song" and "School" are very Five-ish. Roger Hodgson, of Supertramp, explained the thinking behind these two songs in a fascinating interview for *Louder*, published in 2018. Here is an excerpt:

> "The Logical Song" was born from my questions about what really matters in life. It was a very personal lyric for me. Throughout childhood we are taught all these ways to be, and yet we are rarely told anything about our true self. We are taught how to function outwardly but not guided to who we are inwardly. We go from the innocence and wonder of childhood to the confusion of adolescence that often ends in the cynicism and disillusionment of adulthood.

Young Fives, like Fours, feel like loners and misfits. They dodge the in-crowd. They avoid the spotlight. They are too cool for school. They can be melancholy and morbid. They have a dark sense of humor. They are young absurdists. Most Fives can relate to Wednesday Addams, the character from the Addams Family stories played by Christina Ricci and other actors. Wednesday has a Gothic appearance, is aloof and macabre, and psychologists would say she has an antisocial personality disorder (ASPD). She has a pet squid named Socrates. She hates Disney movies. She is fascinated by death. She subjects her young brother, Pugsley, to games like "Is there a God?"

> Wednesday: [hooking up an electric chair] Pugsley, sit in the chair.
>
> Pugsley: Why?
>
> Wednesday: Because we're going to play a game.
>
> Pugsley: What game?
>
> Wednesday: [strapping him in] It's called, "Is There a God?"

The "Need to Know" Driver: Fives have a strong "need to know" driver installed in their ego operating system. Fives are nerdy and geeky, in a good way. They enjoy hobbies and interests that expand their knowledge, e.g., astronomy, birdwatching, computer science, and trading in bitcoin. They absorb information like a sponge. They have strong powers of concentration. They can be encyclopedic with their knowledge. They enjoy sports that require mastery, e.g., golf and chess. And computer games with many skill trees or gates of progression.

"Knowledge is a social currency for me," said Tim, a professor of medicine, who took my Love and the Enneagram program. Tim told me, "Being a specialist in my field gives me the confidence to be part of a community, which in my case, is a hospital." Fives are happy to bring their knowledge to the table. They enjoy sharing their learning with others. They often make great mentors and teachers. When I asked Tim why he became a doctor, he told me, "When I was eleven years old, I fell in love with a girl, and I was afraid she wouldn't love me unless I was good at something. I scratched my head and wondered what to do, and I ended up choosing medicine."

Let's look at some examples of how the "Need to Know" driver operates for Fives in the three biological instincts: (1) Self-Preservation Instinct (SP), which is mostly about lifestyle, material matters, and self-care: (2) Social Instinct (SO), which is mostly about relating to family, society, and the world; and (3) (SX) Sexual Instinct (also called One-to-One Instinct), which is mostly about attraction, relating style, and romance.

Self-Preservation Instinct (SP) *Healthy:* You typically live a minimalist lifestyle, with a light footprint, and have few needs. You've trained yourself to be self-reliant and not depend on people for much. My great uncle Derek Hill, an artist, often said, "All I need is my paints." *Not-so-healthy:* You carefully regulate your contact with others. Booking a restaurant table for one is as much fun as dining out with someone. You can easily strike up a conversation with a stranger and *not* swap addresses. You don't often initiate contact with friends. Some of your best friends are books. *Unhealthy:* You neglect yourself physically, forgo eating when studying, and rarely get enough sleep. You may have a million dollars in the bank, but your only sweater has moth holes in it. You forget birthdays, even your own, because you're so engrossed in your work or studies. You ignore the "final reminder" to pay your house insurance. There's a leak in the roof that needs urgent attention, and you hope it will somehow fix itself.

Social Instinct (SO) *Healthy:* You find humans interesting and are happy to have a reasonable amount of contact with them. You connect with people through shared interests. "I became a sommelier so that I could talk to people about something," says Mike, a Five, who is a Master of Wine. You are more of an open book than SP and SX Fives. You are also motivated to serve and help others. *Not-so-healthy:* At work, you connect with others by adopting the social role of expert, specialist, or mentor, but in everyday life you are more solitary, shy, and socially awkward. You collect friends who are interesting to you, but you don't share much of your personal self with them. *Unhealthy:* You have a lot of virtual friendships. You claim to be great friends with people you've met only once or twice. You're afraid of rejection, and so you minimize your contact with friends and work colleagues. You are quick to reject people who don't appreciate your genius or fail to recognize how intelligent you are.

Sexual Instinct (SX) *Healthy:* You are typically more assertive, intense, romantic, and idealistic than other Fives. At work, you seek out "great minds" who stimulate and inspire you. In social situations, you are drawn to the most interesting person in the room. In romance, you want a companion who is stimulating and safe, a person to confide in, and someone to share your deepest and darkest secrets with. *Not-so-healthy:* "The idea of romance is more appealing than the earthy reality of it all," says Melanie, a Five, who is a forensic investigator. A long-distance relationship with regular rendezvouses or weekends together suits you because it doesn't demand too much of you. You fear that your intensity and your strangeness will be off-putting to others. *Unhealthy:* SX Fives must make sure they channel their libido and vital energy into creative and inspiring projects, otherwise it can turn dark and destructive. SX Fives who are too withdrawn are known for fantasizing about intimacy, and for being attracted to eroticism, to fetish encounters, and for craving contact that is taboo and off-limits.

Passion: Avarice

All nine Types on the Enneagram experience a *passion*, or cause of suffering in the heart, that emerges from a sense of separation and from the basic fear.

The passion for Fives is "avarice," another one of the seven cardinal sins. Avarice comes from the Latin *avarus*, meaning "greedy" and "craving." Paul the Apostle said avarice is the "root of all evil." Other philosophers have said avarice is "everyone's sin."

Evagrius Ponticus (345–399 AD), who lived with the Desert Fathers and Mothers in Egypt, listed avarice in his "eight deadly thoughts," which was a precursor to the cardinal sins. Evagrius is widely thought to be a Five. His classic work *Gnostikos* (meaning "The Knower" or "The Gnostic") is a must-read for Enneagram geeks and scholars. In it, he described in a single paragraph how multilayered avarice is. He wrote,

> Avarice is the parsimony of idols, the prophecy of the crowd, a vote for stinginess, a hoarding mentality, a wealth of captivity, a race of injustice, an abundance of illnesses, a diviner of many years, an enchanter for industriousness, a counsellor of sleeplessness, poverty of the belly, meagreness of foods, insatiable madness, a wickedness of many cares.

Evagrius also observed how the "uprooting of avarice" frees us from fear, poverty, and envy. He described a person who is free of avarice as "a sun without distraction."

Avarice means something different to each Ennea-Type. It arises in Fives when they are gripped by the basic fear of not knowing enough and when they fret about not having sufficient resources or know-how to deal with life. My friend Jerry, a Five, has given me many helpful insights into how a Five might experience avarice in the heart. Here is an excerpt from an e-mail he sent me: "Avarice arises when I feel disconnected from love. A big fear for Fives is that love is not real; it is just a sentimental idea, a heart-shaped candy box, or a bunch of flowers from the grocery store. An even bigger fear for Fives is that love is VERY REAL, the most real thing there is, but that it will forever elude my grasp because I am not capable or competent enough to know what to do with it."

> *Avarice, envy, pride. Three fatal sparks.*
> — Dante, *The Divine Comedy*

As with all the passions in the Enneagram, avarice can harm your sense of self, your emotional well-being, and your relationships. It is vital therefore that Fives shine a light on their avarice to understand it better. Here are five expressions of avarice that Fives commonly experience.

Self and Avarice. Fives fear they are ontologically inept, which is a scholarly way of saying, "I'm afraid I don't have what it takes to do life." This fear convinces Fives to retreat into themselves, and to observe the world from behind their eyes. They keep themselves to themselves and are stingy about giving away their time and energy to others. They fear that being around others too much will cause what Claudio Naranjo, the Enneagram teacher, called a "catastrophic depletion" of psychic energy.

Heart and Avarice. Fives are often more comfortable with a "meeting of minds" than with "heart to heart" connections. "I've had to train myself to give more hugs, kisses, and displays of affection to my family," said Matt, a Five, who took my Love and the Enneagram program. "I'm afraid to admit how much I love them," he told me. When I asked why he was afraid, Matt told me, "Because love is too beautiful to speak of, and our time in this world is too short." Avarice stops Fives from sharing their heart more fully with others, for fear of loss and heartbreak. Working with Matt, I helped him to see that unless he shared his heart with others, he wouldn't know what love is, and his family would never know how much he loves them.

Grief and Avarice. Fives feel sad that they don't know more about everything. They grieve the loss of knowing, and the *degradation of consciousness*, another Claudio Naranjo term, that happens when you live inside a body, with a heart for a pump, and a brain that runs on less than 10 percent capacity. Fives grieve that they don't know how to love others well enough. *What does it mean to say I love you?* They look for answers outside of them. But you can't learn love from a book. "We can only learn to love by loving," wrote author Iris Murdoch in *The Bell*.

Self-Reliance and Avarice. "The Enneagram has taught me that the more self-reliant I try to make myself, the more avaricious I become," said Brian, a Five. Avarice arises from our perceived separateness from an abundant and loving universe. This misperception causes Fives to fear that love is in short supply and that their heart is too small to share with everyone. Meditation teacher Sharon Salzberg is a Five. "If you go deeper and deeper into your own heart, you'll be living a world with less fear, isolation and loneliness," she wrote in *A Heart as Wide as the World*.

Faith and Avarice. "I have enough material to write ten books, but not enough faith to start any of them," said Felicity, a Five, who came to me for mentoring. Avarice is a response to a lack of faith in ourselves and our basic relatedness to the universe. "You don't lack faith; you lack heart," I told Felicity. "What does that mean?" she asked quizzically. For Fives, faith isn't make-believe; it is a genuine knowing in the heart that you are not alone, that inspiration is everywhere, that help is always at hand, and that every work is a co-creative act. *The more you live in your heart, the more faith you have in yourself and what you are capable of.*

Fixation: Retentiveness

In the Enneagram, the *fixation* refers to a mental habit that causes an imbalance in your mental health and well-being. The fixation for Fives has been given different names by Enneagram teachers, and these names include stinginess, hoarding, grasping, clutching, and retention. The name I use is retentiveness.

As we have seen, Fives are knowledge-seekers who enjoy investigating and researching matters that interest them. Fives commonly develop a muscle for retentiveness that assists them greatly in their pursuit of knowledge and love of learning. Indeed, Fives are known for having brains with extra memory storage and astonishing powers of recall. At the drop of a hat, a Five can, for instance, recite the lyrics to any Beatles song; identify the flag of every nation, and tell you which team from East London won the FA Cup in 1980 (even though they have only "a passing interest" in English soccer).

Retentiveness is a gift for Fives. And a source of great joy. I fondly remember the time I took my daughter Bo and her friend, who I will call "J," to the

American Museum of Natural History in New York. Bo and J were five years old, and J was already displaying traits of a Five. Inside the museum, we headed straight for the dinosaurs because J loved dinosaurs. J was the best tour guide ever! He pointed out to Bo and me the rib bones of a *Styracosaurus,* the spine of a *Brachiosaurus,* the skull of a *Tyrannosaurus rex,* and the horn of a *Triceratops*. At one point, J had to correct the official tour guide, who got his facts wrong. J was distressed about this. "He should know his facts," said J, pulling hard on my sleeve. J felt better after the tour guide offered a gracious apology and gave him a special sticker of a *Diplodocus*.

> *I don't need to know everything, I just need to know where to find it, when I need it.*
>
> — Albert Einstein (attributed)

So, what's the problem with retentiveness? Well, I imagine a Five could write a chapter, or even a book, on the perils of retentiveness. For now, here are a few ways that Fives struggle with retentiveness and the effects it has on their mental health and well-being.

Fear of Not Knowing. Did you know there is a term for the fear of not knowing? It's called *agnosiophobia*. Look carefully at this long word and you will see the first five letters of the word *gnosis*, which is the feminine Greek noun for spiritual knowledge and inner knowing. When Fives experience the basic fear of not knowing enough, they defend themselves against the fear by building up as much intellectual knowledge as possible. Unfortunately, this hoarding activity blocks the gift of inner knowing and exacerbates the fear of not knowing enough.

Sense of Deficiency. "Behind the hoarding impulse there is, we may say, an experience of impending impoverishment," wrote Claudio Naranjo in *Ennea-Type Structures*. When Fives fear they are lacking in knowledge, they try to cram their mental hard drive with facts, figures, and statistics to fill themselves up. "It's like we Fives are trying to turn our head into a belly by compulsively feeding it morsels of information," observed Russ Hudson.

Grasping at Knowledge. When Fives fear they don't know enough, they can get highly anxious, which makes them eat books for breakfast (not literally!), fill up notebooks, clutch at ideas, fixate on theories, and grasp at knowing. Anxious Fives try to "get their head around" subjects that are too big for the head to digest by itself. A wise Five understands that knowing comes from a creative mix of lived experience, openheartedness, holy imagination, and everyday curiosity, as well as from deep thinking and reasoning.

Knowledge Versus Wisdom. Fives must be willing to expand their ideas about learning if they are to be wise. For example, they must learn to recognize the difference between memorizing and knowing, information and truth, theory and practice, knowledge and wisdom. Wisdom is not acquired; it is received. It comes from being present and from letting yourself be astonished by things. "Instructions for living a life: Pay attention. Be astonished. Tell about it," wrote Mary Oliver, the poet.

Life Is Not a Theory. When I teach about Point Five, I ask you to visualize yourself standing before two doors. One door has a sign on it that says, "Lecture on Life." The other door has a sign that reads, "Life." What door do you choose? Everyone would do well to attend a few lectures on life. Life is a school, after all. That said, Fives are the Type who would benefit from skipping the lecture on life. They're already up to their eyes on theory. *Life is not just a theory; it must be lived.* Walking through the "Life" door is a wise move for Fives.

LIGHT ON THE PATH

The sole purpose of human existence is to kindle a light of meaning in the darkness of mere being.

– Carl Jung

The Enneagram offers a path of growth for all nine Types that helps you to remember your original nature and be your True Self. For Fives, the path of growth is a path of enlightenment.

Avanti Kumar, my first spiritual mentor, a Five, would often talk to me about light. "Think of yourself as a light," he told me. "When you meditate, focus on a point of light within you. This is the light of your soul." Early on, Avanti gave me a copy of *Light on the Path*. It's an esoteric book that was first published by the Theosophical Society in 1911. It's only 14 pages long. The author is anonymous. "Written down by M.C." appears on the title page. *Light on the Path* offers a collection of short instructions on how to know your soul. I have kept this book with me for the past 40 years and often read from it when I teach about Point Five.

The anonymous author of *Light on the Path* teaches that the purpose of humanity is to experience the full flowering of our consciousness. The term for this is *enlightenment*. The first step on the path is to connect with the light of the soul. "Seek it by plunging into the mysterious and glorious depths of your inmost being," M.C. instructs. At first the soul will appear to be "a dim star that burns within." M.C. continues, "Steadily, as you watch and worship, its light will grow stronger. Then you may know you have found the beginning of the way. And when you have found the end its light will suddenly become the infinite light."

Light is not a metaphor; it's real. Light plays a crucial role in the existence of the universe. "God is light," says the Bible (1 John 1:5 NIV). And creation is a play of light. David Bohm, the theoretical physicist, who might well have been a Five, famously described the universe as "condensed or frozen light." "All matter is a made of light," he observed. He described light as "the fundamental activity in which existence has its ground." This means that we are made of light. Biologists recognize that we are bioluminescent beings. Our body literally gives off a glow, because it is made of light.

> *We only have to go a little beyond the frontier of sensible appearances in order to see the divine.*
> — Pierre Teilhard de Chardin

In *Light on the Path*, the author M.C. says, "For through your own heart comes the one light which can illuminate life and make it clear to your eyes." Mystics and seers refer to it as the uncreated spark of the soul. When we tune in to this light, it helps us to see ourselves without sin, without judgment, without fear, and without shame. This light is pure consciousness. And it reveals to us our divine nature. In this sense, then, we are all on a path of enlightenment.

Virtue: Non-Attachment

Every Ennea-Type has a virtue, or a superpower, that arises naturally as you do your inner work to heal the basic fear, the passion in the heart, and the fixation in your thinking. The virtue for Fives is most often called non-attachment.

Down the centuries, many of the world's great thinkers have recognized that wisdom is not an object that can be grasped by the mind. Evagrius Ponticus, whom we met earlier, observed, "God cannot be grasped by the mind. If he could be grasped, he would not be God." In a similar vein, philosopher Meister Eckhart (1260–1328) said, "I pray to God to rid me of God." Why did he say this? Because he realized that wisdom begins by emptying your mind of your conditioned reasoning, learned ideas, and secondhand knowledge. This is the practice of non-attachment. And isn't it true that often our best thoughts come to us when we are not thinking at all? When the mind is empty, wisdom appears.

One of my favorite books is *Einstein and the Poet: In Search of the Cosmic Man*. It features a series of illuminating conversations between Albert Einstein and William Hermann, the poet. Both are very Five-minded. As they talk, they compare notes on how they think and work. They affirm the importance of being open and available to inspiration. Einstein describes how he waits for a "cosmic religious feeling" to happen inside him before he begins to think. Hermann describes how poetry comes to him without thinking. When reading their conversation, I sometimes need to check who is speaking. Hermann, the poet, sounds like a scientist at times. And Einstein sounds a lot like a poet.

> *Education is the kindling of a flame, not the filling of a vessel.*
> — Socrates

The practice of non-attachment supports Fives—and all of the nine Ennea-Types—in our quest for knowledge. Here are a few observations about non-attachment.

The Original Mind. "There can be no progress, if there is no original thinking, and there can be no original thinking, if you stick strictly to the known," said Einstein. Healthy Fives practice non-attachment to keep their mind open and free of conditioning, bias, and prejudice. One way they do this is by making friends with solitude. "The more powerful and original a mind, the more it will incline towards the religion of solitude," wrote Aldous Huxley, author of *The Doors of Perception*.

Be Not Distracted. Aldous Huxley displayed many Five traits. In his classic work, *The Doors of Perception*, he wrote "I took down my copy of Evans-Wentz's edition of *The Tibetan Book of the Dead*, and opened at random: *'O nobly born, let not thy mind be distracted.'* That was the problem—to remain undistracted. Undistracted by the memory of past sins, by imagined pleasure, by the bitter aftertaste of old wrongs and humiliations, by all the fears and hates and cravings that ordinarily eclipse the Light."

The Wisdom Channel. "I used to think I could collect wisdom in the same way I collected postage stamps as a boy," Dan told me. Dan is a Five, and he is an environmental lawyer. "I believed that my brain was a storage unit, the size of a small box, that I could fill with ideas; but now I think of my brain as a receiving station that can access an infinite supply of ideas and inspiration," said Dan. He continued, "Now, when I work on a case, I tune in to what I call my 'Inner Wisdom Channel,' and I trust that everything I need to know will come to me at the perfect time."

Beyond the Intellect. Returning to the conversation between Einstein and Hermann, the poet, Einstein tells him, "You must warn people not to make their intellect their god." He goes on, "Intuition is the father of new knowledge, while empiricism is nothing but an accumulation of old knowledge. Intuition, not intellect, is the 'open sesame' of yourself." Einstein concludes "... our faculties are dull and can only comprehend wisdom and serene beauty in crude forms, but the heart of man through intuition leads us to greater understanding of ourselves and the universe."

Questioning Your Thoughts. To practice non-attachment, you must be willing to question your beliefs and ideas, e.g., *Are all my thoughts true?, Do I really need to know everything?, Is it wise to spend so much time alone?,* and *Am I still not ready to begin?"* Fives who work with the virtue of non-attachment are less fixed in their opinions, less stuck in their thinking, and less narrow in their approach to life. "The mind that opens to a new idea never returns to its original size," observed Einstein.

Balancing Your Centers

The ancient wisdom of the Enneagram teaches that we have three centers of intelligence—body center, heart center, and head center. Modern science, which can sometimes be skeptical and dismissive of "old thinking," also recognizes the existence of these three centers. Browse the Internet, and you will find many scientific research papers that investigate how "the three brains" work in us. Each brain is interconnected and forms a complex network of intelligence. For instance, the heart is referred to as "the second brain" and has its own neurons and neurotransmitters. And the brain in the gut sends more information to the brain in the head than the head sends to the gut. The bottom line is, we need all three brains to work well together if we are to be healthy, happy, and wise.

Type Fives are called Head Types (along with Sixes and Sevens), and working with the Enneagram can help Fives to use all three brains to optimize their powers of intuition, emotion, and cognition.

The Head Center. Fives tend to describe themselves more as "thinkers" than as "feelers" or "intuitives." Do a poll, and most Fives will vote for thinking as a more reliable processor than feelings or intuition. And yet, when you really think about it, our thoughts are not always true or accurate. Thinking can play tricks on your perception, lead you down rabbit holes, and cut you off from yourself and others. To think clearly, you need to live in all three centers: head, heart, and body. Albert Einstein, in his conversation with poet William Hermanns, said that when his thinking got fuzzy, he'd tell himself, "I must wake up and live more in the world than in my laboratory."

> *It is only with the heart that one can see rightly.... What is essential is invisible to the eye.*
>
> — Antoine de Saint-Exupéry, *The Little Prince*

The Heart Center. Just as the head is capable of fuzzy thinking, so too is the heart prone to emotional reactivity and strange feelings. But this happens only when we live on the surface of these two centers. When you really get to know your own mind, you can easily recognize the difference between a crazy thought and wisdom. Similarly, when you pay attention to your heart, you learn to tell the difference between the sound of fear and the Voice of Love, for instance. You also learn that emotions carry messages, that feelings are a guide, and that love is an intelligent force you can use to guide your thinking.

> *The mind, when housed within a healthful body, possesses a glorious sense of power.*
> — Joseph Pilates, physical trainer, writer, inventor

The Body Center. When Fives are locked away in their head center, they become disembodied, neglectful, and impractical. They detach themselves from everyday life, forget to eat properly, stop exercising physically, don't pay the bills, won't change a lightbulb, and neglect to do everyday menial tasks. "We Fives turn into a disembodied head if we don't pay attention to our body center and our heart center," observes Russ Hudson. Healthy Fives recognize that "the wisdom of the body" is a real thing, not just an old wives' tale. "Healthy-body, healthy-mind" is not only an aphorism; it's an equation. A breath of fresh air, a walk in nature, and daylight on your skin, revives the spirit and increases the flow of blood to the brain.

Spreading Your Wings

Type Five's home base is Point Five, which sits between Point Four and Point Six on the Enneagram symbol. This means Fives have a 4-Wing and a 6-Wing. Typically, one wing is more dominant than the other, but the goal is to balance your wings. Working with the 4-Wing helps Fives to tap into the essential qualities and wisdom

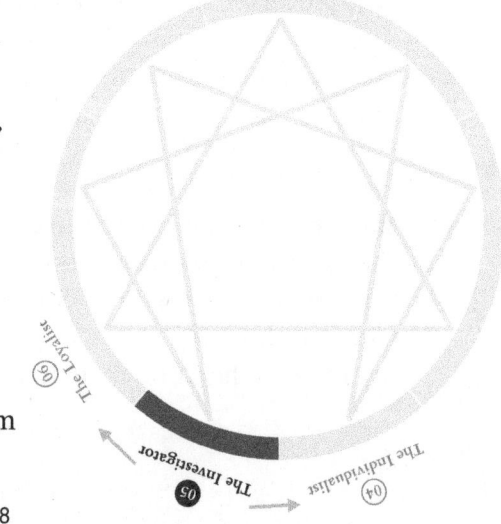

of Point Four, and working with the 6-Wing helps Fives to access the same at Point Six. Learning to live in balance with your wings, by drawing strengths and lessons from both, can help Fives on their path of learning and growth.

Five with a 4-Wing

Fives with a dominant 4-Wing (5w4) are called the Iconoclast. They show up in the world with the main characteristics of Five, plus some traits of Fours. For example:

>**Original Thinker.** A 5w4 combines the healthy qualities of Fives and Fours, such as being original, authentic, unique, and inventive. Fives don't want to be told what to think or be censored by the Thought Police (a reference to *1984*, by George Orwell); they want to learn how to use their own mind, to think deeply on matters, and to express their own ideas. "If you do not express your own original ideas, if you do not listen to your own being, you will have betrayed yourself," said philosopher Rollo May in *The Courage to Create*.
>
>**Eye for Beauty.** 5w4s are known for seeing things differently. Perhaps this is why so many filmmakers, documentary makers, photographers, and storytellers have strong Five and Four energy. 5w4s see beauty in their own unique way. For a 5w4, information is beautiful, a mathematical equation is beautiful, the hexagonal prism of a snowflake is beautiful, and fungi, bacteria, and microbes are beautiful and deadly. An example of this way of seeing is the illustrated book *Life at the Edge of Sight: A Photographic Exploration of the Microbial World*, by Scott Chimileski and Roberto Kolter.
>
>**Emotional Intelligence.** A 5w4 is a combination of a Head Type (Five, Six, and Seven) and a Heart Type (Four, Three, and Two). 5w4s are typically more heart-centered and emotionally expressive than a 5w6. The film *A Beautiful Mind* tells the story of scientist John Nash (played by Russell Crowe), who has a lot of Four and Five energy. At one point in the film, Nash says, "Perhaps it is good to have a beautiful mind, but an even greater gift is to discover a beautiful heart." And later, "It is only in the mysterious equations of love that any logic or reason can be found."

The Reclusive Artist. Both Fives and Fours (along with Nines) are called Withdrawn Types in the Enneagram. They are known for being introspective and introverted. They observe the world, and have a deep love for the world, but they also keep the world at arm's length. Think of reclusive artists like poet Emily Dickinson, *Catcher in the Rye* author J. D. Salinger, and cartoonist Bill Watterson, creator of *Calvin and Hobbes*, all of whom declined interviews and shunned fame.

Deep and Meaningful. 5w4s are known for being deep and meaningful. They are deeply sensitive, and they are on the look-out for deep and meaningful contact with others. They are more image conscious than a 5w6. They don't want to be normal, but they fear being rejected for being different. "I wouldn't have had good scientific ideas if I had thought more normally," said John Nash, the scientist, who wrestled with feelings of alienation and how best to fit in with the world.

Five with a 6-Wing

Fives with a dominant 6-Wing (5w6) are called the Problem Solver. They show up in the world with the main characteristics of Five, plus some traits of Sixes. For example:

Problem-Solving. 5w6s work overtime on solving puzzles and conundrums. *How does this dishwasher work? What do I need to build my own website? How can I upholster this old chair? What does it take to grow a permaculture garden?* They tend to be less introspective than 5w4s and place their focus more on external matters. Sometimes it can be good for 5w6s to take a break from the strain of constant problem-solving. "Life is not a problem to be solved, but a reality to be experienced," said Dutch theosophist Jacobus Johannes van der Leeuw in his 1928 book *The Conquest of Illusion*.

Practical Wisdom. 5w6s are known for being philosophical and practical. Fives wrestle with big *why* questions like *Why are we alive?* and *Why do we go to work?* and *Why do we fall in love?* Because Point Six energy is more about practical wisdom than highbrow philosophy, it helps 5w6s to balance their why questions with practical how questions like *How should we live?* and *How do I find purpose?* and *How do I love someone?* "Never confuse knowledge with wisdom. By wisdom I mean wrestling with how to live," said Cornel West, philosopher and activist.

The Detective. 5w6s often have a bit of Sherlock Holmes and Agatha Christie about them. They combine qualities of Fives and Sixes and are observant and alert, curious and suspicious, and watchful and vigilant. "My mind rebels at stagnation. Give me problems, give me work, give me the most abstruse cryptogram or the most intricate analysis, and I am in my own proper atmosphere," said Sherlock Holmes in Arthur Conan Doyle's *The Sign of the Four*.

Up in the Head. Both Fives and Sixes (along with Sevens) are called Head Types in the Enneagram. So this makes 5w6s a double Head Type. "I am a brain, Watson. The rest of me is a mere appendix," says Sherlock Holmes in Arthur Conan Doyle's *The Adventure of the Mazarin Stone*. As we have seen already, Fives can get stuck in their heads, and this is especially true for 5w6s. Therefore, it's extra important that 5w6s learn to balance the three brains of body, heart, and head.

Collaborative Wisdom. 5w6s tend to be more social and extroverted than 5w4s. They are independent-minded but are also willing to collaborate with people they trust and respect. Their mantra is: "Two heads are better than one." 5w6s take on the outlook of healthy Sixes, who value cooperation, mutual support, and teamwork. They also recognize the importance of being mentored, having therapy, and being coached. They accept that none of us are smart enough to do life on our own.

Moving to Seven and Eight

Following the Inner Lines of the Enneagram symbol, Fives move toward Point Seven (home for the Enthusiast) and Point Eight (home for the Challenger). These Inner Lines are an invitation to visit these Points to explore the gifts and wisdom they have for you.

Moving to Seven

When Fives are healthy and well-balanced, they share some of the higher qualities that Sevens are blessed with.

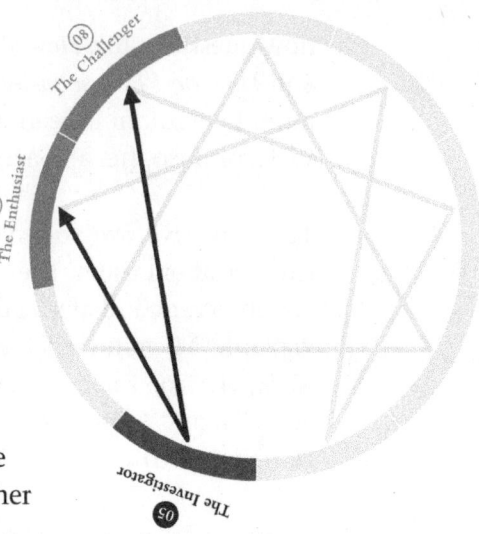

Possibility Thinking. When Fives embrace the expansive energy of Point Seven, it helps them to break free from narrow-mindedness, to broaden their focus, to shift their gaze, to be more open-minded, and to practice possibility thinking. The unknown becomes an adventure rather than something to fear.

More Outgoing. The energy at Point Seven encourages Fives to be more social and extroverted. It's always a good idea for a Five to turn off your screen, put down your book, move away from your desk, and meet a friend for coffee and some stimulating conversation.

Add More Fun. Point Seven is the best meditation seat for tuning in to awe and wonder, enthusiasm for life, and joie de vivre. Fives often get too "bogged down" in themselves and can benefit from some upliftment and gaiety. A healthy dose of Seven energy helps Fives participate more joyfully in the mystery of life.

When Fives are under stress, they may display some unhealthy qualities that are also common to Sevens. For example:

Loss of Focus. When Fives and Sevens get "too heady," they become ungrounded, lose their footing, and trip over themselves. Too much "headiness" causes their thinking to be unfocused, blurred, and "scattered into everydayness," a phrase attributed to philosopher Martin Heidegger.

Driven to Distraction. Sevens and Fives are known for getting distracted and for delaying and not completing tasks. They have too many tabs open in the mind, a pile of half-read books on the desk, too many files open on the computer, and too many good ideas competing for their attention.

You Need to Stop! When Fives are out of balance, they can be very intense, fixated, and detached. They think too much. They work too hard. They get a migraine. Like an unhealthy Seven, they have a lot of Freddie Mercury's "Don't stop me now!" energy. They can also be impetuous, thoughtless, reckless, and out of control.

Moving to Eight

When Fives are healthy and well-balanced, they share some of the higher qualities that Eights embody.

Hello, World! "Being a Five, the Enneagram has taught me to embrace the more out-going energy of Point Eight so that I make more direct contact with the world," said Terry, a geologist, who has two PhDs. "Knowledge comes from reading books, but wisdom comes from living in the world," she told me.

Social Confidence. The energy of point Eight is very physical and can activate in Fives a desire to be more embodied, more in the "here and now," and more engaged with everyday life. It can also empower Fives to overcome feelings of smallness, share their ideas more, and take on leadership roles.

Gut Instinct. The energy of Point Eight draws Fives down into the body center. It helps them contact the intelligence of the body, listen to their gut instinct, and trust their feelings when making decisions. Three brains—head, heart, and gut—are better than one!

When Fives are under stress, they may display some unhealthy qualities that are also common to Eights. For example:

Unhealthy Independence. Fives and Eights both struggle to find the balance between healthy and unhealthy independence. Eights like to be captain of their own ship, and Fives like to rely on their own thinking. Wisdom is knowing when self-reliance and independent thinking are working well for you or not.

Fear of Rejection. Fives and Eights are especially prone to the fear of rejection. For Fives, having their thoughts and ideas rejected, or even questioned, can be especially painful. Hence, some Fives get very defensive and stroppy (like an angry Eight) when others don't see things their way.

Elitist Thinking. Eights can be quick to dismiss people as stupid and unintelligent. Similarly, Fives who are highbrow and full of intellectual pride will label people as muggles, idiots, and halfwits. This shortsightedness is common in Fives who are not in contact with their heart.

HOLY OMNISCIENCE

The eye with which I see God is the same eye with which God sees me.

– Meister Eckhart

The nine Points on the Enneagram each offer a Holy Idea—a universal teaching and higher wisdom—for all nine Ennea-Types to contemplate and practice. Point Five has two Holy Ideas. They are Holy Omniscience and Holy Transparency.

Holy Omniscience teaches that the Universe is the work of an Infinite Intelligence, and that we are all expressions of this intelligence. Since ancient times, thinkers, storytellers, and mystics have observed that we live in a conscious universe. Modern scientists like Sir James Jeans have also helped us to see that universe is more "mind-like" than "matter-like." In *The Mysterious Universe*, he wrote, "The stream of knowledge [modern science] is heading towards a non-mechanical reality; the universe begins to look more like a great thought than like a great machine. Mind no longer appears as an accidental intruder into the realm of matter; we are beginning to suspect that we ought rather to hail it as the creator and governor of the realm of matter."

Holy Transparency teaches that everyone has access to the Infinite Intelligence of the Universe. The mystic Meister Eckhart observed, "Every single creature is full of God and is a book about God." The embryo of a human being is packed with sufficient wisdom to grow a heart, a brain, and a spinal cord so as to make a baby. And babies are born with an innate intelligence that helps them grow through infancy. The point is that babies don't need to read a book about how to crawl or how to stand. And they don't need to study a research paper on smile theory or the meaning of eye contact before they start communicating with someone. We are born with a capacity to be wise, and this inbuilt wisdom is ever-present in our life.

Holy Omniscience is a universe brimming with intelligence. Holy Transparency is a quality of your Original Mind that helps you to tap into this intelligence. The Buddha taught that the mind is pure and luminous in its original state. He encouraged his students to "Be a lamp unto yourself." Jesus Christ offered the same teaching. The word *Christ* comes from the ancient Greek *Christos*, which means "universal light." "You are the light of the world," he told his disciples. Five, at their best, are luminous in their thinking and in their way of being. With their clear lens of perception, and their "seeing mind," they can see life as it really is.

Working with the Enneagram helps every Type—and especially Fives—to practice basic openness, to cultivate inner knowing, and to see with a clear lens of perception. Everything is revealed to one who has ears and eyes to see.

> *You do not need to leave your room.*
> *Remain sitting at your table and listen.*
> *Do not even listen, simply wait, be quiet,*
> *still and solitary. The world will freely*
> *offer itself to you to be unmasked, it*
> *has no choice, it will roll in ecstasy*
> *at your feet.*
>
> – Franz Kafka

Type Six
THE LOYALIST

*It takes courage to grow up and turn
out to be who you really are.*

— E. E. CUMMINGS

The Ennea-Type Six is commonly called Loyalist or Loyal Skeptic. Other names for Sixes include Questioner, Courageous Soul, Security-Seeker, Trooper, and Devil's Advocate.

Sixes are the *Highly Intuitive, Doubting Type*. They are watchful, attentive, and Argus-eyed. In Greek mythology, Argus (or Argos) is the watchman with a hundred eyes. Sixes are looking for something to believe in, for a person who passes their test, for work that is bona fide, and for a sense of purpose. They are known for being faithful and true, for their brave hearts, and for their loyalty to a cause. That said, Sixes are often caught in two minds about life. They oscillate between being committed and cautious, courageous and anxious, dutiful and hesitant. Sixes are the Type most likely to own a copy of *The Worst-Case Scenario Survival Handbook*. Sixes recognize that life is a risky business, and yet they are prepared to risk everything when it really matters. Sixes know in their heart that life is a risk worth taking.

Sixes are always on guard against danger. Their keen sense of vigilance helps them to feel secure and safe. "It's a dangerous business, Frodo, going out of your door," Bilbo Baggins said to Frodo Baggins in *The Fellowship of the Ring*. "You step onto the road, and if you don't keep your feet, there's no knowing where you might be swept off to." Fortunately, Sixes are blessed with a sixth sense—an intuitive wisdom—to guide and steer them through life. Working with the Enneagram helps Sixes build self-trust and live with greater faith and courage. The more they trust their sixth sense, the better it works for them, especially when making important decisions to do with friendships, romance, marriage proposals, job offers, financial investments, and what to believe in or not.

> *Courage is not the absence of fear; it is the making of action in spite of fear.*
> — M. Scott Peck, *The Road Less Traveled*

Sixes often get anxious when they take an Enneagram test. When faced with a lot of questions, they go round in circles, questioning their choices and second-guessing themselves. Sixes are also highly empathic, due to their sixth sense, and can easily mistype themselves. For example, many Sixes think they're an Eight, the Challenger, especially Sixes who are counterphobic and confront their fears. Sixes and Eights may look similar, but on closer inspection you realize their internal operating systems are different. Also, Sixes are known for being a bit down on themselves. I've had Sixes say to me, *"The Loyalist doesn't sound much fun"* and *"I was hoping not to be the Loyalist"* and *"I'd rather be the Individualist."*

Many great Enneagram teachers are Sixes. P. D. Ouspensky, a Russian philosopher, was most likely a Six. He was a real-life Indiana Jones, a seeker after truth, who met George Gurdjieff on his travels across Russia, Turkey, India, and Egypt. He introduced Gurdjieff's teachings on the Enneagram to the West in his classic work *In Search of the Miraculous*. Psychologist Helen Palmer, a Six, wrote the first international bestseller on the Enneagram, called *The Enneagram*. Helen teamed up with

> *The most difficult thing is to know what we do know and what we do not know.*
> — P. J. Ouspensky

Stanford psychiatrist David Daniels, MD, also a Six, to run the Narrative Enneagram community, founded in 1988. She also edited a textbook called *Inner Knowing: Consciousness, Creativity, Insight, and Intuitions*, and taught popular training programs on how to work with intuition in everyday life.

INTRODUCING TYPE SIX

Are you a Type Six on the Enneagram? Maybe you have a family member, a friend, or a work colleague who is a Six.

My grandmother Dorothy, on my mother's side of the family, had a lot of Six energy. She was known to her friends as Topsy. (Sixes have a thing for nicknames.) Granny, as I called her, was a constant in my life. She was always there for me, at the drop of a hat, through thick and thin. She was fiercely loyal, had an acerbic wit, was a bit spikey at times, and had a very kind heart. She often rebelled against Grandpa's authoritarian wishes. She had a close circle of friends that she met up with every week to play bridge and organize activities in the village. Typical of Sixes, she also liked her routines, such as elevenses, which is a British tradition of taking light refreshments at 11 a.m., a cup of Earl Grey tea and slice of cake at 4 p.m., and a tipple of sherry at 6 p.m.

One time, I took a girlfriend to meet Granny. When Granny asked her, "And what do you do?", my girlfriend told her about her work and added, "I am also very psychic." On hearing this, my granny said, "Would you like to see my crystal ball?" I was gobsmacked, as I had no idea she had one, and no one else knew either, not even Grandpa. Sixes are known for being secretive. And yet it made sense because Granny was highly intuitive and had an uncanny wisdom. "Granny, are you psychic?" I asked her. "Oh, I very much doubt that," she said, averting her eyes quickly. "Well, you do win a lot of money on the horse racing," I said. A bet on the horses on Saturday afternoon was another of my granny's routines.

My mother-in-law, Evie, is a Six. As well as being my mother-in-law, she is also my very dear friend. Evie is absolutely devoted to her family and friends. She is steadfast and constant in her love. "You are the heart of our family," I often tell her. She adores her three children, and even more her seven grandchildren. She has always been hands on with our children, Bo and Christopher. She is the head of Health and Safety in our family. All her grandchildren feel safe and loved in her presence. Evie is dedicated to her inner work and personal growth. She is a keen student of the Enneagram. She is also a gifted therapist and counselor. As a Six, her soul gift is helping people befriend their fears, trust their intuition, and be faithful to their True Self.

Healthy Qualities of Sixes

When Sixes are healthy and well-balanced, they display essential qualities we all love and appreciate. Here are a few things healthy Sixes have told me about themselves:

- "I am highly committed and dutiful."
- "I am a loyal and faithful friend."
- "I like to feel safe and secure."
- "I also like to take risks."
- "I am open-minded and skeptical."
- "I am fearful and courageous."
- "I question authority."
- "I trust my intuition to guide me."
- "I am reliable and trustworthy."
- "My motto is: Always be prepared."

Unhealthy Qualities of Sixes

When Sixes are out of balance, they feel ungrounded, indecisive, and lost inside a labyrinth of thoughts. Here are a few things Sixes have told me about themselves:

- "I am more anxious than people realize."
- "I get worried when I am not anxious."
- "I am consistently plagued by self-doubt."
- "I stress myself out when making decisions."
- "I'm always waiting for the other shoe to drop."
- "I see the glass as half empty or as about to break."
- "I tend to accentuate the negative in my life."
- "I don't let many people into my circle of trust."
- "I don't know if I am a pessimist or a realist."
- "I test people to see if they really love me."

RECOGNIZING TYPE SIXES

In Greek philosophy, Heraclitus of Ephesus has a lot of Six traits. He inspired many philosophers and thinkers, including Plato and Aristotle, and, more recently, Hegel and Heidegger. His most famous saying is, "You cannot step into the same river twice." Heraclitus observed that the universe is paradoxical, made of a unity of opposites, and is in a state of constant change. "All is flux, nothing stays still," he said. He also detected a universal intelligence that "steers the totality of all things." He believed that the universe is intelligent, and that we can rely on this intelligence to guide and support us.

In Eastern philosophy, the teachings of the Buddha sit well at Point Six on the Enneagram. In his lifetime, Buddha was asked "Are you a god?" and "Are you a saint?" Buddha replied simply, "I am awake." The name, Buddha, means "the awakened one." After Buddha experienced his enlightenment, while sitting under the Bodhi Tree in Bodhgaya, his first words were "I am enlightened, along with all other beings." Buddha taught that we can all be Buddhas, and that we can all overcome suffering and anxiety, by learning how the mind works, embracing our Inner Buddha, and practicing loving-kindness.

> *The only constant in life is change.*
> — Heraclitus

Buddha has been called a great philosopher, a noble physician, and a founding father of psychology. When I was a studying psychology in my early twenties, I read a paper entitled *"Was Buddha the first psychologist?"* Buddha taught his followers how to think. He instructed them to be watchful, to question their thinking, to observe the mental chatter of the "small mind" (*sem* in Tibetan), and to cultivate a "clear mind" (*rikpa* in Tibetan) that is capable of genuine insight, brightness, and knowing. In the Eightfold Path, the Buddha shared practical wisdom on how to experience, for example, right view, right mindfulness, right concentration, and right intention.

The Dhammapada is the most widely read book in Buddhist literature. Translated, it means "The Path of Truth." It is a collection of aphorisms attributed to Buddha. Chapter 1, called "Contrary Ways," begins with this verse: "What we are today comes from our thoughts of yesterday, and our present thoughts build our life of tomorrow; our life is the creation of our mind." Buddha also said,

> If a man speaks or acts with an unclear mind,
> suffering follows him as the wheel of the cart
> follows the beast that draws the cart.
> If a man speaks or acts with a clear mind,
> joy follows him as his own shadow.

Staying with philosophy, Ralph Waldo Emerson, the Transcendentalist, wrote an essay, "Self-Reliance," published in 1841, that is a must-read for Sixes (and for the rest of us). The chief maxim in Emerson's essay is: "Trust thyself." He believed that our true nature is infused with wisdom, and that our main task in life is to learn to recognize an inner "gleam of light" that can guide our thinking. Emerson encouraged us to know our own mind and to think for ourselves. He also passionately believed that external authority should be disregarded in favor of one's own lived experience. "Whoso would be a man must be a nonconformist," insisted Emerson.

> *To be yourself in a world that is constantly trying to make you something else is the greatest accomplishment.*
> — Ralph Waldo Emerson

In psychology, there have been many thinkers with strong Six traits. William James (1842–1910) is known as the father of American psychology. He said, "The greatest revolution of our generation is the discovery that human beings, by changing the inner attitudes of their minds, can change the outer aspects of their lives." James taught people how to think and how to live. He wrote, "The world we see that seems so insane is the result of a belief system that is not working. To perceive the world differently, we must be willing to change our belief system, let the past slip away, expand our sense of now, and dissolve the fear in our minds."

Erik Erikson's work on psychosocial development is also a good fit at Point Six. In his classic text, *Childhood and Society,* Erikson presented a model of eight stages of growth in the early years. Stage One is called *Trust vs. Mistrust,* and here Erikson pinpointed the need for a child to be raised in a stable "holding environment" that cultivates "a basic trust" in both the goodness of life and

> *Be not afraid of life. Believe that life is worth living, and your belief will help create the fact.*
> — William James

in one's inbuilt capacity to survive life's trials and flourish. Basic trust is vital for the next seven stages of growth that include taking initiative, experiencing intimacy, generating a purpose, and living with integrity. Without basic trust, a child's progress may be hampered by self-doubt, heightened insecurity, and a mistrust in other people and the world.

In leadership, Sixes often have misgivings about taking on leadership positions. Their self-doubt gets in the way. When Sixes do take a lead, it's usually a response to a strong inner calling. Sixes will take a stand, if push comes to shove. Rather like Ones, they have a strong sense of duty; and like Twos, they want to serve. Sixes commonly take leadership positions in politics, law, social services, the police force, and the military. They also serve high up in education and academia. Malcolm X, the African American human rights activist, was most likely a Six. He took a stand against racism and oppression. "I believe in human beings, and that all human beings should be respected as such, regardless of their color," he said.

> *A man who stands for nothing will fall for anything.*
> — Malcolm X

In the arts, Sixes use their creativity to raise questions, make us think, stimulate debate, poke fun at authority, and imagine how life might be if we acted with greater courage and love. Pyotor Ilyich Tchaikovsky, the Russian composer of music for *Sleeping Beauty* and *Swan Lake*, wrote about his anxiety and self-doubt in his many letters. "What I need is to believe in myself again—for my faith has been greatly undermined; it seems to me my role is over," he wrote in a letter to a nephew, shortly before he composed one of his greatest works, Symphony No. 6., *Pathétique*. He also described inspiration as "the guest" that came to him when his mind was perfectly still and clear.

Moving around the arts, think of Auguste Rodin's sculpture *The Thinker*, that is thought to represent Dante, author of *The Divine Comedy*. Think of *Catch-22*, the satire novel by Joseph Heller. Think of actress Julia Roberts and her roles in *Runaway Bride* and *Erin Brockovich*. Also, Marilyn Monroe, actress and model, who said, "It's a make-believe world, isn't it?" Think of Stan Lee, co-creator of the Marvel franchise, and the six Infinity Stones. Think of film director Ava DuVernay, who directed *Selma*, the biopic of Rev. Martin Luther King Jr., and *A Wrinkle in Time*. Also, Bruce Springsteen and his catalog of songs that include "Leap of Faith," "Devils and Dust," "None But the Brave," and "I'll Stand by You."

> *You need a reason to be brave, don't just stand by and watch the world go by.*
> — Bruce Springsteen

Many comedians and humorists have a lot of Six traits. Think of any Woody Allen movie, especially starring actress Diane Keaton, such as *Annie Hall, Manhattan,* and *Love and Death*. Think of the sitcom *Friends*, a tale of enduring friendship, that follows Ross, a Six, played by David Schwimmer, and Rachel, a Three, played by Jennifer Aniston, in their on-off relationship that spans 10 series and 236 episodes. Think of Chris Rock, the stand-up comedian: "Gun control? We need bullet control! I think every bullet should cost five thousand dollars. Because if a bullet cost five thousand dollars, we wouldn't have any innocent bystanders." Also, think of Ellen DeGeneres, who uses her quirky, observational humor to expose follies, tackle taboos, destigmatize, and get her message across. I highly recommend you watch her clip "Anxiety in Restaurants" from her *Relatable* standup show on Netflix.

In film and literature, J. R. R. Tolkien's The Lord of the Rings series has a lot of characters with Six-like traits. In *Fellowship of the Ring*, at the Council of Elrond, nine leaders debate who shall take the Ring to the ominously named Mount Doom, in Mordor. Eventually, it is Frodo Baggins, the hobbit, who steps forward and says, "I shall take the ring, though I do not know the way." Like all Hobbits, Frodo is shy and timid, and craves the safety and security of the Shire, his home. But when the situation calls for it, he responds with great selflessness, courage, and fidelity. Frodo is a reluctant hero, wracked with self-doubt, who nonetheless takes on a treacherous quest, and his courage helps him access a strength of spirit that steers him to a great victory.

> *Find out who you are and be that person. That's what your soul was put on this Earth to be. Find that truth, live that truth, and everything else will come.*
>
> — Ellen DeGeneres

Finally, Shakespeare's *Hamlet* is a play about self-trust and inner knowing. Hamlet, the royal prince, is caught in two minds as to how to respond to his father's murder. He delivers one-third of the lines of the play and speaks very differently when he is in company and when by himself. His "To be or not to be" soliloquy is plagued with self-doubt and uncertainty. He tells himself that he is "thinking too precisely on the event." Will Hamlet follow the word of a ghost or obey the inner promptings of his soul? Will he avenge his father's death and be a murderer, or will he choose a higher path? Only by listening to his soul can he know what to do.

AN AWAKENED MIND

> *Trust that your inner guide is leading you*
> *and guiding you in ways that are best for you,*
> *and that your spiritual growth is*
> *continuously expanding.*
>
> – Louise Hay

Louise Hay was a pioneer of the self-help movement, author of the bestseller *You Can Heal Your Life*, founder of Hay House Publishing Inc., and a Six on the Enneagram. Louise did not have the best of starts in life. She was raised by her mom and a violent and abusive stepfather, was raped as a teenager, got pregnant at 16, gave her child up for adoption, and left school without any qualifications. "I was a high school dropout, and I believed I couldn't think, that I didn't have a mind, and that I didn't know anything, and that I wasn't as good as people who had gone to school," said Louise in her recorded lecture "The Totality of Possibilities."

Louise turned her life around when she discovered the power of her own mind and how to choose her thoughts. Her turnaround happened after she was diagnosed with cervical cancer and her husband of 14 years had left her for another woman. "At the time, I felt completely lost and all alone," Louise told me when we were co-writing *Life Loves You*. She said, "When you are lost, life sends you a wake-up call. I've had a few wake-up calls in my life. And each time, life has whispered in my ear, *'Ding, ding! You must make a choice between fear and love.'*" Louise learned to listen to her intuition, which she affectionately called her "inner ding," and listening to her inner ding set her on her path as a much-loved teacher, author, and leader in her field.

Louise Hay is known for her practical wisdom. She taught people how to practice self-love, change their thoughts, and live an empowered life. Louise founded Hay House when she was 60 years old, and without any previous experience in publishing. In *Life Loves You*, she told me, "When people want to know how I created Hay House, I always tell them, 'I opened my mind. I listened to my inner voice. I followed the signs. I trusted the flow and learned to move with it.'" Her vision for Hay House was clear and simple. She told me, "What

> *The only thing we are*
> *ever dealing with is a*
> *thought, and a thought*
> *can be changed.*
>
> — Louise Hay

I knew then, and still believe today, is that the real purpose of Hay House is to help create a world where it is safe for us to love each other. With each book we print, we bless the world with love."

When Sixes trust themselves, it helps them to have faith, to live with imagination, to call upon an inner strength, and be courageous, wise, and loving. Here are a few of essential qualities that healthy Sixes display.

Healthy Self-Trust. Healthy Sixes have fears and doubts, like everyone else does, but they have learned to cultivate Self-trust, with a capital S. They trust they are equipped with the necessary resources in their spiritual backpack to cope with life, to make wise decisions, to navigate ups and downs, to survive tough times, to solve problems, and to know when to be brave or not. "Self-trust is the essence of heroism," wrote Ralph Waldo Emerson.

Always Be Prepared. Sixes are the original Boy Scout and Girl Guide. Their motto is "Always be prepared." Sixes are watchful and alert. *Who knows what today may bring?* They tend to sweat the small stuff, but in a crisis, they are remarkably cool-headed, resourceful, and capable. Like Batman and his utility belt, which has a compass, a recorder, a camera, and 140 other Bat gadgets, they have enough tools up their sleeve to help them cope when life throws a curveball at them. Sixes make sure they have our backs too. "Don't worry honey, I've got you," says my friend Diane, a Six.

Sixth Sense. Sixes are blessed with a highly developed sixth sense. The sixth sense is an intuitive intelligence that helps you to trust your vibes, to follow your instincts, to decide without thinking, to be open to guidance, and to say yes to life. As a Six, you're good at reading people and knowing who you can trust or not. You are also naturally psychic. For example, you often think about someone the moment before they phone you. Louise Hay encouraged everyone to trust their inner authority. "I trust my intuition with my life. My intuition is always on my side. I trust it to be there at all times," she said.

Practicing Mindfulness. Sixes know all too well that the mind is a mixed bag of fearful and loving thoughts, irrational ideas and intuitive insights, crazy thinking and razor-sharp awareness. They can be calm and clear-headed one minute and then suddenly be swept away by a thought-storm in the next. *Who is the thinker? Who rules my mind? What are thoughts made of?* Sixes appreciate the need to cultivate mindfulness. Jon Kabat-Zinn, a pioneer of mindfulness, says, "Mindfulness is a way of befriending ourselves and our experience." When Sixes meet their doubts and fears with honesty and compassion, it helps them access wisdom and courage.

> *Mindfulness means being awake. It means knowing what you are doing.*
> — Jon Kabat-Zinn

Road Less Traveled. Healthy Sixes follow their inner guidance, choose their own path, and take the road less traveled. Scott Peck, the psychiatrist and author of *Road Less Traveled,* might have been a Six. His best-selling book has chapters on The Risk of Commitment, The Risk of Loss, The Miracle of Serendipity, and The Welcoming of Grace. The first line of his book reads, "Life is difficult. This is a great truth, one of the greatest truths. It is a great truth because once we truly see this truth, we transcend it." Sixes are resilient and resourceful because they accept that life is hard, and they trust they have an inbuilt ability and know-how to survive and thrive.

Healthy Doubt. Sixes are known for being doubtful and uncertain, which has its challenges, but also has some positives. "Doubt is the beginning of wisdom," said René Descartes, the philosopher. Doubt keeps the mind open. It helps you to question things. It stops you having the wool pulled over your eyes. "Great Doubt, Great Awakening; small doubt, small awakening; no doubt, no awakening," states the Zen koan. Similarly, when Sixes embrace uncertainty, it helps them to live with faith, to be open to guidance, and practice even greater mindfulness and appreciation for life.

A Faithful Friend. When Sixes have a basic trust in themselves, they show up in everyday life as a faithful friend and a powerful ally who is loyal, brave, and true. Sixes are known for their cooperative spirit, being a team player, and being dependable and reliable. As a Six, your mantra is "I've got your back" and "I won't let you down." Sixes are also known for being very likeable. It's as if they've got an extra "likeability gene" in their DNA. They make us feel safe and loved because we know they really are here for us.

The Courage to Be. When I teach Point Six on the Enneagram, I feature the classic work *The Courage to Be*, by Paul Tillich, that addresses our relationship to fear and faith. "Fear is the absence of faith," wrote Tillich. Everyone experiences fear, and Sixes are especially aware of their fearful thinking. "My mind is made up of forty-nine percent anxiety, and fifty-one percent faith," said Mike, a Six, who took one of my Enneagram programs. Sixes find that their fears quieten down when they place their faith in a higher wisdom and trust their inner knowing.

LOSS OF GUIDANCE

The gateways to wisdom and knowledge are always open.
— Louise Hay

In Greek mythology, Ariadne, daughter of King Minos of Crete and Pasiphaë, gives Theseus, the prince of Athens, two items to take with him as he ventures into the labyrinth to slay the Minotaur, a beast that is half man and half bull. These two items are a sword and a ball of golden thread. It's obvious what the sword is for. It will come in handy when Theseus meets the Minotaur. But what is the golden thread for? The golden thread will keep our hero, Theseus, connected to the spiritual world while he is inside the labyrinth. It is an amulet for safe passage that will help him tune in to divine guidance, protect him from danger, and retrace his steps out of the labyrinth and back home.

"As a young girl, I read about Ariadne and Theseus, and I have worn a golden thread on my wrist ever since," Karen, a Six, told me in my Soul of the Enneagram program. The golden thread is made of the same substance as the soul, and it is unbreakable. Everybody has a golden thread, not just Sixes. Your golden thread is your connection with heaven. It ties persona and psyche together. When you are mindful of the golden thread, it helps you to tune in to the one infinite intelligence that steers all things. Carl Jung described the golden thread as an invisible telegraph wire. It gives you access to your higher mind, activates your intuition, and helps you to follow your destiny and live your purpose.

When Sixes go through the separation phase in childhood, they feel disoriented and lost. It's as if they have "lost the thread" that binds them to heaven. The ego, or persona, is "hanging by a thread" from the soul, and it feels separate and alone in the world. The ego-mind is mostly fearful and full of dread because it believes it must navigate the world by itself, without soul guidance, without a compass, without a good star to follow, and without support. No wonder then, that Sixes often feel they are "up shit creek and without a paddle," which, by the way, was one of my granny's favorite sayings.

Basic Fear: Not Being Supported

When Sixes experience the sense of separation, a basic fear arises in them of being unsafe, unsupported, and without guidance. As we shall see, this basic fear also gives rise to self-doubt, a feeling of deep anxiety, and foreboding. The perceived loss of support and guidance may cause Sixes to feel ungrounded, ill equipped, and lacking in vital resources to take on the task of living. To make matters worse, this basic fear is accentuated if the holding environment in early childhood is thrown into disarray by a traumatic incident such as parents separating, death of a grandparent, mental illness in the family, immigration, or a war.

Many Enneagram teachers, including Helen Palmer, who is a Six, recognize two types of Sixes: phobic Sixes and counterphobic Sixes. The phobic Six typically moves away from fear, and the counterphobic Six moves toward fear. In *The Pocket Enneagram,* Helen Palmer wrote: "Fear is acted out in two ways—by fight or flight. Sixes who habitually flee (phobic) appear hesitant and want to be protected, like a man or woman who is afraid to fly. Fighting Sixes (counterphobic) who are equally afraid, would be more likely to undertake a kamikaze mission and seal themselves into the plane."

In my experience, no Six is entirely phobic or counterphobic, which can be confusing for Sixes and for their friends and family. For example, Clive is a Six whom I met on a Leadership and the Enneagram program for Heathrow Airport in London. Clive had taken his Enneagram test and was undecided about his Ennea-Type. "I'm either a Six, Eight, or Four," he told me. Clive worked in the Health and Safety Department. When I finished talking about Type Six, he pulled out a book from his briefcase entitled *Aviation Disasters: The World's Major Civil Airliner Crashes Since 1940 (4th Edition).* "Might this be a sign I am Six?" he said with a smile. Clive is counterphobic at work. He is a troubleshooter who seeks to identify possible hazards and risks to people's safety. However, Clive is phobic in his personal life. He hasn't been in a committed romantic relationship since his wife left him over 15 years ago, mostly because he doesn't want to get hurt again.

Sixes are dealing with the same basic fear whether they are more phobic or counterphobic. My friend Susan Jeffers was more of a counterphobic Six. Susan wrote the bestseller *Feel the Fear and Do It Anyway*. "When I was younger, I was always run by fear," she wrote in her Introduction. She continued, "My fear never seemed to abate, and I didn't have a moment's peace. Even my doctorate in psychology didn't seem to do me much good." Susan's turning point came when she made up her mind to face her fears rather than to keep on trying to suppress or ignore them. "I realized I had to befriend my fears instead of seeing them as my enemy," she told me. Susan moved toward her fears, and in doing so she taught millions of people how to be less afraid of fear and be more courageous and authentic.

> *Remember that underlying all our fears is a lack of trust in ourselves.*
> — Susan Jeffers

When Sixes are gripped by the basic fear of not being supported or without guidance, it may cause them to lack Self-trust, block their intuition, be skeptical and cynical, and make fear-driven decisions. Here are a few things Sixes have told me about living with their basic fear:

- "I prepare for worst-case scenarios."
- "I would never walk under a ladder."
- "I like knowing where the Safety Exit is."
- "I still have my childhood security blanket."
- "I like a challenge, but I'm also risk averse."
- "My mind gets quickly hijacked by fear."
- "I test people to see if they really love me."
- "I am surprisingly steady in scary situations."
- "My sense of humor is my saving grace."
- "The next disaster is around the corner."

Childhood Story: Eyes Wide Open

My daughter Bo, who is a Six on the Enneagram, was born with her eyes wide open. "She doesn't want to close her eyes," said Hollie, my wife, as she handed her to me. Bo kept her steady gaze fixed on me while I held her tiny body in my hands. Her eyes were locked on me. I felt like I was under surveillance and being scanned by someone with X-ray vision. Young Sixes are typically wide-eyed, observant, and alert. They scan their environment, using their eyes like a CCTV camera, to take in every detail. Their watchful eye helps them to be fully oriented and aware of the situation they find themselves in. Sixes want to feel safe and secure in their surroundings.

Young Sixes are born with a question mark over their head. They are quizzical and cautious from the outset. They are normally very chatty and full of questions. Early childhood research observes that young children of all types and temperaments ask on average 300 questions a day; I'd add an extra 20 percent on to that figure for Type Sixes. I remember how questions came tumbling out of my daughter Bo's mouth as soon as she could speak. At first, it was mostly "What's that?" questions, as she pointed to a butterfly, a rainbow, a hairclip, or a pencil sharpener. Then came the more practical questions about how things work and then probing cross-examinations about why things are the way they are.

Young Sixes are not just on a fact-finding mission when they ask questions. There is a much deeper purpose to their questioning. Our children's kindergarten teacher, Leigha Hipkin, once explained to me: "When a child is asking questions, they are learning to recognize their own voice. Not just their physical voice, but the voice of their True Self." Leigha told me, "By asking questions, children are sharpening their intuition and fine-tuning their capacity to recognize truth and wisdom."

From a young age, Sixes are training their intuition so that they can navigate themselves safely through life. As they grow up, they will encounter many authority figures, such as parents and grandparents, uncles and aunts, and nannies and teachers. Sadly, not every authority figure is a wise wizard like Gandalf or a good witch like Glinda. If a Six is fortunate, they will be raised by healthy authority figures who encourage them to build Self-trust, practice inner listening, and seek guidance from people who are reliable. However, if Sixes run into unhealthy authority figures, they might give their power away to these people and will enter adulthood with self-doubt, their intuition squashed, and seeking validation and support from the wrong people.

The "Be Safe" Driver: Young Sixes are born with a persistent "Be Safe" driver installed in their ego operating system. They want to know "Am I safe?" and their questioning mind keeps them alert to potential threats and dangers. *Can an electric shock kill you? Can you drown from drinking too much water? Is there* *a monster under the bed? Has an earthquake ever happened here?* On the evening before my daughter Bo's first day of school, I asked her how she was feeling. She was five years old at the time. "I do have some questions, Daddy," she said. Her first question, which was two questions in one, was, "Does the school have a fire alarm, and what should I do if it goes off?"

Going to school is a big deal for every child. For Sixes, the school drop-off can be especially difficult, as it can bring up feelings of separation anxiety. "I used to hug my mum and dad so tight because I was so afraid I wouldn't see them again," said Martin, a Six, recalling his early school days. Once a young Six walks through the school gate, they encounter a world that their parents are not part of. In this new landscape, they seek to attach themselves to a teacher who is kind and fair, and to make friends with children who appear to be confident and capable, or who are even more anxious than they are.

Let's look at some examples of how the "Be Safe" driver operates for Sixes in the three biological instincts: (1) Self-Preservation Instinct (SP), which is mostly about lifestyle, material matters, and self-care; (2) Social Instinct (SO), which is mostly about relating to family, society, and the world; and (3) (SX) Sexual Instinct (also called One-to-One Instinct), which is mostly about attraction, relating style, and romance.

> **Self-Preservation Instinct (SP)** *Healthy:* Your chief concern is physical safety and survival. You work hard and are sharp-eyed when it comes to household bills, bank account statements, family health insurance, and a possible leak in the roof. At work or on the school run, you might worry about, *"Did I put the burglar alarm on?"*, *"Did I switch the oven off?"*, and *"Are the fire alarm batteries working?" Not-so-healthy:* An SP Six has a more phobic tendency than an SO Six and an SX Six. *It's a jungle out there!* It's you against the world. New friends must pass a safety check or security test. *Are they friend or foe?* When new friends make it into your circle of trust, you are less secretive and confide in them about your own fears and worries. *Unhealthy:* Your anxiety flares up quickly around money matters and health issues. Even with a steady income, you scare yourself silly with thoughts about poverty being around the corner. You can be a bit of hypochondriac, and worry yourself sick researching physical symptoms late at night on the Internet.

Social Instinct (SO) *Healthy:* You approach people with warmth and friendliness. *I am a friend, not a foe.* You gain a lot of strength and support from making allies. You believe in the adage "there is safety in numbers." You like to feel plugged in to your family. You initiate regular contact with friends. You stay in touch with old acquaintances. You are a strong networker at work. You like your independence but also like being part of a well-established organization, institution, or profession. *Not-so-healthy:* You have trouble with divided loyalties. For example, you are invited to two parties on the same night. *What should I do?* Your boss wants you to work late, but it's your date night with your partner. *Who will I let down?* Both your children think the other one is your favorite. *I just can't win!* A colleague asks you to cover up a transgression. *Who should I be loyal to? Unhealthy:* Your misplaced loyalty leads to self-sacrifice and self-betrayal. You stay in a safe job for too long. You hold on to friendships that aren't good for you. You remain in social groups that you've outgrown and are holding you back.

Sexual Instinct (SX) *Healthy:* An SX Six is typically more counterphobic than an SP Six or SO Six. They are assertive and adventurous. Their mantra is: "Fortune favors the brave." They feel the fear and go for it anyway! *What's the worst that could happen?* They take a risk, pick up the phone, apply for the promotion, and ask the most beautiful person in the room out on a date. *Not-so-healthy:* An SX Six can resemble a stoic Type One, be intensely romantic like a Type Four, and be strong and confident like a Type Eight. But their "Be Safe" driver is always switched on. The more they try to conceal their self-doubt and anxiety, the more insecure and angsty they are. They stop believing in themselves, they test the people they love, they constantly seek reassurance, and they fear rejection and betrayal. *Unhealthy:* An SX Six can be very reckless and risk everything on bad advice, an impulsive gamble, and poor decision-making. Their psychology is overrun with cynicism, pessimism, and paranoia. When they are untethered and have lost their thread, they are erratic, unreliable, and a danger to themselves and others.

Passion: Angst

All nine Types on the Enneagram experience a *passion*, or cause of suffering in the heart, that emerges from a sense of separation and from the basic fear.

The passion for Sixes is commonly called *fear* or *anxiety*. I prefer to use the words *angst* or *anguish* because I believe it conveys more accurately the intensity of the passion.

Shakespeare's *Hamlet* is a play about existential angst. Hamlet's soliloquy "To be or not to be" is the best-known soliloquy in the world and is called the soliloquy of angst. We can all relate to angst, regardless of our type. Angst is an experience of faintheartedness. It arises from the fear of not knowing what to do. Hamlet's angst is also compounded by feelings of aloneness. Hamlet delivers many soliloquies. The Latin root word for soliloquy is *solus*, which means "alone." In one of Hamlet's soliloquys, he cries, "O, what a rogue and peasant slave am I." Fear has got the better of him. He has lost faith in himself. He is lacking in what psychologist Erik Erikson called "the virtue of hope," which comes from basic trust in yourself and in life. In his anguish, Hamlet becomes hesitant, covert, suspicious, approval-seeking, paranoid, and is at a loss as to how to proceed.

Sixes typically report that they feel angst right from the get-go. "I seem to have come out of the womb with existential angst and I wasn't a happy kid," said Marci Shimoff, the #1 *New York Times* best-selling author and much-loved teacher of psychology and personal growth. Marci is a Six and a big fan of the Enneagram. She was my guest at the International Enneagram Association annual conference, held in San Francisco. During lunch she told me, "As a Six, I've had to do deep emotional healing work on my angst. Eventually, I realized I had a choice. Either I use my angst as a reason to play safe and say no to my miraculous life, or I befriend my angst and make it a powerful ally that helps me to live in the miracle zone where good things happen because I'm courageous, compassionate, and ready to say yes to life."

> *To be, or not to be, that is the question: Whether 'tis nobler in the mind to suffer The slings and arrows of outrageous fortune, Or to take arms against a sea of troubles . . .*
>
> — Hamlet

The passion of angst can be either a friend or foe, depending on your attitude to it. So, let's take a closer look at angst to understand it better, and be less afraid of it. Here are five ways angst can show up, especially for Sixes.

Feeling Lost. Many Sixes report that their angst comes from feeling lost and not knowing what path to take. Dante's *The Divine Comedy* begins: "In the middle of the journey of our life I came to myself within a dark wood where the direct way was lost." Feeling lost can be scary, but it can also be a good thing. When you admit you are lost, doors open within, and you become more receptive to guidance, inspiration, and support. Louise Hay, a Six, told me, "I always felt a little lost in the world until I found my inner ding [her intuition]." She said, "Listening to my inner ding helps me to trust that I am One with the power that created me, and that I am not abandoned or helpless."

Self-Sufficiency. Many Sixes suffer from angst because they confuse self-reliance with self-sufficiency. Self-reliance is about cultivating Self-trust, listening to your intuition, and making wise decisions. Self-sufficiency is more about trying to do life all by yourself, without asking for any help. In *A Course in Miracles*, which is a book about fear and love, it says, "If you are trusting [only] in your own strength, you have every reason to be apprehensive, anxious and fearful." It also says, "If you knew Who walks beside you on the way that you have chosen, fear would be impossible." A wise Six sees fear as a sign that you are doing life too much by yourself and that you need to ask for help.

Cowardice. Oscar Ichazo, the pioneer of the Enneagram of types, used the word *cowardice* to describe the ego-fixation for Sixes, which we'll look at in the next section. It's a close call, but I think cowardice resonates more with the passion for Sixes. Cowardice is a feeling of faint heartedness. It is *the fear of facing your fears*. In the *Wizard of Oz* stories, the cowardly lion believes he has no courage, but that isn't so. When he puts himself in harm's way to protect his friends, he realizes an inner strength that was always there. In facing his fears, his courage was activated in him, and his view of himself was changed.

Pre-Traumatic Stress. Sixes experience angst when they anticipate emotional pain and heartbreak. Actress Helen Mirren once described the feeling of "pre-traumatic stress" or "premature anxiety" when she said, "There is that awful moment when you realize that you're falling in love. This should be the most joyful moment, and actually it's not. It's always a moment that's full of fear because you know, as night follows day, that joy is going to rapidly be followed by some pain or other. All the angst of a relationship." The underlying fear of pre-traumatic stress is that you won't survive emotional pain or heartbreak. But the truth is you will, especially if you trust yourself, listen to your heart wisdom, and let yourself be supported.

Fear of Uncertainty. I have a friend who is a Six that always reads the last chapter of a novel first. "I like to know how things will end," she told me. When Sixes are lacking in Self-trust, their need for certainty increases and can be paralyzing. For example, they want a total guarantee that a relationship will work before they commit, and they want a risk-free investment or nothing. They suffer from anxious hesitation and a postponement of action. Their faintheartedness keeps them safe, but it means they're not living wholeheartedly and flourishing. *Surely, there is more to life than playing it safe, isn't there?*

Fixation: Overthinking

In the Enneagram, the *fixation* refers to a mental habit that causes an imbalance in your mental health and well-being. The fixation for Sixes has been named by different Enneagram teachers as fear, anxiety, and cowardice. Because the fixation is specifically about a persistent habit that disturbs mental well-being, I prefer to use another name: "overthinking."

When Sixes are not in a good headspace, it's often because they have "lost the thread" to their inner guidance and are being pulled in different directions by their thoughts. They overthink, run around in circles, play devil's advocate, invalidate themselves, and get lost in their thinking. Sixes are also known for being caught in two minds, so to speak. They oscillate between being committed and cautious, open and skeptical, dutiful and rebellious, steadfast and ambivalent, friendly and curmudgeon, and heroic and timid.

> *Hold on, let me overthink this!*
>
> — saying on a coffee mug

Who taught you how to think? It doesn't matter what type we are; most of us get into trouble with our thinking at some point. We all suffer from psychology, so to speak. Most of the thoughts we think are not our real thoughts. They are primarily a gaggle of judgments, criticisms, worries, doubts, and fears. Working with the Enneagram helps you to be aware of your mental habits and to notice if your internal chatter is helping or scaring you. When you observe your mind, you see that your thinking is either fear-based or love-centered. A good question to ask yourself is *"Am I thinking with fear or with love?"* and *"Is my thinking ego-driven or soul-centered?"*

"I had to teach myself how to think," Louise Hay told me while we were writing *Life Loves You*. In a chapter on Affirming Your Life, I said to Louise, "Imagine you could teach one class to every child on this planet: What would it be?" Louise clapped her hands with joy. "Oh, what a good question!" she said. She then became very still. Louise would always ground herself in her body and quieten her mind when she wanted to think an especially good thought. "I'd teach a class on 'Making Friends with Your Mind,'" Louise told me with a big smile. She went on, "And parents and teachers would have to come too. And the first thing I'd teach them is *"you are the only thinker in your mind, and you can choose if your thoughts are true or not."*"

> *We cannot escape fear. We can only transform it into a companion that accompanies us on all our exciting adventures.*
>
> — Susan Jeffers

Changing your relationship to your mind changes how you experience your life. This inner change starts with self-awareness. Here are five observations about how the fixation of overthinking plays out for Sixes.

Attachment to Anxiety. "My problem is that I get anxious when I'm not anxious, and I get afraid when I'm not afraid," said Tracy, a Six, a lawyer who took one of my Enneagram programs. Sixes run into trouble when they overidentify with their fear and anxiety. They tell themselves that "fear keeps me safe" and "being anxious keeps me alert." But their constant anxiety and fearfulness can also cause mental instability and physical illness. Healthier options include practicing daily self-care, listening to your intuition more, and learning about mindfulness.

The Negativity Bias. Psychologists recognize that everyone has a negativity bias that makes them alert to danger and keeps them safe. The negativity bias is in our genes, so to speak, and is part of our survival instinct. Sixes are known for "accentuating the negative." They overlook present happiness and rob themselves of joy by focusing on potential dangers real or imagined. "I hate playgrounds. They are an accident waiting to happen," said Jo, a Six, as we sat together watching our two young children play.

Worst-Case-Scenario Thinking. Sixes are the Ennea-Type most likely to own a copy of *The Worst-Case Scenario Handbook*. You know, the book that gives you valuable tips on how to deliver a baby in a taxicab, how to escape from killer bees, and how to survive an out-of-control driverless car. It's one thing to be prepared, but it's quite another to keep scaring yourself silly with imagined scenarios. "I've had a lot of worries in life, most of which have never happened," is a quote attributed to Mark Twain.

Playing Devil's Advocate. When Sixes overthink, they ask lots of questions, but haven't the presence of mind to listen for answers. Their mind jumps around from one point of view to the next, without taking anything in. They play devil's advocate, assume an opposite point of view, and debate things endlessly. This may look intellectually smart or clever, but it's mostly fear-based, directionless thinking. Playing devil's advocate can be constructive, but only if it is a choice, not a compulsion. A good question to ask is, *Why does the devil need an advocate anyway?*

Doubt Attacks. Sixes often experience what Enneagram teacher Helen Palmer calls "doubt attacks." A doubt attack is when the mind is flooded with fear, doubt, worry, and negative self-talk. A Six may write off their chances of success before they take a driving test or go for a job interview, for example. "I just know I won't succeed," they say. And then they pass with flying colors. "I really should believe in myself more," they say. But because Sixes have an "amnesia of success," another Helen Palmer term, they go through the same self-doubt time after time.

PATH OF GUIDANCE

> *There is a thread you follow. It goes among things that change. But it doesn't change . . . and you don't ever let go of the thread.*
>
> — William Stafford, "The Way It Is"

The Enneagram offers a path of growth for all nine Types that helps you to remember your original nature and be your True Self. The path of growth for Sixes has to do with guidance.

When I teach about Point Six on the Enneagram, I give everyone a piece of golden thread to wear on their wrist. The idea is to use the golden thread as a mindfulness practice for paying attention to your life and recognizing when you are being pulled by what Heraclitus called "the intelligence that steers all things." Your golden thread is a spiritual anchor that reminds you that you are not alone, and that guidance and support are always available to you. It may be invisible to the naked eye, but it is always with you. It ties you to your purpose, and it pulls you toward people you are destined to meet, books that inspire you, songs with important lyrics, and places you need to go.

Your golden thread connects you to your "inner voice" and "inner knowing," which are two terms that Carl Jung used when describing how intuition works. Both your inner voice and inner knowing belong to your psyche, which is the essence of you. This means that you come to earth fully equipped with an internal GPS system to guide you, but only if you learn to recognize it and trust it. Jung wrote in *Man and His Symbols*, "Somewhere, right at the bottom of one's own being, one generally does know where one should go and what one should do. But there are times when the clown we call 'I' behaves in such a distracting fashion that the inner voice cannot make its presence felt."

The Enneagram offers Sixes a treasury of deep inquiries, meditation practices, and practical exercises to help them be more soul-centered, trust their sixth sense, embrace uncertainty, affirm the positive, and trust life.

Virtue: Courage

Every Ennea-Type has a virtue, or a superpower, that arises naturally as you do your inner work to heal the basic fear, the passion in the heart, and the fixation in your thinking. The virtue for Sixes is courage.

In Greek philosophy, Plato wrote a Socratic dialogue called *Laches* that presents a debate about what courage is and is not. Socrates presides over the debate. All the parties agree that courage is a noble virtue, but the dialogue ends in *aporia*, which means an impasse, confusion, and puzzlement. No one can "get their head around" courage, because courage is more than a mental concept or an idea. The word *courage* in Old French *corage* and the Latin root *cor* both denote "heart." Courage comes from the heart. It is also a soul quality that is called *thumos* (also spelled *thymos*), which means "spirited and vivacious."

> *Courage is the finest of human qualities because it is the quality which guarantees the others.*
> — Aristotle

When I teach about the virtue of courage on my Enneagram programs, I recommend to everyone, and especially to Sixes, that they read Paul Tillich's classic work *The Courage to Be*. In it, he identifies several different threads of anxiety, including the anxiety of emptiness, meaninglessness, and death. Tillich describes anxiety as "the sting of fear" and explains that the true antidote to anxiety is courage. *The Courage to Be* starts with a summary of Plato's dialogue *Laches,* and then sweeps through the centuries, gathering up inspiration from the Stoic philosophers, from Shakespeare's *Hamlet*, from the works of Spinoza and Nietzsche, and from Arthur Miller's *Death of a Salesman*. He also adds his own deeply mystical thoughts and conclusions on courage.

Here are five reflections on the virtue of courage, featuring some of Tillich's ideas as well as others.

Self-Affirmation. For Tillich, courage is not mental; it is ontological. In other words, courage arises not from your thinking mind, but from the ground of your being. Therefore, courage comes naturally when you are grounded in your I AM, your true nature. "Courage is the universal and essential self-affirmation of one's being," wrote Tillich. Courage is a quality of the soul, and when you are loyal to your soul, you are filled with Self-trust and with an inner knowing that life is guiding you on your journey.

Being Authentic. Tillich's self-affirmation closely resembles Emerson's self-reliance. Both encourage you to trust yourself and use your inner wisdom to make authentic choices. Emerson wrote, "Insist on yourself; never imitate." He said courage comes from being faithful to your innate talent, not "the adopted talent of another." "Nothing is at last sacred but the integrity of your own mind," wrote Emerson. More wise counsel for Sixes comes from *Hamlet* and in Polonius's speech to his son Laertes that begins, "This above all: to thine own self be true."

Being Wholehearted. A big "aha" for Sixes is to realize that the more centered you are in your heart, the less afraid you are. When Sixes go deep into their heart, they discover their heart wisdom. They hear the Voice of Love that is their companion and guide. For Sixes, much fear arises from being half-hearted and from only half-expressing yourself. The more you speak your truth, the safer you are. It can be frightening to speak your truth, but if you really think about it, it's more frightening not to.

> *Speak your mind, even if your voice shakes.*
> — Maggie Kuhn, founder of the Gray Panthers

Saying YES. Sixes often hesitate to say yes right away. They prefer to say "Maybe," "Let's see," and "I'll let you know." This buys them time to gather their thoughts and make up their own mind. Sixes who don't listen to their inner knowing may dither and delay decision-making indefinitely. Sixes who trust their inner guidance find it easier to say a courageous yes or no. One of Louise Hay's favorite affirmations is "I trust my inner wisdom. I say no when I want to say no, and I say yes when I want to say yes."

And Action! Sixes are known for their postponement of action. They think about what to do but don't act. One reason why Sixes procrastinate is that they're waiting for courage to happen. But courage is activated only after you commit yourself. When you take a step, a bridge appears, just like in the scene from *Indiana Jones and the Last Crusade*, when Harrison Ford, the reluctant hero, steps out into the abyss, and his foot lands on a bridge that was always there but could not be seen until he took a step of faith.

Balancing Your Centers

The Enneagram encourages you to work with all three centers of intelligence—head center, heart center, and body center—to help you be happy, healthy, and wise. Sixes are called a Head Type (along with Fives and Sevens) because your primary center of intelligence is the head center. As a healthy Six, you are drawn to mindfulness practices that put you in a good headspace by grounding you in your body and centering you in your heart. Sixes know from experience that the head, heart, and body are like three allies—"All for one, and one for all"—who need each other's support to promote well-being and optimal functioning.

Head Center. When Sixes spend too much in their head center, their "thinking engine" overheats. Their mind goes into overdrive. Their thoughts spin out of control. Their perception is dizzy and distorted. They become irrational and may start to "awfulize" and "catastrophize"—two terms coined by cognitive psychologist Albert Ellis—which exaggerates worst-case scenarios and increases fear. A daily mindfulness practice that includes physical activity, such as a nature walk, a yoga class, singing in a choir, gardening, knitting, or crocheting, can help the head center to cool down, reset, and come back online.

> *If overthinking were a sport, I would be a world champion!*
> — Anonymous

The Heart Center. Jon Kabat-Zinn, the pioneer of mindfulness, notes that "In Asian languages the word for *mind* and the word for *heart* are the same." He goes on, "Mindfulness is about love and loving life. When you cultivate this love, it gives you clarity and compassion for life, and your actions happen in accordance with that." Healthy Sixes drop into their heart center to listen for wisdom, direction, and guidance. Listening to their heart wisdom helps Sixes to be faithful to themselves, befriend their fears, and think less and love more. Love is intelligent, and when you let your thinking be guided by love, it helps you to feel safe and secure.

The Body Center. Healthy Sixes look after their body. They exercise regularly, eat healthily, and get a good night's sleep to regulate their body's nervous system and be ready for a new day. They listen with love to their body's messages. They trust their intuition. They follow their gut instinct. They honor the wisdom in their bones. When Sixes feel safe in their body, they feel safe in the world. "My body loves me. I appreciate my body's wisdom. And I trust my body to guide me," wrote Louise Hay.

Spreading Your Wings

Type Six's home base is Point Six, which sits between Point Five and Point Seven on the Enneagram symbol. This means Sixes have a 5-Wing and a 7-Wing. Typically, one wing is more dominant than the other, but the goal is to balance your wings. Working with the 5-Wing can help Sixes to tap into the essential qualities and wisdom of Point Five, and working with the 7-Wing can help Sixes to access the same at Point Seven. Learning to live in balance with your wings, by drawing strengths and lessons from both, can be very helpful for Sixes.

Six with a 5-Wing

Sixes with a dominant 5-Wing (6w5) are commonly called the Guardian or Defender. They show up in the world with the typical traits of Six, plus some traits of Fives. For example:

> **Original Thinker.** A 6w5 embraces the mental attributes of Fives such as basic openness, perceptiveness, ingenuity, and innovative thinking. A 6w5 is not easily swayed by the thoughts and opinions of others. *I am the originator of my thoughts.* Your mind is a powerful

tool, and it works best when it is in your own hands and not someone else's. "I affirm every day, *I am in charge of mind, and I have the power to think great thoughts,*" says Jane, a 6w5, who is a psychologist and author.

Your Inner Genius. Everyone has a capacity for genius. The Latin root for genius is "to beget, bring forth," and it refers to "an attendant inner spirit assigned to every person at birth." For a 6w5, their genius is the ability to think deeply and see things as they really are. In his essay "Self-Reliance," Ralph Waldo Emerson encouraged readers to engage with their inner genius. He wrote, "To believe your own thought, to believe that what is true for you in your private heart is true for all men—that is genius."

The Problem Solver. A 6w5 uses their mental ingenuity to solve problems. They are naturally attracted to mathematics, philosophy, and ways of thinking that address the question, "How best shall I live?" "As a child, I became obsessed with the Rubik's Cube. I convinced myself that if I could solve the Rubik's Cube, I had the ability to solve every other problem that came my way," said Steve, a 6w5, whom I met at Coaching and the Enneagram. Every problem has a solution, and you don't always have to find the solution by yourself.

The Practical Philosopher. Most 6w5s are practical philosophers. They want to apply their thinking to the problems of the day and participate actively in politics, law, ethics, and education, for instance. "To know and not to do, is not to know," said Goethe a thought echoed by other philosophers such as Jiddu Krishnamurti and Alan Watts. "What's the use of being able to recite the Psalms if you don't know how to fix a flat tire or know someone who can?" says Tim, a 6w5, who is a college lecturer.

Analysis Paralysis. A 6w5 is typically more introverted and withdrawn than a 6w7. They can spend a lot of time locked away in their mind, working on problems, solving riddles, playing computer games. They are also prone to analysis paralysis, which leads to excessive analyzing and an inability to decide or act. And too much overthinking creates problems that don't exist. For 6w5s, the inner work is to think less and live more. It's good to remind yourself to *get out of your head and come out to play.*

Six with a 7-Wing

Sixes with a dominant 7-Wing (6w7) are commonly called the Buddy or Friend. They show up in the world with the typical traits of Six, plus some traits of Sevens. For example:

Positive Outlook. A 6w7 embraces the upbeat energy of Point Seven which is optimistic, buoyant, hopeful, and grateful for life. The positive energy of Point Seven balances the inherent Negativity Bias in Sixes. It helps them to look for positive outcomes in difficult situations. "When I get confused, I train my mind to be positive by asking questions like, *What is the highest thought I can be thinking right now?"* says Karen, a 6w7, who is a psychotherapist.

Being Spontaneous. As a 6w7 you may be anxious about life and worry about the future, but you also seize the day, live in the moment, and say yes to the present. The wisdom of Point Seven encourages you to live in the *now*. It's good to be prepared, but one should also leave room for spontaneity and unplanned happiness. Louise Hay, a 6w7, once told me: "I begin the day with gratitude. And I trust that good things will come to me in delightful and surprising ways."

Extraverted Energy. A 6w7 tends to be more outgoing, social, and communicative than 6w5. They are less insular and more out-and-about in the world. They are less self-sufficient and more collaborative. They share their anxieties and concerns more freely with others. They believe in the idiom: "A problem shared is a problem halved." Think of the lyrics in the Beatles' song "With a Little Help from My Friends." They also make great "Ride or Die" friends, who will be there for you no matter what.

A Higher Plan. The Holy Idea at Point Seven is called the Holy Plan. A 6w7 who works with the higher energies of Point Seven learns to trust the Higher Plan for their life. Susan Jeffers, a 6w7, once told me, "When I trust in a higher plan for my life, I can embrace uncertainty, and this helps me be more open to guidance and inspiration." If your plan isn't working out, maybe life has a better plan for you.

A Racing Mind. A 6w7 can take on some of the unhealthy traits of Sevens, such as hurry sickness, a hyperactive mind, and racing thoughts. The energy at Point Seven requires focus, or it can send the mind spinning in all directions. Thoughts bounce around like a pinball. You feel "at sixes and sevens," which is an old idiom that describes being confused, disorganized, and in disarray. Slowing down, and stilling your mind, will get you back in sync with your inner knowing.

Moving to Nine and Three

Following the Inner Lines of the Enneagram Symbol, Sixes move toward Point Nine (home for The Peacemaker) and Point Three (home of the Achiever). These Inner Lines invite you to visit these Points to explore the gifts and wisdom they have for you.

Moving to Nine

When Sixes go to Point Nine, they access some of the higher qualities that Nines are blessed with. For example:

> **Inner Peace.** The invitation at Point Nine is to connect with the inner peace that exists at the vital core of your being. Sixes benefit greatly from having a regular mindfulness practice that promotes inner peace, e.g., a breathing exercise, a meditation for inner calm, a guided meditation, or a yoga flow.
>
> **Engagement.** The virtue for Nines is called engagement. It takes courage to engage more fully in your life, but doing so also gives you courage to keep going. "All our dreams can come true, if we

have the courage to pursue them," said Walt Disney, a Nine. A helpful daily engagement practice for Sixes is to commit to one daily act of courage. *One way I can be brave today is . . .*

More Embodied. Nines are Body Types on the Enneagram, along with Eights and Ones. A visit to Point Nine is a great reminder for Sixes to be more embodied, prioritize physical wellness, ensure quality sleep, eat healthily, stretch your body, sit under a tree, and be in nature, especially when life is stressful and overwhelming.

When Sixes are stressed, they may exhibit unhealthy qualities displayed by Nines. Knowing about these unhealthy qualities can help Sixes to be more mindful and grounded as they go about their day. For example:

Comfort Zone. Unhealthy Nines are known for living too much inside their comfort zone. They do this to avoid conflict and hold fast to inner peace. Similarly, Sixes try to avoid fear and anxiety by playing safe. A good inquiry for Sixes is to spot the dangers of always playing safe. "Do what you fear and your fear will die," is a line attributed to Emerson.

Reluctant Hero. Sixes are a lot like Nines, who are often hesitant and reluctant to commit to their life. They are like Neo, the character played by Keanu Reeves in *The Matrix,* who is full of self-doubt and ambivalence. "You have to let it all go, Neo. Fear, doubt, and disbelief. Free your mind," says Morpheus to Neo.

Day Dreaming. Unhealthy Sixes, like Unhealthy Nines, will dream big, but not convert their dreams into action. When they fail to act, they may end up like the fictional character Walter Mitty, who has plenty of heroic daydreams but nothing real to show for it. "Don't be pushed by your problems. Be led by your dreams," said Emerson.

Moving to Three

When Sixes move to Point Three, they discover some of the higher qualities that Threes are blessed with. For example:

Inner Directed. The invitation for Sixes at Point Three is to have the courage to be yourself and live an authentic life. One way to do this is to listen within for "the sound of the genuine," a term coined by Howard Thurman, and let yourself be guided and directed by your inner voice. *Authenticity is the courage to be yourself.*

True to Myself. The virtue for Threes is called veracity or truthfulness. The Disney film *Mulan* is based on the legendary Chinese female warrior Hua Mulan, who has lots of Six and Three energy. Mulan's inner journey is from fear to love. She overcomes her self-doubt by listening to her heart and embracing her True Self. Mulan summons inner strength by asking herself regularly, *"Am I loyal, brave, and true?"*

Action-Oriented. Sixes and Threes both want to participate in a worthwhile cause and greater purpose. "I wanna be in the room where it happens," sings Aaron Burr, a character from *Hamilton*, the Broadway musical. The energy at Point Three helps Sixes to be more action oriented and balance contemplation with action.

Also at Point Three, Sixes are made aware of the unhealthy qualities of Type Threes. These act as a warning for Sixes. For example:

Busy Workaholic. Unhealthy Sixes resemble unhealthy Threes, who are manic, busy, and hyperactive. Their constant busyness is usually driven by fear and insecurity. Sixes get over-busy when they don't have faith in themselves, they won't trust life, and they haven't the presence of mind to listen to their inner knowing.

Self-Betrayal. Both Sixes and Threes feel a terrible sense of self-betrayal when they are not true to themselves and don't take the road less traveled. "If you do not express your own original ideas, if you do not listen to your own being, you will have betrayed yourself," wrote Rollo May in *The Courage to Create*.

Half-Heartedness. The Sufi poet Rumi spoke of the dangers of half-heartedness. He said, "Half-heartedness does not reach into majesty. Gamble everything for love, if you are a true human being. If not, leave this gathering." Sixes and Threes must give up their cool self-image, their mask of composure, if they are to live courageously and experience love.

HOLY FAITH

> *Faith is an act of a finite being who is grasped by, and turned to, the infinite.*
>
> — Paul Tillich

The nine Points on the Enneagram each offer a Holy Idea—a universal teaching and higher wisdom—for all nine Ennea-Types to contemplate and practice. Point Six has two Holy Ideas. They are Holy Faith and Holy Strength.

Holy Faith is a joyful feeling of self-affirmation that arises in you from the core of your being. Holy Faith is more than a belief; it is a direct knowing—an inner realization—that you are well made and that even though you have doubts and fears, you are fully equipped to live a good life. The spiritual DNA of your being is packed with Divine Natural Abilities that will support you in your efforts to be wise, courageous, and loving. "Living with my Sixiness isn't always easy, but I also love my Sixiness," says Bo, my daughter. "Life is often scary, but I've learned to listen to my inner voice, and I can tell when I make decisions based on wisdom or fear. I'm also learning to trust life more and to see that life really does want the best for all of us."

Holy Faith is a state of openness and trust. It arises in you when you feel the unshakable bond between your psyche and the cosmos. It comes from "the reunion of the separated," as Paul Tillich puts it. We are fearful when we lose our mooring to our being and feel cut adrift in the universe. But Holy Faith restores the feeling of "basic trust" that psychologists like Erik Erikson speak of. Basic trust is an optimizing force that helps you to trust yourself, follow the golden thread, and let yourself be steered and supported.

> *There is but one cause of human failure. And that is man's lack of faith in his true Self.*
>
> — William James

Holy Faith affirms that you are a child of the universe, and that life loves you. While writing our book *Life Loves You*, I asked Louise Hay about faith. She told me, "I've lived life without faith and with faith. I highly recommend living with faith!" When I asked what faith meant to her, she said, "Faith means knowing that I am lovable, and that life loves me." As we continued to explore faith, we got on to the topic of the friendly universe.

"Is the universe friendly?" I asked Louise.

"There's only one way to find out," she said.

"What way is that?"

"Say yes," she said with a smile.

"What do you mean?"

"If you answer no, you'll never find out if the universe is friendly," she said.

"Because if you say no, you won't see it."

"Exactly. But if you say yes, then you might."

"It's all in the answer."

"The answer is in us," said Louise.

And what about Holy Strength? Well, Holy Strength is the reward you get for practicing Holy Faith. When you place your faith in your I AM and in the intelligence that steers the universe, you discover a strength of spirit within you. Holy Strength increases as you make the inner shift from being ego-driven to soul-centered. Life is impermanent, and full of trials and difficulties, but you are blessed with an inexhaustible inner strength to carry you. When you call upon this Holy Strength, it helps you in delightful and surprising ways, and you discover to your great joy that you have what it takes to grow up and be the person you truly want to be.

> *What lies behind you and what lies in front of you,*
> *pales in comparison to what lies inside of you.*
>
> – Ralph Waldo Emerson

Type Seven
THE ENTHUSIAST

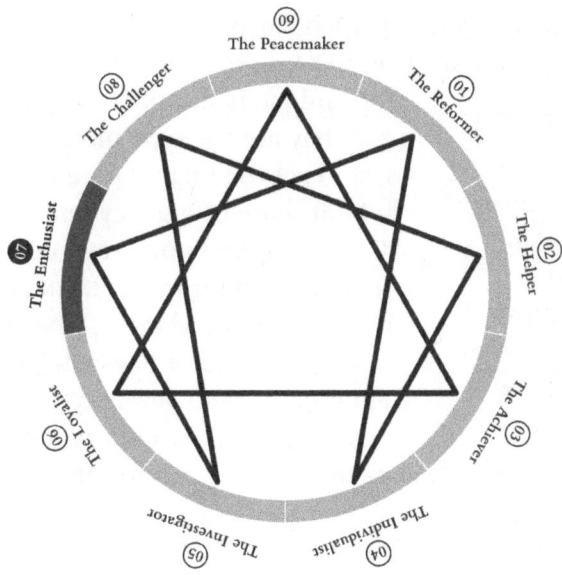

*We shall not cease from exploration
And the end of all our exploring
Will be to arrive where we started
And know the place for the first time.*

— T. S. Eliot, "Little Gidding"

The Ennea-Type Seven is commonly called Enthusiast or Adventurer. Other names for Sevens include Epicure, Joyful Soul, Adventure-Seeker, Pilgrim, Producer, and Energizer.

Type Sevens are the *Highly Enthusiastic, Adventurous Type*. They are known for their upbeat energy, spirit of adventure, positive mindset, fun-loving attitude, and low boredom threshold. Sevens are the most naturally carbonated of all nine Ennea-Types. They are effervescent and full of energy. Sevens really don't need to drink coffee. "I drink espresso to relax," says my friend Paul, a Seven. Sevens are full of life and aim to live life to the full. They are life's great maximizers and are always hungry for more. A 25-hour day would be a wonderful thing. Being able to bilocate would be handy. Sevens are known for being focused and scattered, happy and restless, upbeat and anxious, ready to seize the day, and afraid of missing out.

Sevens see life as a journey. Each day is a new adventure. Their mantra is: "Don't let a day go wasted!" They like to keep their options open. They live with forward momentum. They are constantly on the go. They are the type most likely to skip breakfast to get their day started faster. They have an inbuilt sense of urgency and a Freddie Mercury "Don't stop me now!" attitude. They get easily frustrated and impatient, like Donkey in *Shrek*, played by Eddie Murphy, who keeps asking, *"Are we there yet? Are we there yet?"* Working with the Enneagram helps Sevens to see that life is a journey, not a race. The Enneagram takes Sevens on a journey of self-discovery that helps them stop chasing after happiness and find joy wherever they go.

> *We are travelers on a cosmic journey, stardust, swirling and dancing in the eddies and whirlpools of infinity.*
>
> — Deepak Chopra,
> *The Seven Spiritual Laws*

When Sevens look for an Enneagram test to take, they are typically drawn to tests that are advertised as "short," "quick," "fast," and "easy." Life is short, and Sevens don't like to waste time. That said, Sevens who realize the higher purpose of the Enneagram will dive headlong into it because of their enthusiasm for learning and growth. Also, Sevens are typically the early adopters in their social circles and will enroll friends and family in the Enneagram. One note of caution here: Sevens are tempted to drop their interest in the Enneagram if they suspect it will limit their freedom of choice. "Why can't I be a Type Seven, Eight, and Four?" a Seven might ask. But when Sevens give the Enneagram a chance, they discover that, much to their joy, the Enneagram helps them to discover real freedom and fulfillment.

INTRODUCING TYPE SEVEN

Are you a Type Seven on the Enneagram? Maybe you have a family member, a friend, or a work colleague who is a Seven.

My friend Liz Trubridge is a Seven. She is a TV and film producer who has won a BAFTA, Golden Globe, and Emmy for her work on all six series of *Downton Abbey* and three *Downton Abbey* films. (Sevens are actually called the Producer in some Enneagram circles.) Liz is an enthusiastic student of the Enneagram. "I take my knowledge of the Enneagram with me wherever I go," she says. Being on set with Liz, I watch her display many of the healthy qualities of Sevens. First and foremost, Sevens are natural manifesters who use their creative energy to produce positive outcomes. They are possibility thinkers. They have irrepressible optimism. They uplift everyone's spirits. They think on their feet. They know how to improvise. They turn obstacles into opportunities and don't stop until the task is done.

My sister-in-law Lizzie loves the Enneagram. "I knew I was a Seven as soon as I saw the name Enthusiast," she told me. Lizzie has a bright, positive, happy energy, and I always feel uplifted in her presence. Lizzie is dedicated to her personal growth and is always on the lookout for new inspiration—a book of poetry, a novel, a film, a podcast, or a new artist. My children, Bo and Christopher, light up when they see their Auntie Lizzie. Like a lot of Sevens, Lizzie crams a lot into her life. She is a devoted hands-on mum to her two children, and she has a portfolio career in which she wears many hats, including global head of human resources for her father's music company and senior tutor for Thirdspace, a leadership and coaching group. Lizzie is also a certified coach with a private practice, and she co-hosts a weekly podcast, *Turning Towards Life*, that offers "a week-by-week conversation inviting us deeply into our lives."

Healthy Qualities of Sevens

When Sevens are healthy and well-balanced, they display essential qualities that we all love and appreciate. Here are a few things healthy Sevens have told me about themselves:

- "I have an enthusiastic outlook on life."
- "I want to make the most of life."
- "I don't want to live an unlived life."
- "I am always looking to elevate my life."
- "I like learning and expanding my horizons."
- "I look on the bright side of life."
- "I am looking for happiness and fulfillment."

- "Life is a journey; enjoy the ride."
- "I prefer to live my dreams, not my memories."
- "My mantra is: Be here now!"

Unhealthy Qualities of Sevens

When Sevens are out of balance, they become manic, restless, and afraid of missing out. Here are a few things Sevens have told me about themselves:

- "I am often in a hurry."
- "I wish there was more time in the day."
- "My brain is thinking of the next five things."
- "I suffer from destination addiction."
- "I don't stop to smell the roses."
- "I put a positive spin on sad feelings."
- "I don't take time to rest and heal."
- "I don't like stop signs."
- "I live too fast to connect to my soul."
- "I still haven't found what I'm looking for."

RECOGNIZING TYPE SEVENS

In Greek mythology, Dionysus is a good fit at Point Seven and is helpful for addressing some common misperceptions about Sevens. Dionysus is popularly known as the Greek god of wine, ecstasy, and festivities. He is the god of hedonism and the pleasure of the senses. Short descriptions of Dionysus, as found in schoolbooks and on Google, portray him as a superficial god who is hollow and unsound of mind. Like Dionysus, Sevens are often characterized as being shallow, frivolous, and frothy. But these caricatures of Dionysus and Sevens are shortsighted and misleading. When you dig deeper into who Dionysus is, you find scholarly papers about his heroic enthusiasm and mystical insight. You learn that Dionysus took an inner journey to the center of his being. Dionysus found that God is everywhere. He spiritualized matter. He turned pleasure into joy. He found heaven on earth.

Sevens are attracted to spiritual paths that highlight awe and wonder, a gospel of good news, thanksgiving, and resurrection. For instance, in Hindu mythology, *Lila* is a Sanskrit name for the joy of taking delight in the cosmic play of creation. Krishna is the personification of Lila. Typical of a Seven, Krishna had many adventures in his youth. He played his flute, loved to dance, and wooed his sweetheart, Radha. Later, Krishna transmuted these fun qualities into joy, wisdom, compassion, and love. In the Hebrew Book of Psalms, an anthology of 150 spiritual poems, we are encouraged to "shout joyfully to God," to delight in "the day the Lord has made," and to "serve the Lord with gladness." And in Sufism, the whirling dervishes dance ecstatically in a counterclockwise direction, with their right hand raised to heaven and left hand lowered to the ground so as to channel divine energy deep into the earth. Hazrat Inayat Khan, the 20th-century Sufi scholar and mystic, wrote:

> *When the cares of my heart are many, your consolations cheer my soul.*
> — Psalm 94

> Our souls are only created to dance;
> it is their nature to dance, and it is the tragedy of life
> when the soul is kept from dancing.

His Holiness the 14th Dalai Lama has an abundance of Seven energy. Anyone who has spent time with the Dalai Lama can testify how uplifting it is to be in his presence. He is a pro-activist who chooses to focus on positive outcomes and won't get drawn into negativity or attack. His core teaching is that the purpose of life is to be happy. He has said his favorite Buddhist practice is *mudita*, Pali for "sympathetic joy." Mudita is one of the Four Immeasurable or Boundless Qualities in Buddhism, and it is the practice of finding joy by spreading joy to others. In *The Book of Joy*, co-written with Archbishop Desmond Tutu, the Dalai Lama wrote:

> Joy is the reward, really, of seeking to give joy to others. When you show compassion, when you show caring, when you show love to others, do things for others, in a wonderful way you have a deep joy that you can get in no other way. You can't buy it with money. You can be the richest person on Earth, but if you care only about yourself, I can bet my bottom dollar you will not be happy and joyful.

In psychology, Sevens are interested in positive psychology and models that emphasize personal growth, human flourishing, and self-actualization. Richard Alpert, better known as Ram Dass, had lots of Seven energy. Ram Dass was a prominent Harvard psychologist in the '60s who researched psychedelics, altered states, and higher consciousness. "Psychedelics helped me to free myself, albeit temporarily, from the prison of my ego-self," he told me in an interview. After psychedelics, Ram Dass took a pilgrimage to India, where he met his guru Maharaj-ji. "It was Maharaj-ji who set me free. He was the one who helped me find my spiritual self and learn how to be here now," he said. In his classic book *Be Here Now*, which became a "counter-culture bible" for millions of spiritual seekers, Ram Dass wrote:

> *Our thinking minds deprive us of the happiness that comes when we are living fully in the moment.*
> — Ram Dass, *Be Here Now*

> I think the message is that you don't need to go anywhere else to find what you are seeking.

In leadership, Sevens typically show up as the entrepreneur, energizer, and pacesetter. Richard Branson, founder of the Virgin Group, has bags of Seven energy. He has launched a variety of ventures using the Virgin brand, including Virgin StartUp, Virgin Voyages, Virgin Atlantic, and Virgin Galactic. When I designed and delivered a one-year Leadership Journey for his Virgin Media team, I included a module on the Enneagram. I ran the program for four years in a row, and at the start of each one, Richard Branson issued an enthusiastic rallying cry that was very much in the spirit of a Seven. Some of his key messages were "stay ahead of the curve," "predict the market," "enjoy the journey," and "keep growing." He told his leaders, "Be wise enough to know when to speed up and when to slow down" and "Don't forget to stop and breathe!"

> *Do good, have fun, and the money will follow.*
> — Richard Branson, *Screw Business as Usual*

In the arts, Sevens pour their energy and exuberance into their creative endeavors. Wolfgang Amadeus Mozart lived a LFDY life—*Live Fast Die Young*. He was free-spirited and disciplined, a genius and impish, irreverent and devoted to his music. He produced over 600 works at a rapid pace and died at 35. His Symphony No. 41, called *Jupiter*, is lauded as the pinnacle of his orchestral works. I enjoy listening to it conducted by Leonard Bernstein and by Benjamin Zander, who both have strong Seven energy. Mozart's *Jupiter Symphony* gives you a deep insight into the psyche of Sevens. It is profoundly expressive and full of grand fanfares, quiet passages, melodic invention, emotional depth, and a typically jubilant finish. It is said that Mozart could see the whole composition in a single note. He was in tune with the infinite.

In poetry, read anything by Walt Whitman for an injection of exuberant Seven energy. Whitman was known as the father of free verse. His wondrous odes and ballads are rambling, conversational, passionate, intimate, erotic, honest, and inspiring. His works are enlivening and invigorating. After reading "Leaves of Grass," "Song of Myself," or "Captain, My Captain!" for example, you can't help but want to live more fully and with greater passion, imagination, and daring. His epic poem "Song of the Open Road" starts with these two short stanzas:

> *O Mozart, immortal Mozart, how many, how infinitely many inspiring suggestions of a finer, better life you have left in our souls!*
> — Franz Schubert

Afoot and light-hearted I take to the open road,
Healthy, free, the world before me,
The long brown path before me leading wherever I choose.
Henceforth I ask not good-fortune, I myself am good-fortune,
Henceforth I whimper no more, postpone no more, need nothing,
Done with indoor complaints, libraries, querulous criticisms,
Strong and content I travel the open road.

In music, Sevens are very rock and roll and everything that goes with it. Think of the Rolling Stones and songs like "Start me Up," "Satisfaction," and "How Can I Stop?" Visualize Freddie Mercury and Queen performing their operatic roller coaster "Bohemian Rhapsody." Listen to Elton John's "Rocket Man," Katy Perry's "Firework," and Miley Cyrus's "7 Things." Sing along to "Can't Stop the Feeling," by Justin Timberlake. And book tickets to go see an Earth, Wind & Fire concert. Their fusion of R&B, soul, jazz, and funk is an experience of pure joy. Listening to "Boogie Wonderland," "Let's Groove," "Shining Star," "Sing a Song," and "September" transports you to a higher realm. Gospel music is also full of spiritual Seven energy.

In TV and film, many heroes and rogues have lots of Seven energy. In the Marvel films, Tony Stark (aka Iron Man) is a billionaire playboy scientist. He starts out as self-interested and obnoxious, but along the way he finds his heart and is increasingly compassionate, wise, and altruistic. Sticking with Marvel, the Guardians of the Galaxy series features a more comedic Seven in hero Peter Quill (aka Star-Lord) played by Chris Pratt. Actress Goldie Hawn has bundles of Seven energy. Think of her feel-good films like *There's a Girl in My Soup, Butterflies are Free*, and *Private Benjamin*. Also think of free-spirited Holly Golightly, played by Audrey Hepburn in *Breakfast at Tiffany's*. Oh, and a quick mention for Ted Lasso, the irrepressibly positive and optimistic football manager of AFC Richmond in the comedy-drama series *Ted Lasso*.

> Maverick: "I feel the need."
> Goose: "The need for speed!"
> — Top Gun

Sevens make great entertainers. You find them everywhere in the entertainment industry, backstage and front, in theater, musicals, dance, and variety. Think of Lin-Manuel Miranda, actor, rapper, and creator of the hit musical *Hamilton*. Robin Williams, actor and comedian, registers as a Seven-Plus on the Enneagram! His genius stand-up comedy had a manic, breathless, over-the-top delivery. He also inspired us with his sensitive, heartfelt character portrayals in *Good Will Hunting, Good Morning, Vietnam*, and *Dead Poets Society*. Think of Eddie Murphy, the high-octane comedian, actor, producer, and all-round entertainer. Also, Mike Myers, creator of the swinging-'60s spy character Austin Powers; and Liza Minelli, actress, singer, dancer, and star of Bob Fosse's *Cabaret*; and Bill Hicks, the LFDY satirist and comedian who died at 32. Check out his sketch: "It's Just a Ride."

> Reality is something you rise above.
> — Liza Minelli

In Shakespeare's plays, think of his jesters, such as Falstaff in *Henry IV Part 1 and Part 2*, Feste, the "wise fool" in *Twelfth Night*, and Speed in Two *Gentlemen of Verona*. The dramatic function of Shakespeare's jesters is to offer song and dance, to provide comic relief, to prick folly and pride, and, above all, to speak the truth.

THE JOYFUL SOUL

*There are souls in this world
which have the gift of finding joy everywhere
and of leaving it behind them
when they go.*

– Frederick William Faber

The Enneagram, with its origins in Greek philosophy, teaches that we live in an infinite universe. The circle of the Enneagram is a symbol for the infinite nature of God. "God is an infinite sphere, whose center is everywhere and whose circumference is nowhere," declared Alain de Lille in *The Rules of Theology.* Today's scientists who explore the multiverse theory and projective geometry, for instance, are in awe of our infinite universe. The circle of the Enneagram is also a symbol for the infinite nature of the soul. The ego (persona) is infinitesimally small in the grand scheme of things, but it is connected to the soul (psyche) that is infinite by nature. The greatest joy for Sevens is to be in tune with the infinite and to revel in and enjoy a life of infinite possibilities.

> *In an infinite universe, anything can happen.*
> — Douglas Adams, *The Restaurant at the End of the Universe*

One of my favorite settings for teaching Enneagram retreats is Assisi, Italy. This picturesque medieval town is the birthplace of Saint Francis of Assisi. Saint Francis had lots of Seven energy. In his youth, Francesco Bernardone (his given nickname) was a playboy, a wild Dionysus, and a pleasure-seeker, but he lacked fulfillment. He became a knight but was quickly captured on the battlefield and was thrown into a dungeon for a year. This was his dark night of the soul. Here he was emptied of all sense of self. After his release, Francesco had a profound conversion. He rebuilt a ruined church called San Damiano. He became a "holy fool" for God and spoke of "perfect joy." He made himself into an instrument for peace. "Where there is hatred, let me sow love," he prayed. And "where there is sadness, joy."

Saint Francis could easily be the Patron Saint for Sevens. He sang and danced his prayers, like a Sufi whirling dervish. He treated everyone as an equal and befriended all he met, including bishops and sultans. He worshipped "Brother Sun"

> *What we are looking for is what is looking.*
> — Saint Francis of Assisi

and "Sister Moon." He gave a sermon to the birds, he kissed lepers, and he made friends with a wolf in Gubbio. He took many pilgrimages, and he found love everywhere he went. He is called the "saint of joy," and his life has many teachings and lessons that are a good fit at Point Seven on the Enneagram, which is where we are all encouraged to sit and meditate on happy matters such as abundance, gratitude, freedom, joy, and omnipresent love.

When Sevens are in tune with the infinite nature of their soul, they display positive and vibrant qualities that we all love and appreciate. Here are a few of these essential qualities.

> **Fullness of Being.** Healthy Sevens experience what in ancient Greek is called *pleroma*, which is a natural "fullness of being" and "spiritual completeness." In philosophy, the number Seven represents fullness and completeness, both inner and outer. "Everything in the universe is within you," says Rumi, the Sufi poet. A Seven's sense of inner fullness gives them the freedom to be themselves and to enjoy life to the full. They are a free spirit who is not weighed down or encumbered by any sense of lack, gravity, or craving.
>
> **Enthusiastic Outlook.** Enthusiasm is a hallmark quality of Sevens, hence their name, *The Enthusiast*. The word *enthusiasm* is rooted in three Greek words ἐν (en, "in") and θεός (theós, "god") and οὐσία (ousía, "essence"), which translates as "filled with God" and "inspired by God's essence." A Seven's characteristic enthusiasm is more than a positive mental attitude; it bubbles up from the depths of their being. When Sevens are genuinely in tune with their enthusiasm, they are focused, devoted, inspired, and feel very much on purpose with their life.
>
> **A Grateful Heart.** "Every day, think as you wake up: Today I am fortunate to be alive, I have a precious human life, I am not going to waste it," teaches the Dalai Lama. Sevens are natural epicures who never go hungry or thirsty because they are full of gratitude. On the deepest level, gratitude arises from a spiritual realization that you are created perfectly and that "I am what I seek." Gratitude is also a great blessing because it increases your capacity to be present, to savor your experiences, and to appreciate things as they are.

Joie de Vivre. Sevens are blessed with a natural joie de vivre. Joyfulness is in their spiritual DNA. They have an ageless spirit, a youthful vigor, a playful nature, and a fun-loving attitude. They are spontaneously available to life and know how to maximize the enjoyment of the present moment. "Joy is the noblest human act," wrote Saint Thomas Aquinas. Sevens remind us that inside each of us—all nine Types—lives "a call to joy," and when we follow our joy, it gives our life direction, meaning, and purpose.

Spirit of Adventure. Ask a Seven, "How are you?" and they will tell you life is good, things are going well, and, also, give you breaking news about an exciting new adventure. "*Adventure is worthwhile in itself,*" was the personal motto of Amelia Earhart, the aviation pioneer and the first woman to fly solo across the Atlantic Ocean. A Seven's spirit of adventure gives them courage and resilience to engage fully with life, to behold its miracles, to survive dark times, and to learn and grow along the way.

YES Energy. As a Seven, you have a lot of YES energy. Your YES energy is full of positivity, hope, and love. It helps you to rebound quickly from setbacks and disappointments. You are always ready to go again. You are like the Energizer Bunny in the TV commercial whose batteries never seem to run out. Your YES energy is sacred. It comes not from adrenaline or coffee; but from your soul. It is highly creative, it uplifts everyone's spirits, it replenishes the weary, and it fuels your many productions and enterprises.

Always Growing. In philosophy, the number Seven represents the continuous unfolding of creation. Sevens are committed to personal growth, realizing their potential, and living life to the full. Ram Dass said, "Treat everyone you meet like God in drag." We all have God potential within us. Sevens make great teachers, coaches, mentors, motivators, and cheerleaders who see our wholeness and help us realize potential. Deep down we already are the person we most wish to be. "We are all just walking each other home," said Ram Dass.

SEARCHING FOR HAPPINESS

If there is such a thing as complete happiness, it is knowing that you are in the right place.

— Fannie Flagg, author of *Fried Green Tomatoes at the Whistle Stop Cafe*

The legend of the Holy Grail ignites the spirit of adventure in us. It conjures up images of a sacred journey to a place on a map with an *X* on it. The Holy Grail represents spiritual fulfillment and true happiness. Everyone searches for their Holy Grail. All nine Ennea-Types are on a quest for something. What is your Holy Grail? What purpose does it serve? Do you know? At the start of your quest, you are filled with enthusiasm, positivity, and hope. But the journey takes longer than imagined, and after much searching you still haven't found what you are looking for. If, like Parsifal, the hero in the Grail legend, you fail to ask the right questions and learn from your experiences, you will be frustrated, and your search will be never-ending.

Sevens are known for their itchy feet, their restlessness, and their ceaseless desire to seek and find. They have a "searching outlook," and they are always on the lookout for something new, something exciting, and something more. Everyone can relate to this as we all have some Seven energy in us. Remember, all nine Points of the Enneagram live in you. The trouble with the "searching outlook" is that it can lead you away from yourself. Looking for love, the pursuit of happiness, the search for meaning, and chasing after success are mindsets that place your attention outside of you. The search for something "out there" compounds a sense of inner emptiness and lack. And so, your searching is your suffering.

Searching is not the same as finding. This is one of the central lessons of the Holy Grail myth. It is also a vital life lesson for Sevens. Some people search for love in all the wrong places, for instance, and others are so busy searching for happiness that they overlook what is right in front of them. As the poet Rumi observed,

> *The voyage of discovery lies not in finding new landscapes, but in having new eyes.*
>
> — Marcel Proust

> You wander from room to room
> Hunting for the diamond necklace
> That is already around your neck!

Searching is a symptom of spiritual blindness. You might have "scaled city walls," "run through the fields," "climbed the highest mountain," and "kissed honey lips," just like the person in the song by the Irish rock band U2, entitled "I Still Haven't Found What I'm Looking For." You are still searching because you've looked everywhere outside of you, but not within. The legend of the Holy Grail begins with Jesus and the Last Supper. The Holy Grail is commonly thought to be a precious object, a golden chalice of some sort. In truth, the Holy Grail is far more precious than a cup or bowl. The Holy Grail is your divine substance; it is the essence of you. One of Jesus's key teachings is: "The kingdom of God is within you" (Luke 17:21).

Basic Fear: The Fear of Missing Out

Sevens have a buoyant, upbeat, and positive nature. It appears as if nothing dampens their spirits or gets them down. But like the rest of us, they too have their ups and downs, joys and sorrows, hopes and fears. The basic fear for Sevens is the fear of missing out, commonly called FOMO. When Sevens let FOMO get the upper hand, their enthusiasm gives way to anxiety. They are driven by a fear of being deprived and losing out. They turn up the afterburners and become increasingly busy, manic, compulsive, and scattered into everydayness.

Everyone experiences FOMO, but not as much as Sevens. This basic fear in Sevens arises from a sense of separateness and lack, and it is experienced in many ways. For example, Sevens are super happy when they have freedom of choice, but when their choices are limited, they get fidgety, restless, and anxious. "Freedom of choice means a lot to me," says, Kathy, a Seven and a psychotherapist who took my Happiness and the Enneagram program. She told me, "There is no better feeling than having a full tank of gas in my car because it makes me feel that the world is my oyster." Kathy also told me, "When my gas tank goes below half full, I get anxious because my choices are limited and I don't want to be trapped in the same place forever."

FOMO causes you to focus more on the choices you don't make, and less on the ones you do. Ian, a Seven, told me his story: "My mom took me to the local diner to celebrate my eighth birthday. The menu had three flavors of ice cream: chocolate, vanilla, and strawberry. I asked for all three flavors, and mom said, 'Honey, we can only afford one scoop.'" When I thought about choosing chocolate, I could only imagine eating vanilla or strawberry. When I thought about choosing vanilla, I couldn't stop thinking about strawberry or chocolate. And when I thought about having strawberry, I didn't want strawberry because what I really wanted was what I couldn't have. I didn't know how to choose, and I burst into tears. Even now, as I grown man, I hate making choices off a menu."

FOMO also causes you to feel that wherever you are, you should be somewhere else. "I think I have FOMO and FOLO!" said Tonya, a Seven, who works in the travel industry. FOLO is the fear of losing out. "No matter where I am, my mind is always someplace else," Tonya told me. "When I am at the theater, I think I should have gone out to dinner with friends. If I go away for the weekend, I miss being at home. I guess I'm afraid of not being in the right place, and of missing out on a better option somewhere else." Deep down, Sevens fear they will always be frustrated in their efforts to find happiness. The problem is, though, *if you always think happiness is somewhere else, it will never be where you are.*

Here's a few more examples of what Sevens have said to me about living with FOMO and the fear of losing out.

- "I fear the grass is greener someplace else."
- "I get pulled in too many directions."
- "I can be impulsive and lack focus."
- "My bucket list keeps getting longer."
- "I'm always three days behind on my life."
- "I cram as much as possible into each day."
- "Making choices feels like I am losing out."
- "I don't let the grass grow under my feet."
- "I have a low boredom threshold."
- "My greatest fear is running out of time."

Childhood Story: The Happy Child

Sevens enter the world as a bundle of joy. They are playful babies who show early signs of being bright, responsive, and lively. They commonly have a sanguine temperament that is light and airy, sociable and fun, uninhibited and full of positivity. They are the Ennea-Type that most closely resembles Pollyanna Whittier, the effusive and optimistic orphan in Eleanor Porter's classic novel *Pollyanna*, and Peter Pan, the adventuresome, magical boy from the J. M. Barrie novel

Peter Pan. "Ecstasy is the native condition of the ordinary mind," observed R. D. Laing, a Scottish psychiatrist. Young Sevens are naturally ecstatic and happy, but they soon realize that not everyone is as happy as they are, and their happiness is sorely tested as they experience life's ups and downs—the death of a pet, an upset with a school friend, an illness in the family, their parents' divorce, for instance.

In childhood, Sevens often play the role of the Fun Child. They discover early on that they are blessed with a magical power to make people laugh and be happy. Their irrepressible energy uplifts everyone's spirits. For Sevens, a smile is a universal language, laughter is the shortest distance between two people, and having fun is always a good option. Young Sevens often take on the social role of Entertainer and Jester. Jo, a Seven, who is an actress and comedienne, told me, "Being the Entertainer in my family was my golden ticket. It also got me a lot of friends and opportunities in life. But there was also a catch with my golden ticket, which was I thought I had to wear a "smiley face" all the time or risk losing love and approval."

> *All it takes is faith and trust. And... just a little bit of pixie dust.*
> — Peter Pan

Young Sevens learn to use their positivity as a coping mechanism to manage disappointment, reframe sadness, and bounce back from heartbreak. They use their positive mental attitude to be self-nurturing and independent. "I can make myself happy; I don't need anyone else," they tell themselves. But Sevens run into trouble with their positivity when they use it too often to mask their true feelings. For example, they have difficulty processing so-called "negative emotions" such as fear, anger, and sadness. As they grow up, they must learn that happiness is not the opposite of sadness and that true happiness comes from being able to meet sadness with honesty, compassion, and love.

Sevens often put a positive spin on their childhood story, no matter how difficult it was. Every child meets some unhappiness and heartache, and there is no escaping this, not even for Sevens. A common heartache that young Sevens report is being squashed and put down for their overexcitability. They are told to "tone it down," "rein it in," and curb their enthusiasm. "I was told off by my parents every day for being too bouncy, too positive, and too lively," says Jo, the actress and comedienne. R. D. Laing, the Scottish psychiatrist, observed, "To adapt to this world the child abdicates its ecstasy." How terribly sad this is. Many young Sevens deal with this abdication of ecstasy by being rebellious. The Fun Child turns into a Wild Child. They vow, just like Peter Pan, to escape the clutches of disenchanted adults and to never grow up.

The "Hurry Up" Driver: Sevens have a persistent "Hurry Up" driver in their ego operating system. They are born with "fast genes," so to speak, and race through early milestones such as smiling, laughing, crawling, walking, and talking. "I remember being in a hurry to grow up and find out what my future will be," says Jo. Sevens have high hopes for the future, but they also have the fear of missing out. Some Sevens are like the White Rabbit in *Alice In Wonderland*, who is fretful, in a hurry, and always late. This constant hurrying can cause them to be hyperactive, impatient, and frustrated with life. They may also struggle with focus, discipline, and keeping their attention fixed on one thing at a time.

Let's look at some examples of how the basic fear, childhood story and "Hurry Up" driver operates for Sevens in the three biological instincts: (1) Self-Preservation Instinct (SP), which is mostly about lifestyle, material matters, and self-care: (2) Social Instinct (SO), which is mostly about relating to family, society, and the world; and (3) (SX) Sexual Instinct (also called One-to-One Instinct), which is mostly about attraction, relating style, and romance.

> **Self-Preservation Instinct (SP)** *Healthy:* Your priority is to design a lifestyle that gives you freedom. A 9-to-5 job isn't very appealing to SP Sevens. "A big part of success and happiness is having the freedom to do what I want when I want," says Tim, a Seven, who is a freelance web designer. Getting to financial independence as quickly as possible is an exciting goal. You work hard to make sure you don't go without and are not short of basic pleasures and comforts. *Not-so-healthy:* You focus too much on physical wants and material possessions. You make impulsive purchases. You are overly acquisitive. *"All the money in the world is spent on feeling good,"* said Ry Cooder. You think more about what you want than about what you have. *Unhealthy:* You neglect your physical well-being and are careless with money. "My pattern is go, go, go, collapse!" said Tracy, a Seven, a freelance chef. Your self-care is inconsistent. Your weight might yo-yo up and down. You spend your paycheck as soon as you get it. There's no space in your schedule for a doctor appointment.
>
> **Social Instinct (SO)** *Healthy:* The SO Seven is less self-interested than the SP and SX Seven. You focus your energy more on relationships than on having material things. You get a kick out of being a mom or a dad. You enjoy working on projects that require collaboration

and that bring a smile to others. You are invested in abundance and happiness for everyone. *Not-so-healthy:* Typically, your social role is the Energizer. You enroll others in your enthusiasm. You pour your energy into your friendships, your colleagues at work, and your many social circles. When your social calendar gets too busy, your loved ones don't get your best energy. And you haven't any energy left over for you. *Unhealthy:* You want to be where the action is. You are afraid of missing out. You follow the whole world on social media. You want opening night tickets for the show everyone is talking about. You want to keep up with the Joneses. You try to stay ahead of the curve. You spread yourself too thin.

Sexual Instinct (SX) *Healthy:* You are more impulsive and excitable than the other Sevens. You love to make new friends. You make a beeline for people who are interesting and who inspire you. You are an early adopter in matters that interest you. You have an entrepreneurial "go for it" mindset. You have whirlwind romances. "Where can I find a firework that says, 'Will You Marry me?'" my friend Kirsten, a Seven, once asked me. *Not-so-healthy:* You enjoy novelty. You like new beginnings. You keep your options open. You don't like to feel tied down. "I like the idea of falling in love more than being in love," says Mike, a Seven, a dancer. You have a lot of ideas about how to make a million dollars, but you don't follow through on them. *Unhealthy:* Visualize Freddie Mercury singing "I want to be free!" Listen to the song "Don't Bring Me Down," by rock band ELO. The fear of being "fenced in" or "weighed down" makes you head quickly for the Exit. One minute you are all in, and the next minute you are on the move, you bin the experience, and you don't look back.

Passion: Gluttony

All nine Types on the Enneagram experience a *passion*, or cause of suffering in the heart, that emerges from a sense of separation and from the basic fear. The passion for Sevens is called gluttony, which is another of the so-called cardinal sins. Gluttony is commonly associated with overeating, drinking alcohol to excess, and a passion for guilty pleasures, but these are only presenting symptoms, and, as we shall see, there is much more to gluttony.

Healthy Sevens experience a fullness of being and inner completeness. Sevens are described by some as the Epicure, named after the Greek philosopher Epicurus. To be Epicurean means to relish the adventure of being alive, delight in simple pleasures, and give thanks for life's bounty. Sevens have a big appetite for life. They savor every morsel. Their cup runneth over. They drink in the moment. Healthy Sevens are described as the Ecstatic Appreciators by Don Riso and Russ Hudson in *Enneagram of Personality*. Sevens who experience inner fulfillment, are full of gratitude and have no need to be gluttonous.

Gluttony arises in Sevens when their fullness of being—called *pleroma*, in ancient Greek—is missing from their awareness. When gripped by a feeling of emptiness or inner scarcity, Sevens chase frantically after what I call in my book *Happiness NOW* "the three ego mirages of 'more,' 'next,' and 'there.'" Gluttony is a malaise that comes from a craving for "wanting more." It attempts to fill a hole in your sense of self with external objects of gratification. It also drives our acquisitive societies, excessive consumerism, and the extraction economy that plunders Mother Earth to make more mobile phones, smartwatches, and other consumer objects of desire.

Gluttony is society's most acceptable and encouraged sin. The world of advertising and marketing encourages gluttony to drive sales and boost profits. Think of the advertising slogan for Molton Brown: "More is never enough." Gluttony is the sin we excuse and overlook so that we can "make a dollar" and "bring home the bacon." Gluttony is also recognized as the sin that makes us more likely to commit any of the other sins. Gluttony comes from a loss of internal regulation and self-control and can cause much regret and unhappiness. Let's take a closer look at gluttony so that we can free ourselves of gluttonous tendencies.

> *You can't have everything. Where would you put it?*
> — Steven Wright

The Having Mode. In *To Have or To Be,* psychologist Erich Fromm describes two modes of living: the "being mode" and "having mode." The being mode is natural, and it affirms our inherent fullness of being and fullness of creation. The having mode is a response to the "loss of being" and feeling separate from nature, and it promotes an external focus on getting, possessing, controlling, and hoarding things. "Man is in the process of becoming a *homo consumens*, a total consumer," warns Fromm. In the having mode, there is no cessation from wanting. In the being mode, you appreciate life much more. *What differences do you notice in yourself when you are in the having mode versus the being mode?*

Buying Happiness. Gluttony makes you focus more on having than on being. It sees happiness as a commodity to acquire and own. But joy is not a carrot, and money can't buy you love. True happiness is a quality of your being; it doesn't have a price tag. *Happiness is not in things; happiness is in you.* Hafiz, a Sufi poet, warned:

> Learn to recognize the counterfeit coins
> That may buy you just a moment of pleasure,
> But then drag you for days
> Like a broken man
> Behind a farting camel.

The Thirsty Fish. The Sufi poet Rumi wished to experience the bounty of his soul, which he called the *Infinite* Self. He said, "I have a thirsty fish in me that can never find enough of what it's thirsty for! Show me the way to the ocean! Break these half-measures, these small containers." The ego is a thirsty fish. It searches for something that it can't grasp. Gluttony makes you want things, but prevents you enjoying them. In the search for happiness, we overlook what is already here. *How specifically do you behave like a thirsty fish?*

The Hungry Ghost. In Buddhism, the story of the hungry ghost is used to help students break the addiction to gluttony and its endless cycle of suffering. The hungry ghost is consumed by desire, craving, and attachment to external objects. The ghost is always hungry because it has no stomach and cannot digest the objects. With gluttony, we don't absorb, digest, or metabolize our experiences. Gluttony acts like an antinutrient that prevents us from being nourished and fed by what is all around us.

Soul Food. Gluttony is an emotional escape. It is also a sign that something is eating you up. Gluttony is a spiritual hunger that comes from loss of contact with your soul and feeling deprived of the fullness of your being. "You can never have enough of what you did not want in the first place," said Anne Valley-Fox. What is your soul food? What is your daily bread? What nourishes and inspires you? Stay close to what inspires you, and you will experience daily upliftment and happiness.

Fixation: Over-Planning or Over-Anticipation

In the Enneagram, the *fixation* refers to a mental habit that causes an imbalance in your mental health and well-being. The fixation for Sevens is commonly called planning or anticipation. I prefer the words *over-planning* or *over-anticipation*.

Sevens are known for having an optimistic outlook on life. They place great faith in the future, because the future is full of possibilities. According to Sevens, the future is bright. Their mantra is: "The best is yet to come." The optimistic energy of Sevens is captured in the Leonard Bernstein and Stephen Sondheim song "Something's Coming" in the musical *West Side Story*. Tony Wyzek, the former leader of the Jets, sings the song in Act 1. He is fresh out of prison and dreams of a better future in which "something good" is going to come "cannonballing down through the sky." He doesn't know what it is, "but it's gonna be great." This intense focus on something good that is "around the corner" and "just out of reach" can cause Sevens to over-plan, over-anticipate, and live too much in the future.

Dan is a Seven. He is an entrepreneur who came to me for mentoring at a low point in his life. In our first session he raved about eight exciting projects he had on the go. "I'm going to be a millionaire eight times over," said Dan. I asked Dan to take an Enneagram test. "It turns out I am a raving Seven," he told me. I struck a deal with Dan. I asked him to let go of six of his eight projects and focus on two. "Okay, I'll do it," he said, wincing in pain. I explained to Dan that his excitement for his projects was positive, but it was also masking a fear that none of them would succeed. Together, we simplified his plans. We addressed his anxiety. We focused more on the journey, not only the goal. We prioritized his actions. We made some difficult, but wise choices. And one year later, he was happy in his work, and he had made his first million dollars.

The fixation of over-planning is often driven by a hidden fear that things ultimately won't work out. The fear of missing out (FOMO) and fear of losing out (FOLO) fuel the fixation. Here are five common ways that the fixation for Sevens plays out in their life and work.

Chasing Happiness. Our lifestyles have speeded up significantly in recent times. Each morning, we hit the ground running, we shower with our 3-in-1 shampoo, conditioner, and bodywash, we eat breakfast on the go, and we move quickly through the day. Why are we in such a hurry? One reason is the pursuit of happiness. The problem with pursuing happiness is that the focus is mostly on future happiness. We are fixated on "something just out of reach" and so we fail to slow down, live in the present, and enjoy the journey. "It is an old and ironic habit of human beings to run faster when we have lost our way," wrote Rollo May in *Love and Will*.

Destination Addiction. A few years ago, I coined the term "destination addiction" to describe a compulsive behavior driven by a belief that happiness is somewhere else, "over there," and at the next stop on your journey. Sevens are especially prone to destination addiction. As a Seven, you promise yourself that you will slow down and savor your life "when," "after," and "as soon as" you get to where you are going, but instead you set another destination to strive after. *Until you give up the idea that happiness is somewhere else, it will never be where you are.*

Absent-Mindedness. When Sevens are too full of plans and anticipation, the focus of attention is on what's around the corner instead of what's in front of you. "I used to spend my holidays planning my next holiday. I thought this was fun, until I realized I was missing out on where I was," says Ellie, a Seven. Unhealthy Sevens are psychologically absent and fail to notice that "something good" is already here. Sevens return to health when they come back to living in the now. Wisdom is the power of maximizing the enjoyment of the present moment.

Adrenaline Junkie. Sevens who are gripped by FOMO act like an *adrenaline junkie*, a term used to describe a compulsive desire for excitement and adventure. The more anxious Sevens are, the more restless and reckless they are in their search for the next high, a new thrill, or a quick fix. Constantly seeking stimulation is energy-draining and often leads to a crash. The ups and downs become increasingly intense. Life is a roller coaster, and no one is enjoying the ride.

Too Many Plans. Sevens have great fun making plans, but it's not all fun. Sevens can get anxious without a plan. I met Bonnie, a Seven, in Santorini, Greece, at my Spiritual Growth and the Enneagram retreat. She told me, "From an early age, I learned to believe I had to make my life happen. I was afraid that nothing good will happen if I don't make plans. I overplan my life because I don't trust there is a higher plan looking after me." Too many plans can block the many blessings that come from being open, spontaneous, and present. "A good traveler has no fixed plans, and is not intent on arriving," said Lao Tzu.

ENJOYING THE JOURNEY

> *As you set out for Ithaka*
> *hope your road is a long one,*
> *full of adventure, full of discovery.*
>
> — C. P. Cavafy, "Ithaka"

The Enneagram offers a path of growth for all nine Types that helps you to remember your original nature and be your True Self. For Sevens, the path of growth is about claiming the joys of simply being on the path.

When I teach Point Seven on the Enneagram, I like to read the poem "Ithaka," by Constantine Cavafy, a 20th-century Greek poet. Cavafy wrote "Ithaka" in 1911. He was a recluse who loved to study ancient history, and he displayed a lot of Type Five energy. As you will see, there is an Inner Line from Seven to Five.

The poem "Ithaka" is about the journey of life and the importance of enjoying the whole journey, not just the destination. It is inspired by the Ithaca that is the island home of Odysseus in Homer's *Odyssey*. Odysseus is the king of Ithaca. He leaves Ithaca to fight in the Trojan War. After the war has ended, he sets sail for Ithaca, but the journey back has many twists and turns and it takes him 10 long years. Cavafy's poem "Ithaka" is addressed to Odysseus (and to all of us). In it, Cavafy tells Odysseus to keep his mind on Ithaka, the destination, but remember to enjoy the journey. Cavafy says,

> Keep Ithaka always in your mind.
> Arriving there is what you're destined for.
> But don't hurry the journey at all.
> Better if it lasts for years,
> so you're old by the time you reach the island,
> wealthy with all you've gained on the way.

Cavafy's message in "Ithaka" is that happiness is a way of traveling, not a destination. Happiness is not a place to get to; it's an attitude you travel with. Happiness is not something you find; it's something you realize. Happiness is in you; not in things! Sevens who realize this, experience inner freedom, and they arrive at Ithaka already happy.

Virtue: Sobriety

Every Ennea-Type has a virtue, or a superpower, that arises naturally as you do your inner work to heal the basic fear, the passion in the heart, and the fixation in your thinking. To activate this virtue requires inner work. You must bring forward this virtue by our own efforts. The virtue for Sevens is called sobriety.

Sobriety is often associated with freeing yourself from alcohol and substance abuse, but it is much more than that. Sobriety is freeing yourself from being intoxicated or under the influence of any harmful habit or behavior. Hence, sobriety means something different to each of us and to all nine Ennea-Types. For example, for Ones it might be freeing yourself from an addiction to perfectionism; for Threes it might be to stop chasing external validation; and for Sixes it might be freedom from self-doubt and overthinking. Essentially put, sobriety releases you from a compulsion or habit that causes suffering and heartache. It restores a sense of inner freedom and personal choice, both of which are highly prized by Sevens.

Sobering up starts with self-honesty. As in Twelve Step programs, the first step is being honest about what is *not* working in your life. Kathy is a Seven who juggles running a busy guest house in Martha's Vineyard, with caring for her disabled husband, raising three kids, and looking after two horses, four dogs, and a cat. She shared her story of sobering up at an Enneagram program I taught at the University of Santa Monica. "When I first read about Type Seven, I skipped the section on

> *Dear God,*
> *help me to slow down and notrushpasteverythingthat isimportanttodayamen.*
>
> — The Fast Prayer

sobriety because I don't drink alcohol or do drugs, but now I see that sobering up means much more than this," she told me. For Kathy, her sobriety began with admitting to herself that she was juggling too many tasks. She talked to her family, and was less positive and more honest about how difficult it is to juggle everything on her own.

When I teach about the virtue of sobriety, I ask my students this question: "How do I know when I am sober?" Alternatively, I ask them to complete the following sentence 10 times: "One way I know I am sober is . . ." For Sevens, some common answers are, "When I am not in a hurry," "When I have slept enough," "When I have time to breathe," and "When I am not chasing after something." After doing this inquiry, we look at some ways we can sober up more. Here are five sobering-up actions that are especially helpful for Sevens.

Finding Your Still Point. There's a line from T. S. Eliot's poem "Four Quartets" that reads: "At the still point of the turning world . . . there the dance is." When Sevens cultivate inner stillness, it frees them up from constantly racing about, chasing daylight, and going after life. Being still brings you home to yourself. It helps you to appreciate the fullness of your being. Ram Dass, in *Be Here Now*, wrote, "Our whole spiritual transformation brings us to the point where we realize that in our own being, we are enough."

Ending the Search. Sobering up helps Sevens to shift their mindset from "searching" to "being." A wise person knows that you can't find happiness by searching for it. *Happiness is not a search; it's a way of being.* What you are searching for in the world—joy, love, peace, wisdom, kindness—are qualities of the soul. When you choose to open your heart more, you naturally feel more abundant, happy, and free. When you decide to be more loving, you attract more love into your life.

The JOY of Slow. "As a Seven, my daily spiritual practice is to take off my running shoes, slow down, and enjoy the moment," says Lindsey, a life coach. Healthy Sevens learn to manage their pace. Life is not a race. They make space in their schedule to pause and reflect. They experience the joy of slow. Slowing down helps you to inhabit fully where you are and to savor each moment. Slowing down adds more flavor and richness to your life. Healthy Sevens learn, *if you don't slow down, you might never get there.*

Adding More NOW. "I am always moving forward. Even my handwriting leans forward!" says Nick, a Seven. When you live fast, your focus is more on the future than on the present. "Our thinking minds deprive us of the happiness that comes when we are living fully in the moment," wrote Ram Dass in *Be Here Now*. A healthy practice for Sevens is to add more NOW to your life. When you pay more attention to NOW, it becomes more interesting. Adding more NOW helps you to end the search for happiness. A good mantra for Sevens is, "The grass is greener where you water it."

Simplify Your Life. "Simple joys are holy," said Saint Francis of Assisi, who had lots of Seven energy. He taught his disciplines that simplicity confounds the wisdom of the world, because instead of reducing your happiness; it increases it. Many healthy Sevens have discovered the joy of voluntary simplicity. Less stuff, less clutter, less appointments, less plans, and less distractions are all part of sobering up for Sevens. The decision to simplify your life is a precious gift because it returns you to your essence and helps you to focus on what you truly value.

Balancing Your Centers

Sevens are called a Head Type on the Enneagram (along with Fives and Sixes). Ask a Seven where they spend most of their time (A) in my head, (B) in my heart, or (C) in my body, and they will typically go for option A. Sevens are known for living up in their heads and for rushing headfirst or headlong into life. Working with the Enneagram helps heady Sevens to find their feet and connect with the wisdom of their heart. It encourages them to engage all three centers of intelligence—body, heart, and head—which helps them in the long run to prosper and flourish.

"I'm thirty years old and I should be rich by now, but I've made some poor decisions," said Tony, a Seven. The first question I asked Tony was, "How do you

> *He who works with his hands and his head and his heart is an artist.*
>
> — Saint Francis of Assisi

make a decision?" Tony acknowledged he was often impulsive and quick to act without thinking things through. So, I gave Tony a mindfulness practice that I call Three Green Lights. The idea is that when making decisions, you consult all three centers, i.e., gut intuition, heart wisdom, and headspace. If the decision is a clear "Yes," you should get a green light in your body, heart, and head. A clear "No" will register three red lights. But if you get a red or amber light in one of the three centers, this is a sign to take your time, practice inner listening, and maybe have a conversation with someone to get clear on how to proceed.

Head Center. Sevens have very active minds. They are full of ideas, have a fast mental processing speed, and can be very creative. Sometimes their minds are too busy. "My mind is like a busy airport with ideas flying in and taking off on multiple runways," said Steve, a Seven. Interestingly, Steve took up flying to help him switch off and relax. "When I pilot a plane, I am centered in my body, clear-headed, and completely present," he told me. Healthy Sevens know that their mind works better when body, heart, and head all get a chance to rest and play.

Heart Center. Sevens love to take journeys, to travel afar, and to go on pilgrimages and adventures. The most significant journey a Seven can make is to travel the short distance from their head to their heart. *When Sevens know where their heart is, they find what they're looking for.* Healthy Sevens are emotionally intelligent. They cultivate deep and lasting relationships. They live with the full range of emotions. They care about the happiness of others. "Love and compassion are necessities, not luxuries. Without them, humanity cannot survive," said the Dalai Lama.

Body Center. Billie, a Seven, took my Leadership and the Enneagram program. Twice she broke a toe on her right foot in the first month of the program. At first she didn't let this stop her, but then she broke a toe on her left foot, and now she couldn't hop, skip or jump. "I think my body is telling me to slow down," Billie told me. Sevens will experience migraines, palpitations, and broken toes when their lifestyle is too fast paced, out of balance, and hectic. When Sevens respect their body, they stop, listen, and pay attention to what their body is telling them.

Spreading Your Wings

Type Seven's home base is Point Seven, which sits between Point Six and Point Eight on the Enneagram symbol. This means Sevens have a 6-Wing and an 8-Wing. Typically, one wing is more dominant than the other, but the goal is to balance your wings. Working with the 6-Wing can help Sevens to tap into the essential qualities and wisdom of Point Six, and working with the 8-Wing can help Sevens to access the same at Point Eight. Learning to live in balance with your wings, by drawing strengths and lessons from both, can help Sevens to fly.

Seven with a 6-Wing

Sevens with a dominant 6-Wing (7w6) are commonly called the Entertainer. They show up in the world with the typical traits of Sevens, plus some traits of Sixes. For example:

> **Highly Relational.** 7w6s are known for being relationship-focused and less independent-minded than 7w8s. Like healthy Sixes, they put family first and will consistently nurture their friendships. The positivity of Seven and likeability of Six is a great social combo. 7w6s are great fun to be around. They are committed, loyal, and supportive. They are sensitive and empathic. They stand by you in good times and bad, happy and sad. And they also worry about being disapproved of or rejected.

> **Double Header.** Both the Seven and the Six (along with Fives) are called Head Types on the Enneagram. 7w6s tend to be a bit more "in their head" than 7w8s, who are more "in their body." 7w6s do enough thinking for two people, and so it is vital that they learn to

work with all three centers of intelligence: body, heart, and head. "As a 7w6, I've learned that going for a run helps me to slow down my mind, clear my head, and come back to my center," says Jess, who works in digital marketing.

Future Tripping. "I have a lot of anxiety running through me, and part of me is constantly worried about my future," says Rick, a 7w6, a personal trainer. Sevens and Sixes are known for struggling with anxiety. 7w6s are prone to anticipatory anxiety or future tripping. They worry about the future—financial security, job prospects, people dying, and finding someone to love. 7w6s benefit greatly from mindfulness practices that help them to channel their creative energy into the present moment. "I create my future one thought at a time," taught Louise Hay, a Six.

Inner Listening. Healthy 7w6s find that their 6-Wing helps them to trust their vibes and follow their intuition. The energy of Point Six isn't as mercurial or quick as Seven energy. Kathy, a 7w6, told me, "I was introduced to the Enneagram by my friend Sue, who is a Six. When I learned about the wings of the Enneagram, I asked Sue how I could benefit from my 6-Wing. She shared a mindfulness meditation she uses twice a day to still her mind, practice inner listening, and follow her guidance."

Even Mindedness. Healthy 7w6s find that their 6-Wing offers a steadying and supportive influence. For example, the 6-Wing can help Sevens to be less hasty and misguided. A 7w6 can draw upon the virtue at Point Six, which is courage. They can also tap into Holy Strength and Holy Faith, which are the Holy Ideas at Point Six. When a Seven lives with faith, they are less impatient, twitchy, rash, and anxious. They discover an inner strength that helps them be even-minded and centered in their True Self.

Seven with an 8-Wing

Sevens with a dominant 8-Wing (7w8) are called the Opportunist or Asserter. They show up in the world with the typical traits of Sevens, plus some traits of Eights. For example:

Super Energized. Sevens and Eights are known for being full of energy. A 7w8 is typically energetic and enthusiastic. They are running on double the amount of energy than the rest of us. Sevens have lots of mental energy, and Eights have boundless physical energy. It's vital for 7w8s to channel their energy in a healthy way, or else they get manic, hyperactive, lustful, and drive everyone crazy. A good focus for 7w8s is to meditate on this question: *What is the best use of my energy today?*

Seize the Day. Sevens and Eights are known for their assertiveness. A 7w8 is called the Asserter. They are bold, direct, and confident. They go after what they want and won't stop until they get it. Their mantra is "Carpe Diem," which means to "seize the day." They want to live each day to the full. *Let's make today awesome!* They are less prone to procrastination or overthinking like the 7w6. The philosophy of a 7w8 is *live now, procrastinate later!* A healthy inquiry for 7w8s is: *Knowing I shall die one day, how shall I live today?*

The Pacesetter. I call Sevens and Eights (along with Threes) the Fast Types on the Enneagram. 7w8s live with urgency and immediacy. They like to grab the initiative, take the lead, and get ahead. They are entrepreneurs, pacesetters, and early adopters. It's vital for 7w8s to balance speed with wisdom, adrenaline with grace, and daring with caution. 7w8s can go too fast for their own good and for the health of their relationships. Taking time to slow down and enjoy the journey is always a good idea for 7w8s.

Too Independent. "I think I might be too independent for love," said Angelo, a 7w8, who took my Love and the Enneagram program in London. 7w8s are known for being very independent. They like being *young, free, and single* even when they aren't young anymore. Think of James Bond, 007. People who are very independent in relationships are usually carrying an old wound they won't look at. They're afraid of getting hurt again. A 7w8 must be willing to stop running from their past. Healing old wounds creates a better future with more freedom, intimacy, and love.

Heart Wisdom. Sevens pour a lot of their mental and physical energy into their work. They are career driven, have big plans, and have lots of projects on the go. When Sevens go into overdrive, they are too self-centered, too materialistic, and too work-focused for their own good. A 7w8 on overdrive has plenty of mental focus and willpower, but they are often lacking in heart wisdom. They need to slow down, be still, and engage the wisdom of their heart more.

Moving to One and Five

Following the Inner Lines of the Enneagram Symbol, Sevens move toward Point One (home of the Reformer) and Point Five (home of the Investigator). These Inner Lines invite you to visit these Points to explore the gifts and wisdom they have for you.

Moving to One

When Sevens go to Point One, they access some of the higher qualities that Ones are blessed with. For example:

> **Higher Purpose.** Like Healthy Ones, Sevens are enthused with a sense of mission and purpose. They follow their joy, and they live an inspired life. There are the renaissance workers whose joyful presence helps to make the world a better and more beautiful place to live in.
>
> **Greater Good.** Healthy Sevens focus less on hedonism and pleasure seeking, and more on what the ancient Greeks called *eudaemonia,* which is the deep joy and "good spirits" that arise from focusing on one's highest good and the greater good for all.
>
> **Holy Perfection.** The Holy Idea at Point One is Holy Perfection. For a Seven, this is the realization that life is unfolding perfectly, even in the wonky moments, and that you are always in the right place, at the right time, "The next message you need is always right where you are," said Ram Dass.

When Sevens are under stress, they may exhibit some unhealthy qualities also displayed by Ones. Knowing about these unhealthy qualities can help Sevens to be more self-aware and balanced as they go about their day. For example:

Excessive Self-Control. When happy-go-lucky Sevens get stressed, something snaps inside, and they become less open-minded and more rigid, less spontaneous and more controlled, less flexible and more set in their ways.

Too Idealistic. The ego-ideal for Sevens is to be positive, upbeat, and happy 100 percent of the time. Like unhealthy Ones, they suppress and put a lid on so-called negative emotions such as anger and sadness. Suppressing feelings is unhealthy and it blocks a Seven's wish to elevate their life and experience joy.

Over-Serious. Under stress, Sevens can be critical and perfectionistic. Their excitability turns into irritability. Their humor is spiked with sarcasm and anger. They have a sense of humor failure. They bring the mood down. They can't laugh at themselves.

Moving to Five
When Sevens go to Point Five, they access some of the higher qualities that Fives are blessed with. For example:

Joy of Solitude. When Sevens slow down, they become more introspective and discover the joy of solitude. "When from our better selves we have too long / Been parted by the hurrying world, and droop, / Sick of its business, of its pleasures tired, / how gracious, how benign is Solitude," wrote William Wordsworth.

Deep Thinking. Sevens are known as "generalists" and Fives as "specialists." When the powers of Point Five and Point Seven are combined, it helps Sevens to think wide and deep, to process quickly and methodically, to be objective and intuitive, and have the patience to test their theories and develop their ideas.

Eyes Wide Open. The energy at Point Five helps Sevens to pay attention to where they are, have greater spatial awareness, and take in their surroundings. "To stay in one place and watch the seasons come and go is tantamount to constant travel; one is traveling with the earth," observed Marguerite Yourcenar, the Nobel Prize nominee for Literature.

When Sevens are under stress, they may display some of the unhealthy qualities of Fives. Knowing about these unhealthy qualities can help Sevens be more self-observant and make wiser choices. For example:

Fast Thinking. Both Fives and Sevens tend to speed up their thinking when stressed. They benefit greatly from balancing what psychologist Daniel Kahneman calls Fast Thinking and Slow Thinking. Examples of slow thinking include mulling things over, letting ideas incubate, testing assumptions, and checking for cognitive bias and error.

Brain Overload. Under stress, Sevens and Fives may experience mental flooding or brain overload. When a Seven's mind is swimming with too many ideas, they struggle to keep their head above water. They become overwhelmed, and drown in their own thinking, when they can't stop accumulating more data and knowledge.

Mental Escape. When Sevens and Fives feel dejected and overwhelmed, they may look for mental escape. It might be rereading *Ulysses*, watching the entire catalog of Netflix movies, or playing a computer game like *Sentinel* with 9,999 levels of play. They use their mental powers to create a parallel universe or alternate reality.

HOLY PLAN

This is the day the Lord has made;
We will rejoice and be glad in it.

— Psalm 118

The nine Points on the Enneagram each offer a Holy Idea—a universal teaching and higher wisdom—for all nine Ennea-Types to contemplate and practice. Point Seven has three Holy Ideas. They are Holy Plan, Holy Wisdom, and Holy Work.

Holy Plan points to the Grand Design of the Universe. On the surface of things, life appears to be chaotic, haphazard, and without a plan, but when you look more deeply, you discover there is a wonderful mathematics and divine order at work. Modern scientists like Brian Swimme recognize the omnicentricity of the universe, for example. The universe is omnicentric, meaning its center resides everywhere. *Everywhere in the universe is sacred, but not more sacred than anyplace else.* The best real estate in the universe is right where you are. If you really take this in, your FOMO, the fear of missing out, will give way to a sense of awe and wonder.

Holy Wisdom recognizes there is a Holy Plan at work. We are all part of this Holy Plan, and we must learn to live in accordance with it. Making plans is a basic requirement of life. We make plans about where to live, what job to take, and when to start a family, for example. We also make plans every day about what to do, where to go, and who to meet up with. Sometimes our plans work out, and other times we must pivot and change. *When things don't go as planned, maybe it's a sign that life has a better plan for you.* Holy Wisdom encourages you to be open to guidance and support from the Holy Plan. "We must be willing to let go of the life we planned so as to have the life that is waiting for us," wrote Joseph Campbell, creator of *The Hero's Journey.*

> *A healed mind does not plan. It carries out the plans that it receives through listening to wisdom that is not its own.*
> — *A Course in Miracles*

Holy Work is about discovering your True Self, finding your sacred center, and living from that place every day. Being centered in your True Self gives you the wisdom to recognize the Holy Plan for your life. Holy Work is also about centering yourself in the here and now. The more present you are, the less afraid you are of missing out on life. The Holy Plan is unfolding right where you are, and it reveals itself to you wherever you go. Following the Holy Plan for your life is your ticket to joy, freedom, and fulfillment. On that note, I will give the final word to Mel Brooks, comedian, filmmaker, and philosopher, who has bags of Seven energy. In an interview he did for *The New Yorker* in 1978, with Kenneth Tynan, he said,

What we should do is not *future* ourselves so much. We should *now* ourselves more. "*Now* thyself" is more important than "*Know* thyself." Reason is what tells us to ignore the present and live in the future. So all we do is make plans. We think that somewhere there are going to be green pastures. It's crazy. Heaven is nothing but a grand, monumental instance of future. Listen, *now* is good.

Now is wonderful.

Type Eight
THE CHALLENGER

*If only you could love enough, you would be
the most powerful person in the world.*

— EMMET FOX

    The Ennea-Type Eight is commonly called Challenger. Other names for Eights include the Asserter, Powerful Soul, Protector, Leader, and Confronter.
    Type Eights are the *Strong-Willed, Assertive* Type. They have a big personality, an indomitable spirit, and a commanding presence. An extroverted Eight is typically bullish, in-your-face, and larger than life. An introverted Eight is more like a big bear, is self-possessed, and exudes a quiet power. Either way, Eights are a force of nature. "The force is strong with this one," you could say. Eights are self-reliant and want to be the master of their fate. They are fiercely protective

of their loved ones. They champion the underdog. They hate injustice. Most of all, Eights want to feel powerful and in charge, and they will do all they can to avoid feeling weak or being vulnerable. To be truly powerful, Eights must learn the art of wise power. Above all, they must be willing to surrender to a power greater than that of their ego.

Eights see life as a challenge, a contest of strength, a game of strategy, and something to pit their wits against. As we shall see, Eights have a "Be Strong" driver installed in their ego operating system. *But what is real strength?* The Enneagram challenges Eights to think deeply about this. Eights can learn a lot about real strength from the Bible story of David and Goliath. Goliath, the giant, represents the unhealthy Eight. He relies solely on his armory and brute force to overpower others. David represents the healthy Eight. He is agile and quick because he carries only five stones and no heavy armor. He uses his mental strength to outsmart Goliath. He also calls upon spiritual strength. "Thou comest to me with a sword, and with a spear, and with a shield," says David to Goliath, "but I come to thee with the name of the Lord of hosts" (1 Samuel 17:45).

> *It is excellent to have a giant's strength, but it is tyrannous to use it like a giant.*
>
> — Isabella in *Measure for Measure*, William Shakespeare

You can't make an Eight take an Enneagram test; it must be their idea. Some Types, like Sevens and Twos for example, are happy to jump in and get started straight away. But Eights aren't like that. Eights, along with Fives for example, are more guarded and cautious. When Eights do finally take an Enneagram test, they might resist sharing what Type they are. "I didn't tell my wife or anyone that I took an Enneagram test," Vince, an Eight, told me. "I kept my Type a secret because I thought that if everyone knew I was an Eight, it would put me at a disadvantage somehow." Vince also told me, "I was also afraid the Enneagram would try to make me soft and mushy, and less of a badass!"

Once Eights get over themselves, they discover the Enneagram is not the enemy, and it isn't working against them. They recognize that it can serve as a useful tool for identifying and realizing their strengths. Working with the Enneagram helps Eights to be vulnerable and powerful, sensitive and strong, compassionate and wise, and fully equipped to take on the world.

INTRODUCING TYPE EIGHT

Are you a Type Eight on the Enneagram? Maybe you have a family member, a friend, or a work colleague who is an Eight.

Miriam Holden, my grandmother on my father's side, had bags of Eight energy. My granny was small in stature, measuring only 5 feet 1 inch, but she had a big presence. She was the matriarch of our family, and in her marriage with Grandpa Burt, she "wore the trousers," so to speak. My dad, also an Eight, respected and feared her. She was tough as nails on the outside, but soft as marshmallow on the inside. She was very independent and never asked for help. Amazingly, she was legally blind for three years before anyone knew. She made the family doctor swear not to tell anyone. "She didn't want any sympathy," he told us after we found out. At Granny and Grandpa's diamond wedding anniversary party, granny made the DJ play her favorite song on repeat. The song was "My Way," by Frank Sinatra, which is an anthem for Eights.

My dad was a textbook example of both a healthy and unhealthy Eight. For many years, he was the rock in our family. He was passionately in love with my mum. He loved his two boys very much. Growing up, I always felt safe and protected by him. My dad's love made me feel empowered and self-confident. Like his mum, he was very independent. Dad had only a few close friends. He didn't suffer fools gladly. He had a short fuse. He swore like a trooper. His favorite expletive was "Fuck." In my teenage years, we found out Dad was drinking heavily. His inner demons had resurfaced. In WWII, he had served as a navy officer and was twice torpedoed and lost many friends. I never saw his medals. He never talked about the war. Dad was a proud Eight, he wouldn't accept help, and he drank himself to death.

Healthy Qualities of Eights

When Eights are healthy and well-balanced, they display essential qualities that we all love and appreciate. Here are a few things healthy Eights have told me about themselves:

- "I am self-reliant and strong-willed."
- "I march to the beat of my own drum."
- "I am the master of my own fate."
- "I enjoy taking on a big challenge."
- "I naturally take charge in tough situations."

- "I use my strength to serve and protect others."
- "I hate injustice and fight it with a vengeance."
- "I enjoy empowering people I care about."
- "I can be stubborn and headstrong."
- "I keep my cards close to my chest."

Unhealthy Qualities of Eights

When Eights are out of balance, they are more ego-driven, forceful, defended, and afraid of being vulnerable. Here are a few things Eights have told me about themselves:

- "I can be stubborn and headstrong."
- "When I am sad or hurt, I get angry."
- "Always being 'the strong one' isn't easy."
- "I can be overpowering and intimidating."
- "I think vulnerability is a sign of weakness."
- "I can be a bull in a china shop."
- "I have a hard time asking for help."
- "I make too many decisions by myself."
- "I can be too self-reliant for my own good."
- "I expect people to reject me eventually."

RECOGNIZING TYPE EIGHTS

In philosophy, the teachings of Socrates carry a strong Eight energy. Socrates (469–399 BCE) is recognized as one of the founders of Western philosophy. The maxim "Know Thyself" is attributed to him. Socrates was a philosopher and a soldier in the Athenian army. He was enigmatic, shrewd, nonconformist, and a free thinker. "I am not an Athenian, nor a Greek, but a citizen of the world," he insisted. He taught self-mastery and inner strength. "Strong minds discuss ideas, average minds discuss events, weak minds discuss

> *I cannot teach anybody anything. I can only make them think.*
>
> — Socrates

people," he said. His Socratic Method encourages dialogue and openness. "I know that I am intelligent because I know that I know nothing," he said. Socrates insisted that only by surrendering to a higher power do we become wise, potent, and loving human beings.

> *Two things in life are infinite: the stupidity of man and the mercy of God.*
> — G. I. Gurdjieff

In psychology, George Ivanovich Gurdjieff was an Eight. Gurdjieff taught his own blend of psychology, spirituality, and mysticism, and introduced the Enneagram to the West. Russ Hudson, a longtime student of Gurdjieff's work, described Gurdjieff as the "Socrates of the twentieth century." Those who met Gurdjieff were struck by his big aura and commanding presence. His teaching style was direct and confrontive. "I ask you to believe nothing that you cannot verify for yourself," wrote Gurdjieff in *Views from the Real World*. Interestingly, Gurdjieff taught the Enneagram using his own Gurdjieff Movements or Sacred Dances. He made sure his students embodied the Enneagram by working with all three centers: head, heart, and body.

Like Socrates, Gurdjieff taught self-mastery. In his model called the Fourth Way, he taught people to liberate themselves from the personality or ego-self, which he described as an "automation" and "a machine." Gurdjieff said, "Speaking frankly . . . contemporary man as we know him is nothing more than merely a clockwork mechanism, though of a very complex construction." Being an Eight, Gurdjieff was dedicated to Truth, with a capital *T*, and to living truthfully. He said that most of us are sleepwalking through life and are not truly awake or alive. Gurdjieff said, "You are in prison. If you wish to get out of prison, the first thing you must do is realize that you are in prison. If you think you are free, you can't escape." Getting out of prison is what the Enneagram is for.

> *The Work is about making personality passive, a servant rather than a master.*
> — G. I. Gurdjieff

In leadership, Eights want to be the chief strategist who calls the shots, hires and fires, crunches the numbers, and drives everyone forward. Like Sevens, they are entrepreneurial and want to be their own boss. Over the years, I've worked with many leaders in CEO positions or similar, and most were Eights. Eights are not necessarily better at leadership than the other Types, but they do have a big appetite for it and revel in the challenge. Steve Jobs is a good example of a leader with strong Eight energy. Jobs was the driving force behind Apple Inc.'s meteoric success. His leadership style was autocratic. He was feared and revered. He was empowering and intimidating. He was also good at spotting talent, and he gave people the license to invent and create.

Steve Jobs was a high school dropout who got interested in technology, invented a market, and changed the future. The interface between technology and creativity was what most interested him. He saw technology as a tool that might help humanity think differently. "I would trade all of my technology for an afternoon with Socrates," said Jobs in an article entitled "The Classroom of the Future," published in *Newsweek* magazine. In his commencement speech for Stanford University in 2005, he encouraged the graduates to seize their life. He said:

> *We're here to put a dent in the universe. Otherwise, why else even be here?*
>
> — Steve Jobs

> Your time is limited, so don't waste it living someone else's life. Don't be trapped by dogma—which is living with the results of other people's thinking. Don't let the noise of others' opinions drown out your own inner voice. And, most important, have the courage to follow your heart and intuition. They somehow already know what you truly want to become. Everything else is secondary.

In the arts, Ludwig van Beethoven was a forceful, hot-tempered, ill-mannered, creative genius who flouted social convention and carried on composing against all odds. He wrote nine symphonies—known as Beethoven's Mighty Nine—and was completely deaf by the time he wrote his Ninth Symphony (the one that includes "Ode to Joy" in the final movement). Johann Wolfgang von Goethe described Beethoven as an "untamed personality." He said, "I have never seen an artist more condensed, more energetic, more intimate." "DA-DA-DA-DUM," the iconic four-note motif that begins Beethoven's Fifth Symphony (also called the Victory Symphony) is surely the perfect entrance music for an Eight.

Eights bring their full-on energy, intensity, and attack to every genre of music. Beethoven was the original heavy rocker. He inspired many heavy metal rock bands who, with their stack of Marshall amplifiers, belt out songs at a volume that exceed 120 decibels, which is the equivalent effect of standing on a runway when a jet takes off. Think of AC/DC's "Highway to Hell," Deep Purple's "Smoke on the Water," Led Zeppelin's "Kashmir," and Iron Maiden's "Number of the Beast." For other genres, think of Frank

> *I want to seize fate by the throat.*
>
> — Ludwig van Beethoven

Sinatra and the Rat Pack, who performed "King of the Road"; Aretha Franklin, the Queen of Soul, who sang "Respect"; rapper 2Pac and his album *Me Against the World*; country singer Garth Brooks, who sang "The Thunder Rolls"; and singer-songwriter Pink and her song "Fuckin' Perfect," all of whom display tons of Eight energy.

Pablo Picasso displayed many Eight traits. He tore up the rule book and pioneered new techniques in fine art such as Cubism, constructed sculpture, and collage. The bull, a symbol for virility, was one of his chief motifs. His most famous work, *Guernica*, is regarded by many critics as the most moving and powerful anti-war painting in history. "If only we could pull out our brain and use only our eyes," said Picasso. His contemporary, Ernest Hemingway, author of *The Old Man and the Sea* and *A Moveable Feast*, wrote with similar vigor and gusto. He was known for his outsized personality, his macho swagger, and self-destructive behavior. His writing style was sensitive, blunt, direct, and real. "There is nothing to writing. All you do is sit down at a typewriter and bleed," is a quote attributed to Hemingway.

> *Art washes away from the soul the dust of everyday life.*
> — Pablo Picasso

Toni Morrison was the first Black woman to win the Nobel Prize for Literature. Her novels *Sula*, *Song of Solomon*, and *Beloved* were written with earth-shaking honesty and sensitivity. Hailed as a "visionary force," she has inspired a new generation of writers. "If you have some power, then your job is to empower somebody else," said Morrison. And think of Queen Latifah, songwriter, hip-hop artist, actress, film producer, and activist. Her first single was "Wrath of My Madness," and her film credits include *Living Out Loud*.

In film, Eights deliver powerful and nuanced performances. Think of John Wayne, nicknamed the Duke, in *True Grit* and *The Searchers*; and Clint Eastwood in *The Good, the Bad and the Ugly*, and *Unforgiven*. Also, Samuel L. Jackson in *Unbreakable*, and Al Pacino in *The Godfather*. Think of the spirited Princess Leia in *Star Wars* ("Aren't you a little short for a stormtrooper?" she says to her would-be rescuer, Luke Skywalker); and Captain Marvel, played by Brie Larson, a female Avenger who possesses superhuman strength. And Orson Welles, in *Citizen Kane*, the epic rise-and-fall story of publishing mogul Charles Foster Kane. On his deathbed, Kane utters "Rosebud," which we later discover is the name on his childhood sled. Thompson, the reporter who tries to solve the

> *Life is so much bigger, grander, higher, and wider than we allow ourselves to think.*
> — Queen Latifah

puzzle of Kane's dying word, says, "Maybe Rosebud was something he couldn't get, or something he lost."

In Shakespeare, think of the main protagonist in *Henry V*. The play begins with a Chorus who calls for "a muse of fire" and then introduces us to the "warlike Harry" who is about to take on a seemingly impossible challenge. Leaving behind his misspent youth, Harry ventures forth and grows into a strong and wise leader. He assembles a band of brothers. He gives several powerful speeches. "Once more unto the breach, dear friends, once more!" Against all odds, he wins the Battle of Agincourt. Finally, he woos and marries the princess of France, and he thereby unites two nations.

> *Every subject's duty is the king's, but every subject's soul is his own.*
> — King Henry V

THE IMPERISHABLE SOUL

> *It is perfectly certain that the soul is immortal and imperishable, and our souls will actually exist in another world.*
> — Socrates, *Phaedo*

The Enneagram, with its origins in Greek philosophy, recognizes that truth is eternal, and the soul is immortal. Plato's *Phaedo,* also known as *On the Soul*, features a dialogue with Socrates, who has been imprisoned and sentenced to death by the Athenian Courts for causing civil disobedience among the youth. "Be true to thine own self," he tells them. He encourages them to focus not on worldly power or political gain, but on wisdom, truth, and "care for your soul." The Athenian Courts offer Socrates clemency if he agrees to renounce his teachings, which he refuses to do. Before his execution, Socrates engages in a dialogue on the soul in which he presents four main arguments as to why the soul is immortal and how the soul, being made in the likeness of the divine, is the seat of true wisdom and power.

Martin Luther King Jr. embodied many healthy qualities of an Eight, including what his family described as his "strength of soul," "magnanimous heart," and "enduring love." MLK Jr. was a Baptist minister, political philosopher, and the most prominent leader in the American Civil Rights campaign of 1950s and 1960s until his assassination on April 4, 1968. He was a drum major for justice, brotherhood, and peace. He was opposed to the "triple evils of society" of racism, economic inequality, and militarism. While incarcerated, he wrote "Letter from Birmingham Jail," in which he drew inspiration from Socrates's dialogue on the soul. He cited Socrates's "unswerving commitment to truth," and Socrates's example of being "a nonviolent gadfly" and "an irritant" to injustice anywhere and everywhere.

As we shall see, healthy Eights call upon a power greater than that of the ego. Like Socrates and MLK Jr., they are in touch with an inner strength that is not just muscular or willful. MLK Jr. called it "soul force" or "soul power." This power does not belong only to Type Eights; every Type can access it. For Eights, it is about surrender and service. It is also about love. MLK Jr. called upon everyone to step into their true power and their greatness. He famously said:

> Everybody can be great because everybody can serve.
> You don't have to have a college degree to serve.
> You don't have to make your subject and your verb
> agree to serve. You only need a heart full of grace,
> a soul generated by love.

As with the other Ennea-Types, the healthy qualities and signature strengths of Type Eights arise from being in contact with their True Self. Let's take a closer look at some examples of these healthy traits.

An Indomitable Spirit. Eights are blessed with an indomitable spirit that gives them inner strength and confidence to face life's challenges. In Latin, the word *spiritus* means also "vigor," "soul," and "courage." Eights are powerful souls. They stand firm in their I AM or True Self. They refuse to be dominated or overcome by external forces. They trust that *spirit always prevails over matter* and that *truth always triumphs over deception*. "I thank whatever gods may be / For my unconquerable soul," wrote William Ernest Henley in his famous poem "Invictus."

Sense of Aliveness. Eights have a strong personal magnetism, a big aura, and a bristling sense of aliveness. They are plugged in to universal energy. "It was not I who lived, but life rather that lived me," wrote R. S. Thomas, the Welsh poet and Anglican priest. They're also plugged in to the original energy of the soul. The Hindu bible, the Bhagavad Gita, recognizes the indestructible nature of this soul energy. It declares, "But the soul is indestructible; spades cannot cut it down, fire does not burn it, water does not wet it, and the wind never dries it. The soul is beyond the power of all such things."

Warrior Archetype. Eights embody the Warrior archetype—a masculine energy in the collective unconscious that arms a person with strength, determination, and fight. Eights have a strong sense of fight in them. Healthy Eights will fight for you. They don't hesitate to speak the truth. They relish a lively debate. They butt heads with authority. They oppose darkness and evil. Unhealthy Eights fight only for their own interests or for the sake of fighting. But healthy Eights channel their fight energy into a great work and into something truly worth fighting for.

Big Heartedness. Eights are known for having "a big heart" and for being "hard-hearted." A big life challenge for Eights is to cultivate a healthy relationship with their heart. When Eights are centered in their heart, and their actions are inspired by love, they are at the height of their powers. Martin Luther King Jr., in *Strength to Love*, encouraged everyone to be tough-minded, but not hard-hearted. His message was: *Be tough-minded enough to transcend the world and tender-hearted enough to live in it*. As an Eight, you know in your heart there is no power greater than love.

Bullshit Detector. Eights like to "keep it real" and detest falsity. Their social style is to be up-front, direct, and honest. They have an inbuilt bullshit detector for tackling deception, hypocrisy, and corruption. Another name for their bullshit detector is "gut instinct." As an Eight, you can spot bullshit from a mile away. Your bullshit detector protects you from being harmed. It also keeps you honest with yourself. "My bullshit detector lets me know when I'm being an asshole," Dan, an Eight, told me. Above all, the bullshit detector helps Eights to remember what is sacred and what really matters.

Natural Leader. Eights are called the Leader in some Enneagram circles. Eights make things happen. They are assertive and decisive. "I'm just like my country—I'm young, scrappy, and hungry, and I am not throwing away my shot," said Alexander Hamilton in *Hamilton* the musical. Eights take responsibility for their life. They see obstacles as opportunities. Their mantra is "when the going gets tough, the tough get going." "My world did not shrink because I was a black female writer. It just got bigger," said Toni Morrison, author of *Song of Solomon*.

Higher Power. Eights draw a lot of strength from being independent, but too much independence is an Achilles' heel for Eights. Fortunately, Eights have a superpower, which is the willingness to be vulnerable. An Eight's real strength comes from a healthy mix of self-reliance and vulnerability. "No one is big enough to be independent of others," said Dr. William Mayo. Eights will tell you that being vulnerable feels like the opposite of strength, but in truth, it is a golden key that grants you access to a higher power and a new level of aliveness, strength, inspiration, and love.

LOSS OF POWER

> *We cannot long survive spiritually separated in a world that is geographically together.*
>
> – Martin Luther King Jr., **Strength to Love**

Martin Luther King Jr. believed the greatest challenge humanity faces is overcoming our sense of separateness. In many of his speeches, he began with an affirmation of our Oneness with each other, our planet, and with God. In one of his greatest speeches, "The Birth of a New Age," MLK Jr. said,

> Through our scientific means we have made of the world a neighborhood and now the challenge confronts us through our moral and spiritual means to make of it a brotherhood. We must live together; we are not independent, we are interdependent. We are all involved in a single process. Whatever affects one directly affects

all indirectly for we are tied together in a single progress. We are all linked in the great chain of humanity.

MLK Jr., like a true Eight, spoke the truth as he saw it. "A man dies when he refuses to take a stand for that which is true," he said. He maintained that our failure to embrace our Oneness is the root cause of all humanity's suffering, including segregation and racism, prejudice and injustice, individualism and greed, famine and pollution, and war and conflict. MLK Jr. said that our most pressing challenge is "to rise above the narrow confines of our individualistic concerns, with a broader concern for all humanity." In his "Letter from Birmingham Jail," he wrote:

> In a real sense all life is inter-related. All men are caught in an inescapable network of mutuality, tied in a single garment of destiny. Whatever affects one directly, affects all indirectly. I can never be what I ought to be until you are what you ought to be, and you can never be what you ought to be until I am what I ought to be . . .
> This is the inter-related structure of reality.

The Basic Fear: Not Strong Enough

When Eights experience a sense of separation, a basic fear arises in them of not being strong enough to live autonomously, to be master of their fate, and to overcome life's challenges.

The Eight's basic fear of "I am not strong enough" activates a secondary fear of being dominated or ruled over against their will. For example, by an overbearing parent, an autocratic boss, an external authority figure, or controlling partner. To counteract this threat, Eights may adopt a very defensive outlook on life. They strike a pose of "me against the world." They bristle with anger when someone tells them to do something. They will not be influenced by others. They are wary of giving their power away. "As an Eight, I realize my defensiveness is a double-edged sword," said Tim, a lawyer, who took my Love and the Enneagram retreat in Findhorn, Scotland. He said, "My defenses make me impenetrable. They prevent me being taken advantage of, but they also block intimacy, friendship, and love."

> *Vulnerability is not weakness; it's our greatest measure of courage.*
>
> — Brené Brown

Eights often learn the hard way that being defensive doesn't make you less afraid; rather, it increases fear. The more defensive a person is, the more afraid they are to be vulnerable, for instance. Eights see vulnerability as a weakness. They're afraid that being vulnerable will expose them to being violated or rejected. Professor Brené Brown is a leading researcher on the essential need for vulnerability. I often feature her work when I teach the Point Eight on the Enneagram. Her books include *Rising Strong, Daring Greatly,* and *The Power of Vulnerability.* Her TED Talk on "The Power of Vulnerability" has been viewed millions of times. "True strength lies in acknowledging our vulnerabilities and working through them," says Brené Brown.

Eights will try to counteract the fear of "I am not strong enough" by being independent of others. Being independent is highly prized by Eights because they believe it makes them strong. Independence does have its benefits, but too much independence amplifies separation and aloneness, and causes more harm than it prevents. For instance, independence is a defense against vulnerability. Brené Brown has described vulnerability as the birthplace of connectivity and as the path to connection. "Connection is why we are here," she said. "We are hardwired to connect with others, and without it, there is suffering." She concludes, "Staying vulnerable is a risk we have to take if we want to experience connection."

Here are a few things Eights have told me about living with their basic fear of not being strong enough.

- "I hate feeling small or not strong enough."
- "I get angry when I feel weak or powerless."
- "I actively resist being controlled by others."
- "I operate as if it's me against the world."
- "My motto: 'Stand on your own two feet.'"
- "I am always pushing myself to the limit."
- "I wish I had Wonder Woman bracelets."
- "I armor my heart against getting hurt."
- "I can be too quick to write people off."
- "I struggle with emotional vulnerability."

Childhood Story: Strong-Willed

Eights enter the world like the rest of us, as a fragile baby that is entirely dependent on a parent or parenting figure to feed them and keep them alive. They have dropped out of eternity and into time. Their body is perishable, even if their soul is indestructible. When young Eights enter the separation phase of childhood, they feel weak and vulnerable, and they don't like it one bit. Being in a small body can be alarming and frustrating for Eights. They are keen to grow up quickly. They want to be strong, be independent, and exercise their powers. They aim to cultivate an inner strength, or a show of strength at least, that will help them to survive and take charge of their life.

> *I was a very defensive kid 'cause I was really sensitive underneath and didn't want people to know. So, I came off as very tough and very angry.*
>
> — Pink, singer and actress

Young Eights are often described as being strong-willed or high-spirited children. Their physical circuits hum with energy. They are very active and will keep going until the tank is empty. "My mom would always ask me, 'Aren't you tired?' and Dad would say, 'You must be tired by now,' and I'd tell them, 'No, I'm not,' even when I was on my last legs," says Sam, an Eight. Young Eights can be a handful for their parents and teachers. They are willful and assertive. They resist being told what to do. They have no problem saying no. "You can't make me!" they say. They don't shy away from a conflict. They engage in power struggles. When a young Eight perceives they are being belittled or mistreated, they will fight their corner.

My son, Christopher, has a lot of Eight energy. As soon as he could talk, he asked "big" questions like "When will I be big?" and "How soon will I be bigger?" He was curious to know about the biggest dinosaur, the biggest whale, and the biggest star in the sky. He once asked me, "Daddy, what's bigger than the world?" When I'd wave good-bye to him at the school gates, he would shout, "I love you bigger than space." In my book *Higher Purpose*, I share a conversation I had with Christopher when he was three years old. We were on the beach at Encinitas, California, watching surfers ride waves. "Would you like to be a surfer when you grow up, Dad?" he asked me. We talked some more, and then he said, "I know what I want to be when I grow up." After a short pause, he said, "What I really want to be is a bigger me."

Young Eights are keen to show everyone "I am a big person, and I can make my own decisions." They want to "be big" as soon as possible because they see "being big" as the best defense against being harmed. Young Eights will be adults soon enough, but sometimes life events force them into being "little adults" even sooner. "My dad died when I was thirteen years old," says Alan, an Eight, who did some Enneagram coaching with me. "I channeled all my grief into being 'the man' of the family. I told my mom I would protect her and look after things. I got my first job the week after my dad's funeral. I had three jobs on the go by Christmas that year. Overnight, I became a man, and I put away childish things."

The "Be Strong" Driver: Eights are born with a "Be Strong" driver installed in their ego operating system. Young Eights want to "be strong" to shield themselves against life's slings and arrows. Th ego-ideal for Eights is to be so strong that they never feel weak, get hurt, or are overpowered. In the Marvel movies, Captain America's shield is made of vibranium, the toughest material in the universe, and the Black Panther's suit is composed of a vibranium weave. "Imagine how cool it would be to have a vibranium body," said my son, Christopher, with a big smile while we were watching *Captain America: The First Avenger* for the third time!

The "Be Strong" driver has an upside. It helps young Eights to take responsibility for their life, to know their own mind, to stand up for themselves, and to overcome obstacles and challenges. But the "Be Strong" driver can also cause problems for Eights, especially when it is not tempered with wisdom or love. For example, Eights may internalize messages such as "It is not okay to cry," "It is not okay to ask for help," and "It is not okay to admit mistakes." They then take on the role of the Rock, the Protector, the Strong One, and the Provider in relationships and work. These roles can be a shield that blocks intimacy and causes heartbreak if worn too tightly.

Steve, an Eight, was the school bully, and he made sure everyone feared him. Soon after he left school, he got into trouble with the police. His mum arranged a meeting for Steve and me. I got Steve to take an Enneagram test, and I gave him a challenge. "The real challenge of your life is to work out what real strength is and to put your strength to good use," I told him. "You can use your strength to be destructive or creative. It's up to you. You can either play small or play big. It's your choice." That meeting was over 15 years ago. Today, Steve is a qualified social worker, he has trained in the Enneagram, and he works with young offenders in prisons and in society. He recently received a CBE from HRH King Charles in recognition of his services to disadvantaged and vulnerable children.

Let's look at some examples of how the basic fear, childhood story, and "Be Strong" driver operates for Eights in the three biological instincts: (1) Self-Preservation Instinct (SP), which is mostly about lifestyle, material matters, and self-care; (2) Social Instinct (SO), which is mostly about relating to family, society, and the world; and (3) (SX) Sexual Instinct (also called One-to-One Instinct), which is mostly about attraction, relating style, and romance.

Self-Preservation Instinct (SP) *Healthy:* Your focus is to engineer a lifestyle that gives you autonomy and a license to do things "my way." You prize financial independence. You make sure you control the purse strings. You look after yourself physically. You are the subtype most likely to run a marathon, do an Iron Man, or take up a martial art. It's a jungle out there, and life is about the survival of the fittest. *Not-so-healthy:* SP Eights are typically more introverted and independent than SO and SX Eights. You protect your personal space. You control your calendar. You prioritize work over relationships. You spend so much time managing the finances, ensuring your loved ones are financially protected, that you are often absent from their lives. *Unhealthy:* Eights don't rest; they take power naps. You have a big engine in you, and you often override your body's signals as you charge through the day. You treat your body like an object. You are the type most likely to have high blood pressure and do nothing about it.

Social Instinct (SO) *Healthy:* An SO Eight is typically more extroverted than the other Eight subtypes. Family means a lot to you, and you count your best friends as family. You are known for your love of camaraderie and friendship. Your mantra is: *We are stronger together.* You get a kick out of empowering others so that they can make their mark on the world. You are warm, expressive, and have softer edges than SP and SX Eights. *Not-so-healthy:* You gravitate toward social circles and clubs that swear allegiance, have a code of honor, but are not pretentious or stuffy. You like to be part of the gang, and you naturally assume a role of group leader or chief influencer. You must learn to share your seat of power; otherwise it leads to power struggles. *Unhealthy:* You automatically take on the role of the Rock or Protector, a bit like Jack Byrnes, played by Robert De Niro, in *Meet the Parents*, who keeps his family protected inside his "circle of trust." Your stance is "us against others." Your mantra is: *Know your enemy.* You have a win-lose attitude. You are sensitive to rejection and betrayal. Once someone is out of your circle of trust, they don't get back in.

Sexual Instinct (SX) *Healthy:* An SX Eight is typically more assertive, passionate, and intense than the other Eight subtypes. They are drawn to relationships and to opportunities that are exciting and add spice to life. They are often "gung-ho" and "all in" when starting up businesses and new projects. In romance, if they ever settle down and go steady, they make sure it is with someone they can build a nest with and whom they trust implicitly. *Not-so-healthy*: An Eight's passion, or source of suffering, is lust. SX Eights are prone to being excessive and over-the-top. They can be shameless in their pursuit of pleasure and power. They are pushy and combative. They enjoy a good argument. "A good fight clears the air," they say. But they also fight too hard. "I was only play-fighting!" they insist. An Eight's "too-muchness" can cause irreparable harm and upset. *Unhealthy:* SX Eights who are not in touch with their heart can be possessive, controlling, and abusive. They rule over others. When you cross an Eight, they can be "angrier than God." They can be vindictive, vengeful, and show no mercy.

Passion: Lust or Forcefulness

All nine Types on the Enneagram experience a *passion*, or cause of suffering in the heart, that emerges from a sense of separation and from the basic fear. The passion for Eights is called Lust, which is another of the so-called cardinal sins. Lust is one of the "greedy sins" along with avarice, envy, and gluttony. It describes a feverish pursuit of carnal pleasures such as sex, food, money, and power. Lust is fiery, pulsating, and energetic, but it is always short-lived and ends not with a bang but with a whimper.

> *Love surfeits not, Lust like a glutton dies; Love is all truth, Lust full of forged lies.*
>
> — William Shakespeare, *Venus and Adonis*

Lust is not just an Eight-thing. All nine Types on the Enneagram are prone to lust when out of balance and not centered in their True Self. For instance, Sevens seek adventure and are known for being hedonistic, chasing rainbows, and never feeling satisfied; Threes crave attention, recognition, and fame; Nines are attached to comfort and peace; Fours experience lust as envy and as a deep longing for love that is unrequited or out of reach; and Fives have an insatiable urge to collect and store knowledge. That said, Eights are the most lustful of all Types. No one who is not an Eight can "out-lust" an Eight.

Lust has been described as the most visible of sins. Lust is rarely discreet or modest. When lust has got the better of someone, it's obvious. Lust is a private matter; but it is always played out in public. "Society drives people crazy with lust and calls it advertising," wrote John Lahr, the theater critic and writer. We are lustful when we are acquisitive and in a "having mode" rather than a "being mode." For instance, when we shop for "must-have items," chase after happiness, want to be in control, seek power, and insist that "my will be done."

Eights are lustful when they experience a loss of wholeness and feel disconnected to their original energy. They are like Samson in the Bible story, which is a parable about remembering the source of your true power. Samson is a Nazirite with long hair, and his hair represents his link to God and his vow to serve a higher purpose. He is a great leader who is blessed with immense physical strength. He is also lustful, prone to temptation, and visits a prostitute in Gaza. When Samson is betrayed by his lover, Delilah, his head is shaven by the Philistines, and he is made powerless. While in prison, Samson prays to God for strength, his hair grows back again, and he performs one final act of strength and thus fulfills his divine purpose.

Let's take a closer look at how Eights experience the passion of lust and what they can do to make sure they are not overpowered by lust.

> **Loss of Aliveness.** "Don't ask what the world needs. Ask what makes you come alive and go do it. Because what the world needs is people who have come alive," said Howard Thurman, the philosopher, a mentor to Martin Luther King Jr. An Eight's basic desire is to feel a sense of aliveness. Another name for aliveness is *life force*. When Eights are in touch with their life force, their primal energy, there is no need for lust or excessive forcefulness. It's only when Eights are "not in their true power," so to speak, that the temptation of lust arises. A good inquiry for Eights is, *What makes me come alive?*
>
> **An Armored Heart.** Eights are lustful when they're not in contact with their heart. Eights try to make the heart bulletproof to be

strong and not get hurt. The problem with this defensive strategy is that an armored heart blocks attack and love. Too much emotional armament cuts you off from the wisdom of your heart, it isolates you from others, and you feel weaker, not stronger. Real love, connection, and intimacy only happen when the heart is undefended. When Eights lower their defenses, they realize the heart is not just a muscle, it is a seat of power, and herein lies their true strength.

Love Substitutes. Healthy Eights are forged by their heartbreaks and emerge from them stronger and wiser. When Eights won't deal directly with a heartbreak, they get emotionally blocked and are less able to love and be loved. When Eights resist doing the inner work to heal a heartbreak, they typically become lustful and will lust after "love substitutes" such as sex, shopping, money, fame, status, power, or candy. None of these replacements for love are satisfactory, no matter how much spice they add to life.

Making a Grab. When Eights are lustful, they are grabby. Grabbiness is trying to get something by force. Grabbing is taking without asking. Eights who take the position of "me against the world" don't believe they can ask for anything. Grabby Eights are too independent to join in with the reciprocal flow of giving and receiving. Their mantra is: "I get what I take." Being grabby blocks the capacity to receive. The grabbier you are, the less you can enjoy what you have. A good heart meditation for Eights is to practice gratitude for the blessings that life freely offers you (and that you don't have to grab or lust after).

What Is Sacred. When Eights are overpowered by lust, it is because they've forgotten what is sacred. They have committed adultery, so to speak, and are more interested in matters of the flesh than of spirit. "From whence come wars, and fighting, and factions? Whence but from the body and the lusts of the body?" said Socrates. Eights want to play big and live a larger life, and to do this, they must put spirit before matter. They must live from their sacred center. They don't have to believe in a God in the sky, but they must know in their heart what is sacred and real. And most of all, they must surrender to love.

Fixation: Vengeance

In the Enneagram, the fixation refers to a mental habit that disturbs your mental health and well-being. The fixation for Eights is commonly called vengeance.

Socrates, whom we met earlier, was a philosopher who educated people on how to think. One of his best-known maxims is: "To find yourself, think for yourself." Like a true Eight, he empowered people to "know your own mind" and "not let others tell you what to think." His Socratic Method was based on open-mindedness and humility, and it trained students to question their thinking, challenge assumptions, and test ideas to see if they are valid or not. Healthy Eights nod in approval at Socrates and his school of thinking. By remaining open and humble, Eights learn to recognize what is true or not, and this strengthens their capacity to be wise and loving.

Unhealthy Eights get into trouble when they don't examine their thinking and won't challenge their beliefs or ideas. Instead of being open-minded, they are hard-headed, fixed in their opinions, and unwilling to yield or budge on anything. They would rather be right than be happy. There is a popular saying, *the truth will set you free, but first it will piss you off.* Unhealthy Eights would rather stay pissed off and angry than admit to a mistake or surrender to the truth. Their thinking style is forceful and defiant. Their stance is: *Don't let other people's opinions influence you!* This is when vengeance rears its head in Eights and causes much trouble and woe.

> *Education is the kindling of a flame, not the filling of a vessel.*
> — Socrates

All nine Ennea-Types can relate to vengeance, even Type Nines who are known for being calm and peace loving. We've all experienced the urge to be vengeful, even saints and babies. When you take a toy away from a baby, you're asking for trouble. Eights, however, are the most prone Type to being overpowered by vengeance. Vengeance can ruin an Eight, unless they are willing to examine its causes and go for something better. Here are five ways that the fixation of vengeance plays itself out in Eights.

> *I want to be indifferent to vengeance. It's degrading. Not having a spirit of vengeance protects me, internally.*
> — Ségolène Royal

Seeking Revenge. "As an Eight, when I get hurt, my first impulse is to seek revenge. If I bang my thumb with a hammer, I want to break the hammer. If I cut myself with a knife, I want to throw the knife against a wall so that it feels what I feel," Donna, an Eight, told me. Anger flares up in an Eight when they get hurt physically or emotionally. They hate the feeling of being hurt because it makes them feel small and not strong enough. They want retribution and will take matters into their own hands. They try to numb the hurt or discharge the pain by being vindictive and taking revenge.

Staying Angry. Vengeance has its roots in anger. Anger is a go-to emotion for Eights. When Eights are hurt, they get angry. When they feel sad, they get angry. When Eights are tired, they get angry. When they are anxious, they get angry. When they're afraid, they get angry. Most of all, Eights get angry when they feel small or powerless. "As an Eight on the Enneagram, I've learned that I get angry when I am not grounded in my true power," says Scott, who took my Leadership and the Enneagram program. "And the longer I stay angry, the weaker and more powerless I become."

Love or Hate. Hard-headed Eights are known for having strong opinions and reactions. They blow "hot and cold." They either "love it or hate it." People are either "smart or stupid." They stand "for or against" things. People are either "in or out." "Hate" is a powerful word, and Eights are not afraid to use it. Young Eights will yell "I hate this" and "I hate you," even if they've been told a hundred times not to say the word *hate*. Hatred is often a cover for feelings of heartbreak and powerless. Sam, an Eight, took my Love and the Enneagram program. Sam told me, "After my divorce, I believed that if I hated my Ex enough, I'd forget I ever loved them."

Eye for an Eye. When Eights are hurt, their impulse is to take revenge. They want to fight fire with fire. "An eye for an eye" seems fair to an Eight. But, as Martin Luther King Jr. said, "If we do an eye for an eye and a tooth for a tooth, we will be a blind and toothless nation." Eights, like everyone, must learn to practice forgiveness. Why? Because carrying grievances makes you behave like a victim. Vengeance makes you smaller, not bigger. Forgiveness frees you from your tiny self. It releases you from a prison of pain and hate, and it changes the trajectory of your life.

Dog-Eat-Dog. We humans have many frailties, including how inhumane we are to each other. We try to justify our fear, pettiness, and hate by saying things like *It's a dog-eat-dog world* and *Two can play at that game*. "The best revenge is massive success," said Frank Sinatra, the poster boy for Eights. But surely, the best revenge is to *not* to be like the others. For Eights, especially, the greatest success is to remember your imperishable soul, to stand in your truth, and to act less like a wounded dog and more like the person you truly are.

PATH OF SURRENDER

> *Lead me from the unreal to the real*
> *Lead me from darkness to light*
> *Lead me from death to immortality*
>
> — Pavamana Mantra

The Enneagram offers a path of growth for all nine Types that helps you to remember your original nature and be your True Self. For Eights, their path of growth is a path of surrender.

"When I first read that surrender is the saving grace for Eights, I threw the book across the room and shouted *F*ck that!*" said Mike, an Eight, who took my Coaching and the Enneagram program in New York. Mike is a soldier and was on active duty in Afghanistan at the time. His commanding officer gave him special leave to attend my program. To get to New York from Afghanistan, he had to take two helicopter flights and three journeys by plane. Mike and I talked on stage in front of three hundred people.

"My motto is: *Never surrender*," Mike told me.

"I hear you," I said.

"Surrender is bullshit!" he said.

"Do you believe that?" I asked.

"Hell, yes."

"Why are you here on this program, then?" I asked

"There's a bluebird in my heart," he said.

"What's that?" I asked.

"It's from a poem by Charles Bukowski."

"Oh yes, 'Bluebird.' I know it," I said.

"Then you know why I am here," he said.

Mike recited the poem "Bluebird" to us. He knew it by heart. Tears rolled down his face as he spoke. There was barely a dry eye in the room. The bluebird in Bukowski's poem represents something sacred inside of us. The soul, maybe. Our creative spark, perhaps. Or our original innocence. It's open to interpretation. The poem begins:

> there's a bluebird in my heart that
> wants to get out
> but I'm too tough for him,
> I say, stay in there, I'm not going
> to let anybody see
> you.

Eights are on a path of surrender, whether they like it or not. Many Eights, like Mike, don't like it because they believe surrender is a weakness. Eights must challenge their thinking about surrender if they are to grow and live a larger life. When Eights change their mind about surrender, it becomes a strength, not a weakness. "Surrender is only a good idea if it makes you stronger," I told Mike. In our conversation, we talked about laying down the burden of being strong, dropping the tough-guy act, lowering ego defenses, and giving the bluebird a chance to express itself and spread its wings.

"Socrates was both a warrior and a philosopher," I told Mike. It's not a choice of being one or the other. You must embrace both if you want to be fully human and fully divine." Working with the Enneagram helps Eights to balance ego and soul, and be "a bigger me," as my son, Christopher, put it as we sat on the beach in San Diego that day.

Virtue: Innocence

Every Ennea-Type has a virtue, or a superpower, that arises naturally as you do your inner work to heal the basic fear, the passion in the heart, and the fixation in your thinking. The virtue for Type Eight is commonly called innocence.

The virtue of innocence is a big surprise to Eights, who typically think of themselves as being too big, bad, tough, and hardened by life to be innocent anymore. It's true that we usually associate innocence with youth. It is symbolized as baby lambs, puppies, the white body of a dove, and newborn children. As we grow up, we long for the innocence of youth again. Remember Orson Welles in *Citizen Kane*, who plays Charles Foster Kane, the publishing magnate. Kane's dying word was "Rosebud," the name of his childhood sled, which was a symbol of his lost innocence and happier times. Adult Eights try to make up for their lost innocence by putting away childish things and becoming strong and impenetrable. What they don't know is that their innocence has remained intact. It is not lost, only hidden from view.

> *The truth in you remains as radiant as a star, as pure as light, as innocent as love itself.*
> — A Course in Miracles

Pablo Picasso saw innocence as both youthful and eternal. He depicted innocence in many of his works. For example, *Child with a Dove* was painted in 1901 when Picasso was 20 years old and struggling to make his mark as an artist. The dove symbolizes purity and peace, and the child is innocence and happiness. One of Picasso's happiest childhood memories was watching his father, José Ruiz y Blasco, paint doves. Picasso often talked about the loss of innocence and our ability to rediscover it later in life. He observed, "Every child is an artist. The problem is how to remain an artist once he grows up." He also said, "It took me four years to paint like Raphael, but a lifetime to paint like a child."

Everyone is born with an original innocence. One of life's greatest challenges is staying in touch with this innocence. Here are some reflections on how Eights can experience innocence in everyday life.

Your Original Energy. Eights mistakenly believe that innocence and strength are opposites, but nothing could be further from the truth. *Innocence is your original energy.* When Eights remember their innocence, it revitalizes them and plugs them back into the abundant supply of energy they were born with. Innocence for Eights is the eternal link to the True Self, just like inner peace is for Nines, original goodness is for Ones, and joy is for Sevens. When an Eight stands in their innocence, they are connected to their I AM and to a higher power.

The Indestructible Soul. The innocence of the ego is fragile. Most of us lose our innocence before we know we have it. In childhood, it takes only one trauma, one act of abuse, and one heartbreak to lose your innocence. But the innocence of the soul is strong and mighty. It is indestructible, and not a one-shot deal. This is your original innocence, and it connects you to your unbreakable spirit that is not tarnished or ruined by matter. "The spirit is beyond destruction. No one can bring an end to spirit which is everlasting," says Krishna to Arjuna in the Bhagavad Gita.

The Unstruck Heart. The word *innocent* from its Latin root means "free from harm" and "not wounded." And in the philosophy of yoga, the Sanskrit name for your heart center, or heart chakra, is *anahata*, which means "unstruck, unhurt, and unbeaten." The ego is fragile and suffers many heartbreaks, but your spirit is not ever broken. Your biography is not who you are. The heart of you—your true essence—is forever strong. "Out of the shell of the broken heart emerges the newborn soul," wrote Hazrat Inayat Khan.

A Forgiving Mind. Eights get angry at themselves for not being bigger, stronger, and more able to defend themselves against hurt and pain. Their self-attack is meant to embolden them, but it only makes them weaker. When Eights forgive themselves for their human frailty, it helps them to remember their original innocence and treat themselves with respect and love. Similarly, when Eights forgive others, it helps them to heal the past, step into the present, and create a better future. No one benefits more from forgiveness than the one who forgives. Forgiveness sets you free.

Surrender to Love. "Man must evolve for all human conflict a method which rejects revenge, aggression and retaliation. The foundation of such a method is love," said Martin Luther King Jr. The source of all our suffering is that we do not love enough. Our tragedy is that we will not surrender to love. *But what power is greater than love?* When Eights deny the power of love, they lose sight of their innocence and are made weak. Only by surrendering to love do they discover their true power. "Love conquers all things, so we too shall yield to love," said Virgil, a Roman poet.

Balancing Your Centers

Eights are called a Body Type on the Enneagram (along with Nines and Ones) because their primary center of intelligence is the body center. Eights, as we have seen, are fitted with a powerful physical engine. They have a strong life force and are enormously willful. They rely on their willpower to charge forward, jump hurdles, break down walls, and push on in the face of massive resistance. Eights take "my will be done" to a whole new level, and yet even Eights cannot rely on willpower alone. Adrenaline and forcefulness get you only so far. The Enneagram teaches Eights that the body center works best when it combines forces with the head center and heart center.

I first met Will, an Eight, two weeks after he had double bypass surgery. When I asked him how his heart was, he brushed my question aside. "My heart had a faulty valve, that's all," he told me. Will was head of Global Intelligence for an international law firm. I served as the leadership coach for this firm for four years. In that time, I worked on each board member's Enneagram profile and did Enneagram coaching with them. I told Will that Eights often treat their heart like an object—a piece of equipment—instead of as a seat of intelligence. "Your heart has a message for you," I told Will. Will countered, "Yeah, and the message was I needed a new valve." After a difficult start, Will and I ended up working together for two years. He called me his heart coach, and together we organized a conference on the Heart of Leadership.

> **Body Center.** Unhealthy Eights override their body's messages and fail to harness what psychologists call body intelligence or physical intuition. "We tend to dismiss our sensations, urges, hunches and gut feelings as unimportant or unreliable. We treat our bodies as vehicles to get to the next meeting, objects to polish for the next party or machines that we hire an expert to fix. Rarely do we consider that our bodies might have wisdom worth listening for," writes Amanda Blake in *Your Body Is Your Brain*. Healthy Eights take physical cues from their body before making decisions or taking action. They have learned to trust their gut instinct and to go with what their body intelligence tells them.

Type Eight

Heart Center. Eights are afraid that the heart center is their "soft center" and will put up walls around the heart to protect themselves. "Sometimes you put up walls not to keep people out, but to see who cares enough to break them down," said Socrates. One of the biggest challenges for Eights is to be willing to take down the walls. An open heart is more powerful than a defended heart. When an Eight keeps their heart open, they combine willpower with heart wisdom. "When I truly open my heart to love, I feel a surge of energy in my body, and I am guided by a wise power that directs my thoughts and actions," Will, the lawyer, once told me.

> *Have the courage to follow your heart and intuition. They somehow know what you truly want to become.*
> — Steve Jobs

Head Center. The Enneagram encourages Eights to meditate on what real strength is. Strength isn't only muscular or willful. It includes heart qualities like being vulnerable, being emotionally honest, forgiving others, apologizing properly, and making repair when you hurt someone. It also includes mental acuity and good decision-making. Steve Jobs once said, "For the past 33 years, I have looked in the mirror every morning and asked myself: 'If today were the last day of my life, would I want to do what I am about to do today?' And whenever the answer has been 'No' for too many days in a row, I know I need to change something."

Spreading Your Wings

Type Eight's home base is Point Eight, which sits between Point Seven and Point Nine on the Enneagram symbol. This means Eights have a 7-Wing and a 9-Wing. Typically, one wing is more dominant than the other, but the goal is to balance your wings. Working with the 7-Wing can help Eights to tap into the essential qualities and wisdom of Point Seven, and working with the 9-Wing can help Eights to access the same at Point Nine. Learning to live

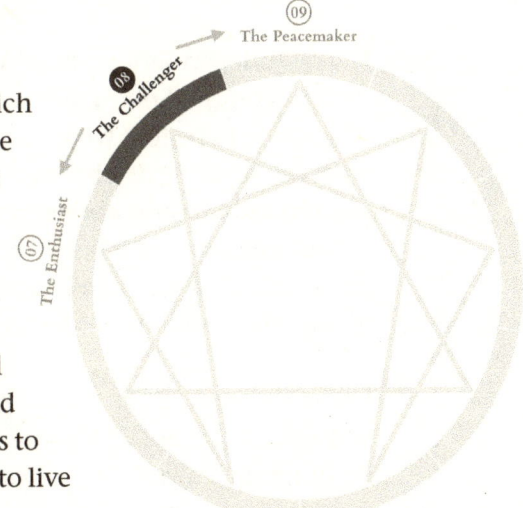

in balance with your wings, by drawing strengths and lessons from both, can be very helpful for Eights.

Eight with a 7-Wing

Eights with a dominant 7-Wing (8w7) are commonly called the Independent or Nonconformist. They show up in the world with the typical traits of Eights, plus some traits of Sevens.

Human Dynamo. An 8w7 combines the essential qualities of Eights with positive traits of Sevens, who are enthusiastic, upbeat, energetic, and fun loving. Both the 8w7 and 7w8 are high-energy personalities. They are known for being a powerhouse, a fireball, and a human dynamo. They have so much energy that they easily lose focus, get scattered, and end up draining themselves. Their challenge is to learn how to use their energy wisely. A good inquiry for an 8w7 is, *How shall I use my energy wisely today?*

Self-Assertive. An 8w7 tends to be more assertive, outgoing, and extroverted than an 8w9. They are the go-getter who is up for a challenge and has a big spirit of adventure. An 8w7 is always on the front foot. They are more lustful than an 8w9. They push themselves to the limit. They can also take things too far. Think of the free-spirited Alexis Zorba in *Zorba The Greek*, played by Anthony Quinn, who says, "Life is trouble. Only death is not. To be alive is to undo your belt and look for trouble."

Fierce Independence. 8w7s are one of the most independent subtypes on the Enneagram. They are dissenters and freethinkers who refuse to be told what to do. They are the type most likely to enjoy horse riding or who own a Harley Davidson motorbike. They want to feel free and not hemmed in. Aretha Franklin, the Queen of Soul, embodied this fierce independence. She said, "Be your own artist, and always be confident in what you're doing. If you're not going to be confident, you might as well not be doing it."

Loose Cannon. 8w7s are known for being a maverick, a rebel, and a loose cannon. They are all-or-nothing people. They don't do things by halves. They often run into trouble because they are too impulsive and don't take time to pause and reflect. They can be their own worst enemy because they won't seek advice and refuse help. Connecting with their heart center, and reaching out to others, is especially helpful for 8w7s.

Entrepreneurial Mindset. 8w7s move mountains when they are connected to a higher power. They are resourceful, pragmatic, and have a great can-do attitude. They challenge themselves to think big and do great things. They also enjoy empowering others to live their dreams. They work hard and play hard, burn the candle at both ends, and go through many ups and downs. They are the type most likely to make a million dollars and lose a million dollars. For 8w7s, this is all part of the fun of taking on big challenges and being willing to learn and grow along the way.

Eight with a 9-Wing

Eights with a dominant 9-Wing (8w9) are commonly called the Bear. They show up in the world with the typical traits of Eights, plus some characteristic traits of Nines.

Inner Strength. 8w9s are known for their inner strength and gentle use of power. This is because they draw upon the calming energy of Point Nine. Like a healthy Type Nine, an 8w9 is self-possessed, cool-headed, and resolute and unwavering in challenging times. They access the essential qualities that give Nines their core strength, such as a gentle spirit, a calm temperament, quiet determination, a positive outlook, and inner peace.

A Big Bear. 8w7s are like a bull, and 8w9s are like a bear. Not like a teddy bear; more like a big bear, a mama bear, or a papa bear. A bull and bear are both strong and powerful, but in different ways. The bull is aggressive and unpredictable, whereas the bear is more laid back and accommodating. A bull is quick to lock horns when it "sees red," so to speak, whereas a bear shows its teeth only if seriously provoked. A bull seeks dominance, whereas a bear can be gentle, tolerant, adaptable, and affectionate. That said, you should never poke a bear.

Even Tempered. An 8w9 and 8w7 have the same core motivations but behave differently in everyday life. For example, an 8w7 tends to charge through the day at a fast pace, whereas an 8w9 is more deliberate and likes to go at their own pace. An 8w7 is choleric and volatile, and they enjoy a bit of "rough and tumble," whereas an 8w9 likes to be calm and even tempered. The speaking style of an 8w7 is direct, candid, and confrontative, whereas an 8w9 is gentle, measured, and softly spoken.

Passive Aggressive. The 8w9 and 9w8 are two of the most stubborn subtypes on the Enneagram. Both Eights and Nines have a sign over them that reads, "Don't mess with me." 8w9s want to be in control and won't be told what to do. They are also less spontaneous and flexible than 8w7s. In a conflict, 8w7s will express their anger directly and won't hold back, whereas an 8w9 will be more passive aggressive and indirect. 8w9s are known for bottling up their anger. Their resistance to anger makes it challenging for them to be emotionally honest, to speak truthfully, and to forgive and let go.

Creature Comforts. Both 8w7s and 8w9s want autonomy and dominion over their surroundings. They are highly territorial and will go to great lengths to mark out "what is mine." 8w7s are more likely to be assertive and want dominion over others, whereas 8w9s are seeking dominion for themselves so that no one bothers them. 8w9s don't want to rule the world; they simply want the world to not interfere with their creature comforts and how they live their life.

Moving to Two and Five

Following the Inner Lines of the Enneagram Symbol, Eights move toward Point Two (home of the Helper) and Point Five (home of the Investigator). These Inner Lines invite Eights to visit these Points to explore the gifts and wisdom they have for you.

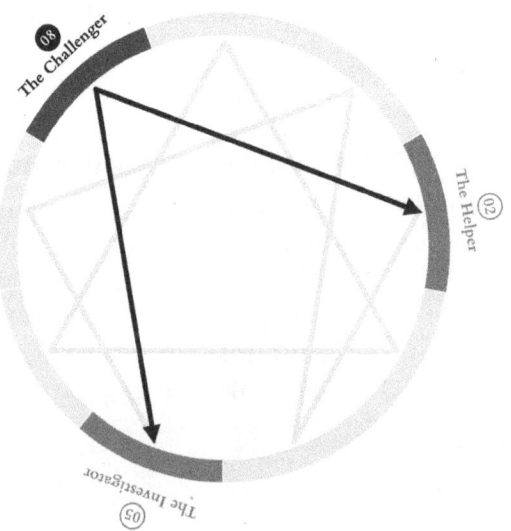

Moving to Two

When Eights go to Point Two, they access some of the higher qualities that Twos are blessed with. For example:

Open-Hearted. When a bold and assertive Eight is connected to their heart center, they come across to others as a big-hearted, benevolent, and well-rounded human being. They naturally demonstrate healthy qualities of a Two such as openheartedness, empathy, compassion, generosity, and love.

Stronger Together. When Eights embrace the higher qualities of Point Two, they become more relationship oriented and service-minded. Their sense of "we" is bigger than their "me." They are naturally more humble, more vulnerable, more open to connection, and more willing to join forces with others.

Love Conquers All. When Eights visit Point Two, they connect with the intelligence of their heart center. They also experience the power of love. "There is no difficulty that enough love will not conquer, no disease that enough love will not heal, no door that enough love will not open," observed Emmet Fox, the philosopher.

When Eights are under stress, they may exhibit some unhealthy qualities of Twos. Knowing about these unhealthy qualities can help Eights to be more centered and conscious as they go about their day. For example:

Letting Love In. Both Eights and Twos find it easier to give love than to let love in. They are more comfortable being the giver than the receiver. Their family and friends often feel hurt and rejected by their resistance to receiving love.

Unhealthy Pride. Both Eights and Twos pride themselves on being "the strong one" who has no emotional needs. Their unhealthy pride forces them to ask indirectly for what they need. When they don't get what they want, they get angry, vengeful, and demanding.

Fear of Rejection. "As an Eight, I don't want to be a burden to others. My personal pain is a secret I try to keep to myself," says Tim, who is a single father of four kids. Eights don't want to let people down by not being strong enough. They're also afraid of being rejected for being weak.

Moving to Five

When Eights go to Point Five, they access some of the higher qualities that Fives are blessed with. For example:

Open-Minded. Eights who are dedicated to inner work and spiritual growth become more open-minded as time goes by. Like a healthy Five, they train themselves to think objectively, to question their beliefs, to recognize the truth, and to see things differently.

Big Mind. Healthy Eights and Fives are naturally in tune with the "big mind," a term used by Buddhists to describe your original mind, higher mind, or Buddha nature. The big mind is calm, composed, and imperturbable. It knows the difference between truth and illusions.

Inner Genius. Deep inside the True Self there is a genius—a spark in the soul—that is bright and luminous. When Eights are in touch with their inner genius, they are like a radiant and healthy Five who is genuinely insightful, perceptive, and aware.

When Eights are under stress, they may exhibit some unhealthy qualities of Fives. Knowing about these unhealthy qualities can help Eights to be more self-aware and mindful as they go about their day. For example:

Too Self-Reliant. Eights and Fives are known for being independent-minded. An overwhelmed Eight will typically try to think things through on their own. They don't ask for help. They won't get a second opinion. They get bogged down in their own thinking.

Socially Isolated. Self-mastery is a core motivation for Eights and Fives. Eights want to be master of their fate, and Fives want to master their mind. Under Stress, they both tend to become introspective, emotionally detached, and socially isolated. Things get better when they come out of their shell.

Closed-Minded. One of the greatest strengths of both Eights and Fives is their open-mindedness. But under stress, they become closed-minded, and their thinking gets increasingly entrenched, skeptical, scornful, and contemptuous.

HOLY TRUTH

And you will know the truth, and the truth will set you free.

– Jesus of Nazareth (John 8:32)

The nine Points on the Enneagram each offer a Holy Idea—a universal teaching and higher wisdom—for all nine Ennea-Types to contemplate and practice. The Holy Idea at Point Eight is called Holy Truth.

Holy Truth is an invitation to know your soul and be your True Self. G. I. Gurdjieff, who was an Eight, famously said, "Life is only real then, when 'I AM.'" In metaphysics, the phrase "I AM" is used to describe your original nature. The I AM is the soul. It is your indomitable spirit. Holy Truth recognizes that we are ONE with each other, and that each person is a soul who has a body, not a body that has a soul. When an Eight lives a soul-centered life, they discover a divine spark—a holy fire within them—that burns away illusions and reveals the truth of what is.

> *We are not human beings having a spiritual experience; we are spiritual beings having a human experience.*
>
> — Pierre Teilhard de Chardin

Holy Truth encourages Eights to discern between truth and ignorance. Socrates taught that everyone has an inbuilt capacity to be wise. Truth is within you. It cannot be extinguished, but it is often forgotten and ignored. Socrates said the best way to recognize Truth is by being truthful with oneself and others. The story goes that Socrates advised his students to use a Triple Filter Test when engaged in a dialogue or when making decisions. The first filter is **truth**, e.g., "Is what I am saying true?"; the second filter is **goodness**, e.g., "Is my motive good?" and the Third Filter is **usefulness**, e.g., "Is this useful?" and "Is it necessary?"

> *The soul is the perceiver and revealer of truth. We know truth when we see it.*
>
> — Ralph Waldo Emerson

Holy Truth recognizes that life is challenging and that everyone experiences pain and heartache.

> *There is a place in the soul where you've never been wounded.*
> — Meister Eckhart

The writer Ernest Hemingway observed, "The world breaks everyone, and afterward, some are strong at the broken places." Heartbreaks are devastating, but they are also an invitation to expand and grow. Holy Truth affirms that *who you think you are cannot overcome this challenge, but who you really are can and will*. The truth is, we are forged by our heartbreaks. As the saying goes, *What doesn't kill you makes you stronger*. When you dedicate a situation wholly to Truth—with a capital *T*—life sends you angels to help you heal and emerge stronger, wiser, kinder, and more as your True Self.

Holy Truth is ultimately about love. Martin Luther King Jr. spoke of the vital relationship between truth and love in his Nobel Peace Prize acceptance speech in Oslo, Norway, in 1964. He said, "I believe that unarmed truth and unconditional love will have the final word in reality. This is why right, temporarily defeated, is stronger than evil triumphant." King Jr. described love as the greatest power we have at our disposal because it is constant and never changing. True Love is eternal, and it has no opposite. And the greatest truth about love is this: *Love has never hurt you*. In truth, what hurts you really is when you turn away from love and stop loving. But the more loving you are, the more your soul enlarges, and every wound becomes a blessing and a source of true power.

> *The world is too dangerous for anything but truth and too small for anything but love.*
> — William Sloane Coffin, *The Courage to Love*

> *When humans truly discover the power of love, it will prove more important than the harnessing of fire.*
> – Pierre Teilhard de Chardin

Type Nine
THE PEACEMAKER

*A great soul serves everyone all the time.
A great soul never dies. It brings us
together again and again.*

— MAYA ANGELOU

The Ennea-Type Nine is commonly called the Peacemaker. Other names for Nines include Mediator, Peaceful Soul, Devotee, Peace-Seeker, and Daydreamer.

Type Nines are the *Peaceful, Easygoing* Type. Point Nine is at the highest point on the Enneagram symbol, and Type Nines are naturally endowed with heavenly attributes such as a gentle spirit, a calm personality, a tranquil disposition, a nonjudgmental nature, a positive outlook, and inner peace. They commonly embody the nine fruits of spirit named by the apostle Paul that include patience, gentleness, kindness, joy, peace, and love. Nines are tempted to preserve their inner peace by withdrawing from others and hanging out on Cloud Nine, but their real work is to help bring heaven down to earth. The message Nines most need to hear is, *the world is not complete without you.*

Nines are known for their holistic outlook on life. They have a deep appreciation for the unity of life and its extraordinary diversity. Oscar Ichazo (1931–2020), the Bolivian psychologist who is recognized as the father of the modern Enneagram, was a Nine. His work in integral philosophy aimed to synthesize modern psychology and ancient spirituality. One of his books is entitled *We Are One: Facing Our Global Crisis with Unity.* It was Ichazo who mapped the nine personality types onto the Enneagram symbol. Ichazo saw the Enneagram as a valuable self-awareness model that can help everyone to heal our sense of separateness, embrace our common humanity, and choose peace over conflict. He wrote:

> *First keep peace with yourself, then you can also bring peace to others.*
> — Thomas à Kempis, *The Imitation of Christ*

> With knowledge we can effect the change needed to face the problems that are unfolding with human dignity, a common purpose, and understanding upon the grounds of Unity and Love for all humanity.

Nines like to go with the flow, but they also insist on doing things at their own pace. For example, when a friend asks a Nine to take an Enneagram test, the Nine will normally say yes, but yes for a Nine could mean in an hour, later today, tomorrow, next week, or in six months' time. The easygoing Nine will not be rushed. Also, Nines are known for having difficulty with recognizing their Type. One reason for this is that Nines find it very easy to step into another person's shoes, even if they do pinch a little. Like Twos, they are highly empathetic and accommodating and can easily forget about their own needs and desires. Nines are also the Type that may have taken an Enneagram test many moons ago and have forgotten what Type they are.

Working with the Enneagram is a great blessing for Nines because it helps them to not forget themselves, to embrace their heart's desires, and to realize their dream of bringing more peace, love, and joy to the world.

INTRODUCING TYPE NINE

Are you a Type Nine on the Enneagram? Maybe you have a family member, a friend, or a work colleague who is a Nine.

Raina Nahar is the Godmother to my two children, Bo and Christopher. She is a Nine on the Enneagram and is deeply loved and appreciated by all the Holden family and many of our friends too. I first met Raina when I was 18 years old. I was struck by her calm presence, her gentle smile, her bright eyes, and her infectious laughter. Raina radiates a natural healing energy, and she is a much sought after meditation and yoga teacher. Two days a week she works as a holistic health practitioner at a children's hospital. She also offers healing sessions to the doctors and nurses who work there. When I describe Raina to friends, I tell them she is an Earth Angel, like the character played by Della Reese in the TV series *Touched by an Angel*.

Raina has an easygoing nature, but she has not had an easy life. In her childhood, she was the Cinderella of her family and suffered terrible abuse and neglect. You would not guess by Raina's calm and happy disposition how challenging her childhood was, which is typical of a Nine. Later, she married a man who suffered from alcoholism

> *I could not have made it this far had there not been angels along the way.*
>
> — Della Reese

and left her to raise her two boys by herself. Somehow Raina found a way to survive and thrive. Her superpower is her inner peace. In a recent conversation, Raina told me, "My inner peace does not come or go; it is always here for me." She said, "Inner peace connects me with my soul and with the divine. My inner peace is a blessing from God, and with God all things are possible. My greatest joy is helping others find their inner peace."

As you can see, Nines identify with inner peace a lot. Inner peace is in everyone's spiritual DNA, but for Nines it is very much a core value, a signature trait, and a soul gift they offer to others.

Healthy Qualities of Nines

When Nines are healthy and well-balanced, they display essential qualities that we all love and appreciate. Here are a few things healthy Nines have told me about themselves:

- "I am a peaceful, easygoing person."
- "I am mostly calm and even-tempered."

- "I dislike disharmony and will avoid conflict."
- "I like to go at my own pace and not be hurried."
- "My motto is: First, do no harm."
- "I rarely, if ever, raise my voice."
- "I am a dreamer, and I'm not the only one!"
- "I imagine a better future for everyone."
- "I like to use my creativity in positive ways."
- "I balance inner peace with social action."

Unhealthy Qualities of Nines

When Nines are out of balance, they shut down, become nonverbal, and live inside a peace bubble. Here are a few things Nines have told me about themselves:

- "I avoid conflict by 'going along to get along.'"
- "I don't find it easy standing up for myself."
- "I have trouble making my own decisions."
- "I wish life would make my decisions for me."
- "I silence my anger in order to keep the peace."
- "I upset friends when I am too calm or passive."
- "I fear that setting boundaries will upset people."
- "I have a hard time turning dreams into action."
- "I stagnate when I don't leave my comfort zone."
- "I withdraw too much and go missing in my life."

RECOGNIZING TYPE NINES

> *The sage lives in harmony with all below heaven.*
> — Tao Te Ching

In philosophy, Taoism sits well at Point Nine. Lao Tzu, the Chinese philosopher born in the 6th century BC, is the legendary founder of Taoism. His name, Lao Tzu, means "old master." The word *Tao* describes the flow of the universe. The 81 verses in the Taoist bible, Tao Te Ching (translated as the Book of the Way), offer a practical, down-to-earth guide for living in harmony with the natural laws of life. The universal precepts of Taoism have inspired millions of people from every culture and faith. They include living life simply, being present in the moment, balancing opposites of yin and yang, observing the path of least resistance, and flowing effortlessly between action and non-action (known as the art of wu wei). Verse 37 of Tao Te Ching begins:

> The Tao does nothing,
> yet leaves nothing undone.
> If powerful men and women
> could center themselves in it,
> the whole world would be transformed
> by itself, in its natural rhythms.

Bhakti Yoga is a Hindu philosophy of devotion and love, and it resonates strongly with Holy Love, which is the Holy Idea at Point Nine. The word *yoga* comes from the Sanskrit root *yuj*, meaning "to join" "to unite" or "to yoke." A disciple of Bhakti Yoga aims to experience oneness with all living beings by following a path of love, devotion ,and service. Swami Paramahansa Yogananda, author of *Autobiography of a Yogi*, and founder of the Divine Realization Fellowship, encouraged his students to embrace a cosmic love that unites us all. "Ignoring all prejudices of caste, creed, class, color, sex, or race, a swami follows the precepts of human brotherhood," said Swami Yogananda.

> *Love alone can transform the world. Love alone can bring peace on this earth.*
> — Swami Sivananda, *Divine Bliss*

The Indigenous wisdom of our ancient cultures is infused with Nine energy. Think of the Métis people of Canada, Celts of Britain, Aborigines of Australia, Maya people of Guatemala and Mexico, Inuits of Alaska and Russia, and Māori of New Zealand. These Indigenous peoples share a holistic spirituality and natural science that encourages deep reverence for life, an appreciation for ancestral wisdom, and a mutual respect for Mother Nature and all living beings. Black Elk (1863–1950) was the son of the Oglala Lakota people. He was known as a visionary, a shaman, a holy man, a healer, and a

> *Know the power that is peace.*
> — Black Elk

warrior. He made it his mission to help the modern world remember its Indigenous roots and native spirituality. He famously said:

> The first peace, which is the most important, is that which comes within the souls of people when they realize their relationship, their oneness with the universe and all its powers, and when they realize at the center of the universe dwells the Great Spirit, and that its center is really everywhere, it is within each of us.

> *Every country my country, and every man my brother.*
> — Quaker saying

In Christianity, the Quakers, also known as the Religious Society of Friends, exemplify the peace-loving outlook of Nines. The Quaker movement was established in 17th-century England, and its first publication was a spiritual manifesto entitled the *Peace Testimony* that was delivered by hand to King Charles II. It declared that peace, not war, is the Will of God. It states, "Conflicts are inevitable and must not be repressed or ignored but worked through painfully and carefully. We must develop the skills of being sensitive to oppression and grievances, sharing power in decision-making, creating consensus, and making reparation."

The Quakers believe in an Inner Christ that everyone has direct access to. They believe that humanity has a shared purpose, which is to love the world and each other. Quakers seek to balance inner peace with social action. They have a long history of working for peace, disarmament, abolition of slavery, social reform, equality for women, and stewardship of the Earth. Famous Quakers include singer Joan Baez, prison reformer Elizabeth Fry, called the "Angel of Prisons," philanthropist Johns Hopkins, and Nozizwe Madlala-Routledge, the South African politician and anti-apartheid activist.

In psychology, Carl Rogers displayed a lot of healthy Nine traits. Rogers was the pioneer of person-centered therapy, also called Rogerian therapy, which offers a powerful, non-directive approach to counseling. In my 20s, I trained in Rogers's model of humanistic psychology that encourages both therapist and client to embody three core principles of (1) *Congruence*: for balancing inner and outer genuineness, (2) *Empathy*: for knowing oneself and understanding others, and (3) *Unconditional Positive Regard*: for practicing self-acceptance and love for others. Rogers proposed that we have within us "an actualizing tendency" that helps us to grow and reach our full potential.

> *What you are to be, you are now becoming.*
> — Carl Rogers

By "launching oneself fully into the stream of life," as he put it, we realize our authentic being and become a fully functioning person.

In leadership, Nines show up where their presence is most needed. Their leadership style is visionary, affirming, determined, and focused on a win-win outcome. Nines operate rather like the conductor of an orchestra. They have a vision, set the tempo, and keep everyone together and in time. Nines make great politicians, diplomats, environmentalists, and activists. Think of Rabindranath Tagore (1861–1941), the Bengali poet, philosopher, and political activist who advocated a universal humanism that has inspired leaders worldwide including Albert Einstein, Mahatma Gandhi, Thích Nhất Hạnh, and Barack Obama. Tagore promoted the ancient doctrine of *ahimsa*, shared by Hindus, Buddhists, and Jains, that affirms "non-violence" and "non-injury" between all living beings.

> *It's important to make sure that we're talking with each other in a way that heals, not in a way that wounds.*
> — Barack Obama

In the arts, there are many famous compositions in classical music that convey the tranquil, heavenly qualities of Point Nine. For example, Claude Debussy's relaxing *Clair de Lune* and *Rêverie*, a solo work for piano, that both transport you into a dream-like realm; Holst's "Venus: Bringer of Peace," from *The Planets* suite, that begins with four ascending notes, and is then joined by harps, flutes, bassoons, and a heavenly choir; and Ralph Vaughan Williams's *The Lark Ascending,* based on George Meredith's poem of the same name. This short, single-movement work features a violin solo that expresses an English Skylark's song of hope while inflight between heaven and earth. It's generally thought that Williams wrote this piece in response to the outbreak of World War I.

In popular music, Nines show up in every genre and especially in folk, country, blues, jazz, soul music, and reggae. Bob Marley, the Jamaican reggae artist and Rastafarian, had a lot of Nine energy. He was a natural mystic whose songbook—"One Love," "Three Little Birds," "Get Up Stand Up," "Redemption Song," and "People Get Ready"—offered a gospel of universal peace and love. He received many awards for his political activism, including the United Nations Peace Medal of the Third World in 1978. Other artists at Point Nine include, Alicia Keys, "We Are Here," James Taylor, "Shower the People," India Arie Simpson, "Steady

> *Me only have one ambition, y'know. I only have one thing I really like to see happen. I like to see mankind live together—black, white, Chinese, everyone—that's all.*
> — Bob Marley

Love," Michael Franti, "Big, Big Love," Norah Jones, "Come Away with Me," and Michael McDonald and the Doobie Brothers, "Takin' It to the Streets."

In painting, think of the famous French impressionists who inspired the music of Claude Debussy, described by some as the first impressionist composer. Claude Monet's *The Water Lily Pond*, Pierre-August Renoir's *Luncheon of the Boating Party*, and pointillist Georges Seurat's *The River Seine at La Grande-Jatte*, each has a soft focus, easy flow, and dreamy quality that is characteristic of Nine energy. *The Birth of Venus*, by Sandro Botticelli, the Early Renaissance Italian artist, is in an entirely different style, but also has a gentle, elegant, otherworldly, and dream-like feel about it.

In literature, I often highlight *The Color Purple*, by Alice Walker, when I teach about Point Nine. The main protagonist, Celie, is a poor African American girl who lives in rural Georgia in the early 1900s. She is beaten and raped by her stepfather. Her two illegitimate children are taken away. Celie survives her abusive childhood by being invisible and mute. She writes letters to God, which is her lifeline. For Celie, it would be easier to die than keep on living, but by grace and good fortune, she rises from the ashes. In the theater version of *The Color Purple,* Celie sings the final song, "I'm Here," a passionate song of self-love, in which she declares herself to be, despite her suffering, a fully empowered spiritual woman. *"I'm beautiful. Yes, I'm beautiful. And I'm here,"* she sings.

> *Why shouldn't art be pretty? There are enough unpleasant things in the world.*
> — Pierre-Auguste Renoir

In film, George Lucas, creator of the Star Wars franchise, has created many films that feature prominent Nine characters. As a child, Lucas was enchanted by classic stories such as Daniel Defoe's *Robinson Crusoe* and Robert Louis Stevenson's *Treasure Island*. He was also a keen collector of science fiction novels. In *Star Wars*, his hero, Luke Skywalker, is very much a Nine. He is a reluctant hero who is valiant and kind-hearted and is often too stubborn for his own good. Yoda, who is Luke's second mentor, helps him to master the force. Yoda's moto "Do or do not. There is no try" is distinctly Taoist in nature.

> *You can't do it unless you imagine it.*
> — George Lucas

Staying with sci-fi: Gene Roddenberry, creator of the Star Trek series, assembled an international crew onboard the USS *Enterprise* to recognize and celebrate the diversity of the human family. The crew comprised most Ennea-Types including Spock (a One), Dr. "Bones" McCoy (a Two), Engineer Scotty (a Six),

Lieutenant Commander Uhura (a Nine), and Captain Kirk (a Seven). Roddenberry said of his creation:

> Star Trek was an attempt to say that humanity will reach maturity and wisdom on the day that it begins not just to tolerate, but take a special delight in differences in ideas and differences in life forms. [...] If we cannot learn to actually enjoy those small differences, to take a positive delight in those small differences between our own kind, here on this planet, then we do not deserve to go out into space and meet the diversity that is almost certainly out there.

Walt Disney, the pioneer of animated cartoon films and creator of *The Wonderful World of Disney* displayed lots of Nine energy. Disney created a whole world from his imagination and his drawing of a little mouse. He assembled a team of talented animators—that he lovingly called the Nine Old Men—to help create happy, whimsical entertainment for "children of all ages." Also, think of Jim Henson, the puppeteer and filmmaker who brought a world of imaginary figures to life with his creation of the Muppets, which was later acquired by the Walt Disney Company.

> *First, think. Second, believe. Third, dream. And finally, dare.*
>
> — Walt Disney

In Shakespeare, think of Desdemona, a young Venetian noble woman who marries Othello, a general in the army. Desdemona is described as "sweet," "gentle," "divine," and as "a maiden never bold, of spirit so still and quiet, that her motion blushed at herself." Desdemona withstands Othello's violent jealousy and false accusations of adultery with great dignity and poise. She stands her ground, like a statue. But is she too submissive? Shouldn't she stand up for herself more? In the final act, Othello smothers Desdemona with a pillow. "O, who hath done this deed?' cries Emilia, her maid servant. Desdemona takes the blame for her own murder, saying with her dying breath, "Nobody, I myself. Farewell. Commend me to my kind lord. O, farewell."

THE PEACEFUL SOUL

> *When you find peace within yourself, you become the kind of person who can live at peace with others.*
>
> – Peace Pilgrim

Nine, in sacred mathematics, is the number closest to heaven. It represents wholeness, harmony, completion, and balance. As a young man, I was tutored in sacred mathematics by Lilla Bek, a healer and mystic. Lilla had the most Nine energy of anyone I've met. To me, she had a striking resemblance to Simonetta Vespucci, the noble woman that was Botticelli's model for his painting *The Birth of Venus*. She was ethereal and at home in her body. She was very feminine and powerful. Her father was a general in the Polish Army. Lilla told me, "During a long and difficult labor for my mother, my father requested all four hundred soldiers in his regiment to be my godfathers. Intuitively, he realized that I needed the grounding energy of four hundred masculine souls to help anchor my feminine soul to Earth."

Together, Lilla and I wrote a book on sacred mathematics called *What Number Are You?* On the symbolism of Nine, Lilla taught me about the Nine muses or creative energies of Greek mythology, the nine divine aspects of Tibetan numerology, the nine heavens of Taoism and Chinese mythology, and the Great Ennead in Egyptian mythology, which is a collection of nine deities or divine energies that Pythagoreans such as Plotinus studied. Very keen students of the Enneagram have a copy of Plotinus's *Enneads* on their bookshelf. Here is an excerpt from *What Number Are You?* on the esoteric meaning of Nine:

> In the history of Creation, numerology states that God, the Creator, invoked the power of nine and thereby finished the initial Work. Nine represents completion, perfection, and the end of a cycle. There now existed, therefore, a cycle and a stairway which could project from God to Spirit into matter, and from Spirit out of matter back to God again. With the advent of nine, the full course for the journey of involution and evolution had now been set.

When I teach about Point Nine, I like to show the painting *The School of Athens,* by Raphael, the Italian painter and architect. Raphael displayed a lot of Nine energy. His famous fresco, painted between 1509 and 1511, features 52 figures from Greek philosophy, including Plato, Aristotle, Pythagoras, and Socrates. Raphael's work has been hailed for its exquisite form, ease of composition, beautiful clarity, and extraordinary diversity. Only a Type Nine could paint such a mix of diverse figures, and on such a grand scale. What's important to note, especially for a Nine, is that these characters aren't just sitting on a cloud contemplating life. They are engaged in a lively debate. Not everyone is agreeing with each other. Differences of opinion abound. And yet they are joined as One in their love of wisdom and desire to see humanity evolve and prosper.

Before we look at some of the essential qualities of Nines, I want to make special mention of one more Nine who I knew personally. Her name is Maya Angelou, the much-loved author, singer, poet, and civil rights activist. I had the good fortune to interview Maya Angelou on three occasions. To be in her presence was a blessing. She was a mentor to many leaders and teachers, including Oprah Winfrey who said, "What stands out to me most about Maya Angelou is not what she has done or written or spoken, it's how she lived her life. She moved through the world with unshakeable calm, confidence and a fierce grace. I loved her and I know she loved me. I will profoundly miss her. She will always be the rainbow in my clouds."

Now let's look at some of the healthy qualities of Nines. Remember, these qualities are not exclusive to Nines, but they are signature traits of Nines.

A Calm Spirit. As a Nine, you treasure your inner peace more than anything. You would not trade in your inner peace for gold or riches. You would not sacrifice your inner peace for fame or fortune. Nines know this to be true: *If you're not at peace with yourself, nothing you attract can bring you peace.* Inner peace is the foundation stone for happiness, health, success, abundance, and all good things. "Never be in a hurry; do everything quietly and in a calm spirit. Do not lose your inner peace for anything whatsoever, even if your whole world seems upset. What is anything in life compared to peace of soul?" said Francis de Sales.

Reverence for Life. Nines feel a natural kinship with all living beings. They enjoy a natural affinity with their environment. They offer a deep bow to everyone they meet. They see the sacred in others. Both angels and humans are worthy of respect and love. For Nines, reverence for life also includes reverence for oneself. "Reverence is the key to understanding our place in the world. It helps a person to show up with self-respect and with a deep love for all beings," says Satish Kumar, author of *Soil, Soul, Society: A New Trinity for Our Time.*

One Human Family. "Humanity is only one spirit," said Oscar Ichazo, the Enneagram teacher. Nines see that we live in an undivided universe that is an expression of unity and diversity. We are different and the same. Maya Angelou wrote her poem "Human Family" to promote civil rights and equality for all people. In her poem, she recognizes differences of skin tone, gender, nationality, politics, and personality, and she concludes, "I note the obvious differences between each sort and type, but we are more alike my friends, than we are unalike."

The Peace Bringer. For Nines, peace is more than just a good feeling or a nice idea. Danny, a Nine, works for a United Nations project called Future of Peace Keeping. I first met Danny in my Leadership and the Enneagram program. He told me, "I see myself as a peace bringer, and it is my inner peace that helps me to live my purpose and do my work." Danny meditates every day, and one of his favorite meditations is listening to *Peace and Purpose*, by John Williams, from the soundtrack for *Star Wars: The Last Jedi*.

The Dreamer Archetype. Nines are greatly influenced by the dreamer archetype. Unhealthy Nines are daydreamers who try to preserve their inner peace by avoiding conflict and distancing themselves from life. Healthy Nines, on the other hand, are visionaries who engage their powers of imagination and creativity to help make the world a more harmonious and beautiful place to live in. Maya Angelou said, "A person is the product of their dreams. So make sure to dream great dreams. And then try to live your dream."

In the Flow. Nines often experience a state of flow when actively engaged in work, sport, and daily tasks. Mihaly Csikszentmihalyi, author of *Flow: The Psychology of Optimal Experience*, wrote, "Flow is being completely involved in an activity for its own sake. The ego falls away. Time flies. Every action, movement and thought follows inevitably from the previous one." Nines make it look easy. They take everything in their stride, let nothing phase them, and remain composed under pressure. Many sports champions are Nines, e.g., tennis players Roger Federer and Naomi Osaka, soccer player Lionel Messi, and teenage darts champion Luke Littler.

Social Activism. Healthy Nines balance inner peace with social action. They pray for peace and actively participate in everyday life to promote peace. Nines believe that our shared purpose is to help bring heaven down to earth. Many of the world's greatest activists, diplomats, and peacemakers have displayed strong Nine energy. "If we are peaceful, if we are happy, we can smile and blossom like a flower, and everyone in our family, our entire society, will benefit from our peace," wrote Thích Nhất Hạnh, the Vietnamese Buddhist and author of *Being Peace*.

A HARMONIOUS UNIVERSE

The goal of life is to make your heartbeat match the beat of the universe, to match your nature with Nature.

– Joseph Campbell

The Enneagram, with its roots in Greek philosophy, recognizes a basic harmony and structural unity in the Universe. Aristotle observed, "A single harmony orders the composition of the whole . . . by the mingling of the most contrary principles." This basic harmony is complex and dynamic. It accommodates a continuous interplay of unity and diversity, space and time, essence and form, and spirit and matter. Modern science also recognizes this basic harmony. Fritjof Capra, in his classic work *The Tao of Physics*, wrote about a "parallel worldview" and "essential harmony" between the spirit of Eastern wisdom and Western science. For Nines, the greatest happiness is to experience this profound harmony both within themselves and the world around them.

Oscar Ichazo taught that the purpose of the Enneagram is to help us remember the basic harmony that exists between psyche and cosmos and heaven and earth. In *Interviews with Oscar Ichazo*, he observed that every human being starts life with an awareness of this basic harmony. He stated, "In essence every person is perfect, fearless, and in a loving unity with the entire cosmos. There is no conflict within the person between head, heart, and stomach or between the person and others." Ichazo also recognized the sense of separation that happens in childhood, and that this is when "man falls from essence into personality." He goes on to say, "Personality forms a defensive layer over the essence, and so there is a split between the self and the world."

Basic Fear: Loss of Harmony

When Nines enter the separation phase of childhood, a basic fear arises in them that has a significant impact on their self-image, relationships, and well-being.

The basic fear for Nines is having their inner peace disturbed so that it causes a loss of harmony, a lack of equilibrium, and discordance between inner and outer.

"When I lose contact with my inner peace, I feel like I break into a million pieces," says Toby, a Nine, who attended my Love and the Enneagram program in London. Nines typically feel fragmented and disunified when their inner peace is rocked. "I'm like Humpty Dumpty in the nursery rhyme who falls off the wall and can't put himself back together again," says Toby. They experience what Internal Family Systems psychology calls "parts" of themselves that are suppressed, unintegrated, and in exile. They struggle with what Carl Jung called an "unintegrated shadow." "Wholeness is not achieved by cutting off a portion of one's being, but by integration of the contraries," said Carl Jung.

When Nines don't feel inner peace, they feel estranged from their True Self and don't feel at home in the world. As we shall see, Nines may avoid doing the inner work to recover their inner peace because they fear it has been shattered beyond repair. Instead, they may create a fantasy self like Walter Mitty in James Thurber's "The Secret Life of Walter Mitty" or live in a dream world like Alice does in Lewis Carroll's *Alice's Adventures in Wonderland* and *Through the Looking Glass*. "A dream is not reality," says Alice, who is described by Carroll as "loving and gentle," "well mannered," and "courteous to all." To which the Mad Hatter replies, "Who's to say which is which?"

Nines typically compensate for their loss of inner peace by being self-effacing and over-adaptable. They present themselves as highly amenable and willing to merge and fit in with their environment. "Would you like a cup of tea?" asks the friend of a Nine. "Only if you are having one," replies the Nine. "How do you like your tea?" the friend asks. "As it comes," says the Nine. "Does this look okay?" asks the friend. "Yes," says the Nine, who doesn't really look. This capacity to over-adapt helps Nines to avoid conflict, but it also heightens the disconnect with their True Self. They end up like the characters in the film *Pleasantville*, starring Tobey Maguire and Reese Witherspoon, where everyone exists peacefully and has a nice life, but no one is fully alive or truly following their joy.

Here's some things Nines have said to me about living with their basic fear of a loss of harmony and inner peace:

- "I don't find conflicts or disagreements easy."
- "I'm not comfortable with being assertive."
- "I often say yes when I mean no."

- "I forget about my own wishes and desires."
- "I like to stay calm and not rock the boat."
- "It's hard for me to stay present when I'm angry."
- "I don't like my routine or rhythm being disturbed."
- "When I withdraw too much, it causes conflict."
- "I mean to connect with people more than I do."
- "I dream my dreams instead of living my dreams."

Childhood Story: The Peaceful Child

Jerry Jampolsky, MD, the much-loved child and adult psychiatrist, authored several best-selling books including *Love Is Letting Go of Fear* and *Children as Teachers of Peace*. Typical of a Nine, Jerry had a gentle smile, bright eyes, and a warm and loving presence. When I teach about the childhood pattern of Nines, I share a story Jerry included in another of his books: *Shortcuts to God: Finding Peace Quickly Through Daily Spiritual Practice.* Here is his story:

> Several years ago, my wife Diane Cirincione and I were in New Jersey lecturing.... A friend of our friend had recently brought home their new baby, their second child. One evening their three-year-old daughter said she wanted to go into the baby's room alone.
>
> At first reluctant because they feared there might be some sibling rivalry, the parents finally granted their daughter her wish. Besides, with the intercom they had in the baby's room, they could listen in on and make sure earthing was okay.
>
> As their daughter tiptoed up to the baby's crib, they heard her softly say: "Baby, remind me what God is like. I am beginning to forget."

Young Nines come down to earth with a bump. They experience their birth as a shock. One moment they're floating in the warm, oceanic bliss of the womb, and then suddenly they're out in the world, forced to breathe, and gasping for air. "My mom said I had the most startled look on my face when I was born," said Sam, a Nine. Nines are known for having a wide-eyed countenance. "I was a quiet baby, and I'm not sure I've ever gotten over the trauma of exiting my mother's womb," Sam told me. Sam had a caesarean birth, and she was pulled out of her mother's womb by the head using forceps. "As a Nine, I tend to be slow in making decisions and resist change until circumstances require me to move forward," Sam stated.

Every family has its ups and downs, its dramas and conflicts, which can be very disturbing for a young Nine who wants to feel peaceful and happy. Everyday life can feel too harsh and abrasive to a sensitive Nine. They're afraid of causing conflict if they assert themselves, voice their opinion, ask for what they want, get angry, or go against a parent's wishes. They withdraw emotionally to not rock the boat. They train themselves to keep their feelings private and forget about their own wishes and desires. They shut out the world and make a peaceful haven inside themselves. They like to daydream, read Jane Austen, play computer games, groom their horse, practice their golf swing, or hang out with an invisible friend.

Maya Angelou had an especially traumatic childhood. When Maya was eight years old, she was sexually abused and raped by her mother's boyfriend, Mr. Freeman. She told her brother, Bailey, who then told the rest of the family. Mr. Freeman was arrested, held in custody, tried in court, and sentenced to one day in jail. Four days after his release, he was murdered. No one was officially charged for his death. Perhaps it was one of Maya's uncles who took the law into his own hands. On hearing the news of Mr. Freeman's death, young Maya became mute, and she didn't speak again for almost five years.

Maya told me, "After I was raped, and the man was killed, I thought my voice killed that man. If I hadn't spoken his name, he would still be alive. So my voice has the power to kill, and so I had better stop speaking." With that, Maya withdrew into herself. She became an invisible child and the forgotten daughter. When I asked Maya about her self-imposed silence, she told me, "I'm not sure I would have left my cage without my brother, Bailey, and my grandmother's love." After Maya wrote her first memoir, *I Know Why the Caged Bird Sings*, she became the most visible Black female leader and teacher of her generation.

The "Be Peaceful" Driver: Nines have a strong "Be Peaceful" driver installed in their ego operating system. Their "Be Peaceful" driver helps them connect to their inner peace, but it also causes problems. In childhood, Nines adopt a social role to avoid conflict and "keep the peace," so to speak. For instance, the Good Child who doesn't upset the apple cart, the Peaceful Child who puts others' well-being first, the Quiet Child who is private and voiceless, or the Invisible Child who avoids attention. Most young Nines wish they had an invisibility cloak, one like the fictional character Harry Potter has. These social roles help a young Nine to avoid conflict but also cause them to feel lonely and to forget their True Self.

The ego-ideal for Nines is to never be angry or upset. A young Nine tries to hold on to this ego-ideal by "avoiding conflict at all costs" and having "peace at any price." But peace is more than just the absence of conflict, and no one knows this better than a Nine who has done their inner work. Dean, a Nine, came to me for Enneagram coaching after his marriage hit a rocky patch. After a few sessions, he invited his wife to join us. He told her in front of me, "I've tried to make our marriage work by avoiding conflict and having no upsets, but I realize this has created distance between us. What I most want is a marriage with you that is wonderful and messy, in which we can resolve conflict and make repair. I am deeply sorry. Please forgive me. I love you."

Let's look at some examples of how the basic fear, childhood story, and "Be Peaceful" driver operate for Nines in the three biological instincts: (1) Self-Preservation Instinct (SP), which is mostly about lifestyle, material matters, and self-care; (2) Social Instinct (SO), which is mostly about relating to family, society, and the world; and (3) (SX) Sexual Instinct (also called One-to-One Instinct), which is mostly about attraction, relating style, and romance.

Self-Preservation Instinct (SP) *Healthy:* SP Nines are known for being comfort lovers. They prioritize physical well-being and feeling comfortable in their skin. They are typically a homebody, one whose life centers on home. They make their dwelling a sanctuary that has soft furnishings, ambient lighting, indoor plants, a cozy fireplace, and, most of all, a comfortable bed. *Not-so-healthy:* SP Nines like a set routine, e.g., green juice for breakfast, a morning walk, meditation time, a daily crossword puzzle, and writing a dream journal. "My morning routines can take up most of my day," says Kate, a Nine. They live at their own pace, don't like being disturbed, and want to be in control. *Unhealthy:* SP Nines can be monastic, hermit-like, and reclusive. They switch on the TV for company. They have an appetite for comfort foods. They have a sweet tooth, like Winnie the Pooh. Their strict adherence to comfort and routine can cause apathy, inertia, and loss of vitality.

Social Instinct (SO) *Healthy:* SO Nines can be highly empathetic like Twos, team players like Sixes, and actively involved like Threes. Instinctively, an SO Nine realizes the vital need to balance their inner and outer life. Bob, a Nine, has a vision board with "Inner Yeses" that include meditation and yoga, and "Outer Yeses" that include meeting up with family and serving in his community. *Not-so-healthy:* SO Nines work hard to promote togetherness, harmony, and a shared vision. They prioritize the well-being of the whole but can forget to include themselves in the whole. "As a Nine, I find it easy to fit into the shoes of all nine Types. The only difficulty I have is fitting into my own shoes," says Juliette, a human resources director. *Unhealthy:* SO Nines take care of everyone else's agenda but neglect their own. Jo, a Nine, has dreamed for 10 years of setting up an animal welfare sanctuary. She hopes to leave her job soon, one day, eventually, when it's okay with her boss.

Sexual Instinct (SX) *Healthy:* SX Nines are known for being comfort-seekers who search for external sources of joy and peace. Socially, they value life-long bonds with friends from school or university days. Romantically, they seek a soulmate. Workwise, they wish to absorb themselves in a creative task or greater purpose. Spiritually, they are attracted to paths that offer mystical union and bliss. *Not-so-healthy*: SX Nines are so externally focused and "other-driven," like Twos can be, that they merge to the point of forgetting themselves. "My first husband was an Eight, who I idealized," says Kathy, a Nine. "I ended up acting like him, speaking like him, and thinking like him. Even my handwriting style was a copy of his." *Unhealthy*: Like Fours, SX Nines develop a Cinderella Complex and fantasize about being rescued by a savior. SX Nines may also disappear into relationships, roles, and projects, erasing their "I AM" in exchange for a feeling of "WE ARE."

Passion: Acedia or Sloth

All nine Types on the Enneagram experience a *passion*, or cause of suffering in the heart, that emerges from a sense of separation and from the basic fear. The passion for Nines is *acedia*, the modern term for which is "sloth" or "inertia."

Acedia is another of the so-called cardinal sins named by Evagrius Ponticus, the Christian monk who lived with the Desert Fathers and Mothers in the Egyptian desert in the 4th century. Remember, the Greek word for "sin" is *hamartia*, an archery term that means "to miss the mark." Thus, a sin is simply a mistake, not a punishable offense. In his classic work *The Praktikos*, Pontius observed that acedia is most common in those who are quiet, withdrawn, and long for inner peace. He noticed that acedia was especially prevalent in monks and nuns who lived a solitary life.

Acedia comes from Greek word *akēdeia,* which means "a lack of care." Ponticus described acedia as "the most oppressive of all demons" that without proper care "will envelop the entire soul." Interestingly, Ponticus observed that acedia is made up of an "entangled struggle of anger and desire." For Nines, the anger arises from not wanting to be in the world. *Stop the world, I want to get off!* And the desire is a temptation to dissociate, or "numb out," from pain and conflict. *Go away world, I'm meditating!* Acedia causes Nines to withdraw too much, to neglect their own suffering, and to forget how much others need their loving presence. On a positive note, Ponticus declared that the rewards are great if you can be bothered to do the inner work to overcome acedia. "A state of peace and ineffable joy ensues in the soul after this struggle," he wrote.

Let's not avoid acedia, then. Let's take a closer look at how acedia, or sloth, may affect Nines in their everyday life. Recognizing how acedia influences them enables Nines to be more proactive, to live with intention, and to manifest their heart's desires.

Emotional Bypassing. "When I feel sad, I can either accept it or resist it. Until I accept it, I will not be at peace," says Tim, a Nine. Emotional bypassing is anything you do to avoid how you really feel. For Nines it may include trying to let go of feelings (i.e., "getting rid of them"), distracting yourself by watching TV, numbing out with alcohol and drugs, suppressing feelings with positive affirmations and meditation, and telling people "I'm fine" when you're not. Nines must learn that happiness is not the absence of sadness; it is the capacity to meet your sadness with honesty and love.

Passive Aggression. Nines present a calm exterior, but they have their hot buttons too. "When I told my therapist I never get angry, he told me 'I don't believe you' and so I stopped seeing him," said Carol, a Nine. Nines disown anger for fear it will disturb their inner peace and cause conflict. They display passive-aggressive behaviors that communicate anger indirectly, e.g., withdrawing emotionally, gaslighting people, giving someone the cold shoulder, ghosting people, and smiling through gritted teeth. Healthy Nines know that real peace comes from reconciling anger, not by avoiding it.

Sin of Omission. Acedia is recognized as a "sin of omission." Doing inner work with acedia, Nines are encouraged to look at what they are not doing that is causing a lack of inner peace. For Nines, some examples of "not doing" include being inattentive to yourself, being too passive in relationships, not honoring your feelings, being too self-effacing and modest, not speaking up, not acknowledging your desires and wishes, not including yourself in your decision-making, and not participating fully in your own life. A good inquiry for Nines is to ask, *What am I not doing that is disrupting my inner peace?*

Spiritual Laziness. Evagrius Ponticus described acedia as the "noonday demon" that tempts you to go through the motions with your inner work and not commit fully to your spiritual growth. Ponticus listed symptoms of acedia that include "laziness in prayer," "muzzling of meditation," "a battle against stillness," and "an opponent of perseverance." Acedia tempts you to withdraw, zone out, and disengage emotionally from life. It makes you robotic in your daily practice. You recite your prayers, but they don't energize you. Your spiritual practice makes you comfortable, but you don't let it transform you.

Comfortably Numb. When I teach about acedia, I play the song "Comfortably Numb," by Pink Floyd, from their album *The Wall*. Both the album and the song struck a chord with people who experience modern life as cold and impersonal. *Welcome my son, welcome to the machine!* The temptation is to withdraw socially and detach yourself from everyday matters. *Hello, is anybody in there? Just nod if you can hear me. Is there anyone at home?* The trouble with being comfortably numb is it disconnects you from yourself. Emotional numbing offers temporary relief, but if you do it too much, it becomes a block to inner peace.

Fixation: Indolence or Daydreaming

In the Enneagram, the *fixation* refers to a mental habit that causes an imbalance in your mental health and well-being. The fixation for Nines is commonly called indolence or daydreaming.

The Odyssey is an epic poem, attributed to Homer, that follows the Greek hero Odysseus, King of Ithaca, on his journey home after the Trojan War. In Book Nine of *The Odyssey*, Odysseus and his shipmates encounter the Lotus Eaters. Odysseus recounts, "I was driven thence by foul winds for a space of nine days upon the sea, but on the tenth day we reached the land of the Lotus-eaters, who live on food that comes from a kind of flower." The Lotus Eaters are peaceable and accommodating. They offer Odysseus's men food made from the lotus plant "which was so delicious that those who ate of it left off caring about home." Odysseus's men become intoxicated, but Odysseus sees what is happening and forces them back to the ship. Eventually, his men wake up and remember their voyage home and "took their places and smote the gray sea with their oars."

> *You cannot find peace by avoiding life.*
> — Virginia Woolf in the film *The Hours*

The story of The Lotus Eaters is an allegory that warns of the dangers of indolence, comfort, and addiction on the spiritual path. At first glance, the Lotus Eaters look like they are enlightened and are living in paradise. On closer inspection, they are more like a commune of hippies, or "flower children," who want to "make love, not war," but are also intent on "getting high," "dropping out," and "blowing their mind" on drugs. The Lotus Eaters are in a state of spiritual slumber. They have forgotten themselves. The island they inhabit is not their original home. They are addicted to a pacifier, the lotus flower. They ignore the summons of the soul. They have lost all sense of direction and purpose. They lack urgency or aliveness. They are comfortable and have no wish to participate in the world.

The Lotus Eaters story has been retold many times because it speaks to everyone, not just Nines. For example, in the original series of *Star Trek*, Episode 24 ("This Side of Paradise") sees the crew of the USS *Enterprise* visit a planet where the inhabitants are under the influence of a strange plant life. The crew are quickly intoxicated and forget about their voyage "to boldly go where no man has gone before." Fortunately, Captain Kirk, like Odysseus, remembers his original mission and helps his crew come back to their senses.

> *The opposite of home is not distance, but forgetfulness.*
> — Elie Wiesel

Odysseus, and Captain Kirk, are our heroes because they encourage us to beware of indolence, to stay awake, and not take the easy way out. Jungian analyst James Hollis, who has a lot of Nine energy, in his book *What Matters Most: Living a More Considered Life*, tells us:

Our enemies are the same old familiar gremlins: fear and lethargy. What makes Odysseus a hero to us, a prototype of our journey, is that he is willing to face his fears and persist, always persist. In his greatest peril he says, "I will stay with it and endure though suffering hardship, and once the heaving sea has shaken my raft to pieces, then will I swim."

Let's take a closer look at how Nines give in to indolence and resist the spiritual task of being fully present in their life.

Cloud Nine. Nines are either actively engaged with life, or they are hanging out on one of their favorite escapes called Cloud Nine. Cloud Nine is a place in your mind—like a space station or satellite—where you teleport yourself to get away from it all. You can get to Cloud Nine in many ways, e.g., putting on your earbuds, sitting in meditation, visiting your allotment, picking up your crochet needles, gazing up at the stars. Being on Cloud Nine is a lovely retreat, but it's not meant to be your permanent residence. The real work of your life doesn't happen on Cloud Nine; it happens here on earth. You are an Earth angel, not a space cadet.

Comfort Zone. Nines are known for being comfort-seekers. Seeking comfort can be a good thing if it helps you to engage with life. For example, Jesus described the Holy Spirit as the Comforter. "I will send you a Comforter," said Jesus. If, however, seeking comfort is an attempt to avoid life, then it becomes a distraction and a trap. "As a Nine, I have to remind myself there is more to life than seeking comfort," says Kim. Nines need reminding that *life begins outside of your comfort zone*. A good inquiry for Nines is: *What means even more to me than being comfortable?*

Day Dreaming. G. I. Gurdjieff, the philosopher who brought the Enneagram to the West, told his students repeatedly, "You do not remember yourselves." He taught that most people live in a state of "waking sleep" and that we must "wake up" if we are to not live an unlived life. Nines can slip into endless daydreaming. The inner work for Nines is to make sure you are not just "dreaming your dreams" but also "living your dreams." A good motto for Nines is,

Don't let your dreams be dreams! Remember what Walt Disney said, "If you can dream it, you can do it!"

Psychological Inertia. Nines who are emotionally disengaged are not sure what they desire or want. They are prone to what psychologists call psychological inertia, or cognitive inertia, symptoms of which include being slow to initiate things, delaying decision-making, and putting off action. For example, a Nine friend tells you they are "hoping" to come on holiday with you, but they keep delaying booking their ticket. Nines are often fatalistic. They want life to make their decisions for them. "Let's see what wants to happen," your Nine friend says. This can be very frustrating and painful for friends of Nines, who wish that their Nine friend would be more proactive and decisive.

Non-Participation. When Nines are too withdrawn and insular, they forget how much their presence matters to others. They tell themselves, "I'm nobody special," "No one will mind if I don't attend," "I won't be missed," and "My vote doesn't make a difference." A powerful remedy for this form of indolence is to watch the Frank Capra film *It's a Wonderful Life*, which tells the story of George Bailey, played by James Stewart, who discovers with the help of Clarence, his apprentice angel, how interconnected we are and what a big difference one person can make. A good inquiry for Nines is to notice some concrete ways how your presence makes a difference to others.

PATH OF PEACE

> *The big question is whether you are going to be able to say a hearty yes to your adventure.*
>
> – Joseph Campbell

The Enneagram offers a path of growth for all nine Types that helps you to remember your original nature and be your True Self. For Nines I call this the Path of Peace.

When I teach about Point Nine, I feature the work of Joseph Campbell, the world-renowned mythologist and creator of the Hero's Journey. Campbell was very Nine-like, and his work has been an inspiration to many philosophers and storytellers. He was a friend and mentor to George Lucas, creator of Star Wars, for example. Lucas calls Campbell "my Yoda." During the Great Depression, Campbell lived as a recluse in a rented log cabin in Woodstock, New York, where he studied mythology, creation stories, and the hero archetype. Many years later, he published his classic work *Hero With a Thousand Faces*. Shortly before his death in 1987, he recorded a six-part PBS special *Joseph Campbell and The Power of Myth*, with Bill Moyers. Much of the series was filmed at George Lucas's Skywalker Ranch, and it is one of the most viewed series in the history of American public television.

Joseph Campbell taught that we are all on a hero's journey. The journey has three parts to it, like the three-act structure of dramatic theory in Aristotle's *Poetics*. Part One is the Departure; Part Two is the Road of Trials, and Part Three is the Return. In Part One, there is a wake-up call that stirs the hero to action. "The hero journey always begins with a call," said Campbell. "One way or another, a guide must come to say, 'Look, you're in Sleepy Land. Wake. Come on a trip. There is a whole aspect of your consciousness, your being, that's not been touched. So, you're at home here? Well, there's not enough of you there.' And so it starts."

> *You are the hero of your journey.*
> — Joseph Campbell

Campbell described Part One of the hero journey as Kicked Out of Ordinary and the End of Normal. An inciting incident upsets the balance of normal life and takes you out of your comfort zone. It might be a happy event, such as going on a first date with the person you will marry one day, becoming a parent, starting a new project, or meeting an inspirational figure, like a Gandalf in *The Hobbit*. Or it may a painful event, such as losing your job, a major illness, the death of a loved one, or your house burning down in a wildfire. This chapter of your life is now over. You are not in Kansas anymore. There is no going back to normal. Campbell said you now have a choice: Either you say yes to your call to adventure, or you say no and refuse the call.

Refusing the Call is one of the stages Campbell cites in Part One of the hero's journey. In Tolkien's *The Hobbit,* the refusal stage is depicted in the first chapter, "An Unexpected Party," when Bilbo Baggins meets Gandalf. Bilbo Baggins, the hobbit, has a lot of Nine energy. He is accustomed to the hobbit way of life, which is mostly peaceful and predictable. He is living inside his comfort zone when Gandalf the wizard pays him an unexpected visit and invites him on an adventure.

> Gandalf: I am looking for someone to share in an adventure that I am arranging, and it's very difficult to find anyone.
>
> Bilbo: I should think so—in these parts! We are plain quiet folk and have no use for adventures. Nasty disturbing uncomfortable things! Make you late for dinner! I can't think what anybody sees in them . . .

Bilbo Baggins refuses his call to adventure as politely as possible. He tells Gandalf, "Sorry! I don't want any adventures, thank you. Not Today. Good morning! But please come to tea—any time you like! Why not tomorrow? Goodbye!" Refusing the call for a little while is okay. We all need time and space to accept *what is* and to prepare for *what's next*. But dormant forces are now awakening in you, and if you persist with your refusal for too long, you fall out of sync with life. You lose your mojo. There's no creative flow. You are stuck in a rut. Life is monotonous. And every day is Groundhog Day. In the end, you must choose to live or die. Campbell said, "Refusal of the summons converts the adventure into its negative. Walled in boredom, hard work, or 'culture,' the subject loses the power of significant affirmative action and becomes a victim to be saved."

> *The fates lead him who will; him who won't they drag.*
>
> — Latin proverb

One of my favorite programs to teach is Hero's Journey and the Enneagram. All nine Types on the Enneagram are on a hero's journey. We each have a hero archetype in our psyche. Our inner work is to recognize what sort of a hero we are. Nines are the Peacemaker, and they are called to show up in the world as healers, counselors, mediators, diplomats, leaders, artists, environmentalists, and activists. A Nine's inner work is to find their inner peace and then offer this peace to the world. It takes a lot of discipline and devotion to do this heroic work. It starts with saying a "hearty yes to your soul's adventure," as Campbell put it, and a willingness to engage fully with life.

Virtue: Engagement

Every Ennea-Type has a virtue, or a superpower, that arises naturally as you do your inner work to heal the basic fear, the passion in the heart, and the fixation in your thinking. The virtue for Type Nine is commonly called action or engagement. This virtue has two aspects to it that are complimentary and equally important: inner engagement and outer engagement.

> *Am I living in a way which is deeply satisfying to me, and which truly expresses me?*
> — Carl Rogers, *On Becoming a Person*

Inner engagement for Nines is about doing the inner work that helps you to know yourself and be yourself. It requires paying close attention to your inner landscape. It is noticing when you *are not at peace* or *not in harmony with yourself.* As Carl Jung observed, we "can meet the demands of outer necessity in an ideal way only if he is also adapted to his own inner world, that is, if he is in harmony with himself." Inner engagement helps you to find the inner peace that cannot be disturbed. It helps you to say yes to your call to adventure and living your dreams. And the good news is that one small step can activate all manner of help, inspiration, and grace on your journey.

Outer engagement for Nines is turning toward life and becoming what Carl Jung called "actors in the divine drama." As we have seen, Nines are tempted to preserve inner peace by withdrawing from life and hanging out on Cloud Nine, but this only creates inertia, a loss of vitality, and a lack of harmony between inner and outer. Healthy Nines realize that their inner peace is strengthened when they share it with others. To this end, Joseph Campbell advised us to "participate joyfully in the sorrows of the world. We cannot cure the world of sorrows, but we can choose to live in joy. The warrior's approach is to say "yes" to life: "yea" to it all."

> *The journey of a thousand miles begins with a single step.*
> — Lao Tzu

Thích Nhất Hạnh, the Vietnamese Buddhist monk, had a strong Nine presence, and he consistently modeled inner and outer engagement in his life. He advocated what he called Engaged Buddhism, which is connecting your meditation practice with social action. His thinking on Engaged Buddhism, which he later outlined in the manifesto

> *That gives peace, when people feel ... that they are living as actors in the divine drama.*
> — Carl Jung

The Fourteen Precepts of Engaged Buddhism, began when he was a peace activist during the Vietnam War. In an interview for *Lion's Roar* magazine, he recalled,

> When I was a novice in Vietnam, we young monks witnessed the suffering caused by the war. So we were very eager to practice Buddhism in such a way that we could bring it into society. That was not easy because the tradition does not directly offer Engaged Buddhism. So we had to do it by ourselves. That was the birth of Engaged Buddhism.

When Nines are equally engaged in their inner and outer life, it helps them become an integrated and whole person. Here are a few ways Nines can practice the virtue of engagement in their life.

Participatory Universe. In *The Tao of Physics,* Fritjof Capra observed how quantum physics has superseded particle physics and given us a new appreciation of our place in the universe. Physicist John Wheeler wrote in a similar vein, "To describe what has happened, one has to cross out that old word 'observer' and put in its place the new word 'participator.' In some strange sense the universe is a participatory universe." Healthy Nines realize that we are meant to participate in life, not just watch it go by. "You are not an observer, you are a participant," writes Thích Nhất Hạnh in *Being Peace.* A healthy inquiry for Nines is: *How can I participate more in my life today?*

The Gift of Peace. "Peace is our gift to each other," said Elie Wiesel, Holocaust survivor and Nobel Peace Prize winner in 1986. The citation called Wiesel "a messenger to mankind: his message is one of peace, atonement, and dignity." Inner peace is strengthened not by keeping it to ourselves, but by sharing it with others. Some good questions for Nines to ask include: *Who did I give my smile to today? Who did I pray for today? What kind words have I spoken? What was my peace offering? Who did I reach out to? How has my presence made a difference?*

Be a Rainbow. "I want to be a good representative of my species," Maya Angelou told me in an interview shortly before her death. Maya recognized as much as anyone how hard it is to keep on living after being wounded or heartbroken. She acknowledged that life is too hard to do by yourself, and that she couldn't have survived and thrived without the help of friends, healers, and angels who she described as "rainbows in my clouds." Maya said, "I've had rainbows in my clouds. And the thing to do, it seems to me, is to prepare yourself so that you can be a rainbow in somebody else's clouds."

Get Up, Stand Up! Engaged Nines recognize a basic truth in life: *What you are seeking for, is also what you are asked to give.* Nines are peace-seekers and peace-bringers. The great work for Nines, and for all of us, is to be the thing you want to experience. If you want peace, be a peaceful presence in the world. If you want love, offer love to others. If you want joy, help others to find their smile. "Get up, stand up!" sang Bob Marley. "I made a stand for equality and peace," said Rosa Parks. A healthy inquiry for Nines is to ask: *What is the conversation that is happening in the world right now that I want to be part of? What do I stand for?*

Follow Your Bliss. Nines must choose between "blissing out" or "following your bliss." Blissing out refers to avoidance tactics Nines use to bypass pain, get high, and forget about life. Following your bliss is a term coined by Joseph Campbell who said, "If you do follow your bliss you put yourself on a kind of track that has been there all the while, waiting for you, and the life that you ought to be living is the one you are living. When you can see that, you begin to meet people who are in your field of bliss, and they open doors to you. I say, follow your bliss and don't be afraid, and doors will open where you didn't know they were going to be."

Balancing Your Centers

Nines are called a Body Type on the Enneagram (along with Eights and Ones) because their primary center of intelligence is the body center. When Nines are living in their body, so to speak, they achieve what biologists call homeostasis, a point of balance, that supports the optimal functioning of a person's whole being. But when Nines are having an out-of-body experience, and are not in tune with their physical self, it can cause a lack of harmony between the body center, heart center, and head center.

At Point Nine, I teach a Self-Remembering exercise that helps all nine Types, and especially Nines, to engage their three centers of intelligence. It's a simple, easy-to-do breathing exercise that has three parts to it. First, you place your hand on your solar plexus, take a deep breath in, and imagine your body is filled with life force and spirit. And affirm: *Breathing in, I am here in my body.* Second, place your hand on your heart, breathe in, and imagine your heart is open and full of love. And affirm, *Breathing in, I am here in my heart.* Third, place your attention on a spot between your eyes, breathe in, and imagine your mind is filled with light. And affirm: *Breathing in, I am here in this present moment.*

Doing this simple and easy-to-practice exercise once a day, preferably in the morning, helps you to inhabit your whole being and be more present in your life—but only if you remember to do it!

The Heart Center. Here, in the heart center, we practice Bhakti Yoga, which, as mentioned earlier in this chapter, is the yoga of devotion and love. Healthy Nines find inner peace by listening to the Voice of Love within and by recognizing what their heart most desires. Bhakti Yoga encourages us to practice compassion for ourselves and others. We strengthen our inner peace by meeting our fears with love and also by reaching out to others, staying in the difficult conversations, and making their inner peace as important as our own. Peace in our hearts creates peace in the world. Remember this: *Every argument, every war, every hate, every wound, every grievance, every conflict ends in love.*

The Body Center. *"Stop the world—I want to get on!"* is a line said by Leo Bloom in Mel Brooks's musical *The Producers*. Leo Bloom, who is played by Gene Wilder, is an accountant with a lifelong dream to be a producer, but will his dream ever become a reality? Here, in the body center, we practice Karma Yoga, which is the yoga of action and service. When Nines are centered in their body, they experience inner peace as a core strength and an inner power. Their inner peace helps them to be assertive, live with intention, take a risk, make a phone call, send an e-mail, knock on someone's door, apply for a vacancy, and participate in life.

The Head Center. Here in the head center, we practice Jnana Yoga, which is the yoga of mental clarity and enlightenment. Healthy Nines engage in mindfulness practices like tai chi, yoga, art, and prayer that strengthen inner peace. "Peace emanates from your soul," observed Paramahansa Yogananda, who taught his students how to uncover the peace of the soul by cultivating stillness, quietening the mind, and meditating on the indwelling presence of God. "The first proof of God's presence is an ineffable peace," he wrote in *Inner Peace: How to Be Calmly Active and Actively Calm*.

Spreading Your Wings

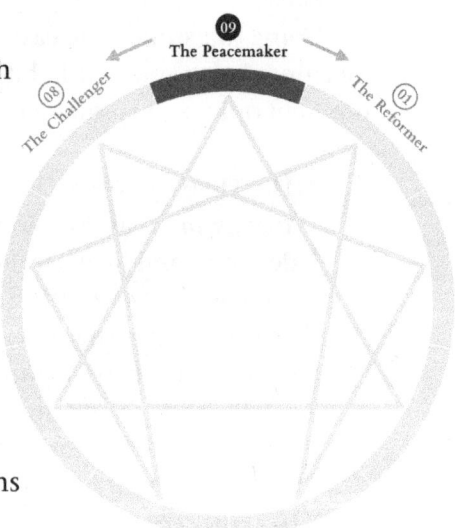

Type Nine's home base is Point Nine, which sits between Point Eight and Point One on the Enneagram symbol. This means Nines have an 8-Wing and a 1-Wing. Typically, one wing is more dominant than the other, but the goal is to balance your wings. Working with the 8-Wing helps Nines to tap into the essential qualities and wisdom of Point Eight, and working with the 1-Wing helps Nines to access the same at Point One. Learning to live in balance with the wings, by drawing strengths and lessons from both, can be very helpful for Nines.

Nines with an 8-Wing

Nines with a dominant 8-Wing (9w8) are commonly called the Facilitator or Mediator. They show up in the world with the typical traits of Nines, plus some traits of Eights.

> **Down to Earth.** 9w8s tend to be more earthy and rough around the edges than 9w1s. They are more grounded and have a practical

approach to life. 9w8s are just as idealistic as 9w1s but are more likely to describe themselves as a realist, who accepts and deals with things as they are. They won't judge you for being imperfect. Saying the word *f*ck* is not a sin. They are unpretentious and never holier-than-thou. They have friends in high and low places. When you most need a friend, they will be by your side.

The Peaceful Rebel. 9w8s embrace their inner rebel more easily than 9w1s. 9w1s judge rebelliousness as a disorderly trait that is destructive and a stain on their good character. "We don't need rebels in heaven, but we do need them here on earth," says Camilla, a 9w8, who describes herself as a spiritual rebel. Her favorite fashion label is Spiritual Gangster. "Rebelliousness is a positive behavior because it helps me to speak up when things are not right and to stand up for what I believe in," Camilla told me. A good inquiry for Nines is: *How can I unleash my rebellious soul and spread more peace and love in the world?*

Embodied Spirituality. 9w8s gravitate toward faiths and philosophies that want you to be "down here" on earth, not "up there" floating on a cloud. They focus on incarnational spirituality that brings heaven down to earth. They practice embodied spirituality that integrates lower and higher aspects of yourself. The ancient Greeks called this work *anthropos*, which means being fully human and fully divine. "People usually consider walking on water or in thin air a miracle. But I think the real miracle . . . is to walk on earth," said Thích Nhất Hạnh.

Owning Your Anger. Martin Luther King Jr. said, "The strong man is the man who can hold in a living blend strongly marked opposites. Very seldom do men achieve this balance of opposites. The idealists are not usually realistic, and the realists are not usually idealistic." Nines struggle with their ego-ideal of being peaceful *and* expressing their anger. The energy of Point Eight activates the fire in your belly. It wants you to be assertive and to own your anger. When Nines deny their anger, it depletes their life force, but when they integrate anger, it lifts their spirits. At Point Eight, the message is: *Use the power of your anger to channel more love into the world.*

Claim Your Power. "People give up their power by thinking they don't have any," wrote Alice Walker, author of *The Color Purple*. Nines can be so self-effacing and modest that they forget their superpowers. The energy of Point Eight helps Nines to be more self-assured and confident. It helps them to be a peace-seeker and a peace-bringer. They use their inner peace not to avoid conflict but to resolve conflict. The energy of Eight reminds Nines that your soul chose to be here on Earth at this exact time. Therefore, be willing to listen to what your soul tells you, and be ready to play your part.

Nines with a 1-Wing

Nines with a dominant 1-Wing (9w1) are commonly called the Diplomat or Idealist. They show up in the world with the typical traits of Nines, plus some traits of Ones.

Higher Purpose. 9w1s are drawn to faiths and philosophies that encourage you to see the bigger picture and embrace a higher purpose. As in transcendental philosophy, they have a reverence for life, a faith in human goodness, a belief in a higher power, and an optimism for the future. They "look up" to the heavens for inspiration and are prepared to work hard "down here" on earth to help make the world a better place. They are fully focused and quietly determined. "In a gentle way, you can shake the world," said Mahatma Gandhi, a One.

Social Activism. Nines are tempted to live inside their peace bubble and not get too involved with the world. They will surf 900 channels of TV entertainment as the world tackles global warming and the threat of mass extinction. Fortunately, the influence of the 1-Wing stirs the good conscience of Nines. Being an activist in the world is a moral obligation for 9w1s. "Take off your bedroom slippers. Put on your marching shoes," said Barack Obama. "Shake it off. Stop complainin'. Stop grumblin'. Stop cryin'. We are going to press on. We've got work to do."

Holy Imagination. 9w1s are dreamers who envision a better future for everyone. A key to their success is engaging their imagination. "My imagination is very holy. Using my imagination helps me to engage with my Higher Self, to channel inspiration, and let God work through me," said Terry, an artist, and a 9w1. Imagination and action combined are a powerful mix for 9w1s. George Lucas, the filmmaker, said, "You can't do it unless you can imagine it. Working hard is also very important. You're not going to get anywhere without working extremely hard."

Good Anger. 9w8s are prone to sudden outbursts of anger. They will erupt with anger, and then quickly move on as if nothing happened. 9w1s try to internalize their anger. They are stoic and unemotional. Their ego-ideal is to be peaceful *and* never angry. They are afraid that anger is destructive. They judge anger as a bad or negative emotion. Suppressed anger makes 9w1s more judgmental, critical, and bitter. The inner work for 9w1s is to practice good anger, which means using anger to be more engaged and proactive.

Too Idealistic? Both 9w1s and 1w9s are known for being idealistic and starry-eyed. The word *idealism* has an ancient Greek root that means "to see." 9w1s are visionaries who live with integrity, and who have a strong sense of mission and purpose. However, 9w1s can also be too idealistic, which makes them perfectionistic, impractical, unworldly, naïve, and impossible to please. A good inquiry for 9w1s is: *How can I be less idealistic and more compassionate and loving?*

Moving to Three and Six

Following the Inner Lines of the Enneagram Symbol, Nines move toward Point Three (home of the Achiever) and Point Six (home of the Loyalist). These Inner Lines invite you to visit these Points to explore the gifts and wisdom they have for you.

Moving to Three

When Nines go to Point Three, they access some of the essential qualities that Threes are blessed with. For example:

Self-Actualization. When Nines move to Point Three, they pay more attention to themselves. *"Who am I?" "What matters to me?" "What is my heart's desire?"* The inner work at Point Three is about embracing your I AM, showing your true face to the world, and becoming more of the True Self. As a Type Three myself, I like to tell my Nine friends, *We will all disappear back into the Oneness one day, but before we disappear, we must first appear!*

Power of Intention. The energy of Point Three helps Nines to live with a greater sense of intention and purpose. Wayne Dyer, who had a lot of Three energy, penned a bestseller, *The Power of Intention.* He wrote: "When you're connected to the power of intention, everywhere you go, and everyone you meet, is affected by you and the energy you radiate. As you become the power of intention, you'll see your dreams being fulfilled almost magically, and you'll see yourself creating huge ripples in the energy fields of others by your presence and nothing more."

Being and Doing. The energy of Point Nine is about *being* and the energy of Point Three is about *doing.* When Nines allow themselves to be influenced by the energy of Point Three, it helps them to align being and doing. Being without doing can cause a Nine's energy to become sluggish and sloth-like, whereas being and doing in balance helps Nines to participate more fully in the dynamic flow of life. Nines need to remember, *I am not a member of the audience; I am an actor on the stage of life and here to play my part.*

When Nines are under stress, they may exhibit some unhealthy qualities displayed by Threes. Knowing about these unhealthy qualities can help Nines be more present in their life. For example,

Always Busy. *Busy, busy, busy, busy, busy . . . dead!* Nines and Threes are prone to habitual busyness and using busyness as a distraction. Unhealthy Nines use constant busyness to "trance out" and get through the day in a semiconscious way. "I served three hundred coffees today, but I don't remember a single face of my customers," said Kim, a Nine, who came to me for Enneagram coaching on how to be more engaged with life.

Pleasing Others. Unhealthy Nines and Threes present a pleasing image to others. Threes slip into approval-seeking to win friends and influence people, and Nines over-adapt and blend in with others to keep the peace. Both are chameleons and change their colors to suit themselves and others. Nines also shift the focus of attention away from themselves so as to keep everything sweet and harmonious. Being more authentic and emotionally honest in relationships is important inner work for Nines and Threes.

Low Self-Worth. Both Nines and Threes experience low self-worth when they forget their inner peace and inner gold. Self-knowledge and self-acceptance are vital medicines for both these Types. When Threes realize their inner gold, they experience intrinsic self-worth; and when Nines experience inner peace, they feel more confident and better able to participate in life. "Success is liking yourself, liking what you do, and liking how you do it," said Maya Angelou.

Moving to Six
When Nines go to Point Six, they access some of the essential qualities that Sixes are blessed with. For example:

Inner Knowing. Healthy Sixes do the inner work to strengthen their sixth sense and trust their intuition to guide them through life. When Nines integrate the energy of Point Six, it helps them to develop their sixth sense and inner knowing too. "At the center of your being you have the answer; you know who you are and you know what you want," said Lao Tzu.

Wide Awake. The energy of Point Six helps Nines to be more mindful and awake. It counteracts the tendency in Nines to be dreamy and soporific when they withdraw too much from others. In Antonio Machado's poem "Is My Soul Asleep?" the answer comes: "No, my soul is not asleep. It is awake, wide awake. It neither sleeps nor dreams, but watches, its eyes wide open far-off things, and listens at the shores of the great silence."

Holy Faith. The Holy Ideas at Point Six are Holy Faith and Holy Strength. When Nines tap into these two holy ideas, it helps them to have faith in their inner peace and to trust that they have what it takes to heal wounds, reconcile differences, and resolve conflicts. "I am a spiritual warrior, and my chief weapon is my inner peace," said Sam, a Nine, who took my Leadership and the Enneagram program.

When Nines are under stress, they may exhibit some unhealthy qualities displayed by Sixes. Knowing about these unhealthy qualities can help Nines act with greater mindfulness as they go about their day. For example:

Psychological Inertia. When Nines and Sixes experience stress, they both suffer from psychological inertia that includes getting stuck in familiar patterns of thinking and being reluctant to change old habits that are unhealthy and destructive. In the *Fight, Flight, or Freeze* model that describes the three broad responses to stress, Nines and Sixes commonly get trapped in the Freeze response.

Playing It Safe. Sixes are known for playing safe, and Nines for living in their comfort zone. The virtue at Point Six is courage. Both Nines and Sixes must be willing to be "half a shade braver," to quote poet David Whyte, if they are to experience a happy life. "Courage is the most important of all the virtues because, without courage, you can't practice any other virtue consistently," said Maya Angelou.

Reluctant Hero. All nine Types on the Enneagram are on a hero's journey. Sixes and Nines are often reluctant heroes. Sixes experience self-doubt and Nines ask, "Who, me?" They both resist the call to adventure and will delay saying yes to their soul's high adventure. Self-trust and self-remembering help both these Types to be the hero they are. "Act as if what you do makes a difference. It does," said William James, the father of American psychology.

HOLY LOVE

*Love recognizes no barriers.
It jumps hurdles, leaps fences, and penetrates walls
to arrive at its destination full of hope.*

– Maya Angelou

The nine Points on the Enneagram each offer a Holy Idea—a universal teaching and higher wisdom—for all nine Types to contemplate and practice. The Holy Idea at Point Nine is Holy Love.

The first time I met Maya Angelou, we talked about Holy Love. Our meeting was on Valentine's Day, which was also the launch date for my book *Loveability: Knowing How to Love and Be Loved*. Early on in our conversation, I referred to a piece of writing by Maya that reads: "Love builds up the broken wall and straightens the crooked path. Love keeps the stars in the firmament and imposes rhythm on the ocean tides. Each of us is created of it and I suspect each of us was created for it." Maya and I talked about love as humanity's shared identity, love as our common purpose, and love as the muse that inspires every great work in our world. "Love is a great doing," Maya told me.

Holy Love is a daily spiritual practice, not just a lofty philosophy. Practicing Holy Love helps Nines, and all the other Types, to get in sync with the energy of love at the vital core of the True Self. Holy Love is the divine spark in each of us. It is what the soul is made of. Practicing Holy love is listening to the Voice of Love within you. *Love is intelligent and love will guide you, if you let it.* Practicing Holy Love is letting yourself be transformed by love. *Love helps you become the person you truly are.* Practicing Holy Love is being an instrument for love and letting love do its work through you.

There are no small acts of love, according to Holy Love. "All acts of love are maximal," teaches *A Course in Miracles*. Every act of love has an endless ripple effect. This is an important message for Nines because they often convince themselves that their presence doesn't really matter. The truth is that every act of love matters and is equally valuable. Why? Because it's not about the action; it's about the love that gets expressed through the action. Holy Love is about being present. It's about how you greet people, the energy you bring, and how you make people feel about themselves when they are in your presence.

Holy Love is being a loving presence in the world. "To love is to be present," said Thích Nhất Hạnh. In his book *True Love* he wrote, "The most precious gift you can give to one you love is your true presence." Holy Love is the realization that GOD IS LOVE and, because you are made of God, the acceptance that I AM LOVE. In essence, you are an expression of the all-embracing love of the universe. God is here, because you are here. Peace is here, because you are here. Love is here, because you are here.

> *I am a place where God's love turns up in this world.*
> — M. Basil Pennington

Holy Love is the genesis—or driving force—of creation. It is the cosmic energy that births galaxies, solar systems, planets, birds, plants, and people. Holy Love brings heaven down to earth. It unites spirit and matter. It transforms egos into souls. It helps us create a climate change from fear to love both in our mind and in the world. On that note, I give the final word to Thích Nhất Hạnh, who said:

> There's a revolution that needs to happen and it starts from inside each one of us. We need to wake up and fall in love with Earth. Our love and admiration for the Earth has the power to unite us and remove all boundaries, separation, and discrimination. We need to re-establish true communication—true communion—with ourselves, with the Earth, and with one another as children of the same mother.

Glossary of Terms

The Enneagram

The Enneagram is a geometric figure consisting of nine points. The word *Enneagram* comes from two Greek words: *ennea*, meaning "nine," and *gram*, meaning "drawing" or "figure." The Enneagram symbol features a circle with a triangle, a set of six inner lines called a hexad, and nine points around the circle. The Enneagram symbol represents universal laws and spiritual principles that help you to realize your potential and become your True Self.

Traditional Enneagram

The Traditional Enneagram has its origins in ancient times. Think of the Enneagram as a mandala, like you find in sacred art, designed to help you know yourself better and experience God. The circle symbolizes the unity of Creation, your soul's wholeness, and your Oneness with the Divine. The nine Points stand for nine essential qualities of the soul, like the nine fruits of the spirit mentioned by the apostle Paul in the Bible. For instance, Point One reveals a holy perfection in you and all of creation; Point Four reminds you of your secret beauty and eternal loveliness; and Point Nine connects you to inner peace and universal love for all beings.

Modern Enneagram

The Modern Enneagram outlines the nine personality Types that correspond to the nine Points on the Enneagram symbol. Psychologist Oscar Ichazo was the first person to map the nine Ennea-Types on the Enneagram, in his work in the 1960s. The nine Types are the Reformer (Point 1), the Helper (Point 2), the Achiever (Point 3), the Individualist (Point 4), the Investigator (Point 5), the Loyalist (Point 6), the Enthusiast (Point 7), the Challenger (Point 8), and the Peacemaker (Point 9). The name given to each Type gives you a clue as to the life outlook and social role the Type plays in their family, relationships, and work.

The Essential Qualities

Each of the nine Types on the Enneagram has some essential qualities, or healthy traits, that are characteristic of the Type. For example, Eights have an indomitable spirit; Twos love to be helpful and be of service; Sixes have a highly developed sixth sense or intuition; and Sevens have a natural joie de vivre and enthusiasm. These essential qualities are encoded in your spiritual DNA. They blossom and bloom naturally in you when you are healthy, when you heal and grow, and as you become your True Self.

The Basic Fear

Each Type has a basic fear in their ego operating system. The basic fear emerges from a feeling of separateness and aloneness. Every child enters a separation phase in their infancy. Normally this happens at two or three years old, when the child begins to say "I," "me," and "mine." The basic fear perpetuates a feeling of loss and a sense of deficiency and "not enough-ness." For instance, Ones are afraid they're not good enough and that something is wrong with them; Threes fear they have no intrinsic value; Fives are afraid of not knowing enough and being incompetent; and Sevens have a fear of being deprived and of missing out.

The Three Instincts

Each Type has three instincts that significantly affect how they operate in the world. These three instincts are commonly referred to as "subtypes." They are: (1) Self-Preservation Instinct, which prioritizes lifestyle, material matters, and self-care; (2) Social Instinct, which focuses on relating to family, society, and the world; and (3) Sexual Instinct (also called One-to-One Instinct), which is about attraction, relating style, and romance. Typically, you have a dominant instinct, the one you lead with, and also a weak instinct that is your blind spot. Working with the Enneagram helps you to cultivate a healthy relationship with all three instincts.

The Passion

Each Type has a "passion" that is an emotional wound or a source of suffering in the heart. The passion emerges in response to the feeling of separateness and the basic fear. For instance, the passion for Type Two is pride; for Type Three, it is vanity; for Type Five, it is avarice; and for Type Eight, it is lust. The passions correspond to the so-called cardinal sins of the Christian religion. The Greek word for "sin" is *hamartia*, which is an archery term that means "to miss the mark." In other words, sin is an error. Working with the Enneagram helps you to heal your emotional wound with greater compassion, honesty, and love.

The Fixation

Each Type has a "fixation," which is an ingrained mental habit that dominates their thinking and upsets their mental well-being. The fixation is a lens of perception through which each Type sees the world. For instance, the fixation for Ones is excessive judging or perfectionism; for Threes it is a pressure to perform, to win admiration, and be the best at everything they do; for Sixes, it is overthinking and being indecisive; and for Nines it is daydreaming and not engaging fully with life. Working with the Enneagram promotes greater mindfulness, better mental health, and more confidence in your True Self.

The Virtue

In the Enneagram system, the "virtue" is your superpower. It is the highest, most authentic expression of each Type. You can't make your virtue happen; it appears naturally as you do your inner work and grow. Your virtue unlocks all your essential qualities. It also helps you to heal your passion and fixation (see above). For instance, the virtue for Threes is veracity or truthfulness; for Fours it is equanimity; for Sixes it is courage; for Sevens it is sobriety; for Eights it is innocence; and for Nines it is participation and engagement.

The Wings

Each Ennea-Type has two wings. The wings are on either side of your main Type. For instance, a Two has a 1-Wing and a 3-Wing, and a Five has a 4-Wing and 6-Wing. Working with your wings helps you to access the vital energy, lessons, and gifts of the neighboring Points of your Type. For example, when a Two engages their 1-Wing, they access the positive qualities of Ones, which include clear personal values, a strong moral compass, commitment to doing good, and the virtue of serenity. Typically, a person has one dominant wing and one lesser wing. Working with the Enneagram encourages you to balance your wings and to fly with both wings.

The Centers

The three centers of intelligence in the Enneagram are the Head (Thinking), Heart (Feeling), and Body (Instinct). The body center is about gut instinct, intuition, will power, and right action; the heart center is about emotional intelligence, compassion, and love; and the head center is about thinking, perception, and being in a good headspace. Each Type has a primary center of intelligence: Eights, Nines, and Ones are Body Types; Twos, Threes, and Fours are Heart Types; and Fives, Sixes, and Sevens are Head Types. Working with your primary center helps you to function better in all three centers. Balancing all three centers helps you to enjoy physical, emotional, and mental well-being.

The Inner Lines

In the Enneagram, the "Inner Lines" or "arrows" represent pathways for growth and development for the nine Types. Initially, most Enneagram teachers taught that one inner line went to a disintegration or stress point; and the other one went to an integration or growth point. Nowadays, more Enneagram teachers favor the idea that both Inner Lines do the same job and help you both to integrate healthy qualities and to address unhealthy qualities of the Point they go toward. For example, Type Ones have an Inner Line to Point Four and Point Two. When a Type One is healthy and in balance, they embrace the essential qualities of Fours and Twos; but when they are unhealthy and out of balance, they often display the unhealthy qualities of Fours and Twos.

The Holy Ideas

The Holy Ideas are aligned with the nine Points of the Enneagram. Each Point has at least one Holy Idea, and some have two or three Holy Ideas. A Holy Idea describes an aspect of higher consciousness and an enlightened point of view about life. For instance, at Point One, the Holy Idea is Holy Perfection, which teaches that the essence of who you are is perfect, whole, and complete; at Point Five, the Holy Idea is Holy Omniscience, which encourages open-mindedness for eurekas, epiphanies, and greater understanding; and at Point Seven, one of the Holy Ideas is Holy Plan, which recognizes there is a higher plan for your life that is more wonderful and far greater than any plan you come up with.

Frequently Asked Questions

Here are some frequently asked questions about the Enneagram.

Where does the Enneagram come from?
The Enneagram is at least 2,500 years old. It has a paperless trail. It does not belong exclusively to one school of philosophy. It does not favor one religion. It offers a perennial philosophy. It works with universal principles and values. It offers a model for self-awareness that helps you to better understand the personality and the soul.

What are the Enneagram numbers?
There are nine Points on the Enneagram. Each Point is home to one of the nine personality Types. The numbers have no numerical ranking. One is not low, and Nine is not high. No number is more important than another. The number isn't meant to define you or label you; it simply represents a path of self-discovery and growth.

Is one Type better than another?
The Enneagram is like a family, and each Type is essential to the harmony and well-being of the whole. No Type is more important or better than another.

What does the name of the Type mean?
The name given to each Type describes the life outlook and social role of the Type. Occasionally, different names are given to the Types. In *Becoming Yourself*, I list the names commonly given to the Type at the start of each chapter. For instance, Twos are commonly called the Helper, the Carer, the Giver, the Caring Soul, and the Samaritan. Type Twos typically want to be of service and be helpful to others. One of their soul gifts is their genius for empathy and genuine caring.

Do Types have a gender bias?
No. A gender bias has not been detected among the Types. However, some cultures favor and celebrate one Type more than another. For example, Type Threes, the Achiever, often feel at home in the culture of the United States with its emphasis on achievement and hard work and its success ethic.

Am I born with my Type?
This question points to the age-old debate about nature or nurture. Am I born with my personality Type, or does my Type form itself after I am born? The honest answer is, we don't know for sure. However, most Enneagram teachers favor the nature theory. Just like we are born with a temperament that is choleric, melancholic, phlegmatic, or sanguine, we are born with a personality type. Your Type is the innate coding of your personality. And it is the lens through which you see yourself and experience the world.

Does my Type change?
Most Enneagram teachers believe that your Type does not change. The aim of the Enneagram is not to change your Type; it is to grow and become even more of your True Self. The healthier you are, the less you are boxed in by your personality. You are less ego-driven and more soul-directed. Your personality becomes a clear instrument for the soul to express itself. In Latin, the word *persona* comes from *per sonare*, which means "to sound through." Always remember that your soul is untypable!

Are some Types more compatible?
The simple answer is, the better you know yourself, and the healthier you are, the easier it is to relate to all nine Types. Working with the Enneagram helps you to meet your basic fear, to heal old wounds, and to open your heart so that you can enjoy more loving relationships and friendships with anyone, whatever their Type is.

What's the best job for my Type?
The Enneagram helps you to recognize the essential qualities, natural talents, and soul gifts of your Type. These signature strengths may explain why you are motivated to do the work you do. However, no Type is necessarily better at one job than other. All nine Types can excel as chefs, actors, or teachers, for instance, with each Type bringing their unique talents and energy to their work.

How should I work with the Enneagram?
The Enneagram offers you a path of lifelong learning and growth. You can work with the Enneagram in many ways. For instance, start by taking an Enneagram test to find out your Ennea-Type. My Enneagram Quiz, which I created for Hay House, is quick and easy to do. We beta tested it with ten thousand people before the launch, and it has a very high accuracy rating. Other options are: signing up for an Enneagram course online; working with an Enneagram coach; or reading a great book, like *Enneagram Made Easy*, by Deborah Egerton (check out the Bibliography on page 323).

Bibliography

Almaas, A. H. *Facets of Unity: The Enneagram of Holy Ideas*. Berkeley, CA: Diamond Books, 2000.

Chestnut, Beatrice. *The 9 Types of Leadership: Mastering the Art of People in the 21st Century Workplace*. Post Hill Press, 2017.

Chestnut, Beatrice. *The Complete Enneagram: 27 Paths to Greater Self-Knowledge*. She Writes Press, 2013.

Egerton, Deborah Threadgill, with Lisi Mohandessi. *Enneagram Made Easy: Explore the Nine Personality Types of the Enneagram to Open Your Heart, Find Joy, and Discover Your True Self*. Carlsbad: Hay House, 2024.

Egerton, Deborah Threadgill, with Lisi Mohandessi. *Know Justice, Know Peace: A Transformative Journey of Social Justice, Anti-Racism and Healing through the Power of the Enneagram*. Carlsbad, CA: Hay House, 2022.

Ichazo, Oscar. *Interviews with Oscar Ichazo*. Oscar Ichazo Fndt, 1982.

Maitri, Sandra. *The Spiritual Dimension of the Enneagram: Nine Faces of the Soul*. New York: Tarcher, 2000.

Naranjo, Claudio. *Ennea-Type Structures: Self-Analysis for the Seeker*. Nevada City, CA: Gateways Books & Tapes, 1991.

Ouspensky, P. D. *In Search of the Miraculous*. San Diego: Harcourt, Inc., 2001.

Palmer, Helen. *The Enneagram: Understanding Yourself and the Others in Your Life*. New York: HarperOne, 1991.

Price, Virginia, and David Daniels. *The Essential Enneagram: The Definitive Personality Test and Self-Discovery Guide*. New York: HarperOne, 2009.

Riso, Don, and Russ Hudson. *Discovering Your Personality Type: The Essential Introduction to the Enneagram*. New York: Houghton Mifflin Harcourt, 2003.

Riso, Don, and Russ Hudson. *The Wisdom of the Enneagram: The Complete Guide to Psychological and Spiritual Growth for the Nine Personality Types*. New York: Bantam, 1999.

Riso, Don, with Russ Hudson. *Personality Types: Using the Enneagram for Self-Discovery*. New York: Houghton Mifflin, 1996.

Rohr, Richard, and Andreas Ebert. *The Enneagram: A Christian Perspective*. PublishDrive, 2001.

Vuong, Nhien. *The Enneagram of the Soul: A 40-Day Spiritual Companion for the 9 Types*. Hampton Roads, 2025.

Wagele, Elizabeth, and Renee Baron. *The Enneagram Made Easy: Discover the 9 Types of People*. New York: HarperSanFranciso, 1994.

Wagele, Elizabeth. *The Enneagram of Parenting: The 9 Types of Children and How to Raise Them Successfully*. New York: HarperOne, 1997.

Index

A
abdication of ecstasy, 225
absent-mindedness, 231
Achiever (Type Three)
  description of, xviii, 71–73
  Glory and, 81–93
  Golden Soul and, 78–81
  path with heart and, 93–105
  qualities of, 73–74, 79–80
  recognizing, 74–78
acquisitive ingratiation, 56
action
  orientation toward, 208
  postponement of, 201
Adler, Alfred, 147
adrenaline junkies, 231
Adventurer. *See* Enthusiast (Type Seven)
adventurous spirit, 221
Advocate, 27. *See also* Reformer (Type One)
Alice's Adventures in Wonderland (Carroll), 226, 292
aliveness, 253–254, 262
Altruist. *See* Helper (Type Two)
ambition, 96
amends, making, 28
analysis paralysis, 204
Angelou, Maya, 289–290, 294, 307, 313, 314, 315
anger, 17–19, 265, 274, 297, 309–310, 311
angst, 194–196
anxiety, 197, 200, 238
appearances, success through, 89
Apple Inc., 112, 249
Aquinas, Thomas, 31, 58, 104, 221
Argus. *See* Loyalist (Type Six)
Ariadne, 188
Aristocrat, 134–135
Aristotle, 5, 44, 52, 58, 74, 146, 181, 291, 302
armored heart, 262–263
Artist. *See* Individualist (Type Four)
As You Like It (Shakespeare), 114
asking indirectly, 56
Asserter, 238–240. *See also* Challenger (Type Eight)
assertiveness, 239, 272
Atman, 150
Augustine, Saint, 24, 52, 58
Aurelius, Marcus, 5
Authentic Success (Holden), 81, 98
authenticity, 30, 64–65, 81, 94–97, 99–100, 109, 115, 121, 134, 200–201, 207
avarice, 159–161
awakened mind, 185–188

B
Bach, Johann Sebastian, 7
Ban Breathnach, Sarah, 96
Barks, Coleman, 23, 130
Barrie, J. M., 224–225
"Be Helpful" driver, 49–50
Be Here Now (Ram Das), 216, 234, 235
"Be Peaceful" driver, 294–296
"Be Perfect" driver, 14–17, 64
"Be Safe" driver, 192–193
"Be Strong" driver, 246, 259–260
"Be Unique" driver, 108, 120–122
Bear, 273–274
beauty, 116, 169
Beckett, Samuel, 148
Becoming (Michelle Obama), 6, 10
Beethoven, Ludwig van, 250
being and doing, 312–313
being mode, 228–229
being on trial, 20
Being Peace (Thích Nhất Hạnh), 291, 306
Bek, Lilla, 288
Bennett, Roy T., 80
Berenson, Bernard, 143
Berlin, Isaiah, 143
Bernstein, Leonard, 216–217, 230
Berry, Thomas, 46–47
Berry, Wendell, 64
best life, living, 80–81
bettering yourself, 10–11
Bhagavad Gita, 75, 150, 254, 269
Bhakti Yoga, 283, 307
"big mind," 276
big-heartedness, 254
biophilia, 40
Black Elk, 283–284
Blake, Amanda, 270
Blake, William, 152
blessing, original, 9–10

Index

bliss, following your, 307
"Bluebird" (Bukowski), 266–267
Bohemian, 135–136. *See also* Individualist (Type Four)
Bohm, David, 164
Borg, Marika, 72–73
Botticelli, Sandro, 286, 288
boundaries, healthy, 66
brain overload, 242
Brown, Brené, 257
Browning, Robert, 149
Buber, Martin, 55
Buddha/Buddhism, 9, 39, 93, 129, 131, 146, 174, 181–182, 215, 229, 276, 285
Buddy, 205–206
Bukowski, Charles, 266–267
bullshit detectors, 254
Burr, Aaron, 208
Burton, Robert, 127
Buscaglia, Leo, 57, 65
busyness, 313

C

calmness, 289
Campbell, Joseph, 243, 302, 303, 304, 307
can-do attitude, 134
Capra, Frank, 301
Capra, Fritjof, 291, 306
Caretaker. *See* Helper (Type Two)
Caring Soul. *See* Helper (Type Two)
caring souls, 45
Carpenter, Tom, 10, 23, 24
Carroll, Lewis, 292
Cassidy, Eva, 113
Castaneda, Carlos, 93–94, 134
catastrophizing, 202
Cavafy, Constantine, 232–233
Challenger (Type Eight)
  description of, xviii, 245–247
  Holy Truth and, 277–278
  imperishable soul and, 252–255
  loss of power and, 255–266
  path of surrender and, 266–277
  qualities of, 247–248
  recognizing, 248–252
change, 181
Charmer, 99–100
Chestnut, Beatrice, 52, 68
Childre, Doc, 62
Chimileski, Scott, 169
Chopin, Frédéric, 112
Chopra, Deepak, 76
Citizen Kane, 251–252, 268

closed-mindedness, 277
Cloud Nine, 300
Clueless, 42
coaches, 99
Coelho, Paulo, 62
collaboration, 171
Color Purple, The (Walker), 286, 310
comfort, seeking, 300
comfort zone, staying in, 207
comparisons, negative/unfavorable, 68, 124
compassion, 152
Complete Enneagram, The (Chestnut), 52, 68
Confronter. *See* Challenger (Type Eight)
congruence, 284
connected universe, 43–46
connection
  loss of, 46–56
  path of, 57–70
conversationalists, 151
courage, 188, 199–201, 238, 314
Courageous Soul. *See* Loyalist (Type Six)
Course in Miracles, A, 10, 92, 137, 140, 195, 316
Covey, Stephen, 10
cowardice, 195
Creative, 100–101
creativity, 100, 116, 134, 135
Crusader. *See* Reformer (Type One)
crusades, 11
crying/tearfulness, 138
Csikszentmihalyi, Mihaly, 290

D

Dalai Lama, 215, 220, 236
Dalí, Salvador, 148
Daniels, David, 179
Dante Alighieri, 58, 103, 183, 195
David and Goliath, 246
Daydreamer. *See* Peacemaker (Type Nine)
daydreaming, 207, 298–301
de Lille, Alain, 219
de Sales, Francis, 289
Death of a Salesman (Miller), 91, 200
death temptation, 103
Debussy, Claude, 285, 286
deceit, 91–93
deep and meaningful contact, 169–170
Deep I, 111, 115
Deep Soul. *See* Individualist (Type Four)
deep thinking, 241
Defender, 203–204
defensiveness, 256–257
deficiency, sense of, 162

deforming mirror, 20
depression, 31, 128
Descartes, René, 145, 187
destination addiction, 231
detectives, 170
devil's advocate, 198
Devil's Advocate. *See* Loyalist (Type Six)
Devotee. *See* Peacemaker (Type Nine)
Dhammapada (The Path of Truth), 181
Dharma, 93
Dickinson, Emily, 142, 169
Dion, Celine, 99–100
Dionysus, 214
Diplomat, 310–311
directness, 66
disconnection, 65
Discovering the Enneagram (Rohr), 13, 18
Disney, Walt, 206, 287, 301
distraction, 165, 172
Divine Comedy, The (Dante Alighieri), 58, 183, 195
Doer. *See* Achiever (Type Three)
dog-eat-dog world, 266
dominion, seeking, 274
Doors of Perception, The (Huxley), 150, 165
doubt, 187, 198, 315
down-to-earth, being, 29
downward spirals, 31
Doyle, Arthur Conan, 170, 171
dreamer archetype, 290
Dryden, John, 46
duty, sense of, 63–64
Dyer, Wayne, 76, 91, 96, 99, 102, 312
Dylan, Bob, 113, 118

E

Eckhart, Meister, 147, 150, 165, 174
Ecstatic Appreciators, 228
Edwards, Gill, 15, 26
Egerton, Deborah, 9, 19
8-Wings, 238–240, 308–310
Einstein, Albert, 147, 150, 152–153, 156, 165, 166, 167, 285
Eliot, T. S., 92, 234
elitist thinking, 173
Ellis, Albert, 202
embodied spirituality, 309
embodiment, 206–207
Emerson, Ralph Waldo, 182, 186, 200–201, 204, 207
emotional bypassing, 297
emotional honesty, 68

emotional intelligence, 116–117, 169
emotional invoices, 56
empathy, 284
empiricism, 145
Enabler, 64–65
Energizer. *See* Enthusiast (Type Seven)
energy
  Challenger (Type Eight) and, 272
  increased, 239
  innocence and, 268
Engaged Buddhism, 304–305
engagement, 48, 206, 305–306
Engoldenment (Kabir), 77
enlightenment, 145, 164
Enneads (Plotinus), 288
Enneagram
  description of symbol of, xv–xvi
  Modern, xvii–xviii
  Traditional, xvi–xvii
Enneagram, The (Palmer), 178
Enneagram: A Christian Perspective, The (Rohr), 9
Enneagram and Grace, The (Rohr and Hudson), 18
Enneagram Made Easy (Egerton), 19
Enneagram of Personality (Riso and Hudson), 228
Ennea-Type Structures (Naranjo), 17, 89, 123, 162
entanglement, 43
Entertainer, 237–238
enthusiasm, 220, 239
Enthusiast (Type Seven)
  description of, xviii, 211–213
  enjoying the journey and, 232–242
  Holy Plan and, 242–244
  joyful soul and, 219–221
  qualities of, 213–214, 220–221
  recognizing, 214–218
  searching for happiness and, 222–232
entrepreneurial mindset, 273
envy, 123–125
Epictetus, 5
Epicure, 228. *See also* Enthusiast (Type Seven)
Epicurus, 228
equanimity, 129–131
Equanimity Prayer, 131
Erikson, Erik, 147, 182–183, 194, 209
even mindedness, 238
even-tempered nature, 274
external valuation, 89
extremes, moving between, 265
extroversion, 99, 172, 205, 261
eye for an eye, 265
eyes wide open, 191–193, 241–242

Index

F

Facilitator, 309–310
failure, 101, 102, 103
faith, 104, 161, 209, 314
False Self, 75–76
fast thinking, 242
feeling lost, 195
Fellowship of the Ring, The (Tolkien), 42, 178, 184
Feynman, Richard, 151
5-Wings, 135–136, 203–204
flattery, 54–56
flow, state of, 290
focus, loss of, 32, 172
FOLO (fear of losing out), 224, 230
FOMO (fear of missing out), 223–224, 224, 230, 231, 243
Fonteyn, Margot, 7
forcefulness, 261–263
forgiveness, 30, 131, 265, 269
4-Wings, 100–101, 168–170
Fox, Matthew, 9–10
Francis of Assisi, 219–220, 235
Franti, Michael, 285
Freud, Sigmund, 147
Friend, 205–206
Fromm, Erich, 40, 44, 47, 90, 228
frustration, anger and, 19
Fry, Elizabeth, 284
fullness of being, 220, 228
fun, 172
Fun Child, 32, 225
future tripping, 238

G

Gandhi, Mahatma, 5–6, 32, 285, 310
Garden, as symbol, 117–118
Gautama, Siddhartha, 146
generosity, 45
Genesis, 9
genius, 204, 276
genuine, sound of the, 95, 207
Gerwig, Greta, 113–114
Gibran, Khalil, 58, 74–75, 81, 95, 105
Giver. *See* Helper (Type Two)
glory, 81–93, 90
gluttony, 227–230
Gnostic. *See* Investigator (Type Five)
Gnosticism, 111, 147
Goddard, Neville, 95
Goethe, Johann Wolfgang von, 147, 204, 250
going with the flow, 29
Golden Rule, 10
Golden Soul, 78–81. *See also* Achiever (Type Three)
golden thread, 188–189, 199
Goliath, David and, 246
good, greatest, 64
"good enough" parents, 49
Good Samaritan, 39
Good Soul. *See* Reformer (Type One)
goodness
 loss of, 11–21
 Original, 8–11
 path of, 21–34
Gowrie, Grey, 144
grabbiness, 263
grace, 33–34
gratitude, 220
Great Work, 80
greater good, 137, 240
Greenleaf, Robert, 41
grief, 18, 160
groundedness, 309
growth, continual, 221
Guardian, 203–204
guidance
 loss of, 188–198
 path of, 199–208
Guide, 99–100
Gurdjieff, George Ivanovich, xvi–xvii, xxi, 7, 94, 178, 249, 277, 300

H

Hafiz, 40, 46, 60–61, 70, 229
half-heartedness, 208
Hamilton, Lewis, 76
Hamlet (Shakespeare), 184, 194, 200, 201
happiness, 222–232, 229, 231
Happiness NOW! (Holden), 12–13, 228
Happy Child, 224–227
harmonious universe, 291–301
harmony, loss of, 291–293
Harry Potter series, 7, 42, 77–78
Harvey, Andrew, 77
having mode, 228–229
Hawking, Stephen, 147
Hay, Louise, 57, 104, 185–186, 195, 197, 201, 203, 209–210
heart, avarice and, 160
heart coherence, 61
heart wisdom, 240
Hegel, 181
Heidegger, Martin, 146, 172, 181
Heisenberg, Werner, 147
help

pride and, 53–54
refusal to ask for, 54
Helper (Type Two)
connected universe and, 43–46
description of, xviii, 35–36
examples of, 36–37
loss of connection and, 46–56
path of connection and, 57–70
qualities of, 38, 44–46
recognizing, 39–43
helper, role of, 53
helper's high, 46
Helpful Child, 48–52
Hemingway, Ernest, 95, 251, 278
Henley, William Ernest, 253
Henry IV Part 1 and *Part 2* (Shakespeare), 218
Henry V (Shakespeare), 252
Heraclitus of Ephesus, 181, 199
Hermann, William, 165, 166, 167
Hermeticism, 80
hero, reluctant, 207, 315
higher purpose, 310
Higher Purpose (Holden), 3, 258
highly sensitive people, 136
Hill, Derek, 143–144, 157
Hinduism, 93, 215, 253–254, 283, 285
Hipkin, Leigha, 191
Hippocrates, 125
Hobbit, The (Tolkien), 302–303
Hodgson, Roger, 156
Holden, Hollie, 132, 137, 191
Holden, Miriam, 247
holding environment, 49, 183
Hollis, James, 299–300
Holy Faith, 209–210, 238, 314
Holy Freedom, 69–70
Holy Grail, 222–223
Holy Harmony, 104–105
Holy Hope, 104, 105
Holy Law, 104
Holy Love, 102, 283, 315–316
Holy Omniscience, 173–175
Holy Origin, 139–140
Holy Perfection, 33–34, 240
Holy Plan, 205, 242–244
Holy Strength, 209–210, 238, 314
Holy Transparency, 174
Holy Truth, 277–278
Holy Will, 69–70
Holy Wisdom, 243–244
Holy Work, 243–244
home, longing for, 113, 118, 120
homeostasis, 307

Homer, 232, 299
hope, virtue of, 194
Houston, Jean, 45
Hudson, Russ, xvii, 18, 127, 142–143, 151, 153–155, 162, 168, 228, 249
Hulnick, Mary and Ron, 79–80
human dynamo, 272
"Human Family" (Angelou), 289–290
Hume, David, 145
humility, 28, 58–61
hungry ghost, 229
hurry sickness, 206
Huxley, Aldous, 2, 150, 165
hyperactivity, 206

I

Ichazo, Oscar, xvii–xviii, 195, 280, 289, 291
Iconoclast, 168–170
idealism, 241, 311
Idealist, 28–29, 310–311. *See also* Reformer (Type One)
image, selling, 90
image consciousness, 65
imagination, 155, 311
imperishable soul, 252–255
independence, 67, 136, 151, 173, 239, 261, 272, 276
Independent, 272–273
indirect asking, 56
Individualist (Type Four)
description of, xviii, 107–110
examples of, 112–113
journey home and, 128–140
Original Face and, 114–117
original wound and, 117–128
qualities of, 110–111, 115–117
recognizing, 111–114
individuation, 111, 128–129
indolence, 298–301
indomitable spirit, 253
Infinite Self, 229
ingratiation, 54–56
inner guidance, 187
inner knowing, 313–314
inner lines of growth, introduction to, xx
inner listening, 238
inner strength, 273–274
innocence, 267–269
instinct, 173, 254
intention, power of, 312
interconnectedness, 43–46
intrinsic value, 89
introversion, 169, 204, 261

Index

intuition, 186, 199
Investigator (Type Five)
   description of, xviii, 141–144
   Holy Omniscience and, 173–175
   light on the path and, 163–173
   qualities of, 144–145, 150–152
   recognizing, 145–149
   separate mind and, 152–163
   universal mind and, 149–152
isolation, social, 276

J

James, William, 104, 182, 315
Jampolsky, Jerry, 293
Jeans, James, 147, 174
Jeffers, Susan, 190, 205
Jerome, Saint, 21
Jnana Yoga, 308
Jobs, Steve, 249–250, 271
John, Book of, 90, 104, 164
Johnson, Robert, 79, 84
Jones, Edward E., 56
joy, 31–32, 221
Joyce, James, 112–113
Joyful Soul. *See* Enthusiast (Type Seven)
judgment/judging, 12–13, 19–21, 23, 137, 138
Julian of Norwich, 11, 24
Jung, Carl, 111, 128–129, 147, 150, 188–189, 199, 292, 304

K

Kabat-Zinn, Jon, 187, 202
Kabir, 77, 102
Kahneman, Daniel, 242
Kant, Immanuel, 145
Karma Yoga, 75, 93, 308
Keats, John, 125
Kerouac, Jack, 125
Khan, Hazrat Inayat, 131, 215, 269
Kierkegaard, Søren, 108, 146
King, Martin Luther, Jr., 81, 95, 252–256, 262, 265, 269, 278, 309–310
King, Stephen, 42–43
King Lear (Shakespeare), 43
Knost, L. R., 45
knowledge, fear of insufficient, 153–154, 162–163
Knowledge-Seeker, 151. *See also* Investigator (Type Five)
Kolter, Roberto, 169
Krishna, 215, 269
Krishnamurti, Jiddu, 204
Kumar, Avanti, 149–150, 152, 163
Kumar, Satish, 289

L

Laches (Plato), 200
Ladinsky, Daniel, 25–26, 40, 70
Lagnado, Silvia, 6
Lahr, John, 262
Laing, R. D., 225
Lao Tzu, 29, 232, 282, 314
laziness, spiritual, 298
Leader, 254–255. *See also* Challenger (Type Eight)
leaders, natural, 254–255
"Letter from Birmingham Jail" (King), 253, 256
life
   as gift, 44–45
   as good, 10
   reverence for, 289
life force, 262
Life Loves You (Holden and Hay), 185, 197, 209
Light in the Heart, The (Bennett), 80
light on the path, 163–173
Loner, 154–158
loose cannons, 272–273
Lord of the Rings, The (Tolkien), 7, 78, 184
Lost Child, 120
Lotus Eaters, 299
love
   Bhakti Yoga and, 283
   Challenger (Type Eight) and, 275
   earning, 54
   fear involving, 47–48
   first, 59
   Holy, 315–316
   made visible, 81
   substitutes for, 263
   surrender to, 269
   truth and, 278
   unconditional, 46
Loyal Sceptic. *See* Loyalist (Type Six)
Loyalist (Type Six)
   awakened mind and, 185–188
   description of, xviii, 177–180
   Holy Faith and, 209–210
   loss of guidance and, 188–198
   path of guidance and, 199–208
   qualities of, 180–181, 186–188
   recognizing, 181–184
Lucas, George, 286, 302, 311
Luke, Gospel of, 22–23
Luks, Allan, 46
Luminous Soul. *See* Investigator (Type Five)
lust, 261–263

M

Macbeth (Shakespeare), 78

Machado, Antony, 314
Madlala-Routledge, Nozizwe, 284
Maitreya Buddha, 39
Mandela, Nelson, 6
Martyr. *See* Helper (Type Two)
martyr, playing the, 64
Mary Poppins (Travers), 7, 14
May, Rollo, 169, 208, 231
Mayo, William, 255
McGuiness, Elaine, 150
McPherson, Christine "Ladybird," 113–114
Mead, Margaret, 116
meaning, from ambition to, 96
Mediator, 309–310. *See also* Peacemaker (Type Nine)
meditation, 150, 163, 305
melancholia, 125–128
mental escape, 242
mentors, 99
Meredith, George, 285
Merton, Thomas, 100, 111, 115, 139, 150
Metamorphoses (Ovid), 88, 124
metanoia, 84
metaphysics, 146
Meyer, Joyce, 60
Miller, Arthur, 91, 200
Milne, A. A., 155
mindfulness, 20, 186–187, 202, 236, 314
Miranda, Lin-Manuel, 218
mirroring, 84–85
misfits, 120–122
missing piece, 124
Mitchell, Joni, 113, 118
Monet, Claude, 286
Moralist. *See* Reformer (Type One)
Morrison, Toni, 251, 255
Morrison, Van, 113, 117, 126
Mother Teresa, 64
Motivator. *See* Achiever (Type Three)
Mozart, Wolfgang Amadeus, 216
Mulan, 207–208
Myss, Caroline, 11, 28, 33–34
mysticism, 146

N

Nahar, Raina, 281
Naranjo, Claudio, xvii, 17, 53, 56, 89, 121, 123, 125, 137, 160, 162
Narcissus, 88
Nash, John, 169, 170
"Need to Know" driver, 156–158
needs
 denial of, 53
 expressing, 68
 humility and, 60
negativity bias, 197–198
Nicomachean Ethics (Aristotle), 74
Nietzsche, Friedrich, 90, 200
night-sea journey, 128–129
9-Wings, 28–29, 273–274
noesis, 146
non-attachment, 164–165
Nonconformist, 272–273
non-participation, 301
nostalgia, 127
Nouwen, Henri, 54, 59, 97
NOW, adding more, 235

O

Obama, Barack, 285, 311
Obama, Michelle, 6, 10
observation, 151, 170
Observer. *See* Investigator (Type Five)
Odyssey (Homer), 232, 299
Oliver, Mary, 148, 163
omission, sin of, 298
omnicentricity of universe, 243
On the Soul (Plato), 252
1-Wings, 63–64, 310–311
openheartedness, 275
open-mindedness, 171, 276
openness, 150–151
Opportunist, 238–240
Original Face, 114–117
Original Goodness, 8–11, 136–137
original wound, 117–128
originality, 90, 115, 118–119, 124, 165, 168–169, 203–204
Originality-Seeker. *See* Individualist (Type Four)
Othello (Shakespeare), 287
Other-Enhancement, 55–56
othering, 54–56
Ouspensky, P. D., xvi, 178
outcast state, 124–125
outgoing energy, 134, 172
outlook, positive, 29
over-anticipation, 230–232
over-planning, 230–232
overthinking, 196–198
Ovid, 88, 124
oxytocin, 49

P

pacesetters, 239
pain, listening to, 130
Palmer, Helen, xvii, 178–179, 189, 198

passive aggressiveness, 274, 297
Paul (apostle), 5, 17, 159
peace
   gift of, 306
   inner, 28, 206, 207, 289, 290, 292, 297–298, 304, 308
   path of, 301–315
Peaceful Child, 293–296
peaceful soul. *See* Peacemaker (Type Nine)
Peacemaker (Type Nine)
   description of, xviii, 279–281
   harmonious universe and, 291–301
   Holy Love and, 315–316
   path of peace and, 301–315
   peaceful soul and, 287–291
   qualities of, 281–282, 289–291
   recognizing, 282–287
Peace-Seeker. *See* Peacemaker (Type Nine)
Peck, Scott, 187
people pleasing, 55, 313
perfectionism, 18, 21
Perfectionist. *See* Reformer (Type One)
Performer. *See* Achiever (Type Three)
persona, 114
personal best, 65
Peter Pan (Barrie), 224–225
Petrarch, 101
Phaedo (Plato), 252
Picasso, Pablo, 45, 251, 268
Pilgrim. *See* Enthusiast (Type Seven)
plans, too many, 232
Plato, 5, 9, 146, 181, 200, 252
playing it safe, 314
Plotinus, 288
Pocket Enneagram, The (Palmer), 189
Poetics (Aristotle), 52, 302
Points, introduction to, xvi–xvii
Ponticus, Evagrius, 159, 165, 296–297, 298
positivity, 205
possibility thinking, 171
power
   claiming your, 310
   loss of, 255–266
Powerful Soul. *See* Challenger (Type Eight)
practicality, 170, 204, 309
preparation, 186
pre-traumatic stress, 195–196
pride, 52–54, 275
Problem Solver, 170–171
problem solving, 204
Prodigal Son, 22–23
Producer. *See* Enthusiast (Type Seven)
Professional, 100–101
projection, 21

Prophet, The (Gibran), 58, 74–75, 105
Protector, 259, 261. *See also* Challenger (Type Eight)
Provider, 259
Psalms, 9, 215
psyche, 114
psychological inertia, 301, 314
psychosocial development, 182–183
purpose, sense of, 240
Pythagoras, 146, 147, 152

Q

Quakers, 284
Questioner. *See* Loyalist (Type Six)
questioning your thoughts, 166

R

rainbows, 307
Ram Das (Richard Alpert), 216, 221, 234, 235, 240
Rank, Otto, 111, 118, 128, 147
Raphael, 5, 288
reasoning, 145–147
rebellion, 33, 309
receiving, joy of, 60–61
reciprocity, 69
Reformer (Type One)
   description of, xviii, 1–2
   loss of goodness and, 11–21
   Original Goodness and, 8–11
   path of goodness and, 21–34
   qualities of, 4, 9–11
   recognizing, 5–8
rejection, 67, 173, 275–276
relationships
   centering, 27, 99–100
   Enthusiast (Type Seven) and, 237
   gift of, 60
   nurturing, 28
reliability, 187–188
Renoir, Pierre-August, 286
Republic, The (Plato), 5
rescue, longing for, 138–139
resentment, anger and, 19
rest, 29
restlessness, 32–33, 222
retentiveness, 161–163
revenge, 67, 264–265
Richardson, Cheryl, 44, 57, 58, 100
Riso, Don, xvii, 108–109, 117, 120, 142, 153, 155, 228
Rock, 259, 261
Roddenberry, Gene, 286–287
Roddick, Anita, 6

Rodin, Auguste, 183
Rogers, Carl, 284
Rohr, Richard, 9, 13, 18, 20, 34
Romeo and Juliet (Shakespeare), 43, 114
Rubinstein, Arthur, 143
Rumi, Jelaluddin, 23, 58, 92, 96, 113, 117, 130, 208, 220, 222–223, 229

S

sacredness, 263
Sad Child, 126
sadness, 126, 127
Salzberg, Sharon, 161
Samson and Delilah, 262
Schopenhauer, Arthur, 146
Schrödinger, Erwin, 43, 147, 151
search, ending, 234
Security-Seeker. *See* Loyalist (Type Six)
Seeker. *See* Enthusiast (Type Seven)
self, avarice and, 160
self-acceptance, 10, 24, 30, 137
self-actualization, 312
self-affirmation, 200
self-betrayal, 208
self-compassion, 68–69
self-control, excessive, 241
self-deception, 91, 92
self-directed anger, 18
self-doubt, 104
self-empowerment, 66
self-forgetting, 102
self-hate, 137
self-image, poor, 137
self-reflection, 100–101
self-reliance, 161, 276
"Self-Reliance" (Emerson), 182, 204
Self-Remembering exercise, 307
self-sufficiency, 195
self-trust, 104, 178, 184, 186, 196, 200
self-worth, 80, 83, 91, 313
Seneca the Younger, 5
separate mind, 152–163
separateness, 152–153
separation, 12, 118, 189, 256, 258, 291
separation anxiety, 192
Serenity, 23–25, 137
seriousness, excessive, 241
Servant, 63–64. *See also* Helper (Type Two)
Servant Leadership model, 41
service, 41, 45–46, 81, 99, 138, 253, 275
7-Wings, 205–206, 271–273
shadow, meeting your, 131

Shakespeare, William, 8, 43, 78, 114, 124, 127, 148–149, 184, 194, 200, 201, 218, 252, 287
shame, 24, 31
Shimoff, Marci, 194
"shoulding" on yourself, 24
sighs, 31, 127
simplifying life, 235
6-Wings, 170–171, 237–238
sixth sense, 103, 186
sloth, 296–298
slow thinking, 242
slowing down, 234
sobriety, 233–235
social activism, 11, 290–291, 310–311
social confidence, 173
Socrates, 248–249, 250, 252–253, 263, 264, 267, 271, 277
solitude, 241
soul
  deep, 117
  Fives and, 150
  gluttony and, 229–230
  imperishable, 252–255
  indestructible, 268–269
  joyful, 219–221
  made visible, 96
  peaceful, 287–291
soul friends, 138
soul gifts, 45
Soul Voice, 103
Specialist. *See* Investigator (Type Five)
Spezzano, Chuck, 60
Spinoza, 200
spontaneity, 32, 205
Star Child, 84–88
Star Trek, 7–8, 42, 78, 286–287, 299
Star Wars, 251, 286, 302
Status Seeker. *See* Achiever (Type Three)
still points, finding, 234
Stoic philosophers, 5, 200
strength
  fear regarding, 256–257
  group, 275
Strong One, 259
Strong-Willed Child, 257–261
success
  authentic, 81
  imitation of, 90
  through appearances, 89
Success Intelligence, 98
Sufism, 9, 40, 93, 111, 215
support, lack of, 189–190

Index

surrender, path of, 266–277
Swift, Taylor, 77, 79, 87, 100

T

Tagore, Rabindranath, 285
Tao Te Ching, 29, 282–283
Taoism, 9, 93, 102, 282–283
Tchaikovsky, Pyotor Ilyich, 183
Teachings of Don Juan, The (Castaneda), 93–94, 134
team players, 103
Tempest, The (Shakespeare), 148–149
territorial nature, 274
Theseus, 188
Thích Nhất Hạnh, 102, 285, 291, 304–305, 309, 316
Thinker. *See* Investigator (Type Five)
Thinker, The (Rodin), 183
thirsty fish, 229
Thomas, R. S., 253–254
Three Green Lights, 236
3-Wings, 64–65, 134–135
Thurman, Howard, 95, 103, 207, 262
Tillich, Paul, 188, 200, 209
Timaeus (Plato), 5
time for self, 67–68
Tolkien, J. R. R., 7, 42, 78, 178, 184, 302, 302–303
Tragic Romantic. *See* Individualist (Type Four)
Travers, P. L., 7
Triple Filter Test, 277
Trooper. *See* Loyalist (Type Six)
Trubridge, Liz, 213
True Love (Thích Nhất Hạnh), 316
trust, 182–183, 209
truth/truthfulness, 94–97, 95, 207–208, 277
"Try Harder" driver, 85–86
Tutu, Desmond, 39–40, 45, 63, 215
Twain, Mark, 88, 198
Twelfth Night (Shakespeare), 8, 218
Two Gentlemen of Verona, The (Shakespeare), 218
2-Wings, 27, 99–100

U

Ubuntu, 39–40
uncertainty, 92, 196
unconditional positive regard, 284
uniqueness, 116
universal mind, 149–152
unstruck heart, 269

V

vainglory, 90

Valley-Fox, Anne, 230
values, living your, 10
van der Leeuw, Jacobus Johannes, 170
Van Gogh, 112, 117–118
vanity, 88–91
vengeance, 264–266
Virgil, 269
Vivekananda, Swami, 75
vulnerability, 255

W

Walker, Alice, 11, 286, 310
warm-heartedness, 27, 138
warrior archetype, 254
Weil, Simone, 59
Welles, Orson, 251, 267–268
Wheeler, John, 306
Whitman, Walt, 217
wholeheartedness, 201
Whyte, David, 314
Wiederkehr, Macrina, 30, 119, 124
Wiesel, Elie, 306
Wilde, Oscar, 135
Williams, John, 290
Williams, Ralph Vaughan, 285
Winfrey, Oprah, 65, 76, 80–81, 94, 103, 289
Winnicott, Donald, 49, 75–76, 84
wisdom, 163, 166, 170, 171, 243
Wisdom of the Enneagram (Riso), 120, 142, 153, 155
Wittgenstein, Ludwig, 146
Woodman, Marion, 21, 26, 133
Woolf, Virginia, 112, 139
Wordsworth, William, 82, 83, 241
work-life balance, 87
worst-case-scenario thinking, 198
worthiness, 83–84
wounds, honoring, 130–131
wrath, 17

Y

Yeats, W. B., 114
yes, saying, 201
YES energy, 221
Yoga Sutras, 9
Yogananda, Paramahansa, 283, 308

Z

Zen/Zen Buddhism, 111, 114–115, 146
Zohar, Danah, 151
zoning out, 102

Acknowledgments

A very big thank-you to everyone who has helped me to write *Becoming Yourself*, especially to my friends, family, students, teachers, and mentors who I mention by name in this book.

Thank you to all my Enneagram teachers and mentors. Deep thanks to Marika Borg for introducing me to the Enneagram at Robert's Café in Helsinki many moons ago. You said I'd be grateful to you for the rest of my life for introducing me to the Enneagram. How right you were. Thank you, Marika. Thanks to Oscar Ichazo, the father of the modern Enneagram, whom I never met, but have learned so much from. A special thanks to Johanna Jenkins, who studied with Oscar Ichazo for several years and shared her student notes with me.

Thanks to Don Riso and Russ Hudson for your exquisite teaching of both the Traditional Enneagram and Modern Enneagram. Your workshop on *Wisdom of the Enneagram* in London, at the Study Society, was the first Enneagram course I took. Russ Hudson, thank you a thousand times for your friendship and mentoring these past 20 years. Thank you, Claudio Naranjo, for your inspiring teachings that I revisit often. I am blessed to have studied with you. Thank you to Helen Palmer, David Daniels, Richard Rohr, Beatrice Chestnut, A. H. Almaas, and Sandra Maitri, whose workshops and lectures have inspired and helped me.

Over the years, I've co-presented Enneagram courses with other teachers. Thank you, Hollie Holden, for our many collaborations. Thanks to Russ Hudson for co-leading trainings and retreats with me. Thanks to Jessica Dibb for joining Russ and me on our Living as Love program, hosted by the Shift Network. Thanks also for the many years you hosted the online Enneagram Summit. Thank you to Caroline Myss, for teaching the Enneagram with me. Thank you, Deborah Egerton, for the programs we've taught online and in person. I look forward to teaching more programs with you in future.

I've been fortunate to teach the Enneagram around the world, and I am grateful to the hosts of these events. Thank you, Venetia David, and the Alternatives team, for taking me to Santorini, Greece, and Montserrat, Spain. Thank you, Nina Hirlaender, for inviting me to teach the Enneagram in Assisi, Italy. Thanks to everyone at magical Findhorn, especially John Willoner and Sylvia Black, for hosting Enneagram events in the Universal Hall. And thanks to

Acknowledgments

Ron and Mary Hulnick for inviting me to teach a 5-day *Soul and the Enneagram* retreat to your students at the University of Santa Monica.

I've taught the Enneagram to organizations worldwide. My Leadership and the Enneagram program evolved from the work I did with brands and companies such as Google, Virgin, Heathrow Airport, Allen & Overy, and IBM. Thanks to Sylvia Lagnado, Fernando Acosta, and Ale Manfredi for inviting me to teach the Enneagram to everyone at Dove and the Real Beauty Campaign. Thanks to Jean-Laurent Ingles, who I worked with for fifteen years at Unilever. Jean-Laurent gave me the opportunity to teach and coach over 500 leaders on the Enneagram in that period.

Thank you to the students who have attended my Enneagram programs. And to everyone I have coached and mentored on the Enneagram. The more I teach the Enneagram, the more I learn.

The seeds for writing this book were sown when I taught the Enneagram to the Hay House leadership team in Napa Valley, back in 2013. Thanks to Reid Tracy and Margarete Nielsen for inviting me to be Enneagram Ambassador for Hay House. Thanks to Kenneth Browning for your legal work on the contract. Thanks to everyone at Hay House for your work on my Enneagram Quiz and on building the Enneagram platform. Thanks to Patty Gift, my commissioning editor, for your friendship and for having such a great surname. Thanks to Anne Barthel, for your editorial support. If this book were a baby, I'd ask you to be its godmother. Thanks to Devon Glenn for your masterful editing. Thanks to Jemima Giffard-Taylor for your cover design and your illustrations.

Thanks to all the Hay House authors for their interviews, endorsements, and support for my work with the Enneagram. Thank you to Louise Hay, Wayne Dyer, Caroline Myss, Deborah Egerton, Eugene Egerton, Colette Baron-Reid, Gabrielle Bernstein, Mindy Perls, Kyle Gray, and Rebecca Campbell, for helping to get the Enneagram out into the world. Thanks also to Trent Thornley, Nicola Albini, Kisser Paludan, Nhien Vuong, Tamar Zanaty, Helen English, Teresa Daniels, and the many other great Enneagram teachers and authors I know.

The next round of thanks goes to my team. Thank you to Laura Samuel, Sohini Sinha, and Diane Haworth for helping me to make the space to write *Becoming Yourself.* It's been a long journey, and I've needed your support every step of the way. Sohini, thank you also for organizing so brilliantly the Enneagram workshops and retreats in London, Findhorn, and Assisi. Thanks again to Jemima Giffard-Taylor for your beautiful designs for our Enneagram events and this book.

Thank you to my dear friend Liz Wenner. You know what it takes to birth a whale-of-a-project. Your supportive texts, our lovely dinners, and your ongoing support have kept me energized and on track. Thank you to Merete Mace for your loving holding and support. Our weekly IFS sessions lifted the burden that my "parts" labored with during two years of daily writing. And thank you, JT, for getting me out on a golf course and for teaching me that golf is a spiritual practice. Now I can finally put down my pen and relax!

Lastly, thank you, Hollie Holden. Hardly a day goes by when we don't talk about the Enneagram. Our mutual interest and appreciation for the Enneagram is so supportive, fun, and inspiring. And thank you, Bo Holden and Christopher Holden. You are both my muses. I've written this book for you both. Everything I do, I do for you.

About the Author

Robert Holden's work on psychology and spirituality has been featured on *Oprah*, *Good Morning America*, a PBS special *Shift Happens!*, and in two major BBC-TV documentaries. Robert is an Accredited Professional Member of the International Enneagram Association (IEA). He has given the opening keynote at two IEA conferences in 2009 and 2021.

Robert teaches public programs on the Enneagram worldwide. He has led Enneagram retreats in Greece, Jerusalem, Assisi, Montserrat (home of the Black Madonna), and Findhorn. He offers a **Coaching & Enneagram** training for psychologists, health carers, educators, and coaches. He also teaches a **Leadership & Enneagram** program for clients including Dove & the Real Beauty Campaign, Unilever, IBM, and Google.

Robert teaches public programs on the Enneagram worldwide. He leads a certified Coaching and the Enneagram training for health professionals, educators, and coaches. He is a *New York Times* best-selling author of 15 books, including *Happiness NOW!*, *Shift Happens!*, *Authentic Success*, *Loveability*, *Life Loves You* (co-written with Louise Hay), *Higher Purpose*, and a book of poetry, *Finding Love Everywhere*.

Robert writes a weekly newsletter called *Shift Happens!* You can sign up for free at: **www.robertholden.com**

Who Are You Really?

Beneath all the roles you play and the goals you chase lies your true self, the part of you that longs to be seen and understood.

Take the free Enneagram Quiz designed by **Robert Holden** and uncover the deeper patterns that shape your thoughts, emotions, and relationships. Your personalized results will offer clarity, compassion, and the first steps toward lasting transformation.

Find out your Enneagram Type here!

Scan the QR code or visit
https://hayhouse.com/enneagram
to discover your Ennea-Type and
begin awakening your true potential.

Hay House Titles of Related Interest

YOU CAN HEAL YOUR LIFE, the movie,
starring Louise Hay & Friends
(available as an online streaming video)
www.hayhouse.co.uk/louise-movie

THE SHIFT, the movie,
starring Dr Wayne W. Dyer
(available as an online streaming video)
Learn more at www.hayhouse.co.uk/the-shift-movie

***

THE 9 POINTS OF POTENTIAL:
The New Enneagram Test to Discover Your Strengths and
Master Leadership, Communication and Collaboration in the Workplace
by Ingrid Stabb

ARCHETYPES: Who Are You?
by Caroline Myss

KNOW JUSTICE, KNOW PEACE:
A Transformative Journey of Social Justice, Anti-Racism and
Healing through the Power of the Enneagram
by Deborah Threadgill Egerton, PhD

YOU'RE IN THE RIGHT PLACE:
Let Go of the Past, Make Friends with Uncertainty and Discover
the Magic of an Uncharted Future
by Colette Baron-Reid

All of the above are available at your local bookstore,
or may be ordered by contacting Hay House (see next page).

***

CONNECT WITH
HAY HOUSE
ONLINE

🌐 hayhouse.co.uk   f @hayhouse

📷 @hayhouseuk   🦋 @hayhouseuk.bsky.social

♪ @hayhouseuk   ▶ @HayHousePresents

Find out all about our latest books & card decks • Be the first to know about exclusive discounts • Interact with our authors in live broadcasts • Celebrate the cycle of the seasons with us • Watch free videos from your favourite authors • Connect with like-minded souls

'The gateways to wisdom and knowledge
are always open.'

Louise Hay